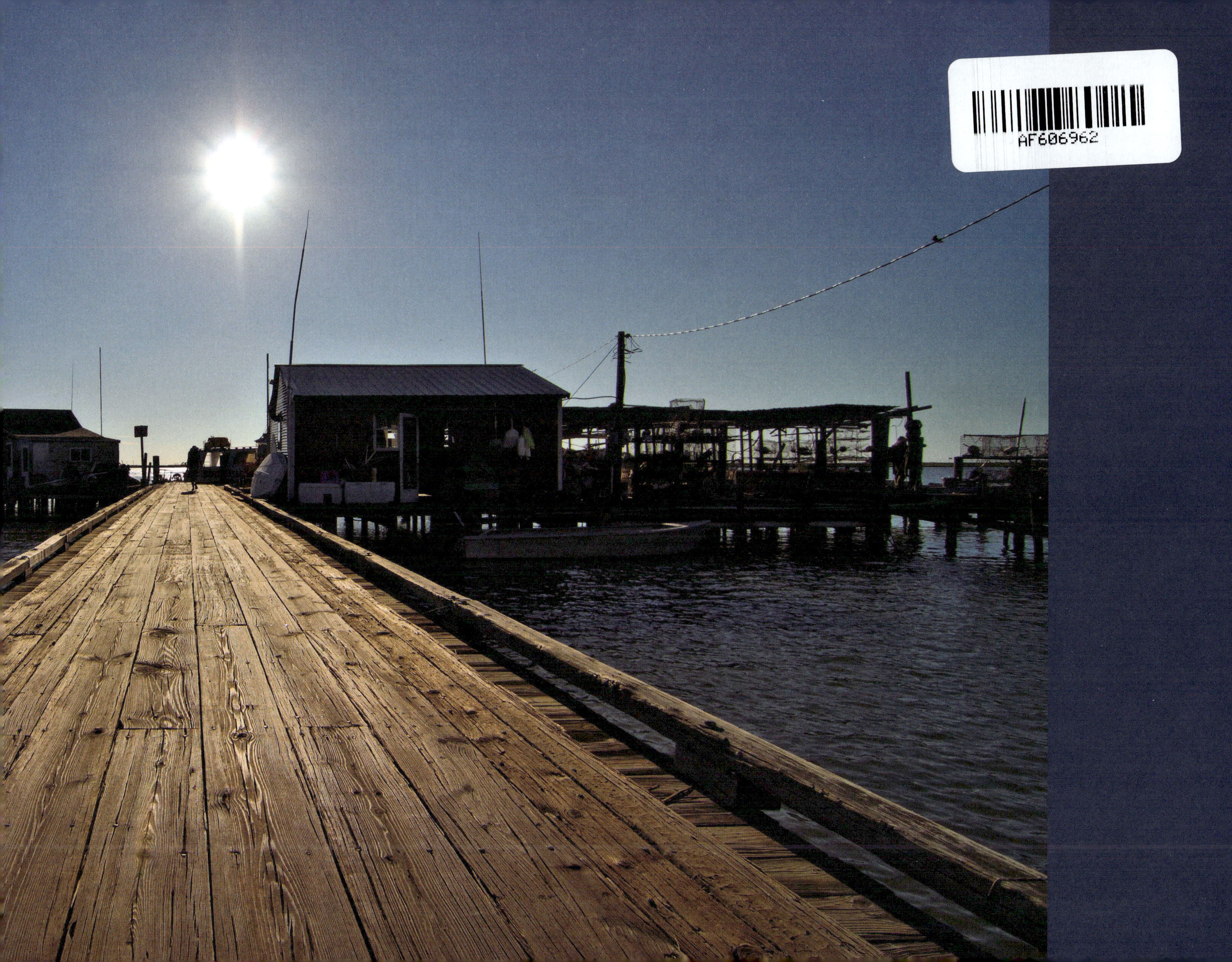

# Chesapeake Views

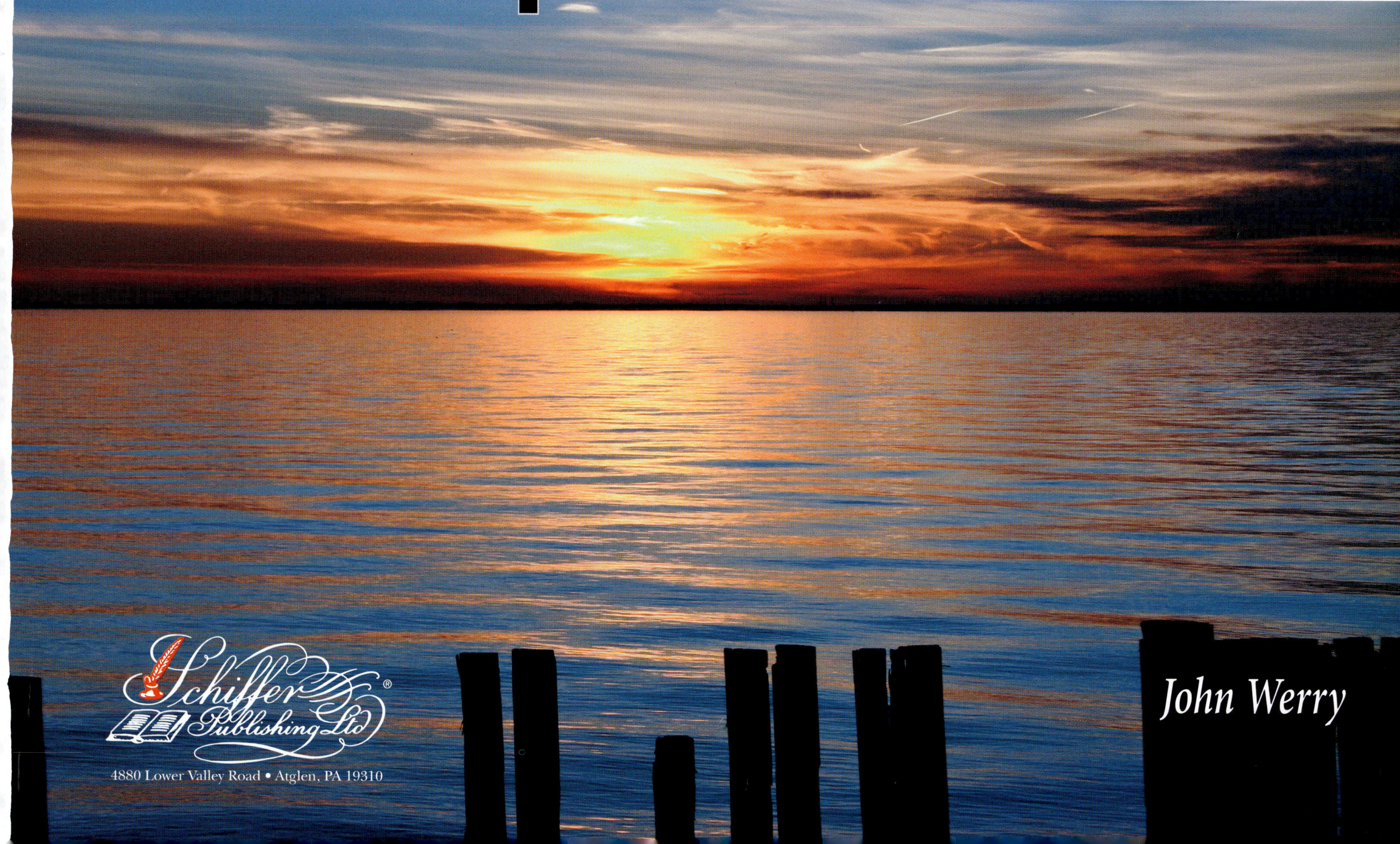

**Other Schiffer Books on Related Subjects:**

*Just Passing Through*, 978-0-7643-3991-2, $14.99



Library of Congress Control Number: 2012931403



Designed by Mark David Bowyer
Type set in Myriad Pro / Minion Pro

ISBN: 978-0-7643-4070-3
Printed in China

Schiffer Books are available at special discounts for bulk purchases for sales promotions or premiums. Special editions, including personalized covers, corporate imprints, and excerpts can be created in large quantities for special needs. For more information contact the publisher:

Published by Schiffer Publishing Ltd.
4880 Lower Valley Road
Atglen, PA 19310
Phone: (610) 593-1777; Fax: (610) 593-2002
E-mail: Info@schifferbooks.com

For the largest selection of fine reference books on this and related subjects,
please visit our website at **www.schifferbooks.com**
We are always looking for people to write books on new and related subjects.
If you have an idea for a book, please contact us at
***proposals@schifferbooks.com***

This book may be purchased from the publisher.
Include $5.00 for shipping.
Please try your bookstore first.
You may write for a free catalog.

In Europe, Schiffer books are distributed by
Bushwood Books
6 Marksbury Ave.
Kew Gardens
Surrey TW9 4JF England
Phone: 44 (0) 20 8392 8585; Fax: 44 (0) 20 8392 9876
E-mail: info@bushwoodbooks.co.uk
Website: www.bushwoodbooks.co.uk

# Contents



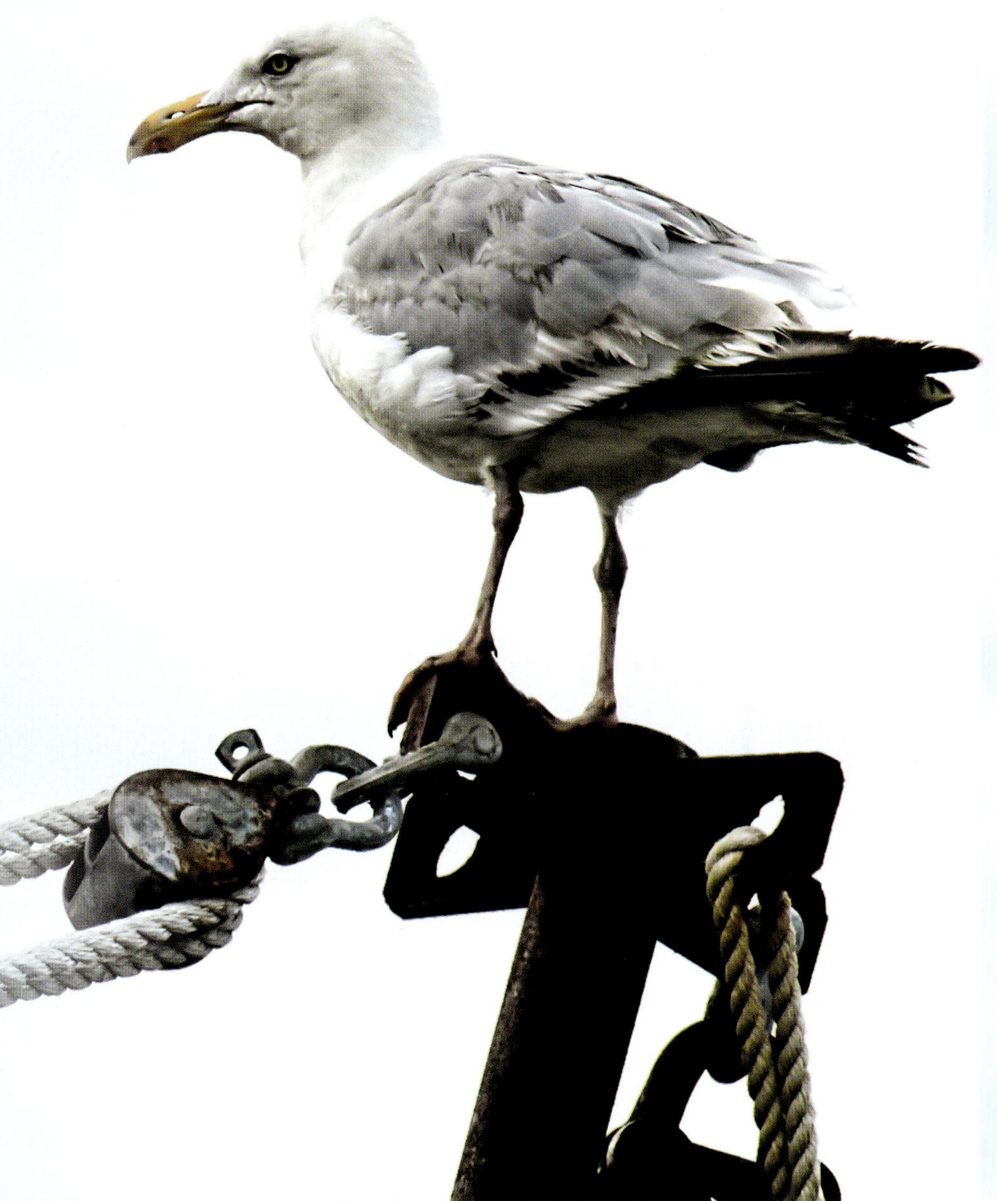

A herring gull rests high above Knapp's Narrows in Tilghman, Maryland.

# Dedication

This book is dedicated with love to my wife, Dawn. I'm glad that back in marching band you chose this drummer to hold the cymbals for.

To Mom, Dad, Brandon, and Heather: What amazing times we have had together across almost four decades on the Bay with many more to come. Our blood runs brackish.

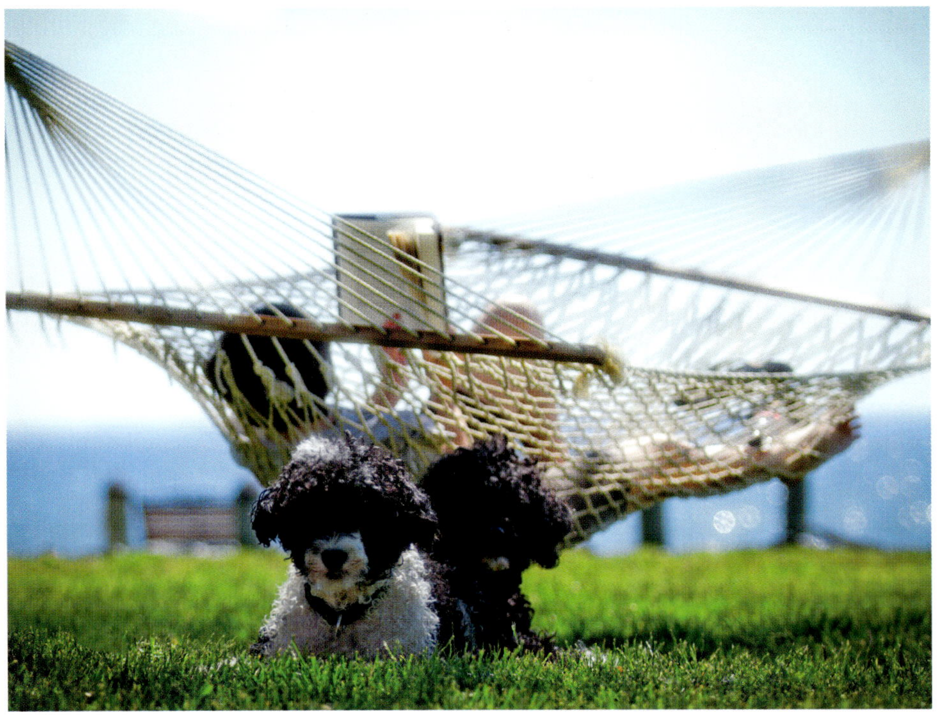

Dawn, Lizzie, and Taylor: My favorite Chesapeake days are those spent with them.

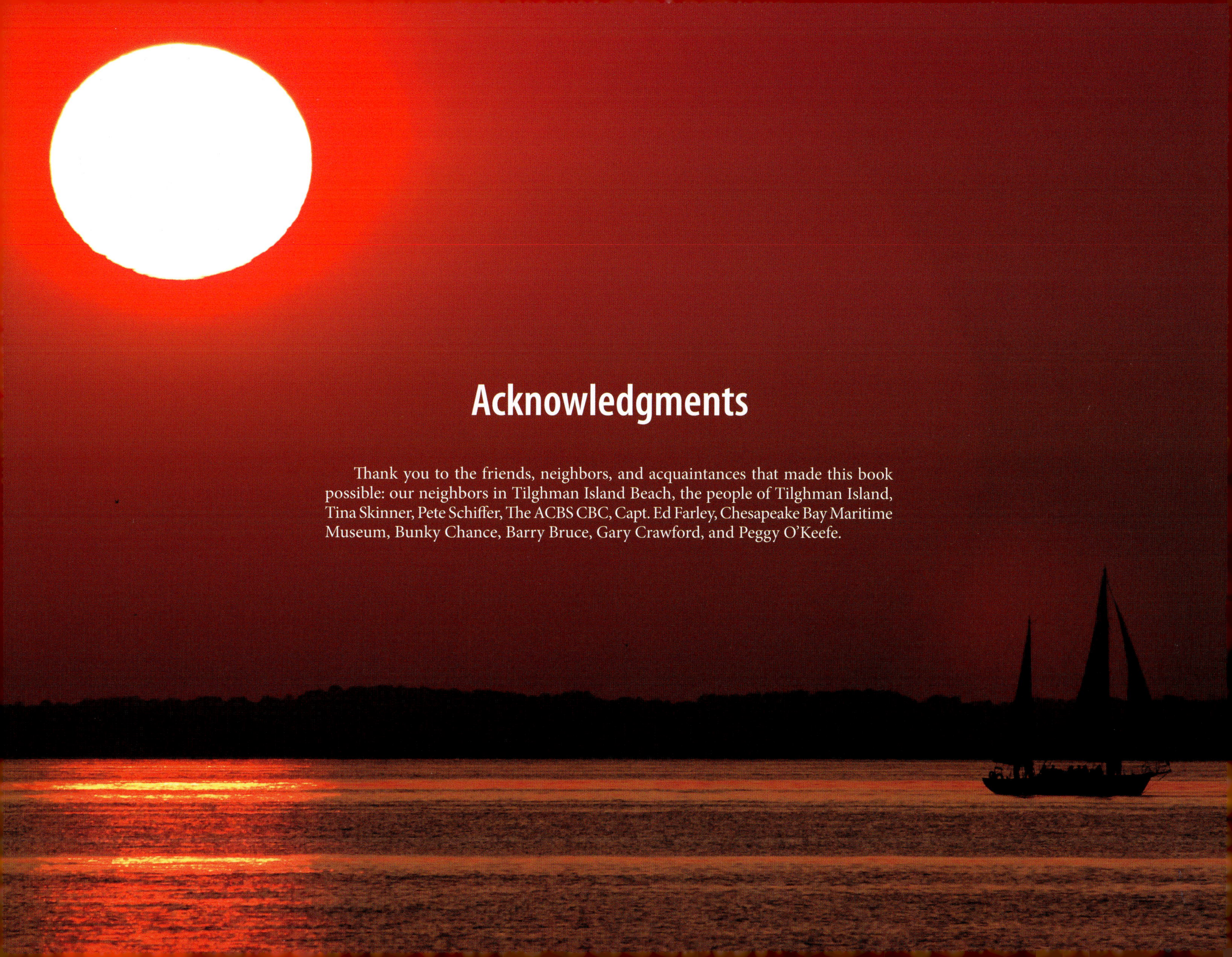

# Acknowledgments

Thank you to the friends, neighbors, and acquaintances that made this book possible: our neighbors in Tilghman Island Beach, the people of Tilghman Island, Tina Skinner, Pete Schiffer, The ACBS CBC, Capt. Ed Farley, Chesapeake Bay Maritime Museum, Bunky Chance, Barry Bruce, Gary Crawford, and Peggy O'Keefe.

# Introduction

## Dorchester County

The Werry family era on the Chesapeake started around 1971, when my grandparents built a home in which to retire on the Little Choptank in "Pig Neck" near Cambridge, Maryland. Time stood still for my brother Brandon, sister Heather, and I as we spent every moment that we could outside, on and around the water. The neighbor's dog, Mattie, roamed free and was a frequent companion.

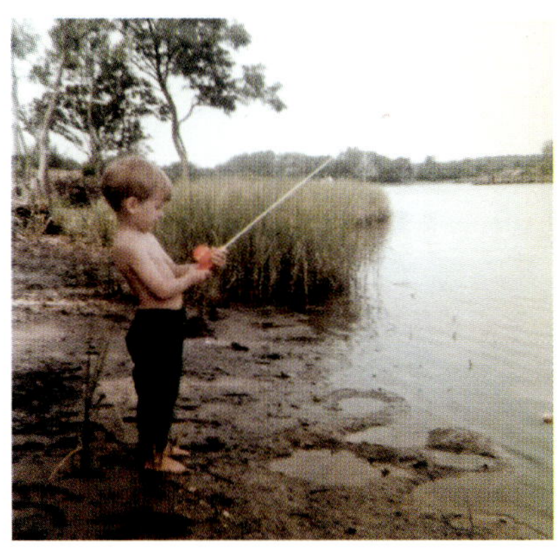

The author as a child on the shores of the Little Choptank at the home of John Werry I and Dorothy Werry, our grandparents.

This is where we learned to fish and crab and just enjoy every little discovery and adventure that the Bay brought to us. This magical place started a 40-year love affair between the Werrys and the Chesapeake Bay.

## Anne Arundel County

In the late '70s, our next-door neighbor in Crofton, Maryland, took us to his boat in Deale, Maryland, and exposed us to the hardcore weekend boater lifestyle. We were immediately hooked with the fishing, crabbing, and socializing and by 1980 we had our own boat, a 28-foot Luhrs. Crabbing from the marina piers became a dawn-'til-bedtime activity.

Although the boat seldom had to leave the dock for us to have fun, many of our best weekends were spent away from it with the "Fox Flotilla"—several of the neighboring boats from the marina who would tie up together, anchored for the weekend surrounded by family, friends, and the water.

A promotion for my father meant a move to Ohio, prompting a temporary leave of absence from the Bay and the sale of our second boat, a 36-foot Trojan. This boat soon ended up on the front page of the newspaper in flames after a bilge blower mishap (they didn't run it) involving the boat broker and a prospective buyer taking it out for a test drive. Everyone was fine but the boat was toast.

After a handful of years, the magnetic force of the Bay must have been at work again because my family found themselves leaving Ohio for the East Coast, and after college I returned as well.

Time passed by in Pennsylvania and Delaware and the Werry clan, which now included my wife, was boatless. Time spent on or near the Bay was not what it had historically been when we were living within a reasonable driving distance. However, by 2002 my wife and I were in the market to buy a second home, and I made a case to break with the regional norm of it being at the Atlantic coast beaches. I wanted it to be on the Chesapeake.

We spent two years looking for a waterfront home on the Chesapeake, spending weekends driving what seemed every mile of shoreline along the Western and Eastern shores within three-hours driving distance of our home in Wilmington, Delaware. We walked our share of muddy lots and dodged swarms of strawberry flies looking for the perfect spot.

## Talbot County

After years of searching, I altered my online searches to include Talbot county, an entire region that I felt would surely be out of our modest waterfront budget and thus had previously excluded. To my surprise, a few houses in the county were meeting our price range requirements, so we took a look at them.

The house we eventually purchased on Tilghman Island needed work, but we were able to see through the wagon-wheel dining table chandelier, wood paneling, orange carpet, and yellow '70s appliances. We knew we could fix these cosmetic problems—but you can't fix the location—which we have always found to be spectacular and which has served as a source of inspiration and subject matter for my photography.

The images within this book were all taken during this third chapter on the Bay, during which my interest in photography grew.

## The Next Chapter

To me, the Chesapeake is a part of who I am and from which I cannot be separated. I always envisioned myself retiring there somewhere as my namesake grandfather had, completing the circle that was started for me in Dorchester county 40 years ago. At the moment, that seems improbable as my wife and I embark on a new phase of life in South Carolina, but somehow the Bay seems to always draw us right back.

—John Werry

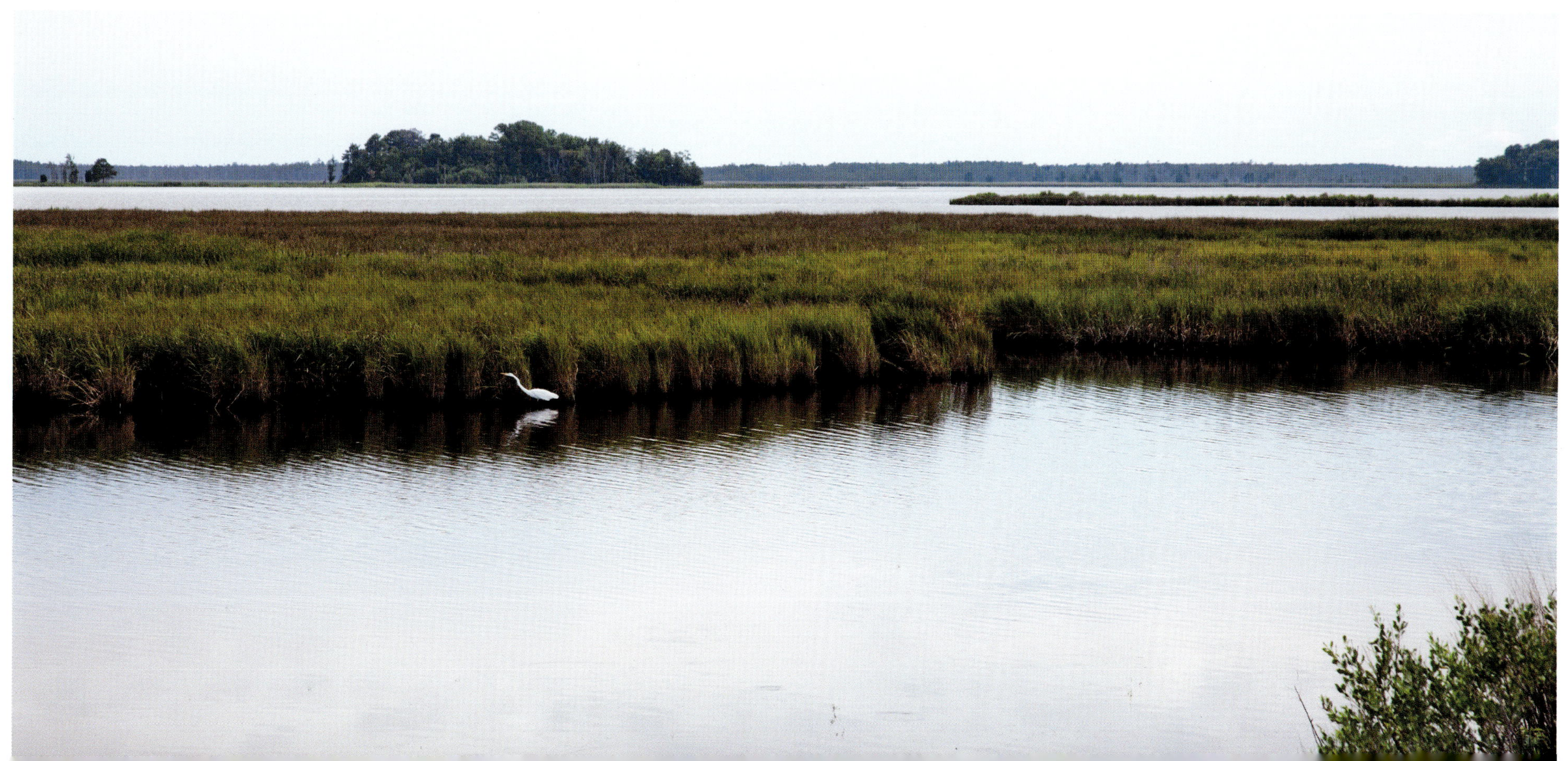

# Boats of the Bay

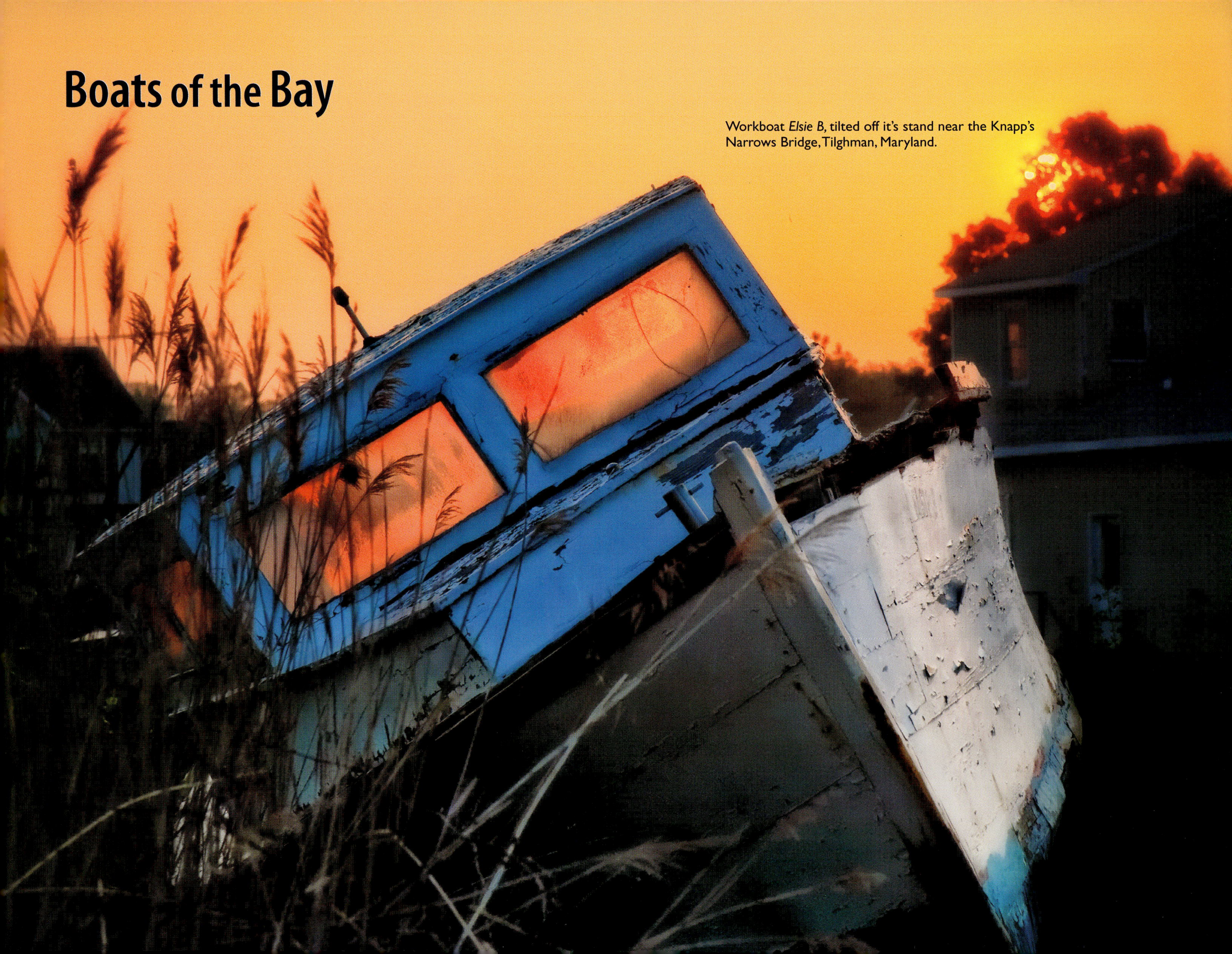

Workboat *Elsie B,* tilted off it's stand near the Knapp's Narrows Bridge, Tilghman, Maryland.

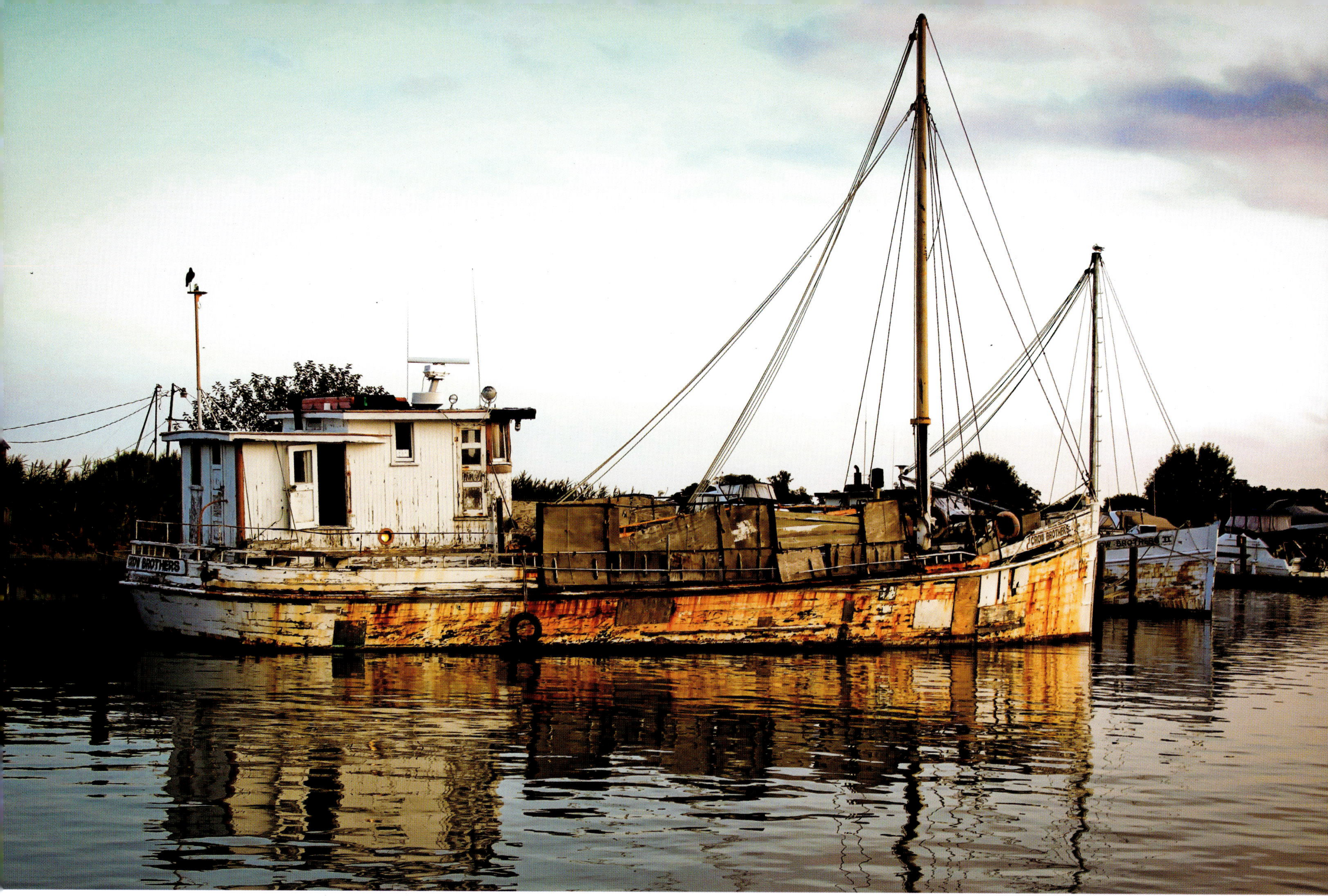


The 1929 Chesapeake buyboat, *Crow Brothers,* when it was still floating in Tongers Basin, Tilghman Island.

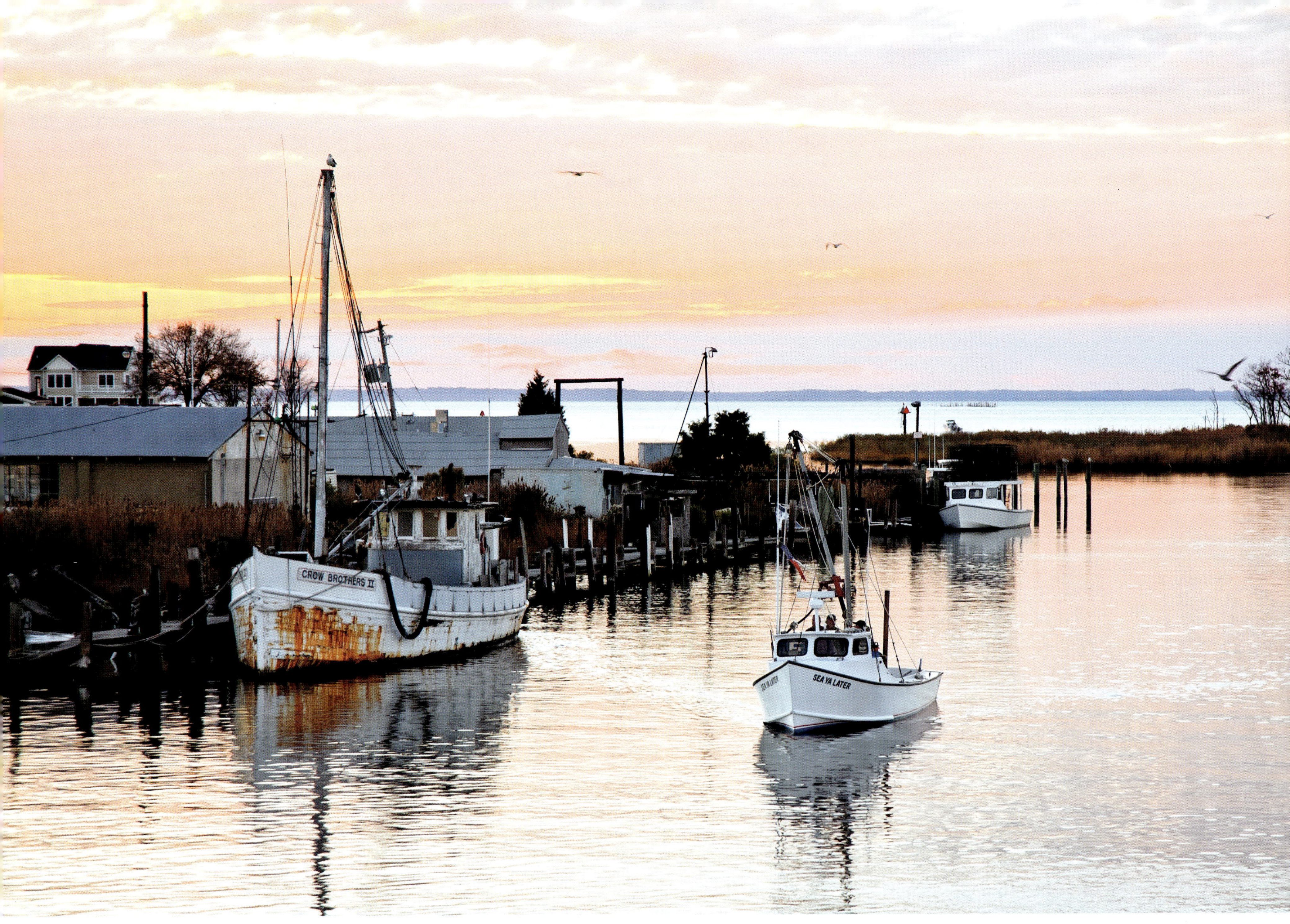


Looking out over Knapp's Narrows, Tilghman Island, from the bridge at sunset.

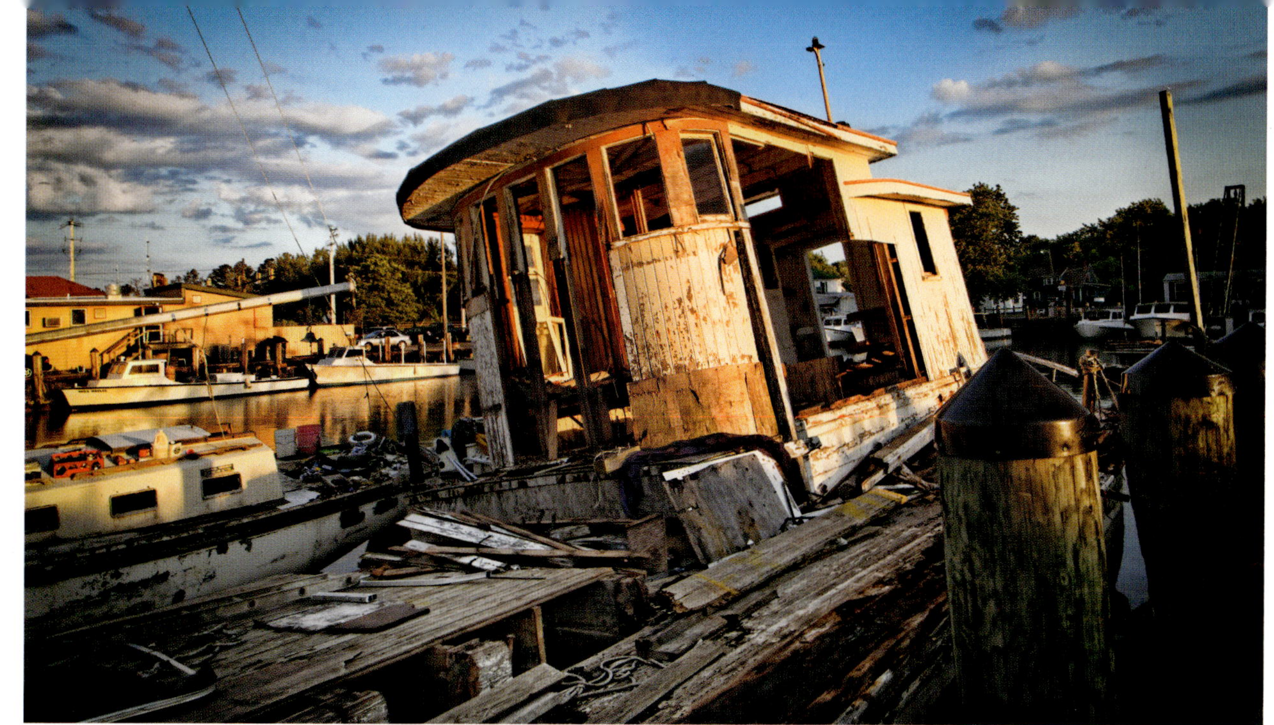

*Crow Brothers* sits on the bottom partially disassembled, just days away from disappearing completely.

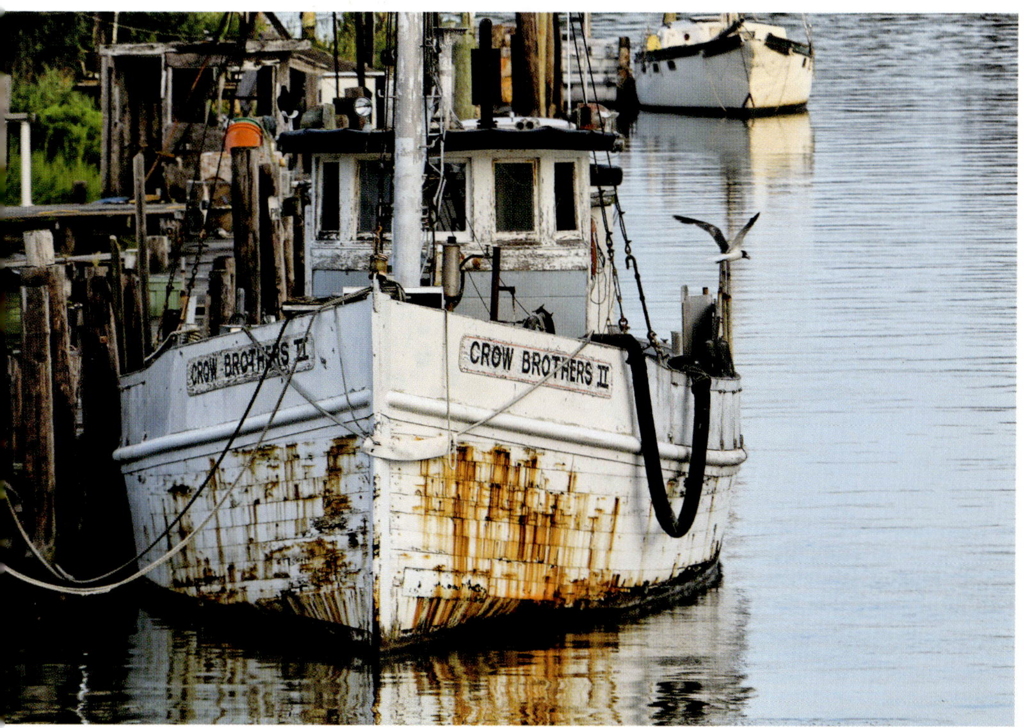


*Crow Brothers II* in it's usual spot along the Narrows, watching boat traffic pass under the bridge.

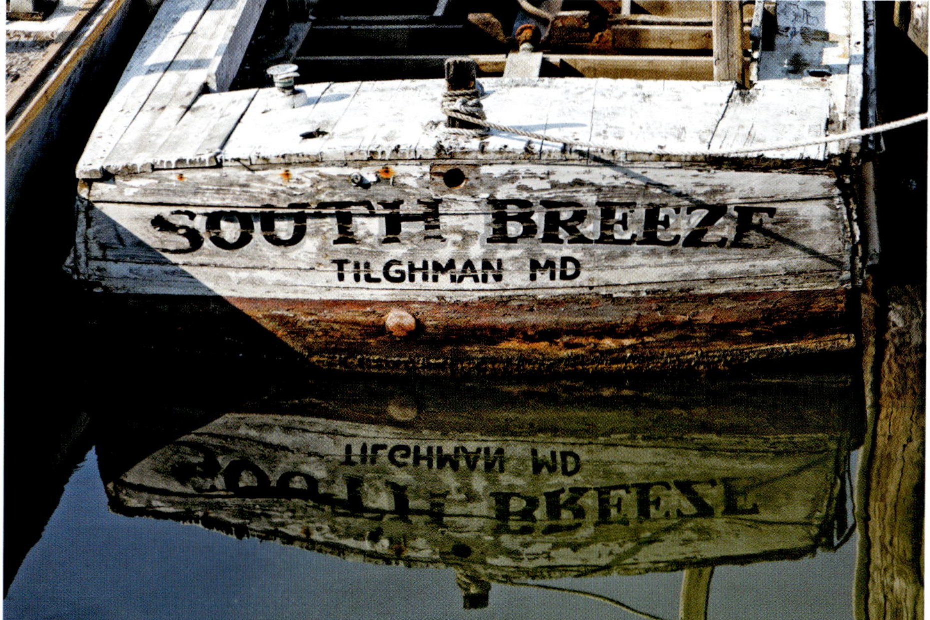


*South Breeze* in Tongers Basin, Tilghman Island.

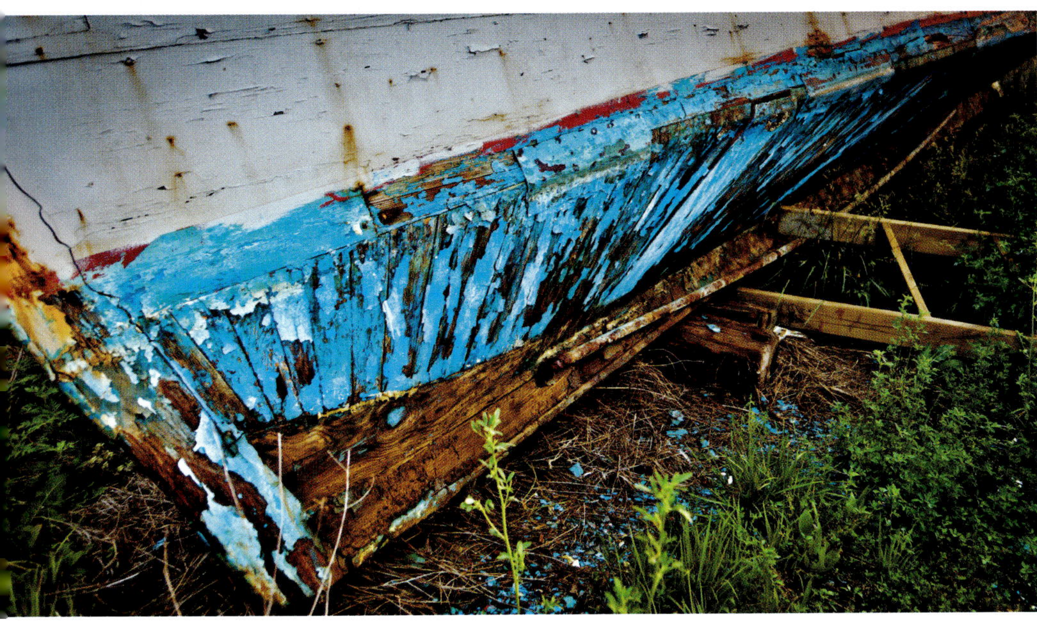

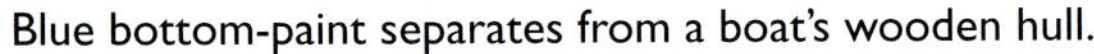

Blue bottom-paint separates from a boat's wooden hull.

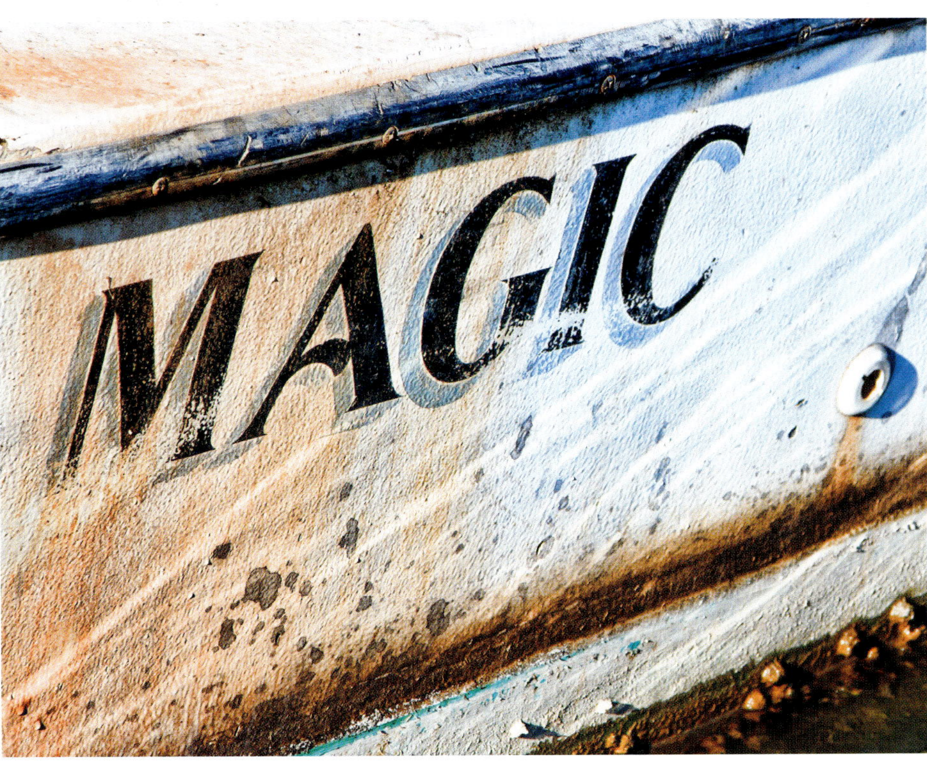


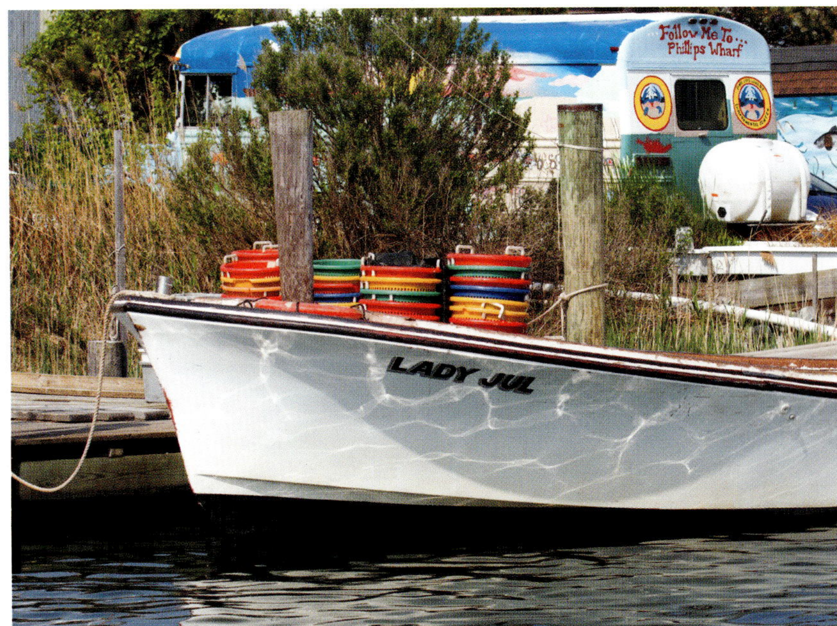


*Lady Jul* and the Phillips Wharf Environmental Center's "Fishmobile" on Tilghman Island.

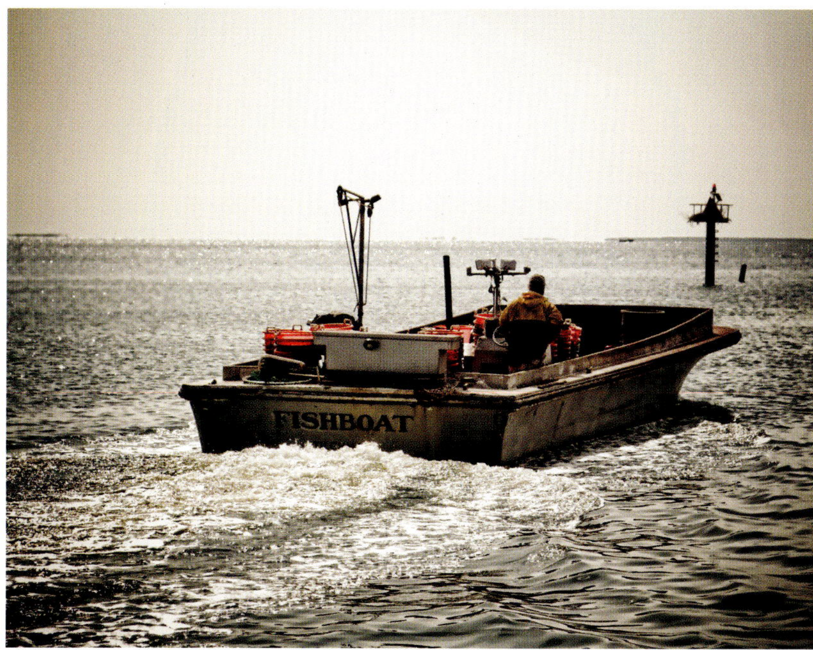


*Fishboat* heads out on a late April morning from Knapp's Narrows.

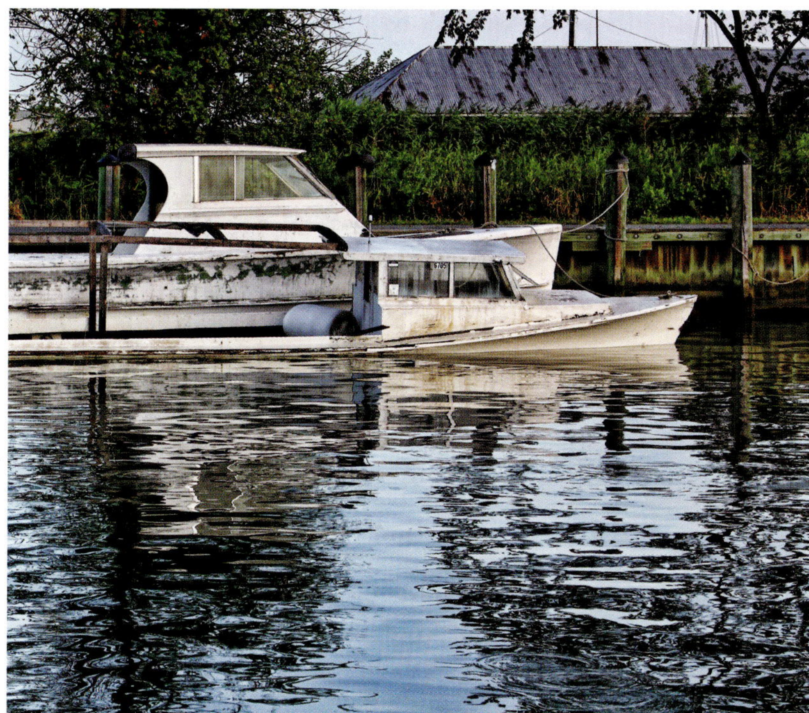

Tongers Basin often finds itself berthing boats in various states of readiness.

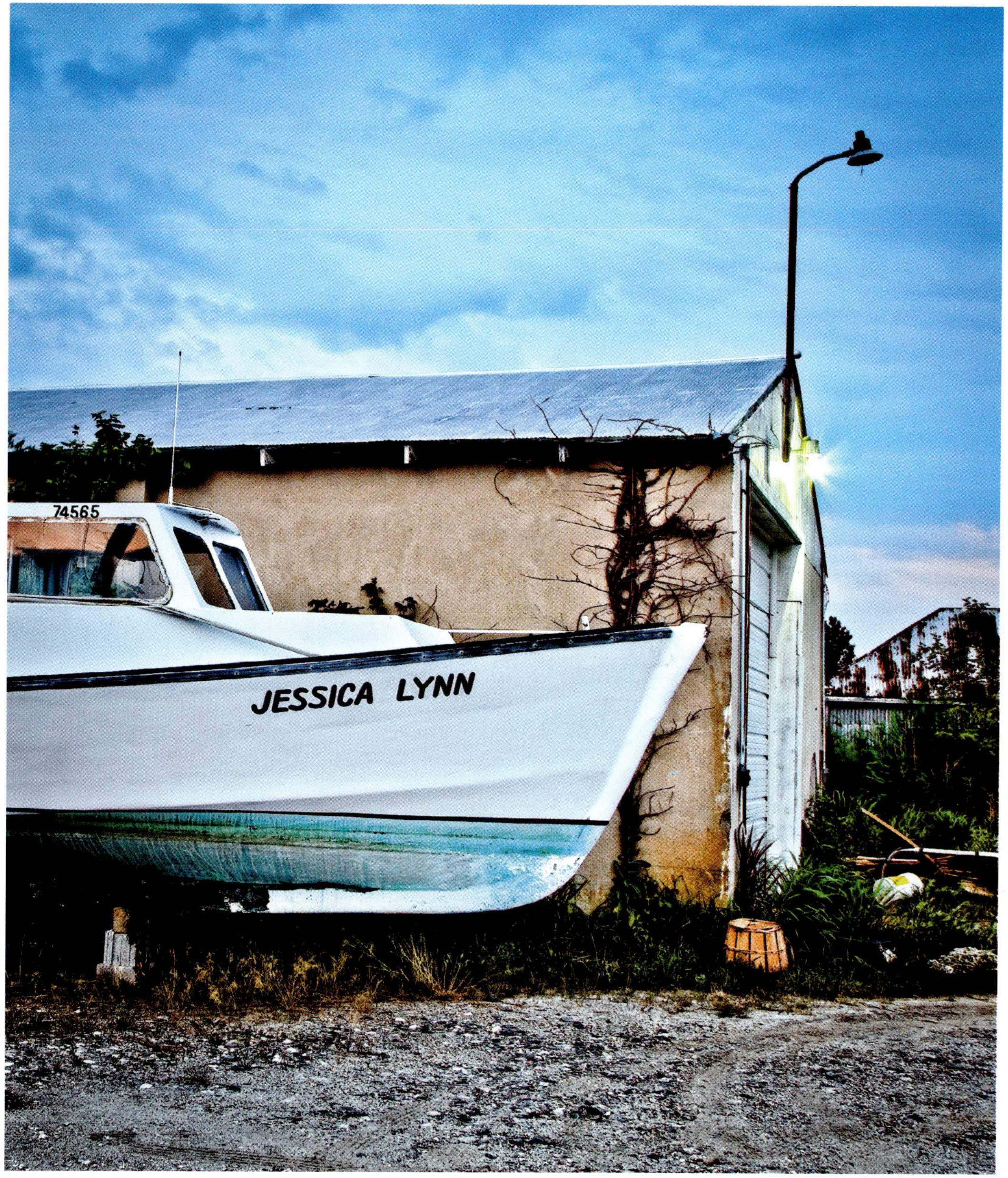

*Jessica Lynn* waits patiently on the hard.

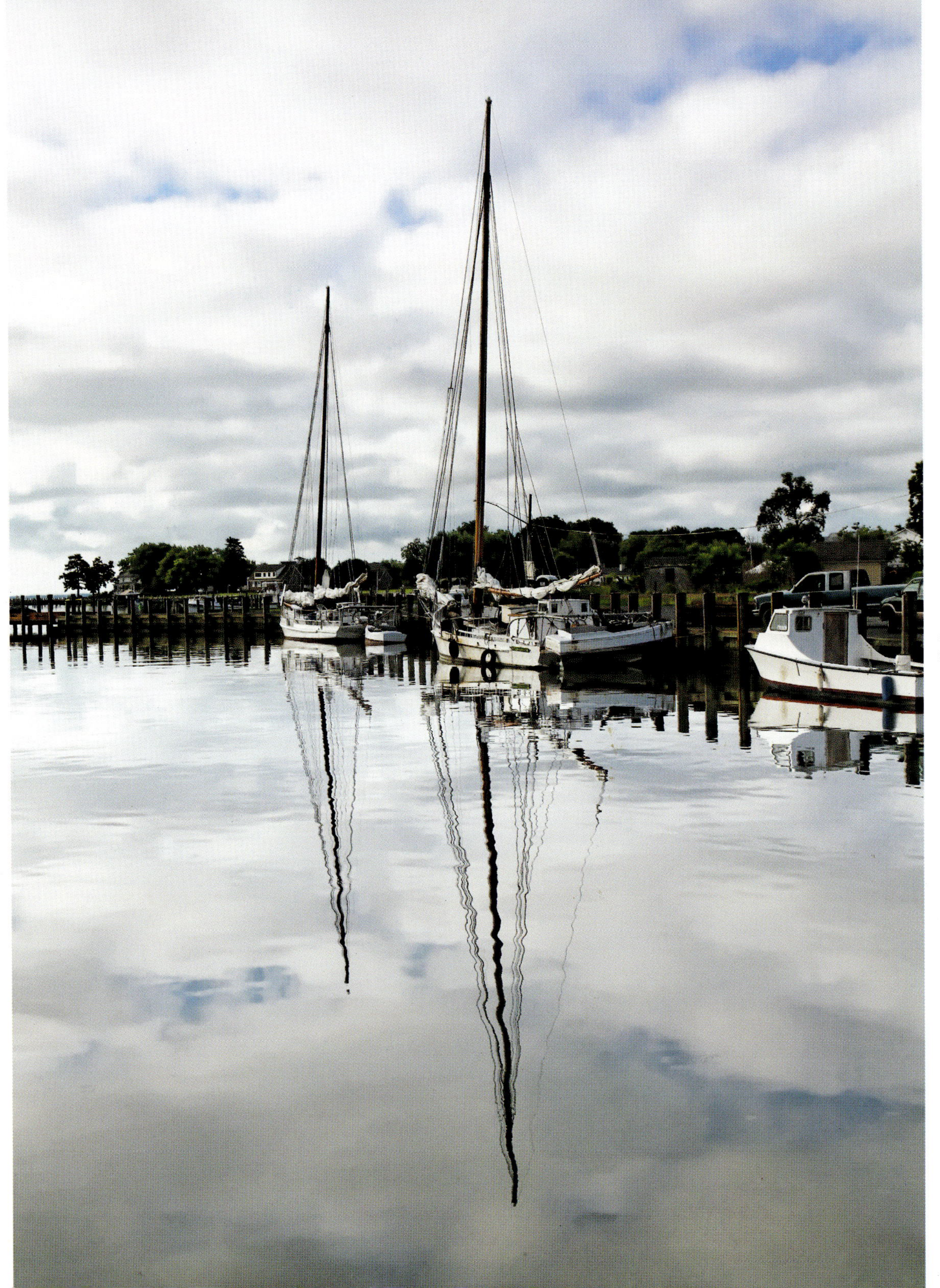

*Rebecca T. Ruark* and *Thomas Clyde* accompanied by their pushboats in Dogwood Harbor.

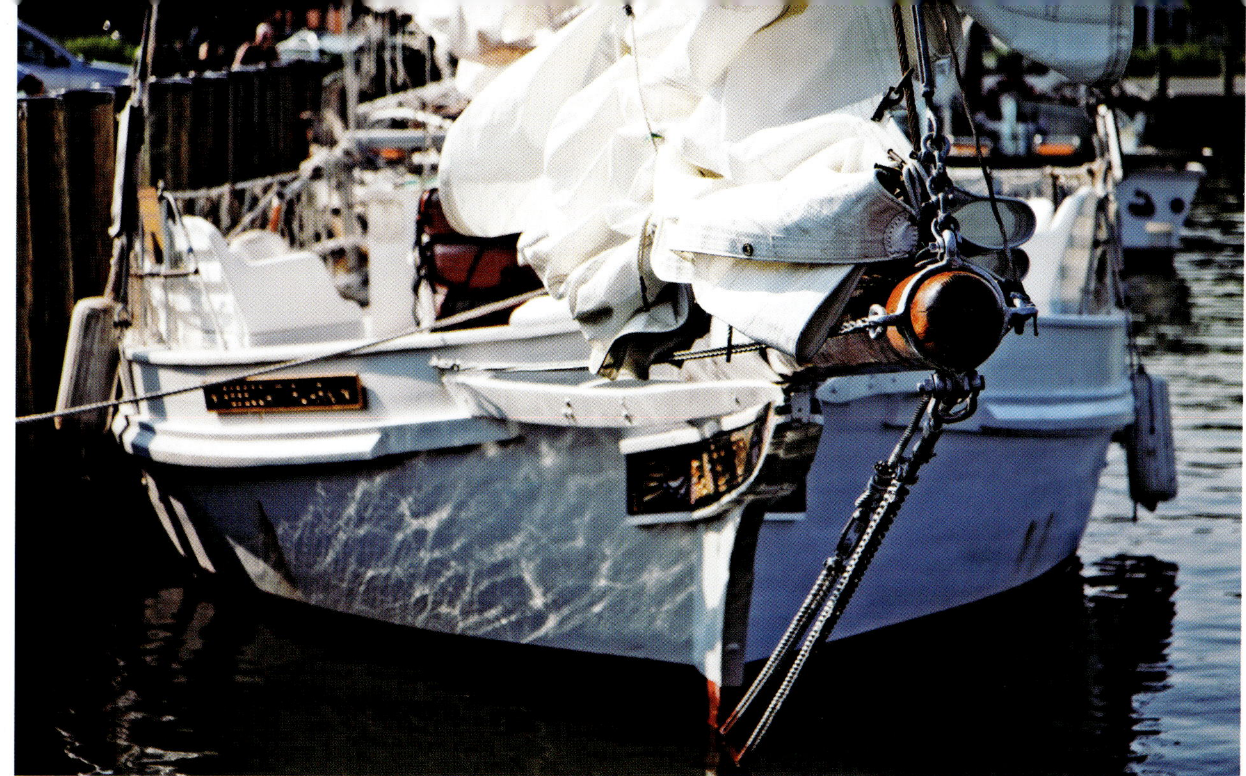

*Rebecca T. Ruark*, built in 1886, is the oldest working skipjack left on the Bay.

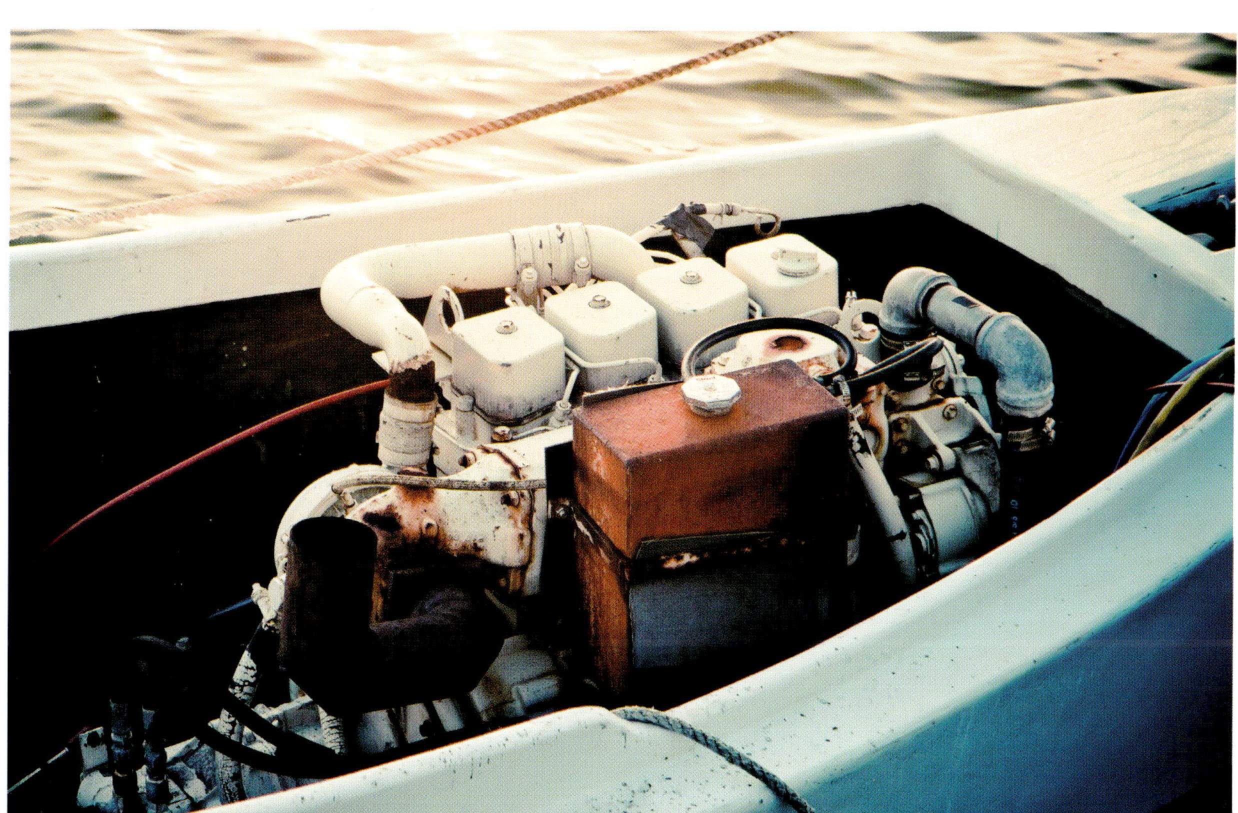

A pushboat motor can sometimes live its life exposed to the elements.

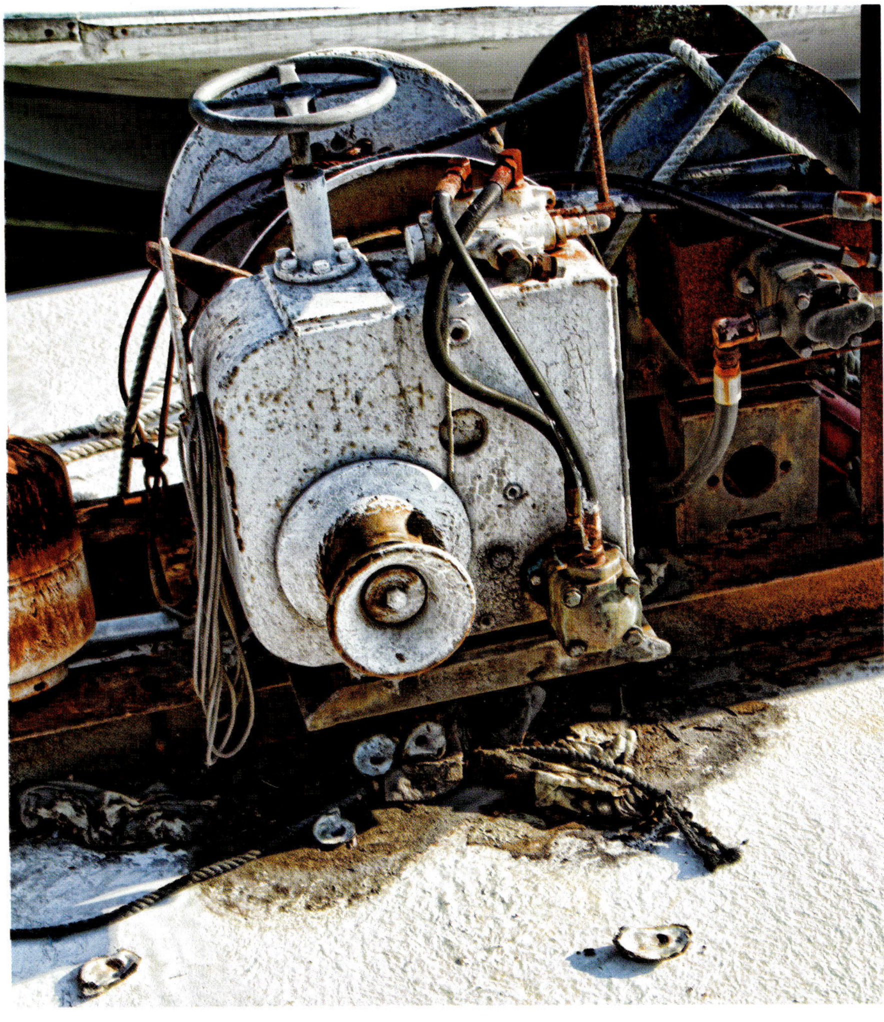

Equipment aboard a waterman's boat sits above evidence of its past oystering excursions.

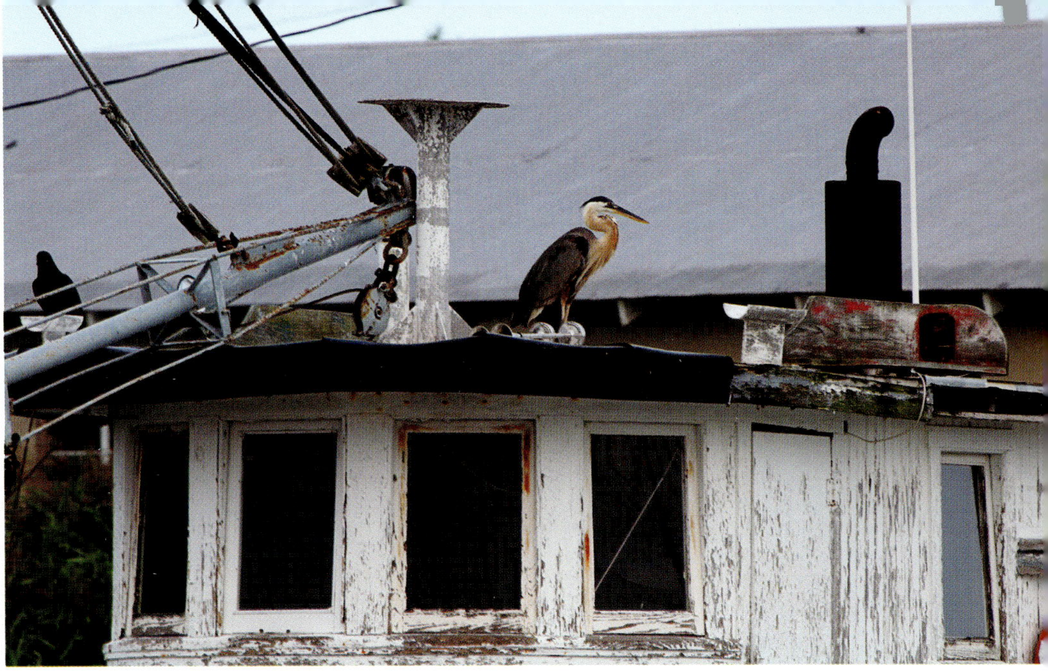

*Crow Brothers II* acts as a resting spot for many of the area's birds, including this great blue heron.

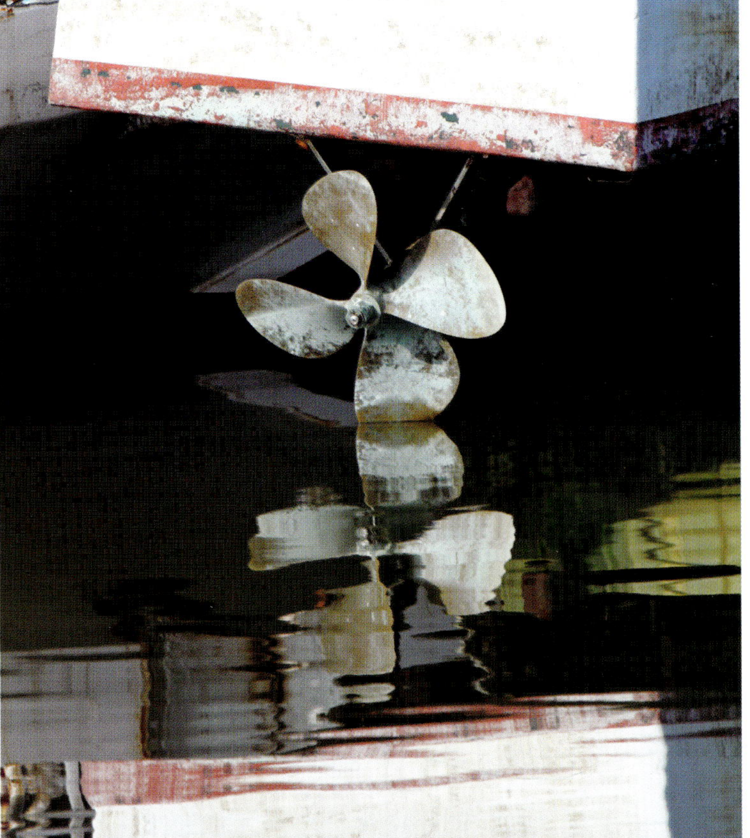

A pushboat prop touches its own reflection in Dogwood Harbor, Tilghman Island.

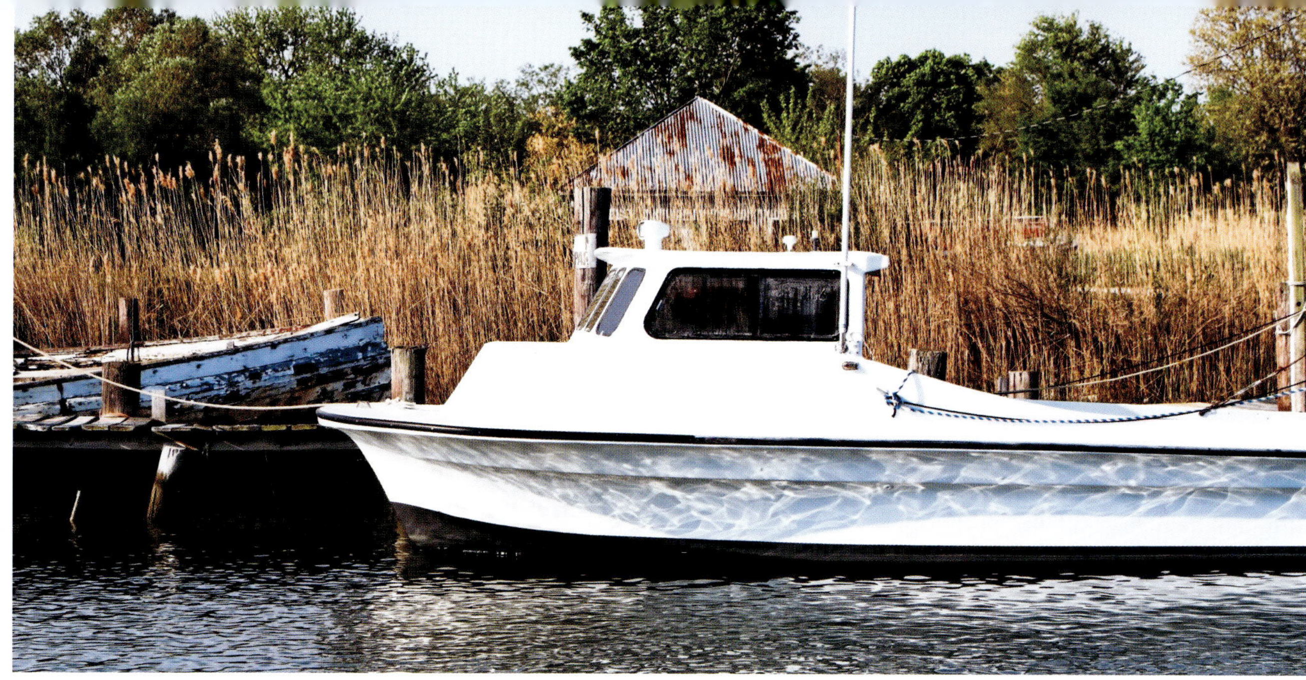

The water's reflection dancing on a boat along Knapp's Narrows.

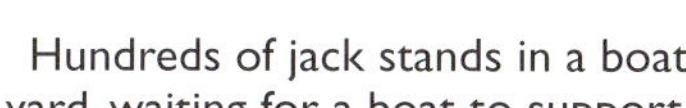

Hundreds of jack stands in a boat yard, waiting for a boat to support.

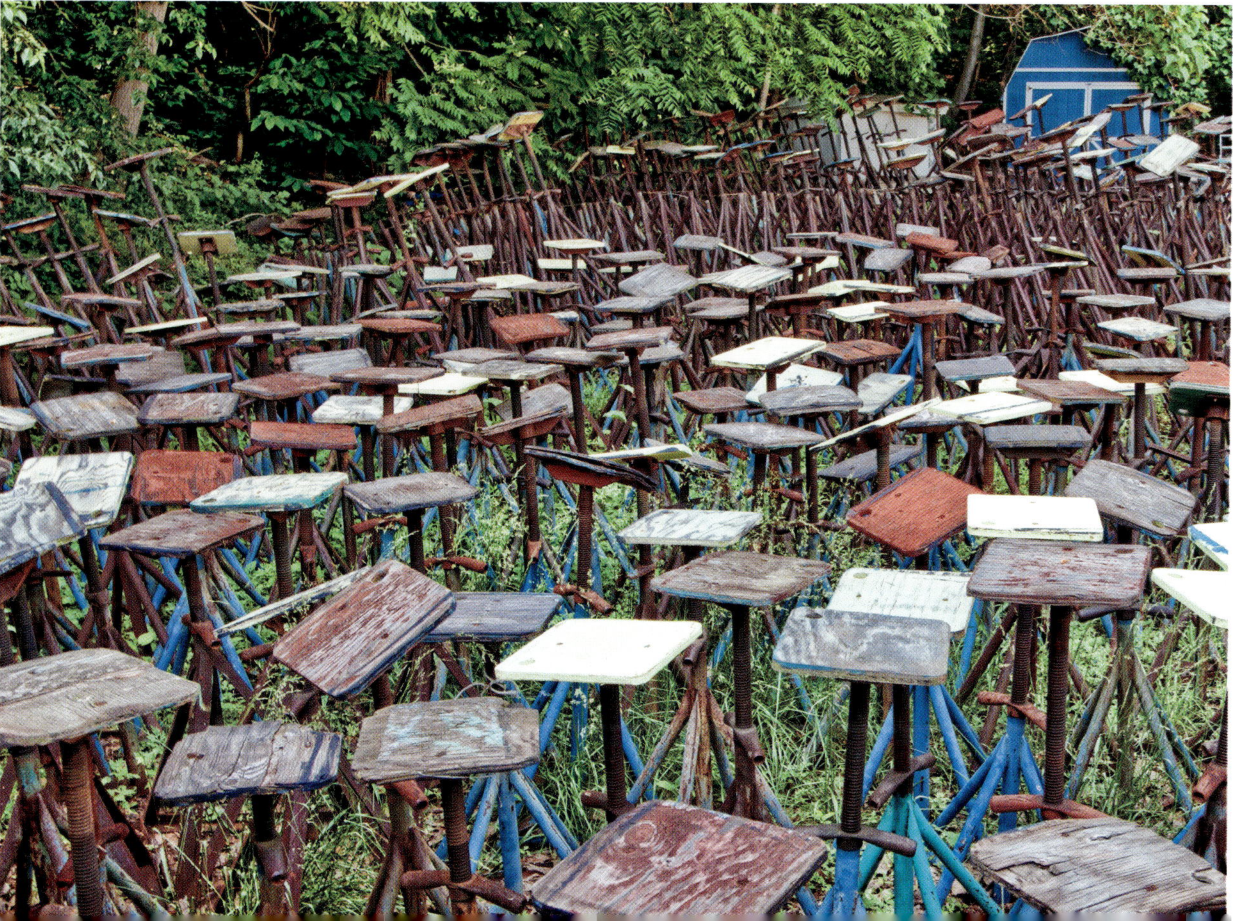

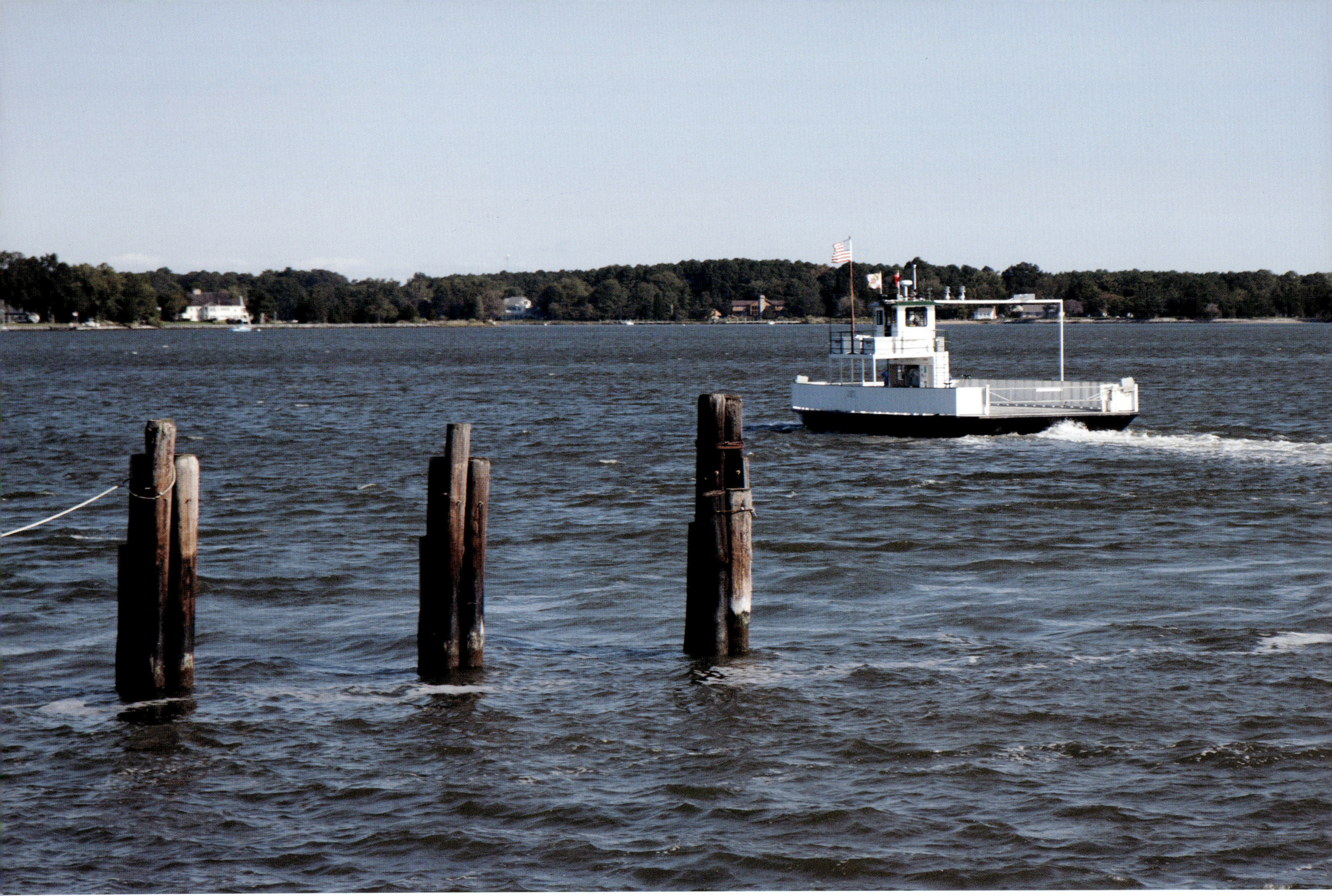

The Oxford–Bellevue ferry was established in 1683 to ferry horses and men across the Tred Avon River in Maryland.

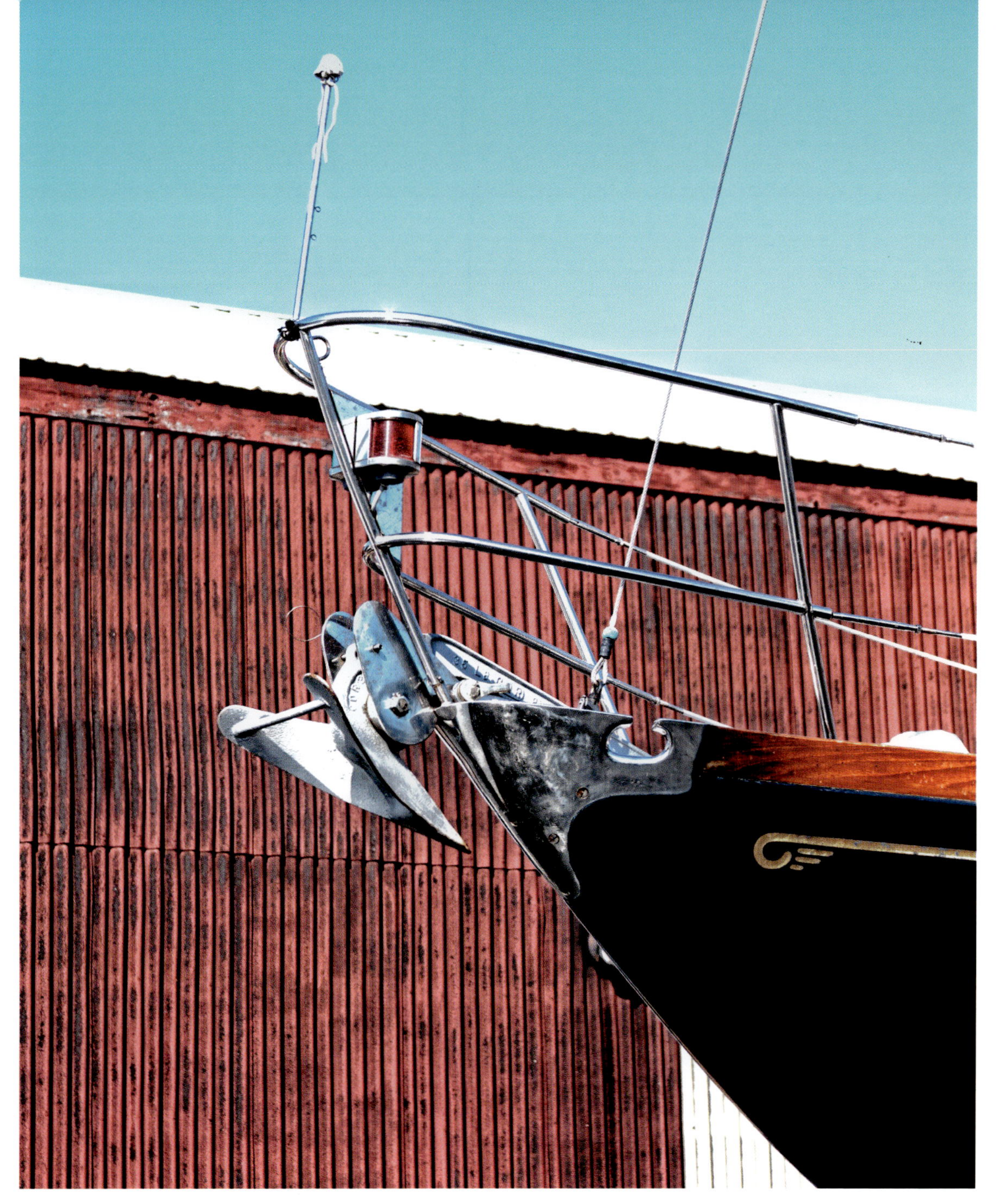

A Hinckley sits in a yard in Oxford, Maryland.

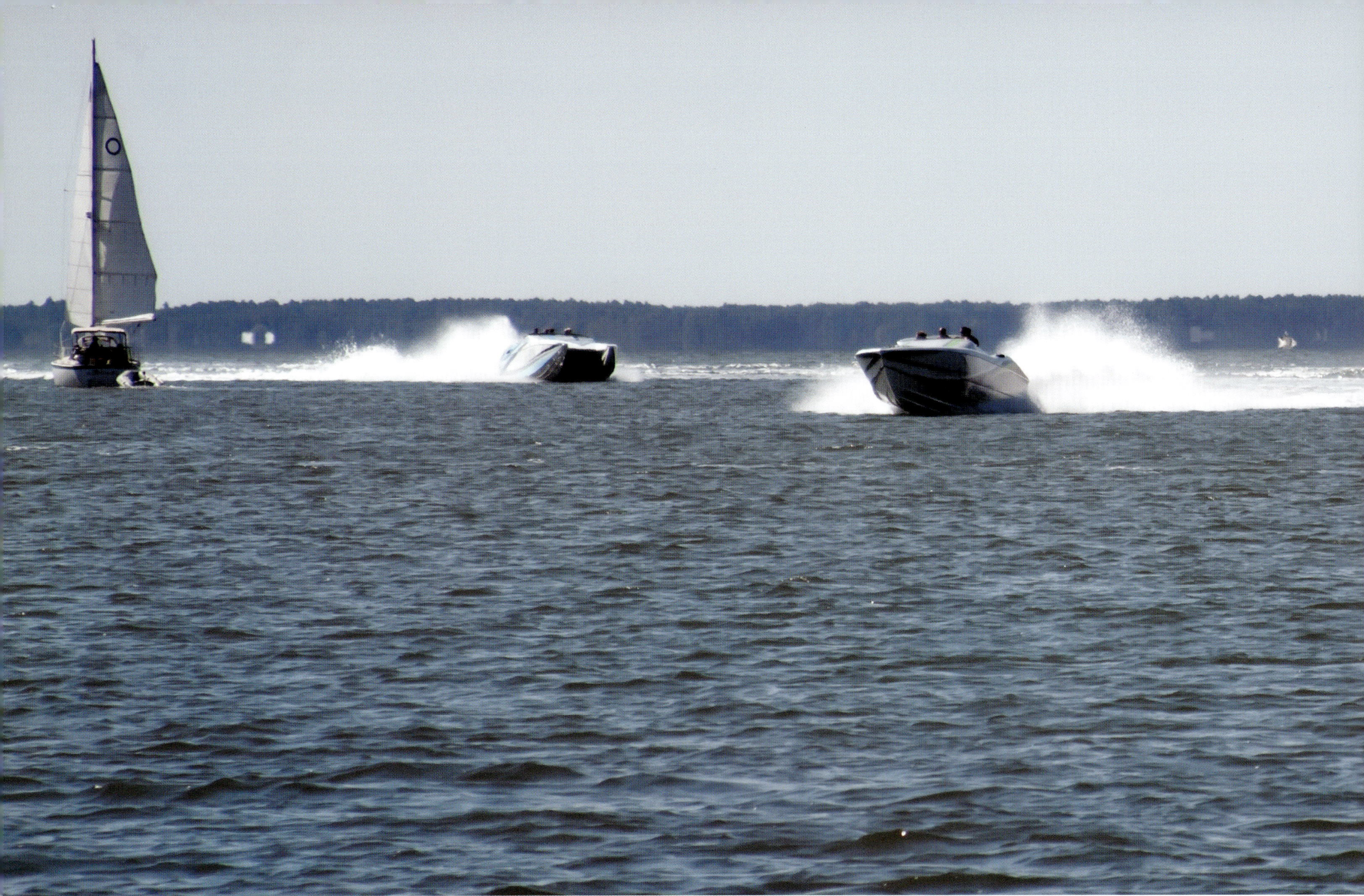

Racing powerboats on the Tred Avon.

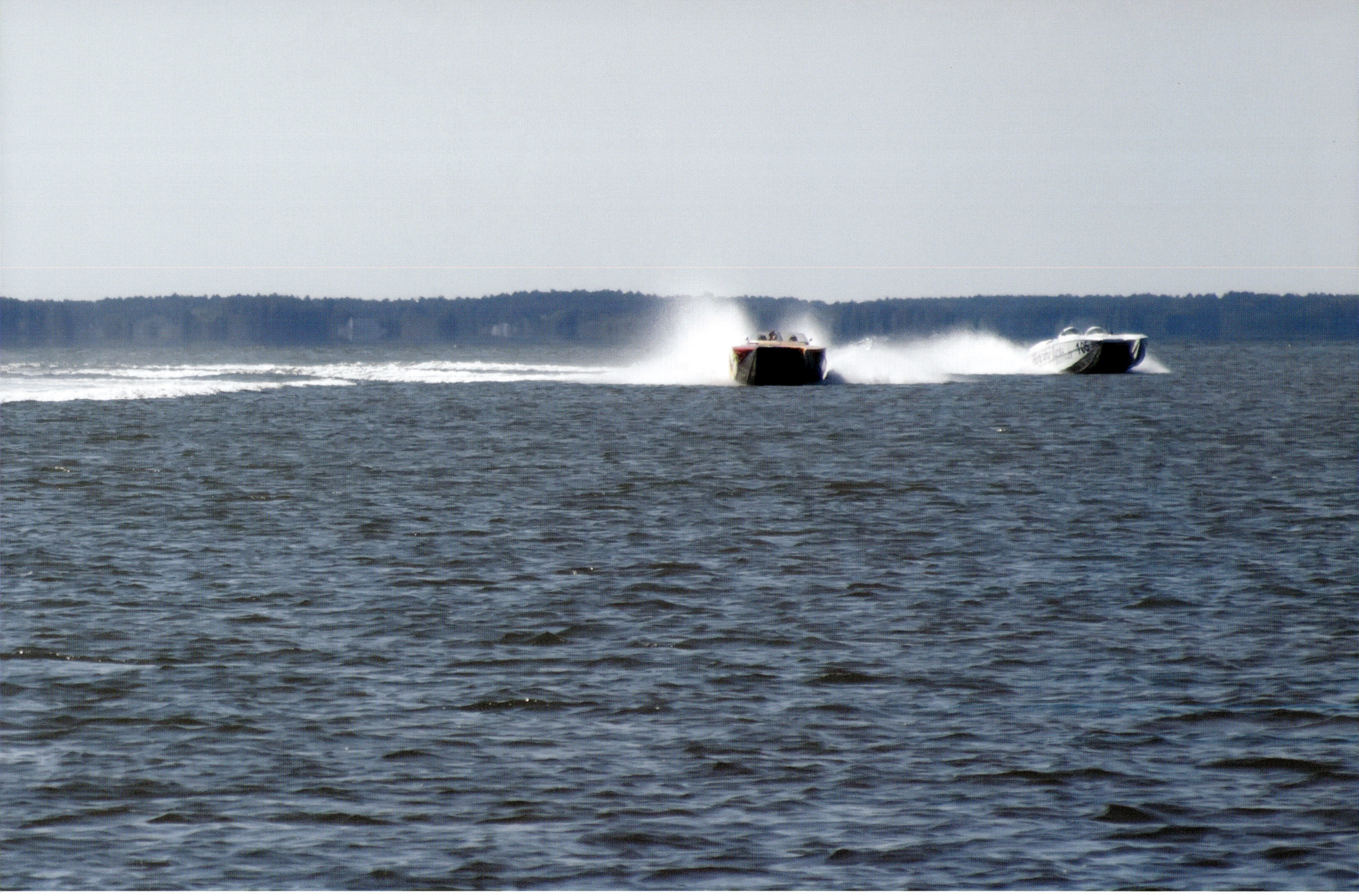

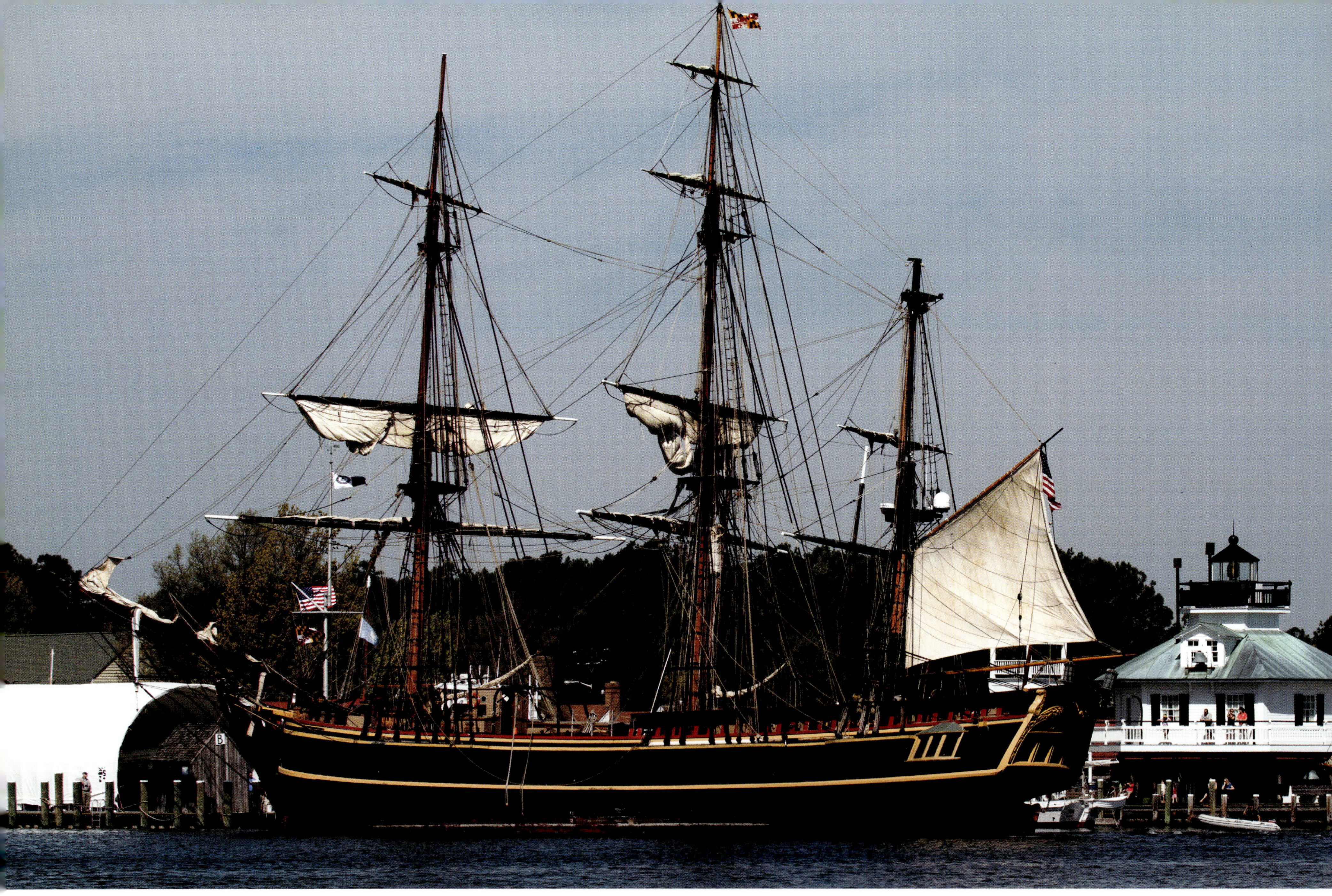

*The Sultana* docked in St. Michaels at the Chesapeake Bay Maritime Museum.

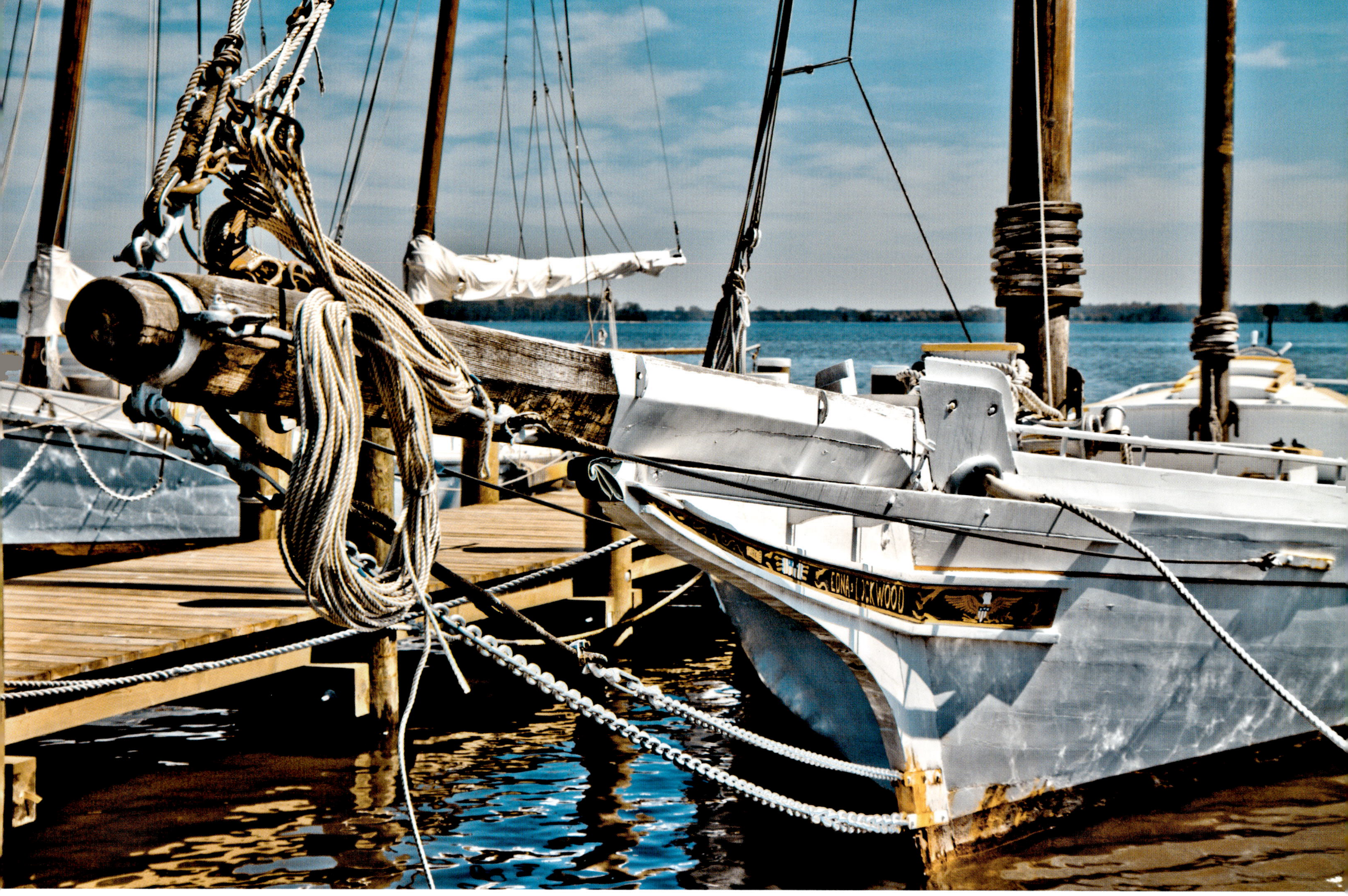

*Edna E. Lockwood* docked at the Chesapeake Bay Maritime Museum.

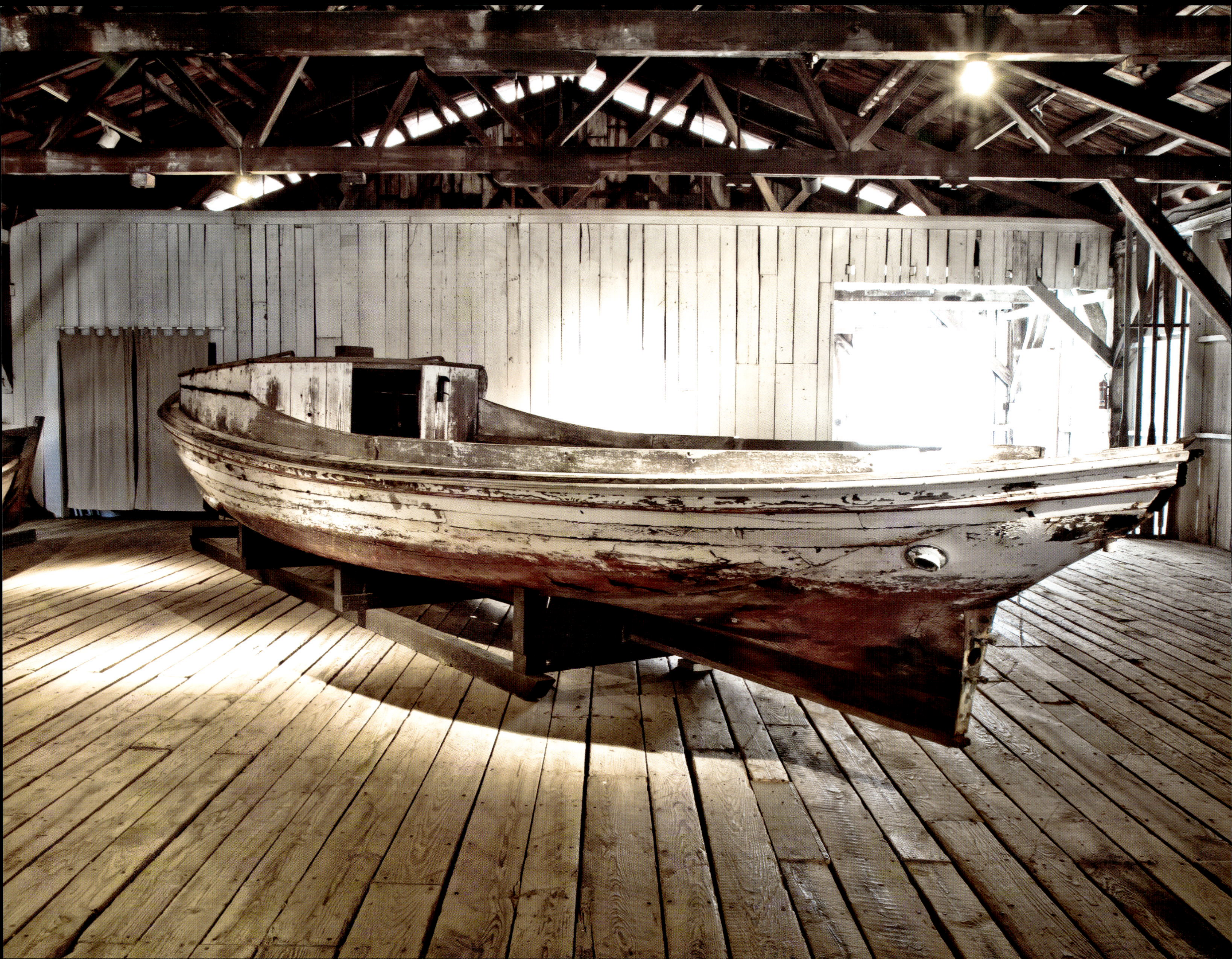

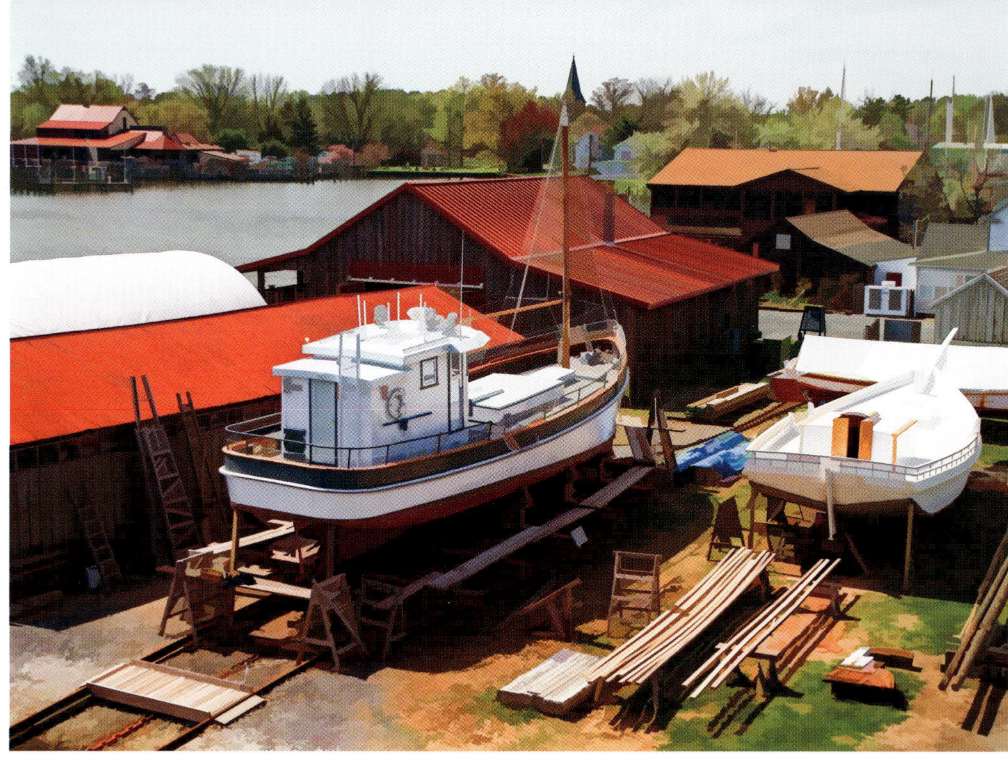

Looking out from the Hooper Strait Lighthouse exhibit at the Chesapeake Bay Maritime Museum, over the replica buyboat *Mister Jim* and the boat yard.

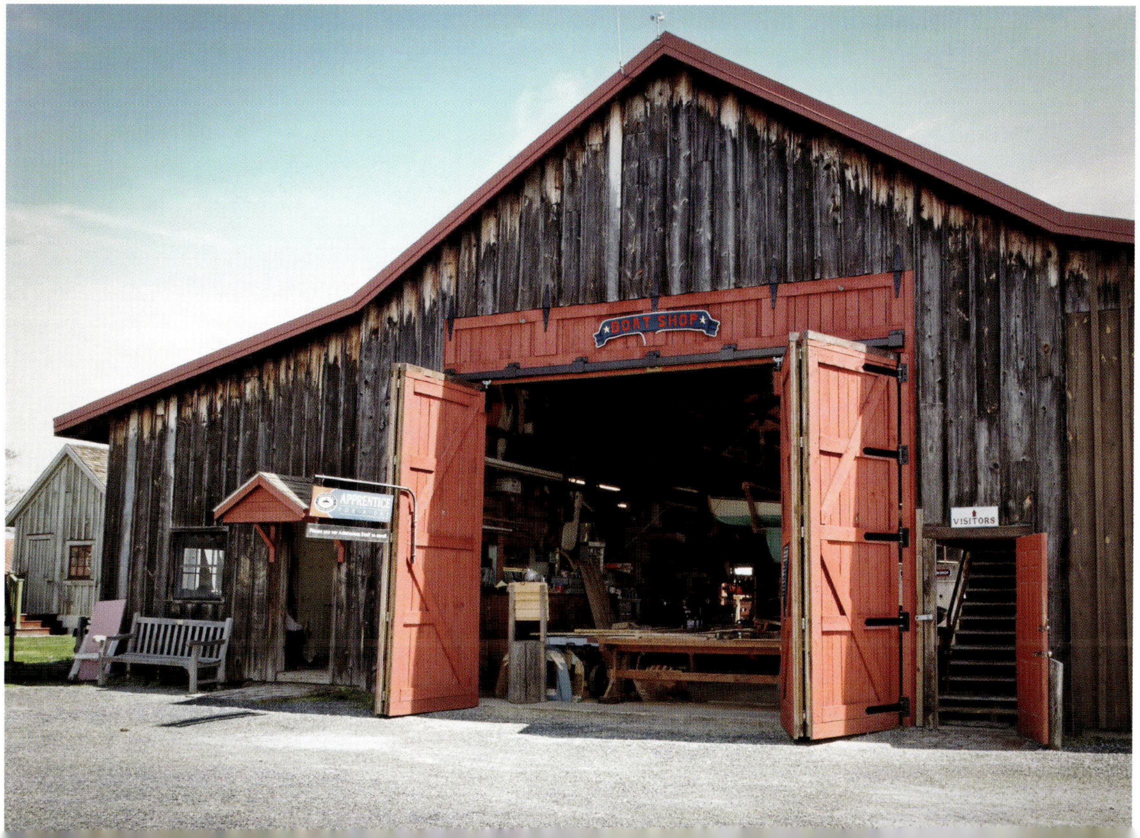

The Boat Shop at the Chesapeake Bay Maritime Museum.

The small boat shed at the Chesapeake Bay Maritime Museum.

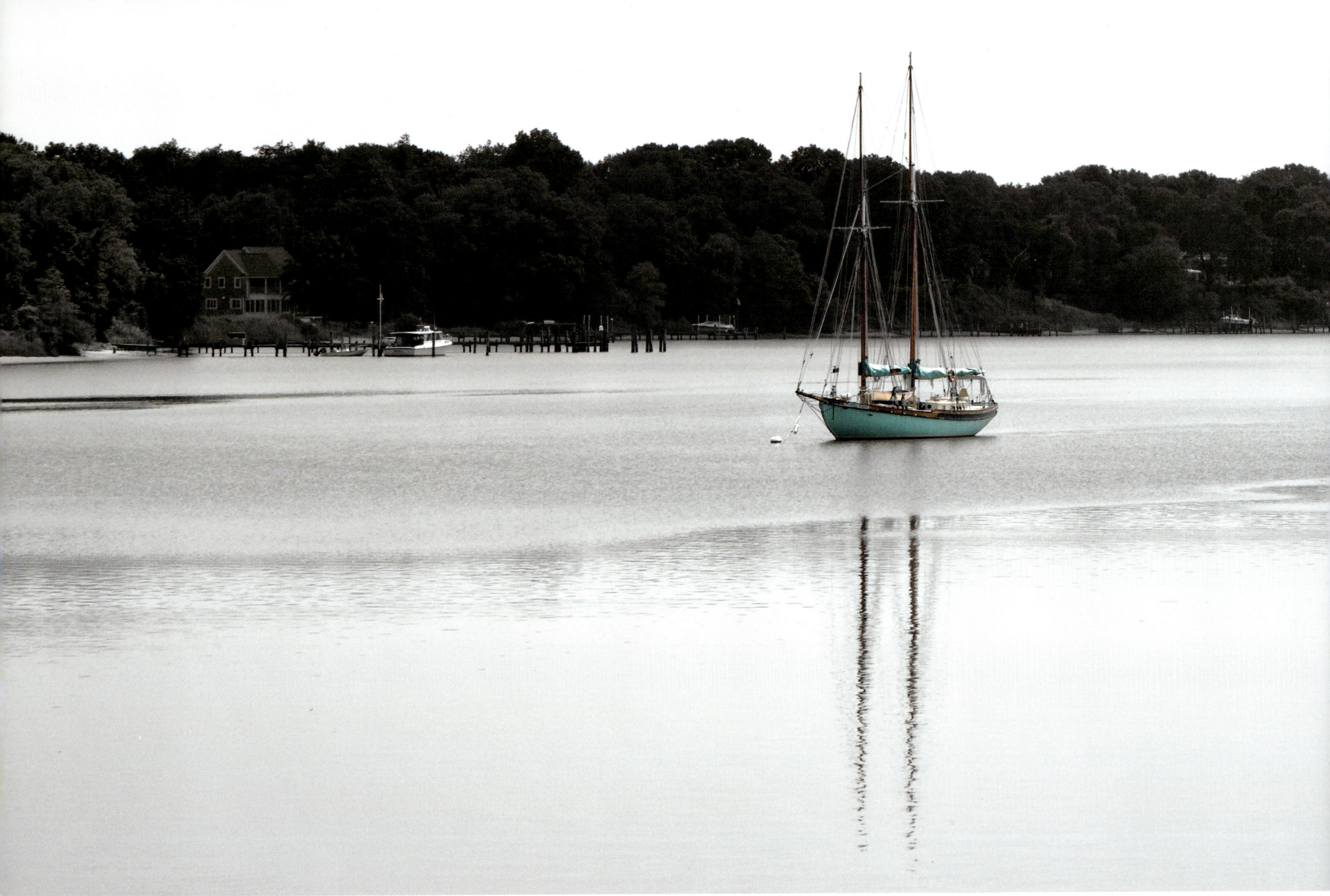

A schooner moored in the Chester River near Chestertown, Maryland.

A feral cat on Smith Island finds a houseboat a safe place to sleep as the sun prepares to go down for the day.

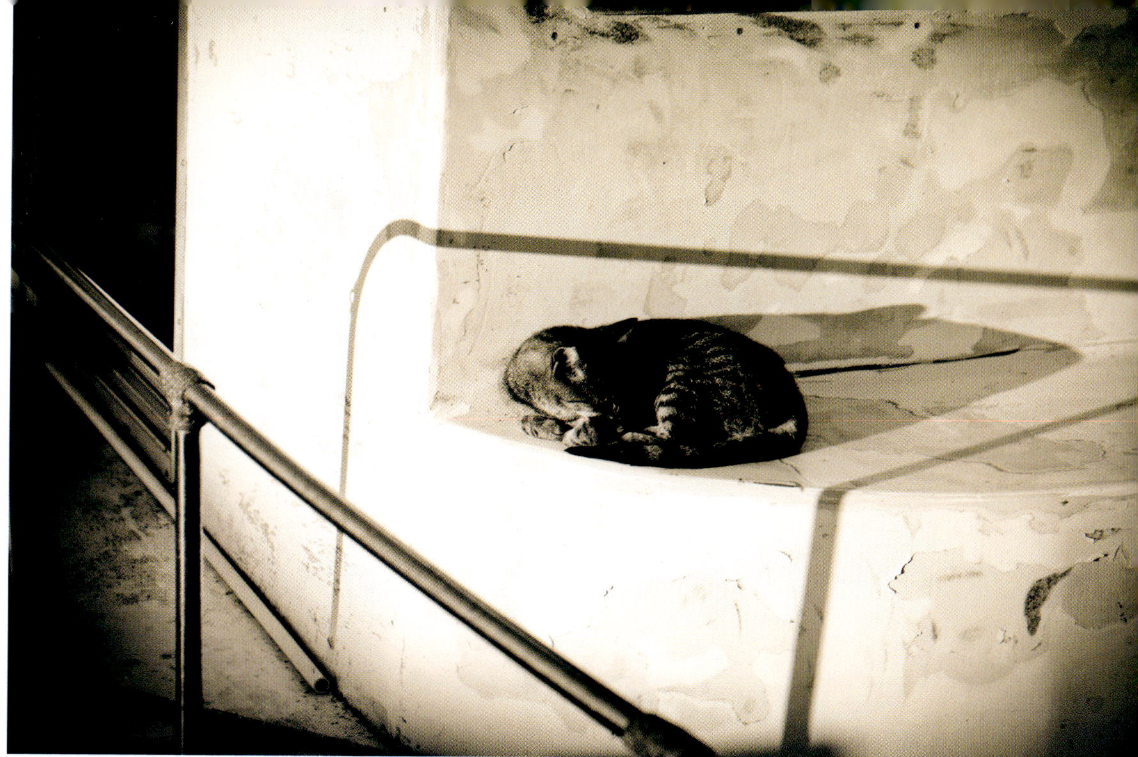

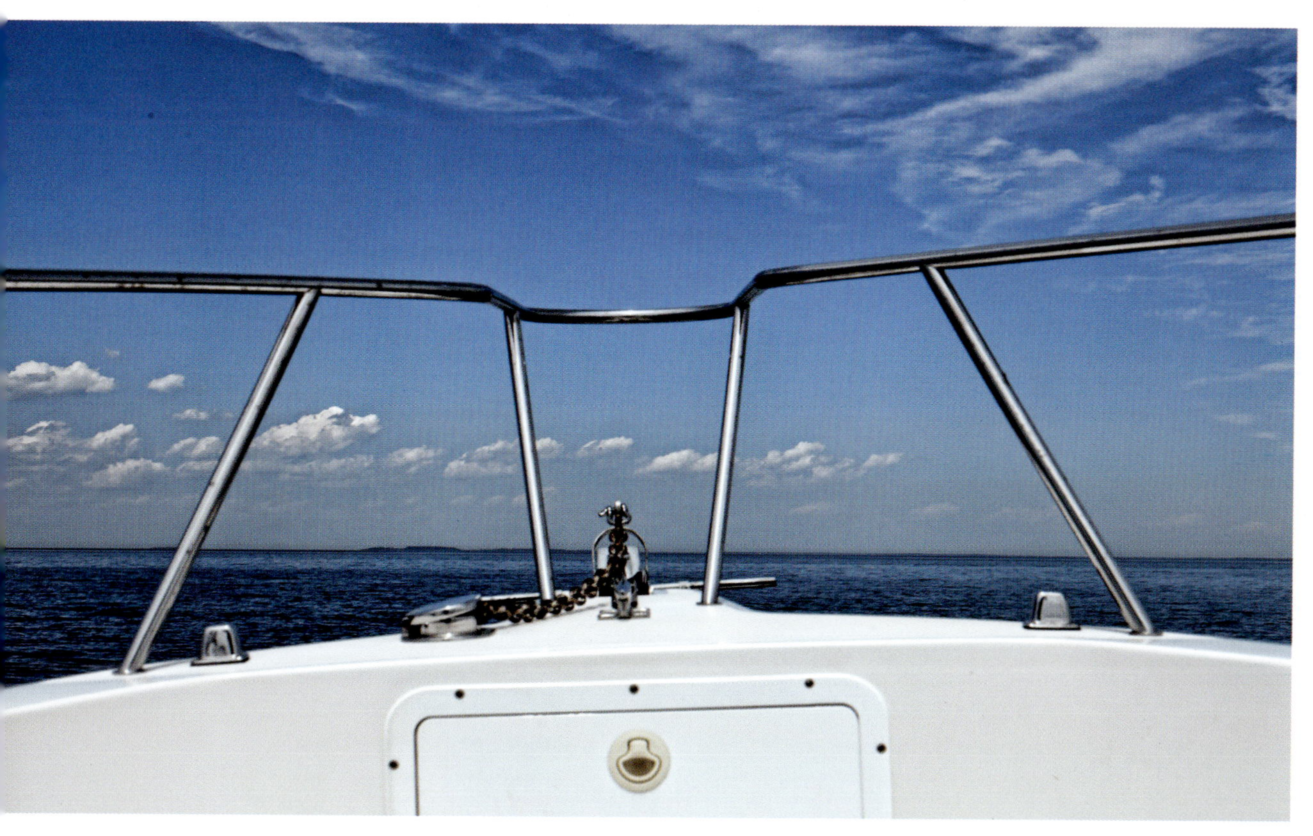

A quick ride from the western shore fishing grounds back to Tilghman Island.

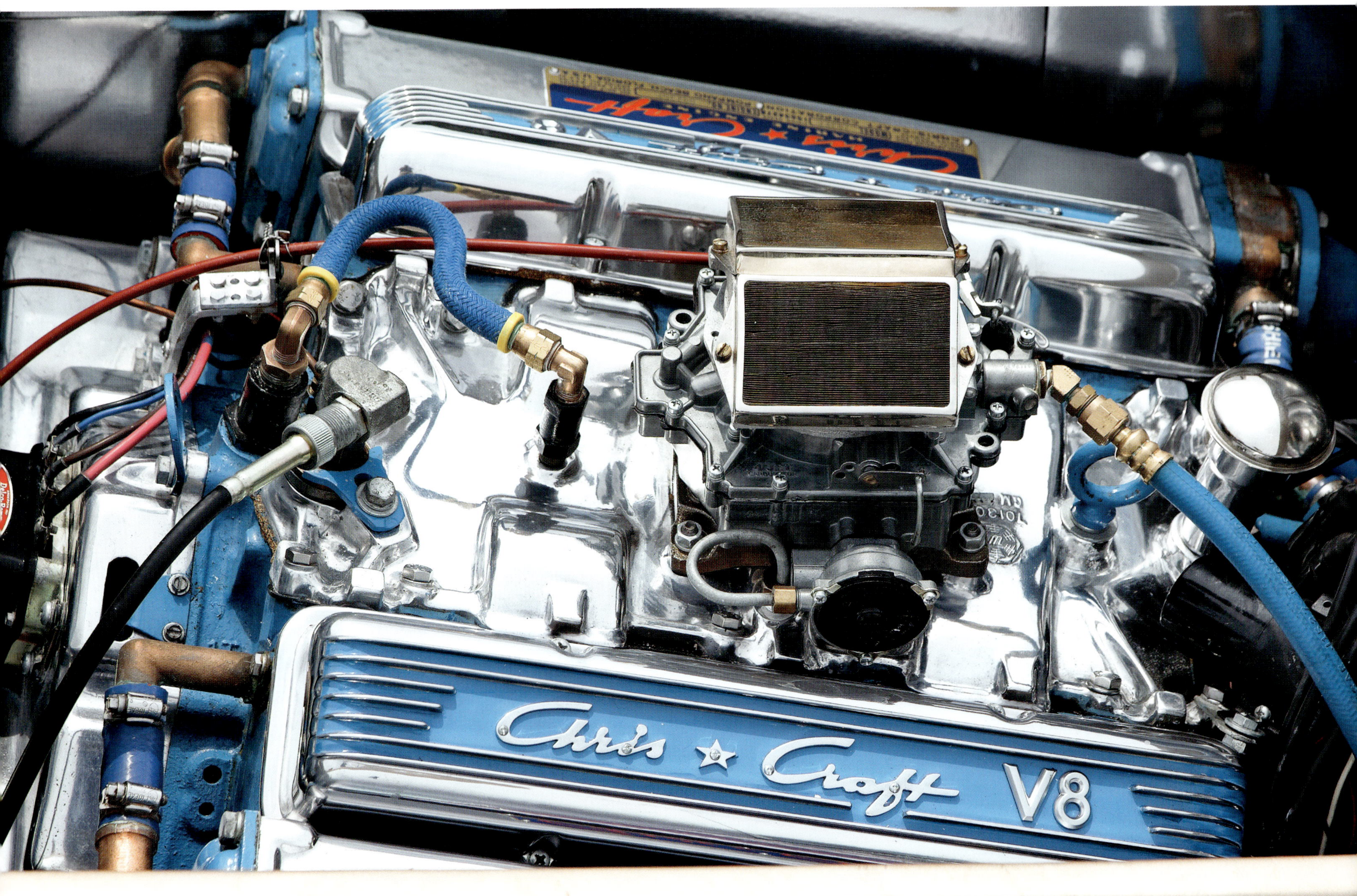


*Cool's* V8

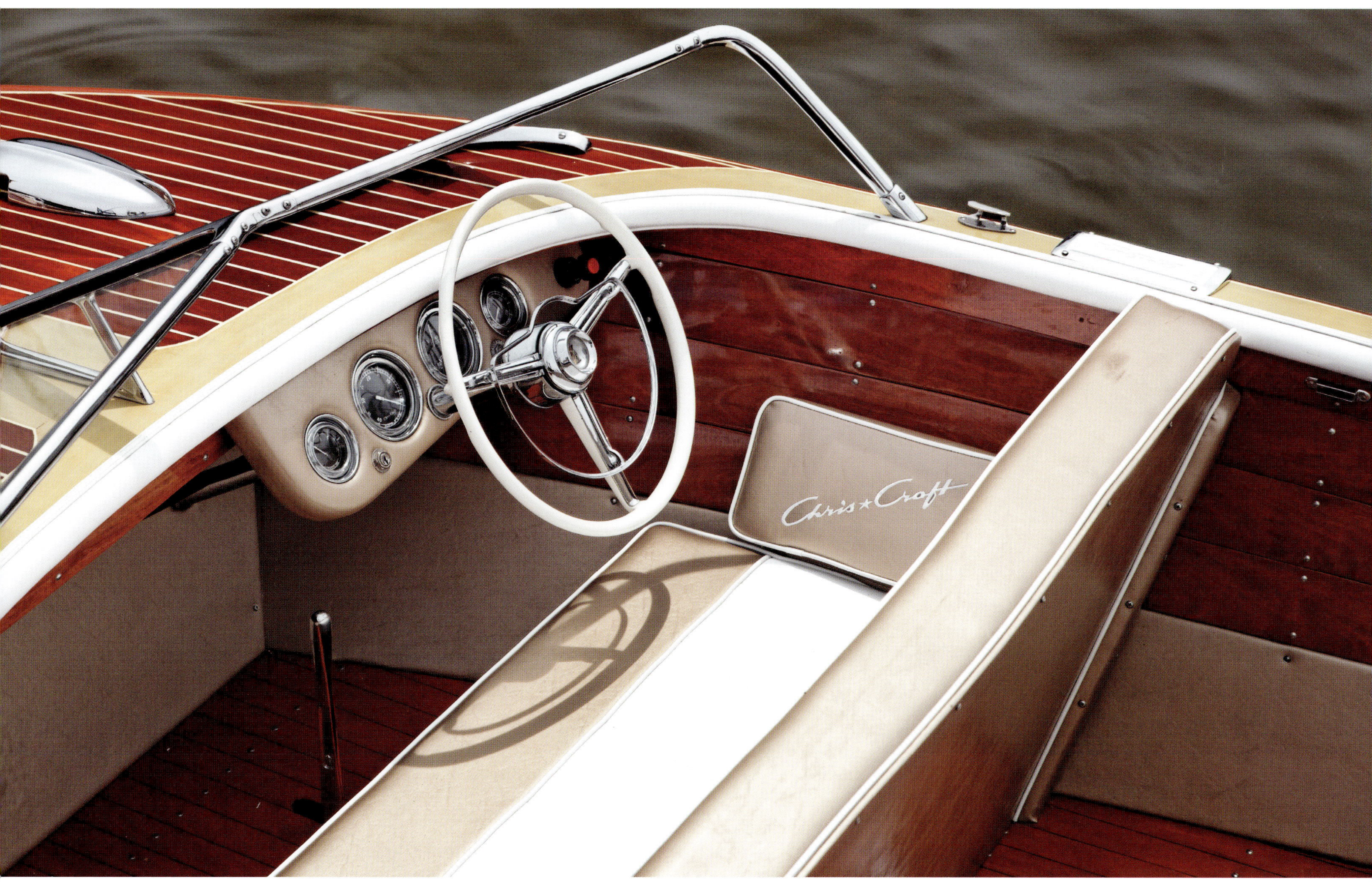


*Cool*, a classic 1955 Chris Craft Continental.

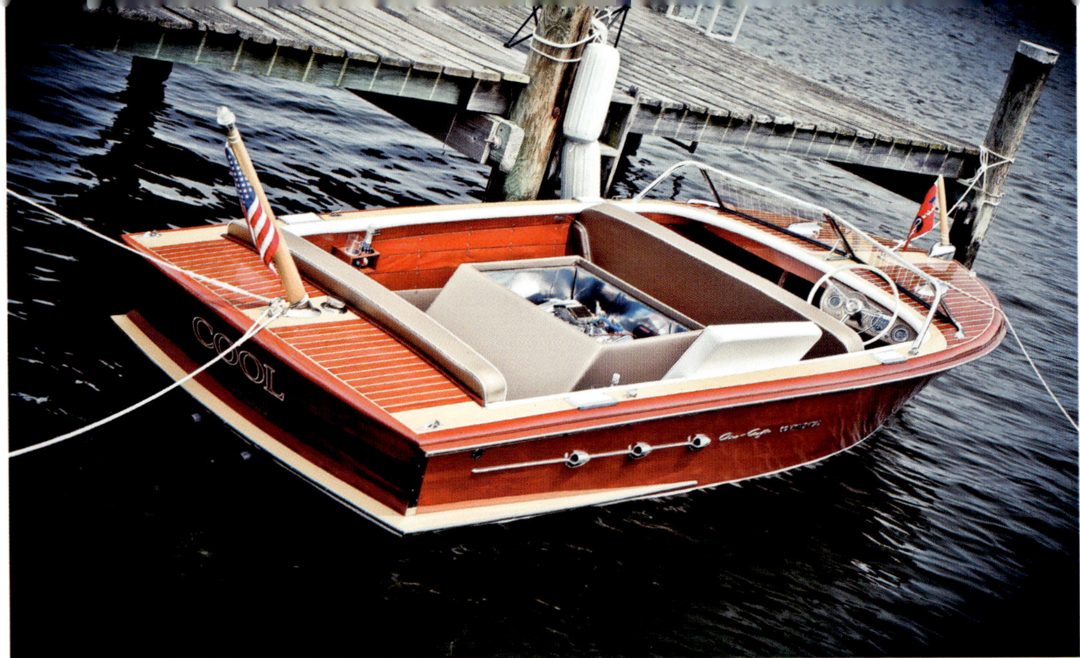


*Cool* on display for the public's admiration.

*Penn Yan Swift*

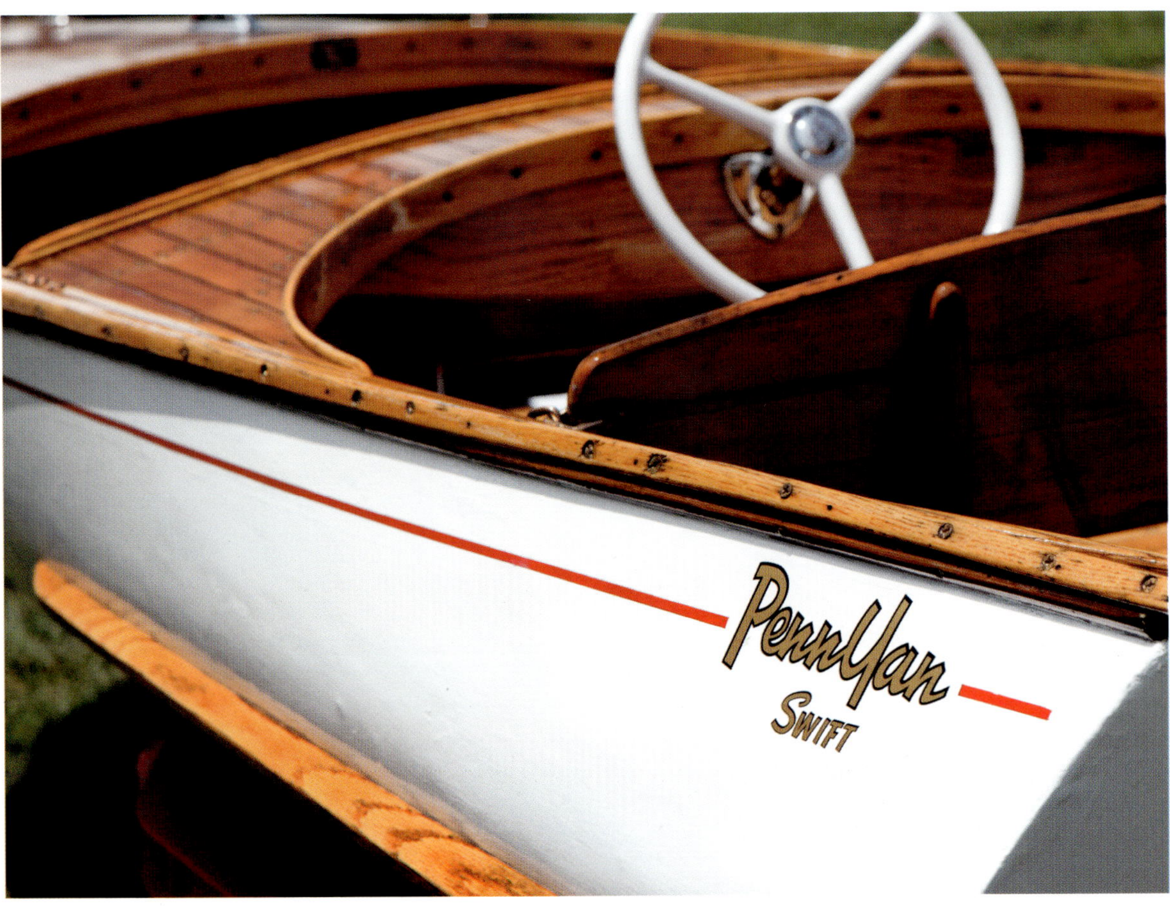

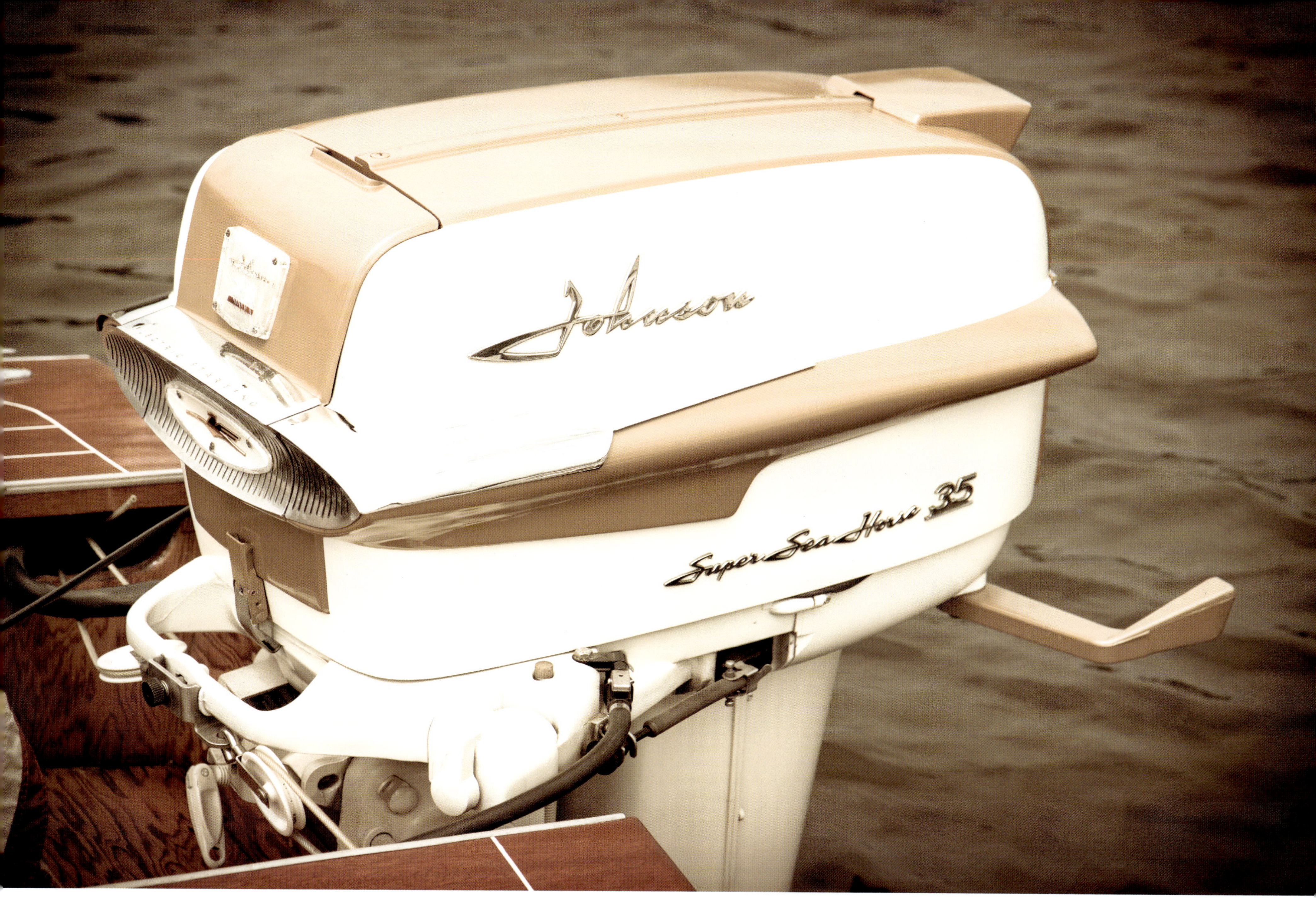


Johnson 35-hp Super Sea Horse on *Sweetie*, a 1958 Berglund Sports Flyte.

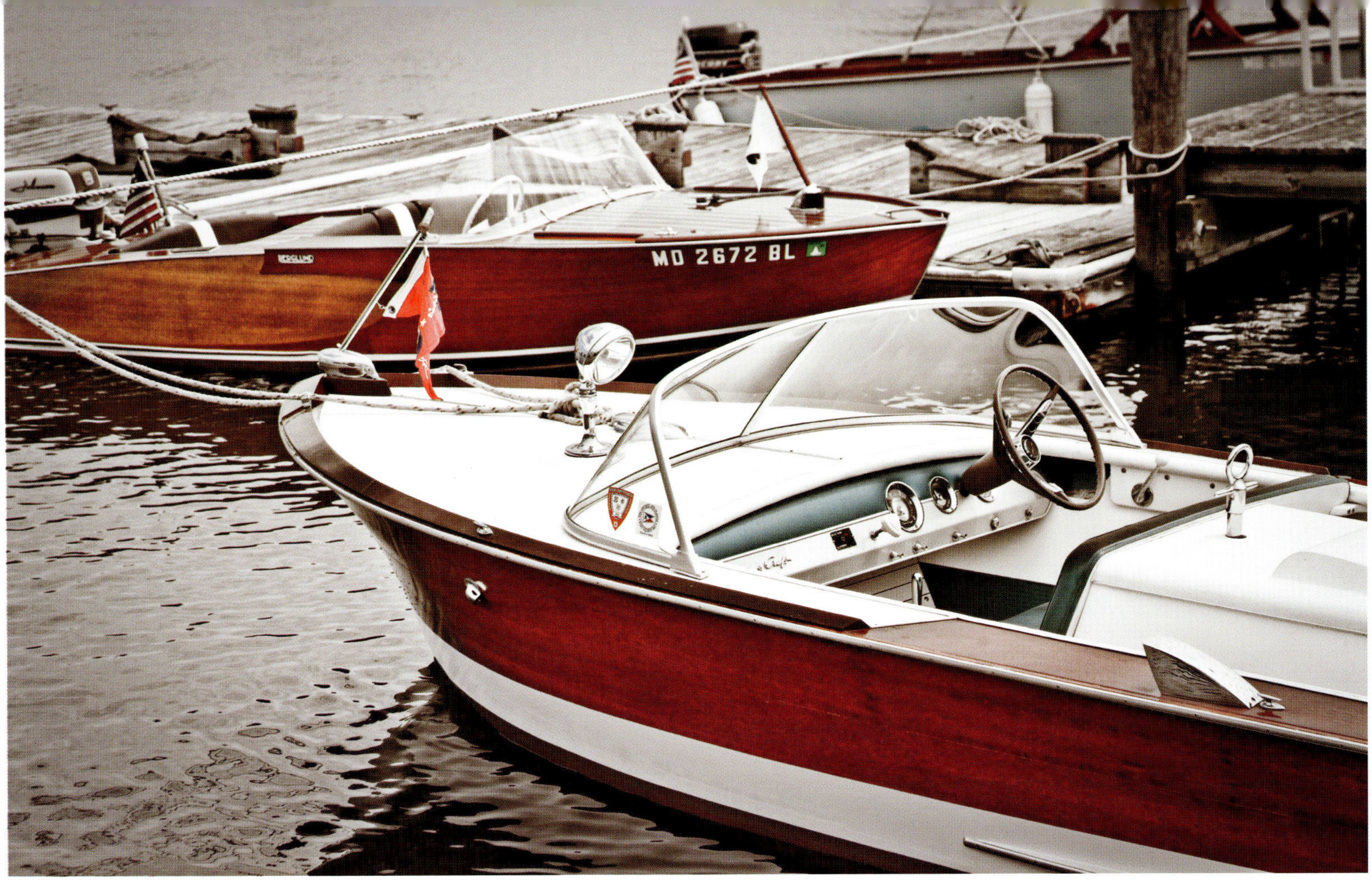

*Red Vaughn* and *Sweetie*

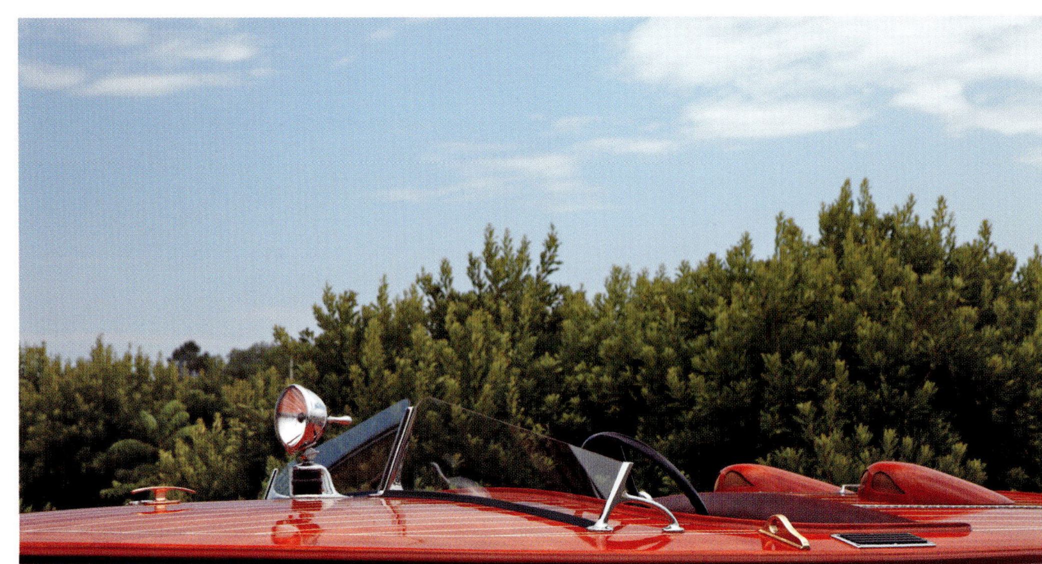

*Betty Boop*, a 1948 runabout by U.S. Plywood, visits the antique boat show at the Chesapeake Bay Maritime Museum in St. Michaels.

*Honey*, a 1942 Chris Craft Special Runabout.

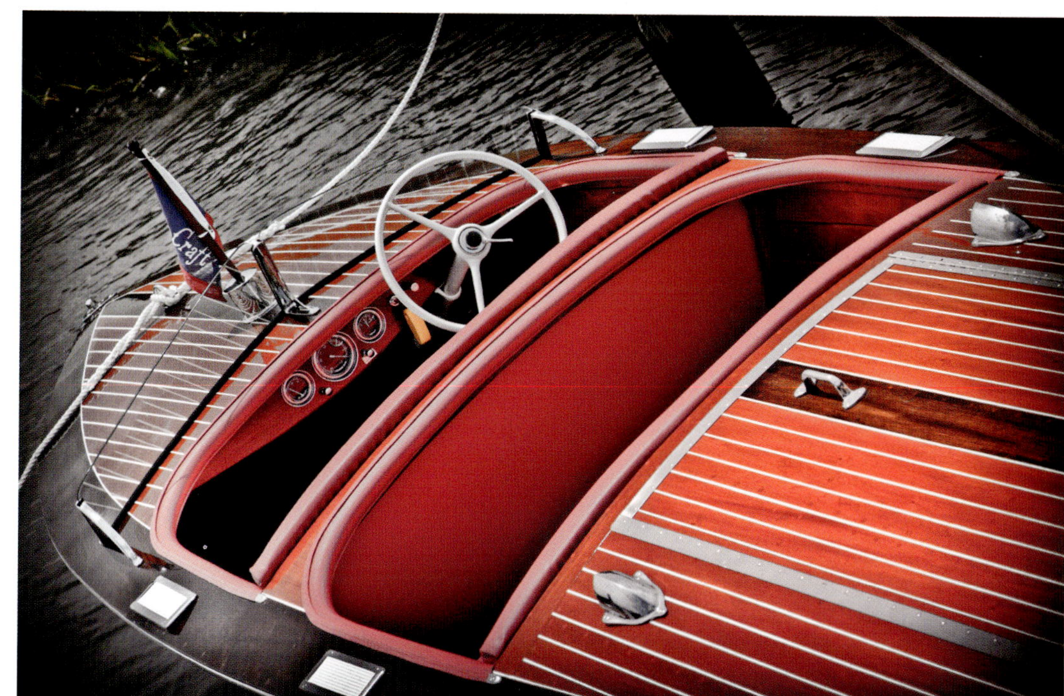


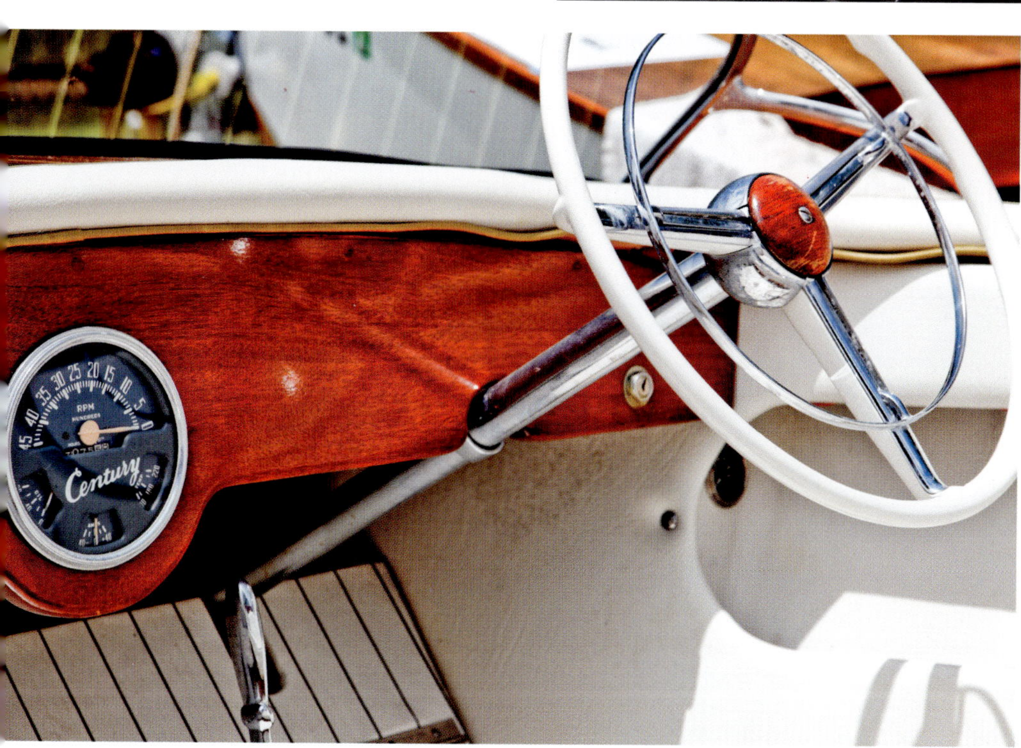


A classic 1949 Century Resorter.

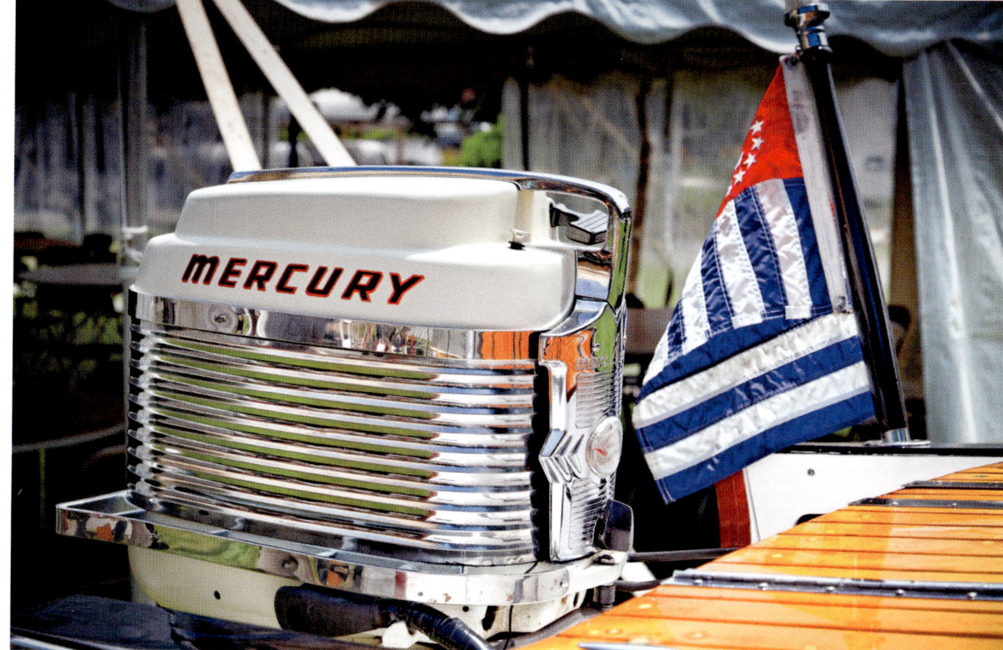


Attention-grabbing chrome on this Mercury outboard.

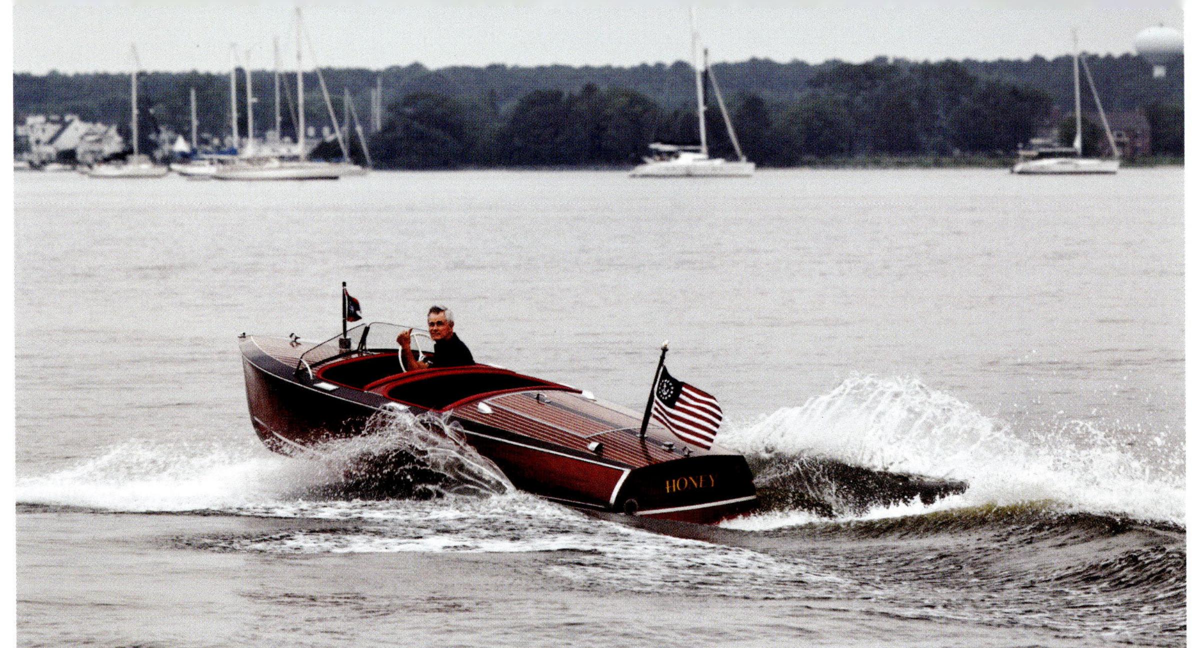

*Honey* and its owner head back to the docks.

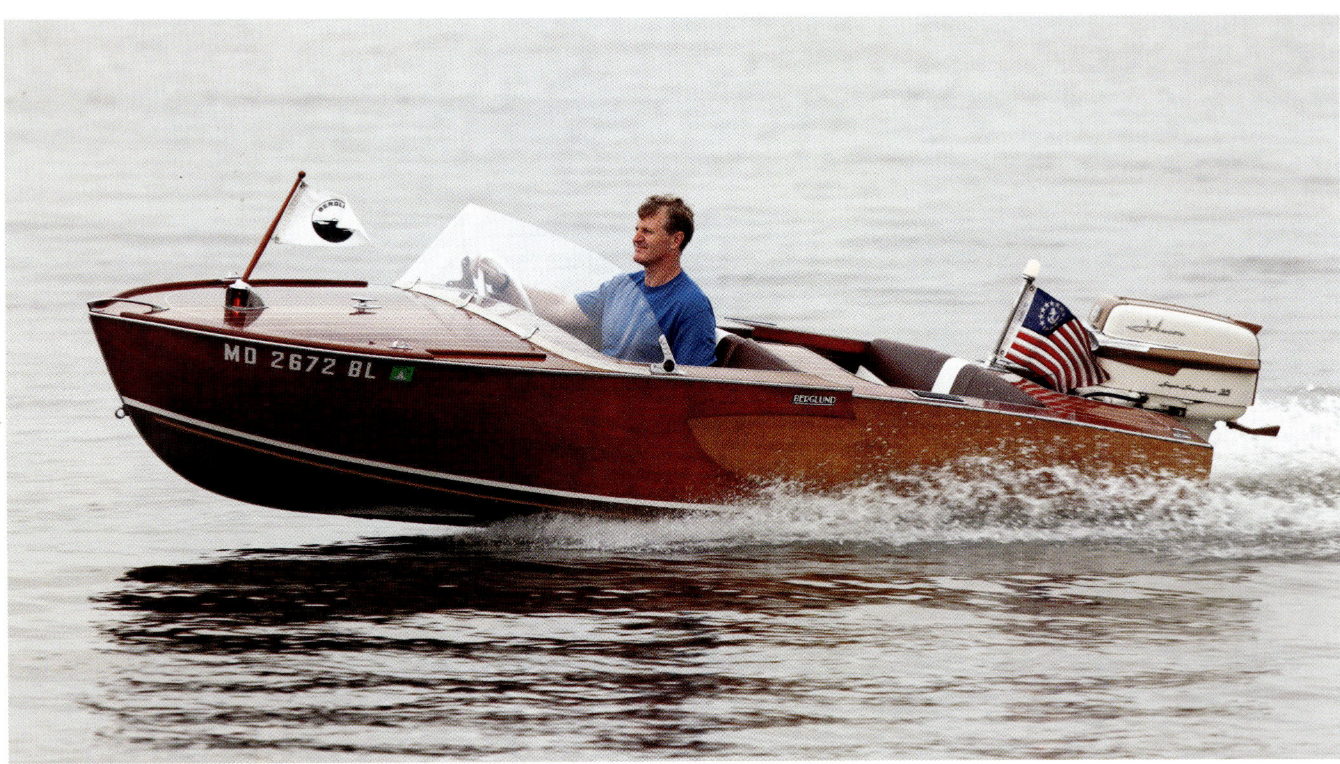


*Sweetie* and its owner go out for a spin.

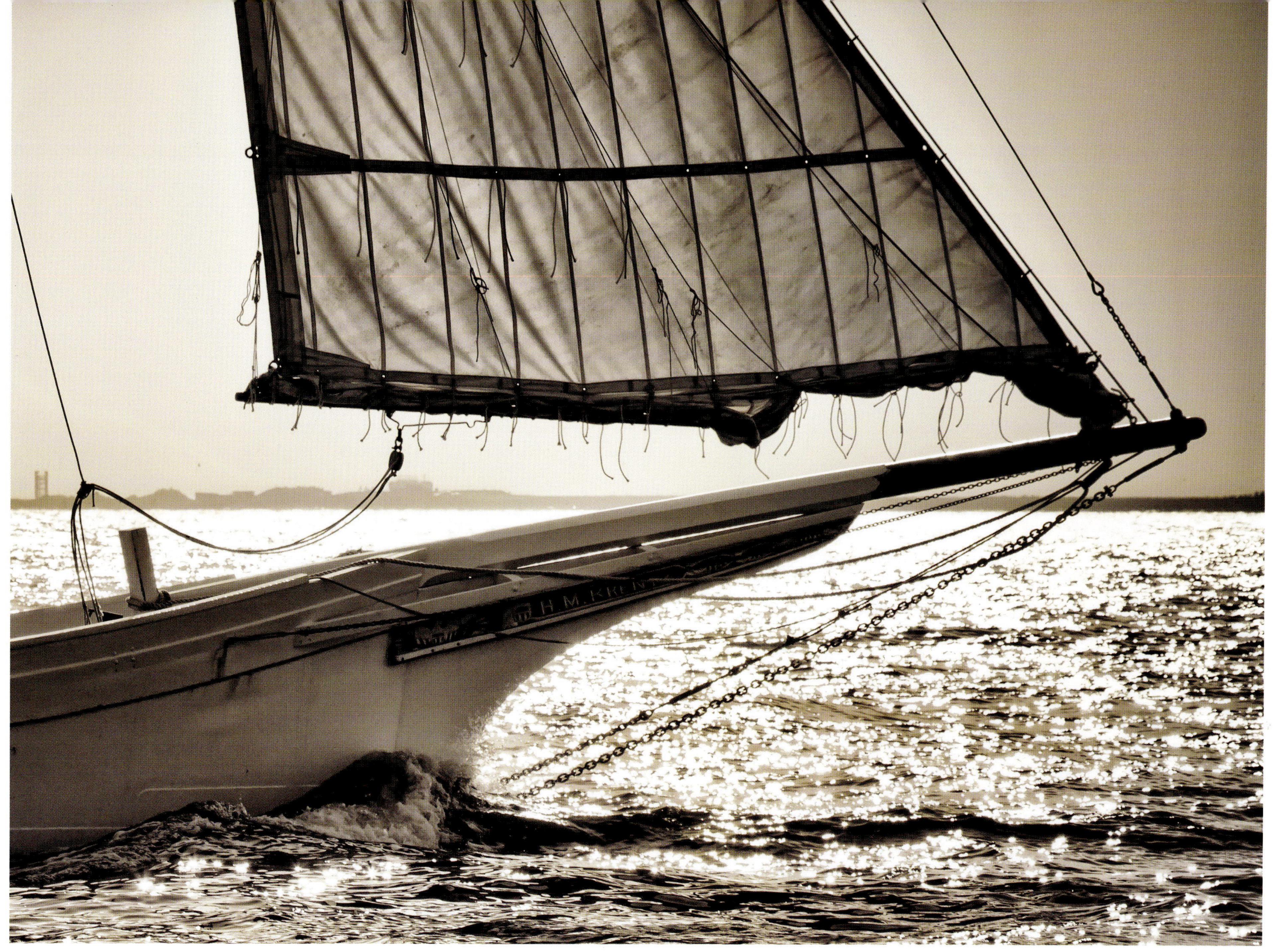


Captain Ed Farley's skipjack, *H.M. Krentz,* out on the Bay.

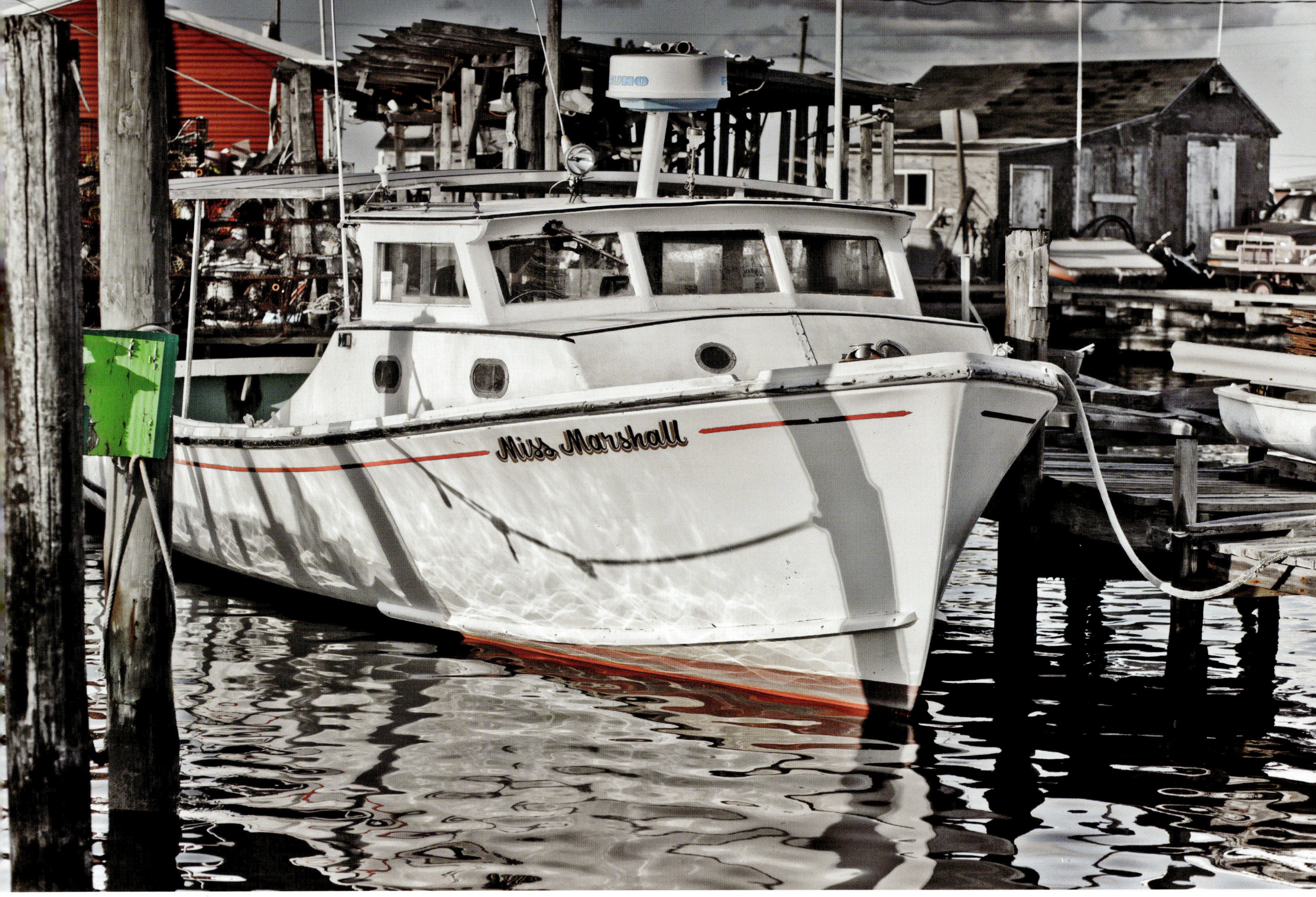


*Miss Marshall* docked on Smith Island.

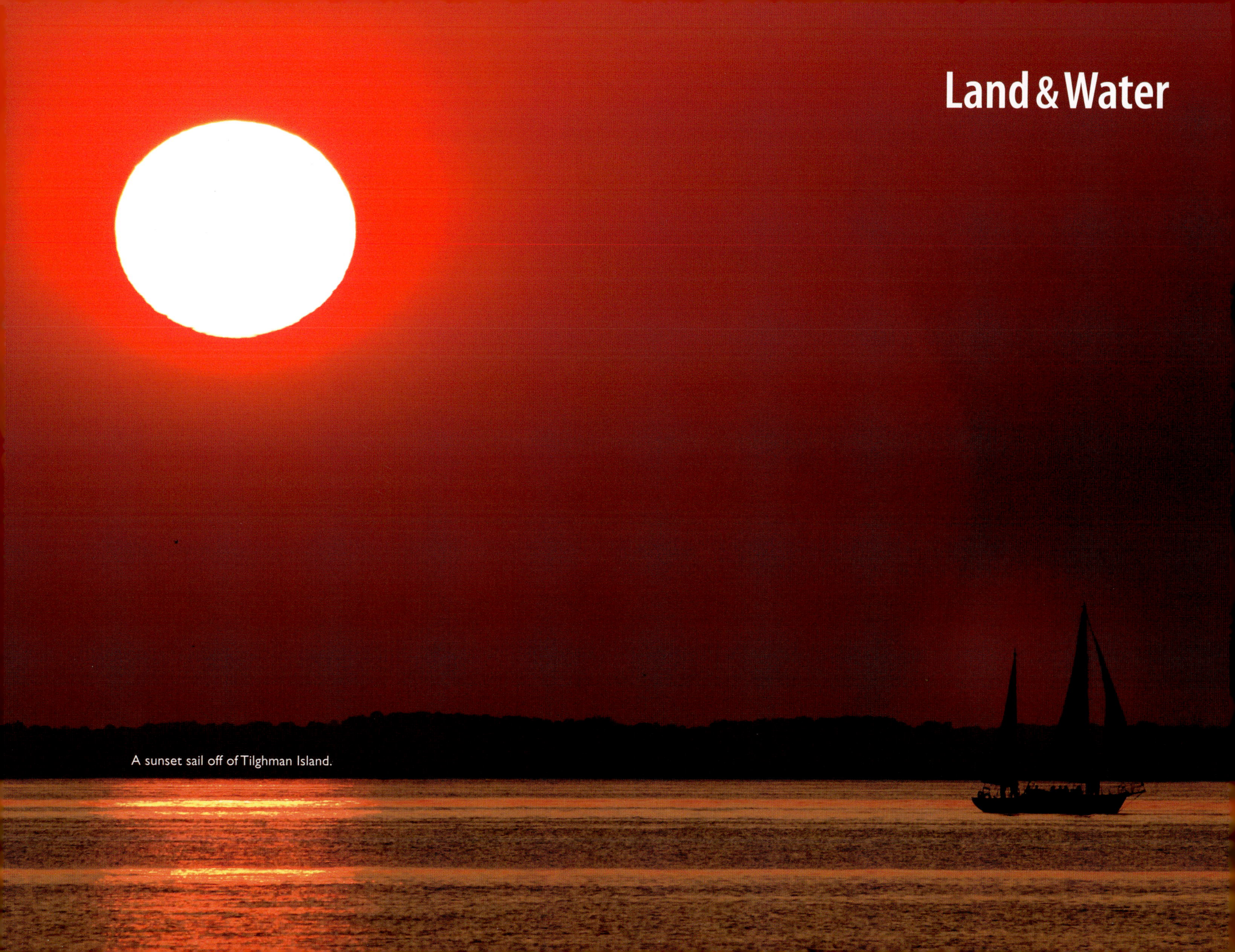

# Land & Water

A sunset sail off of Tilghman Island.

Ice accumulates on a pier in Paw Paw Cove, Tilghman, in January.

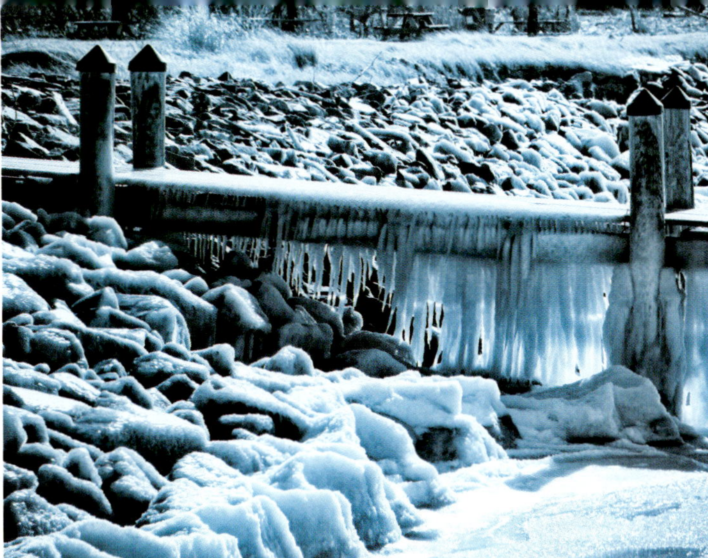

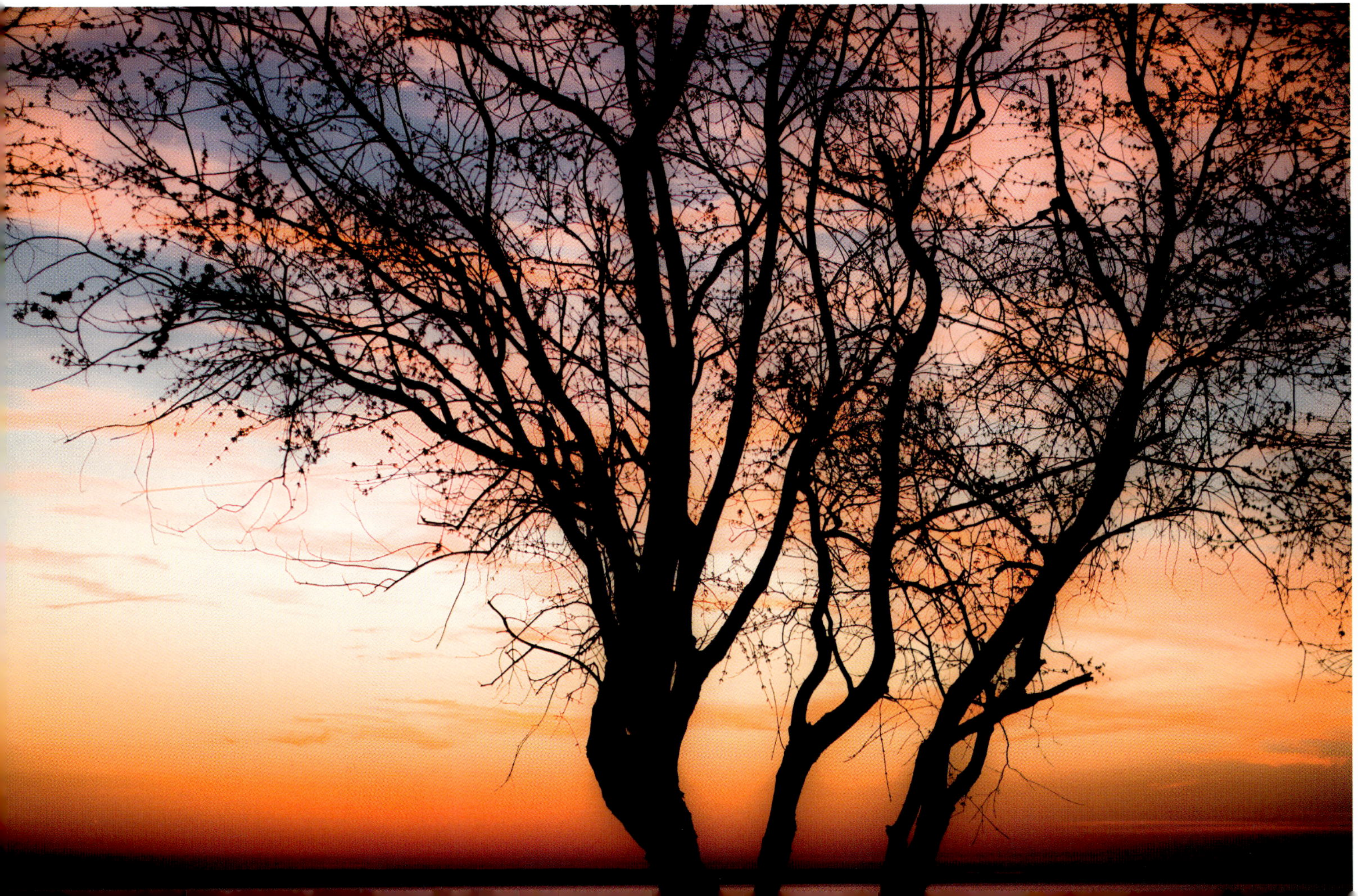

The sky continues to glow during the "Golden Hour."

The sun sets over the western shore of the Chesapeake.

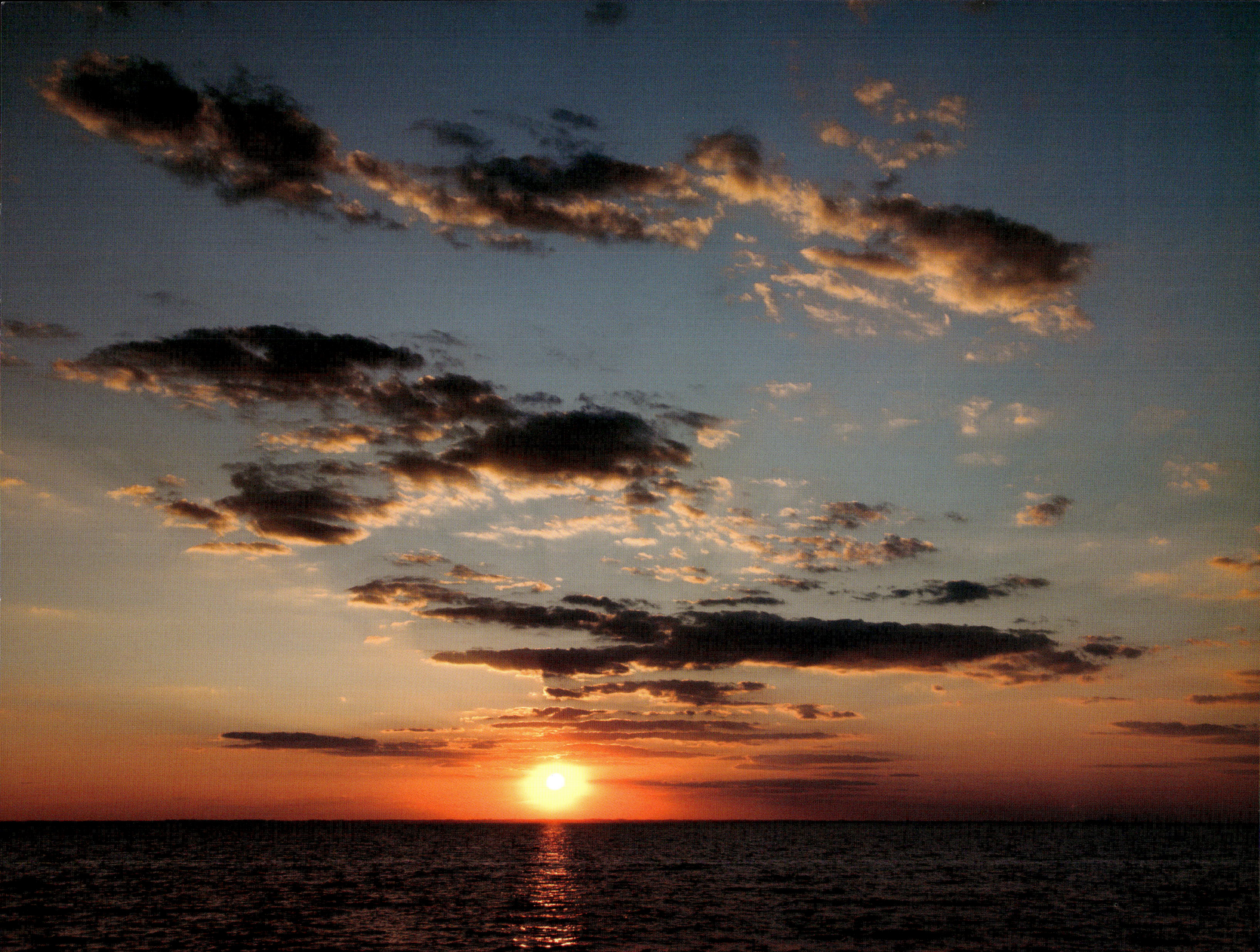

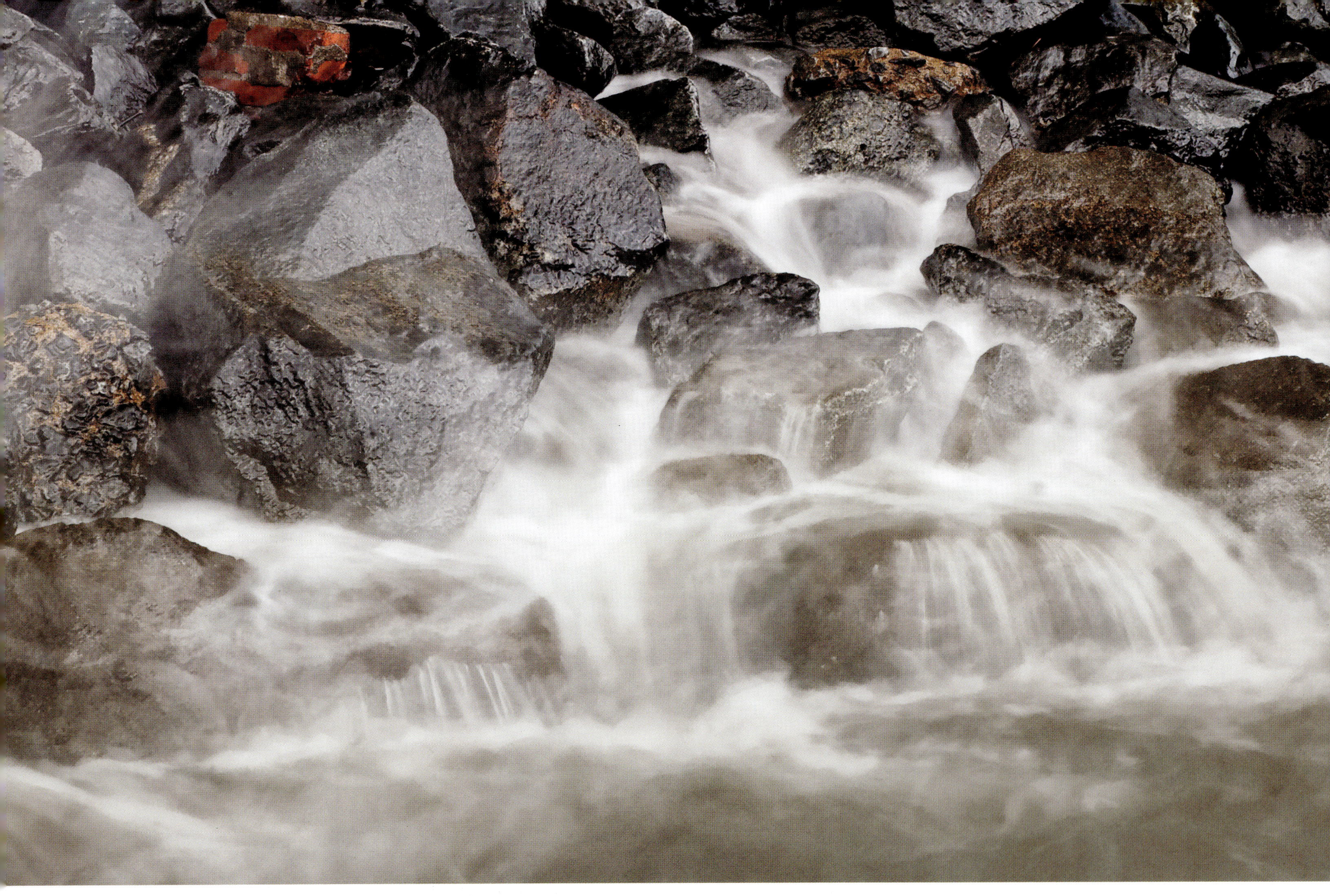

Wave action slowed down, resembling mini-waterfalls.

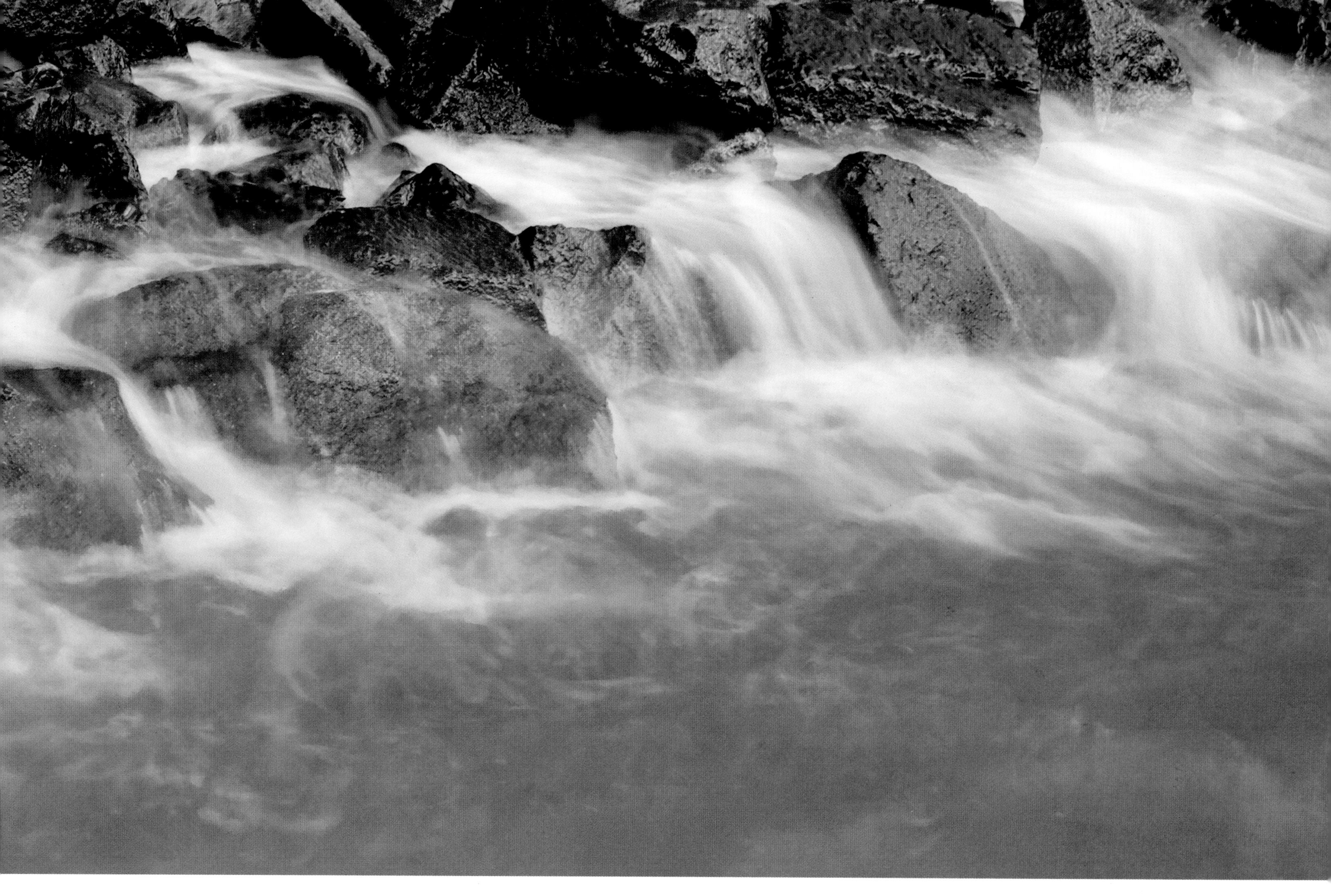

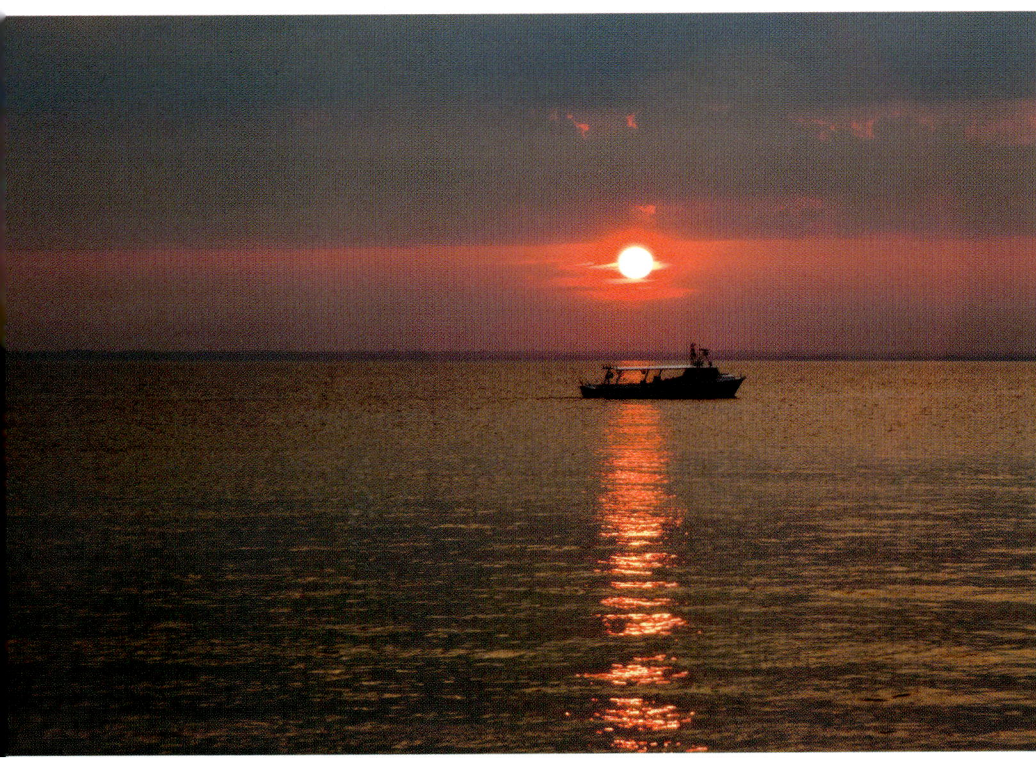

With its lines pulled-in, this fishing boat heads back to its slip.

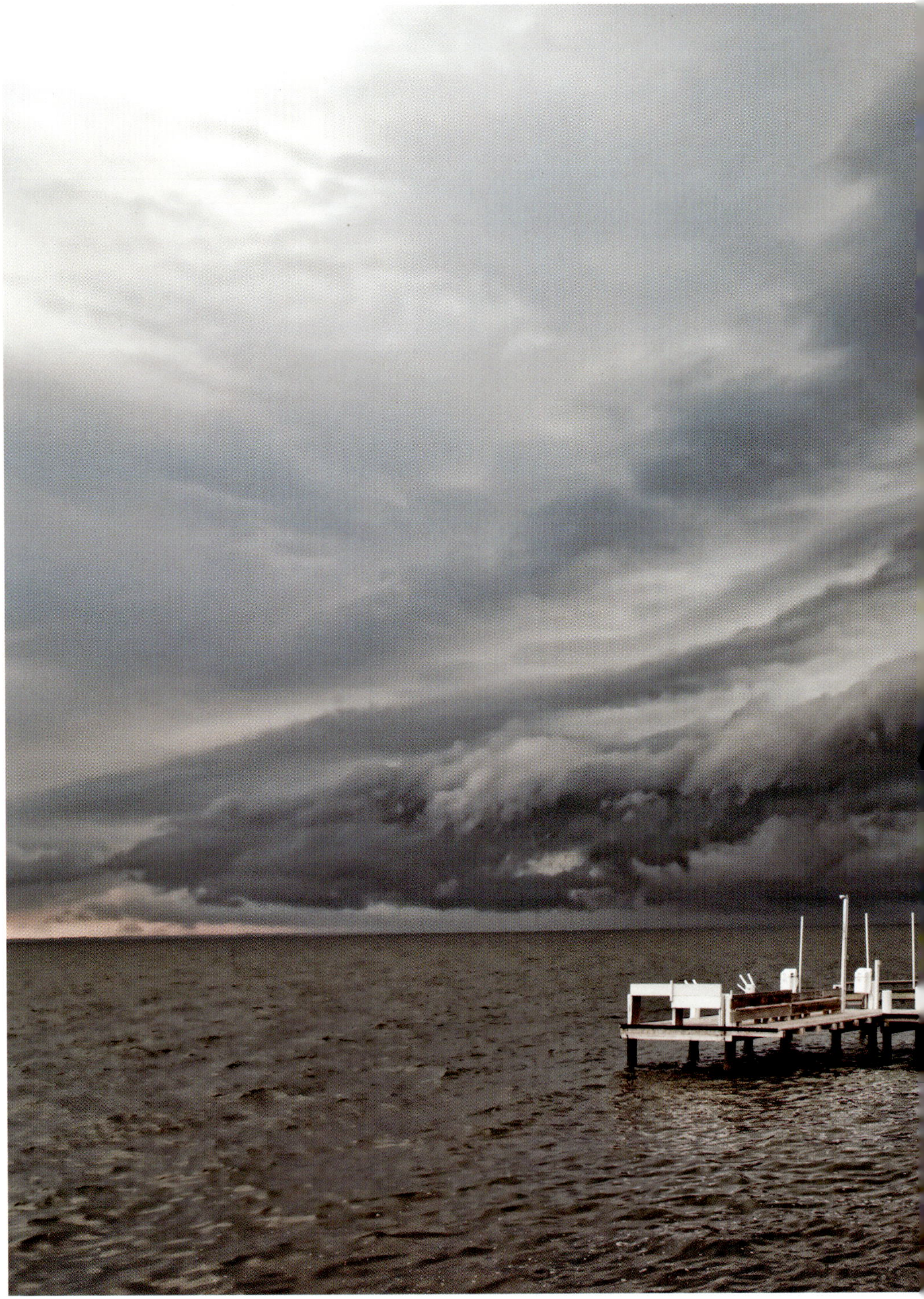

Storm clouds hint ominously
of what's to come.

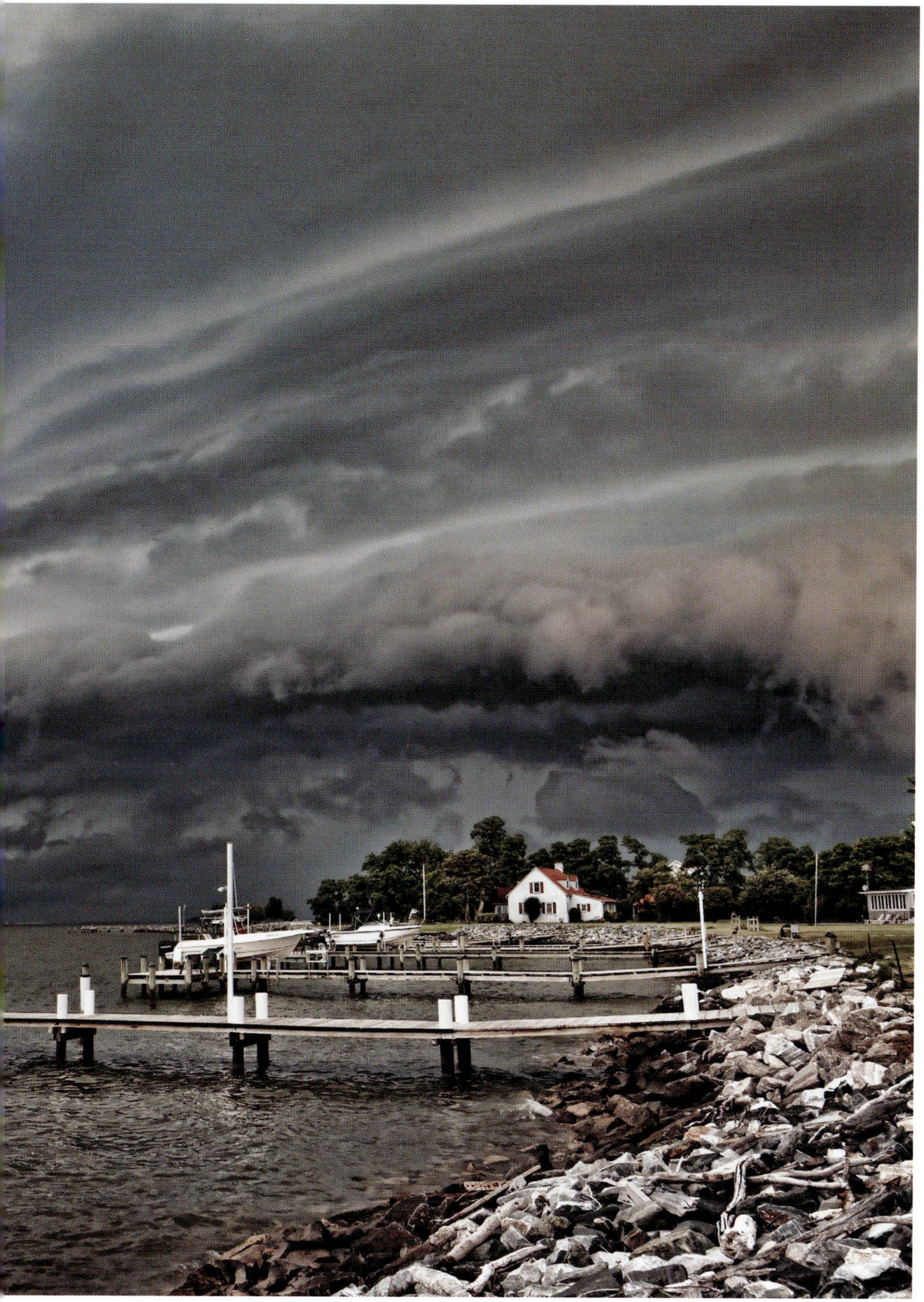

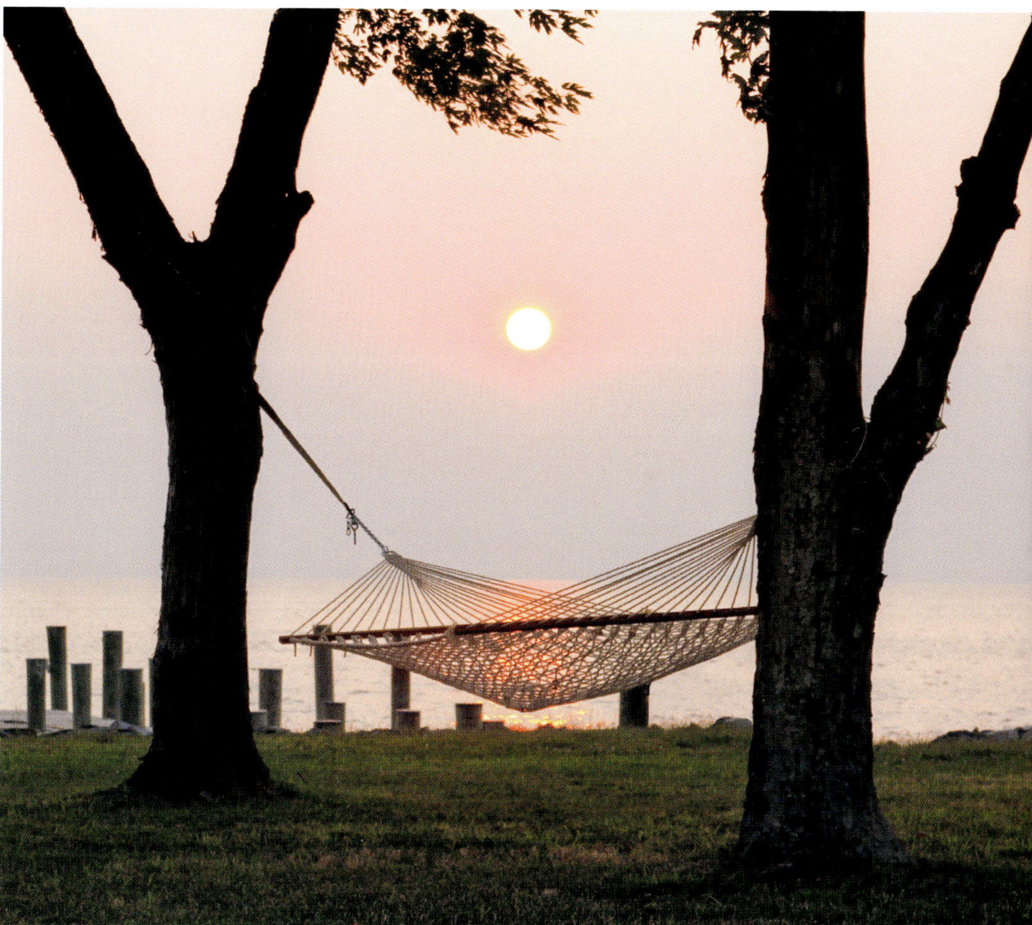

Our ever-present hammock waits for Taylor, our Portuguese Water Dog who can't stand not to be in it with you.

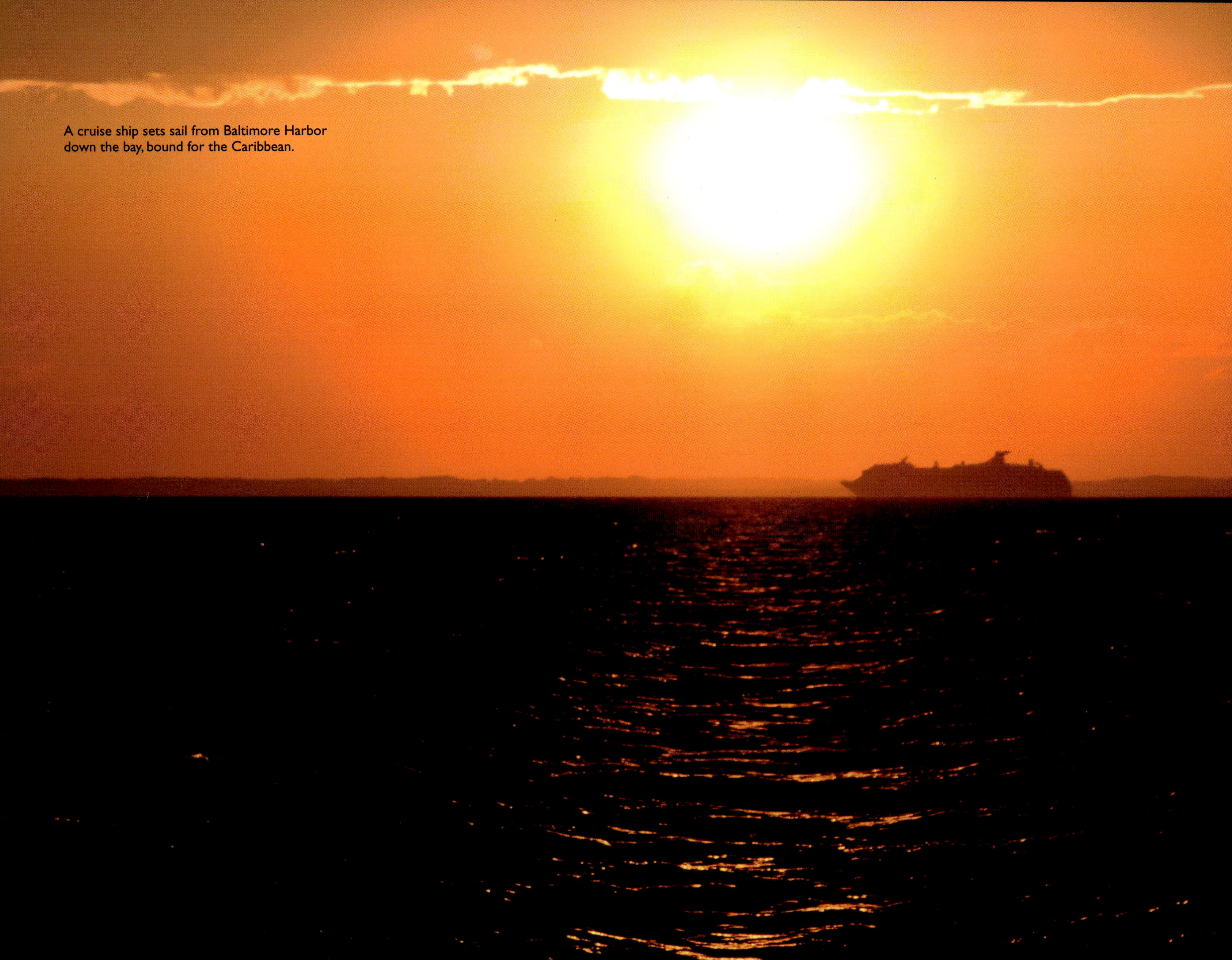

A cruise ship sets sail from Baltimore Harbor down the bay, bound for the Caribbean.

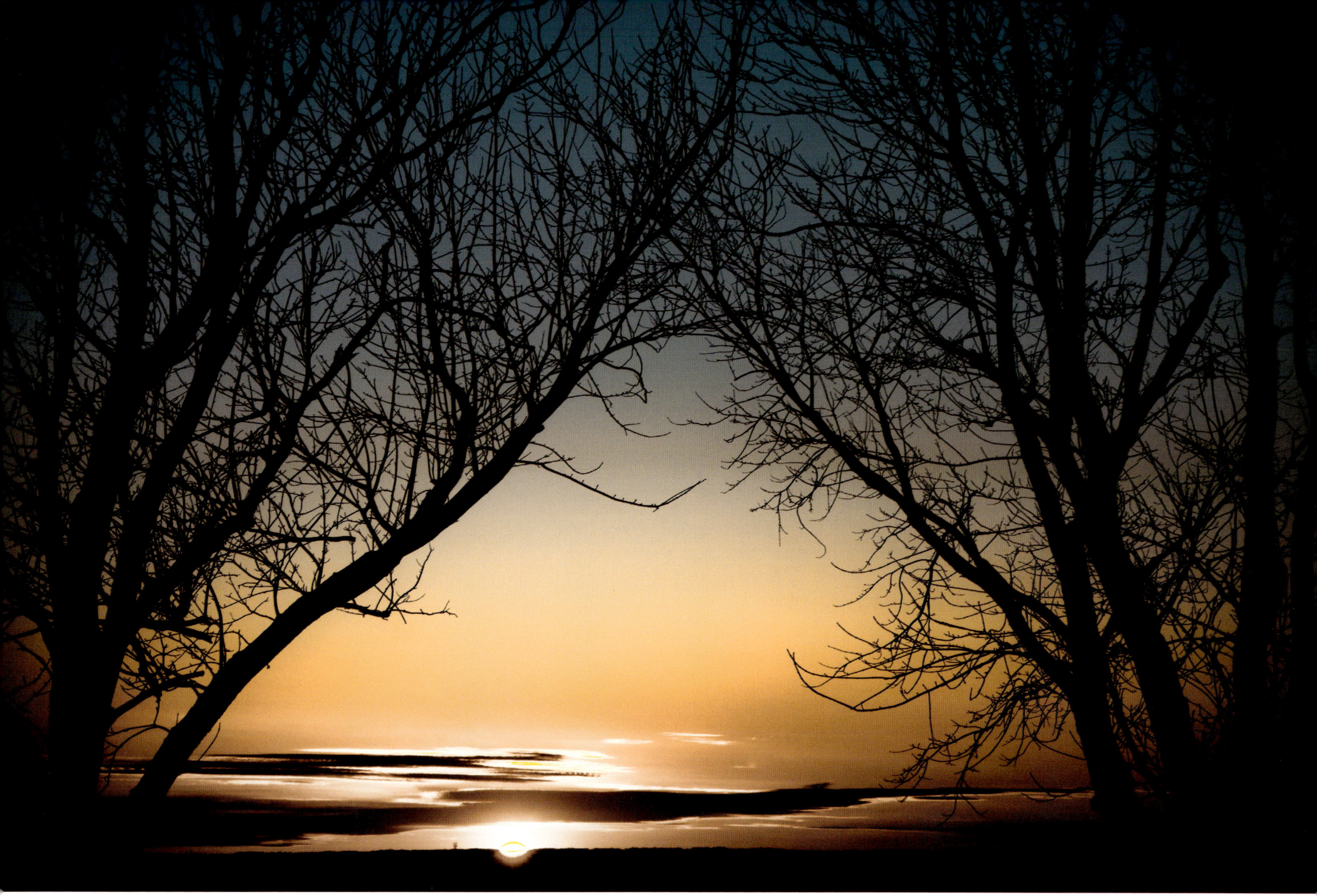

A maple tree arch frames the sun dropping below the horizon.

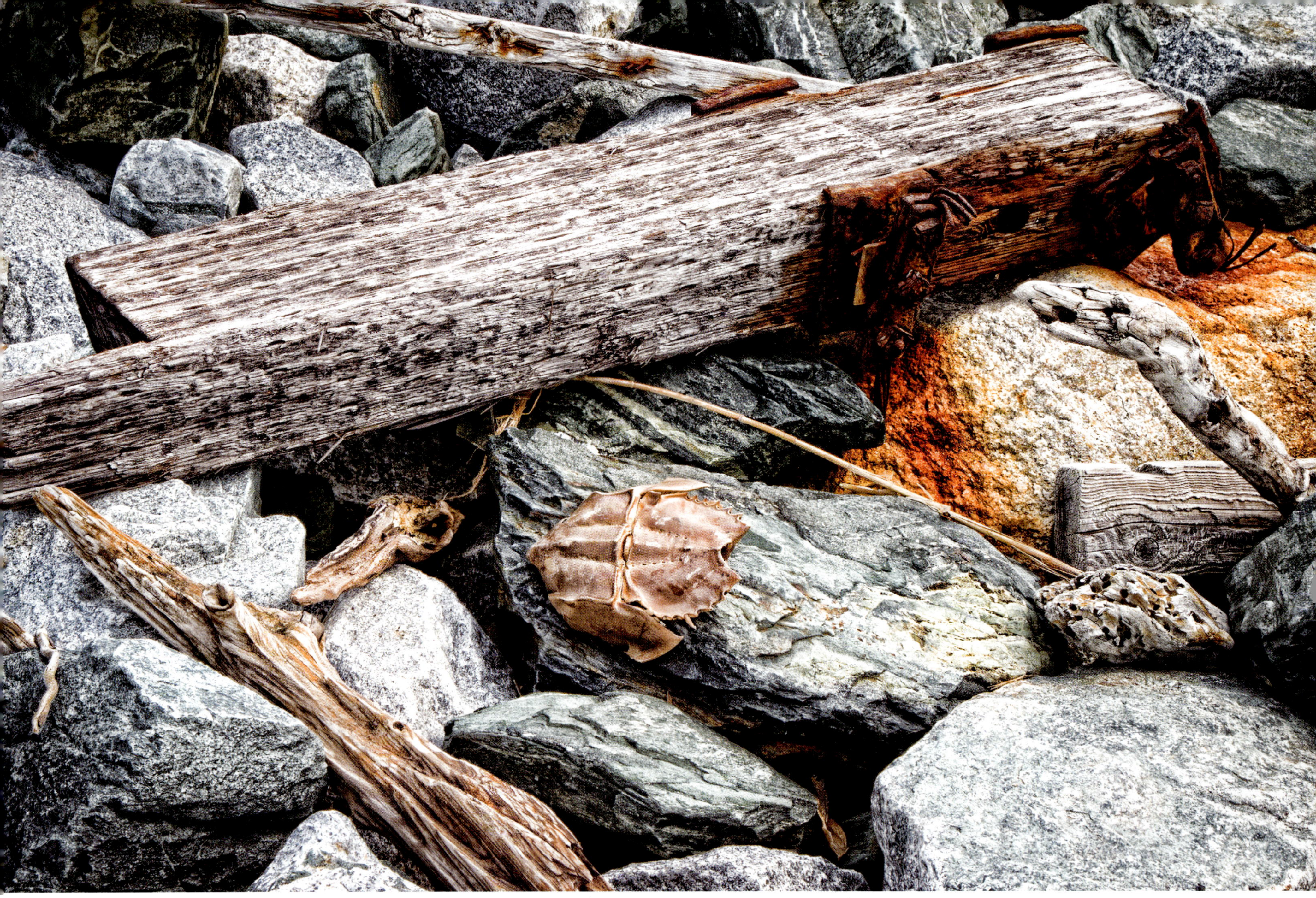

Gifts from the Bay wash in to shore and accumulate on the gradually sloping rip-rap.

A disintegrating bulkhead near Black Walnut point on Tilghman Island.

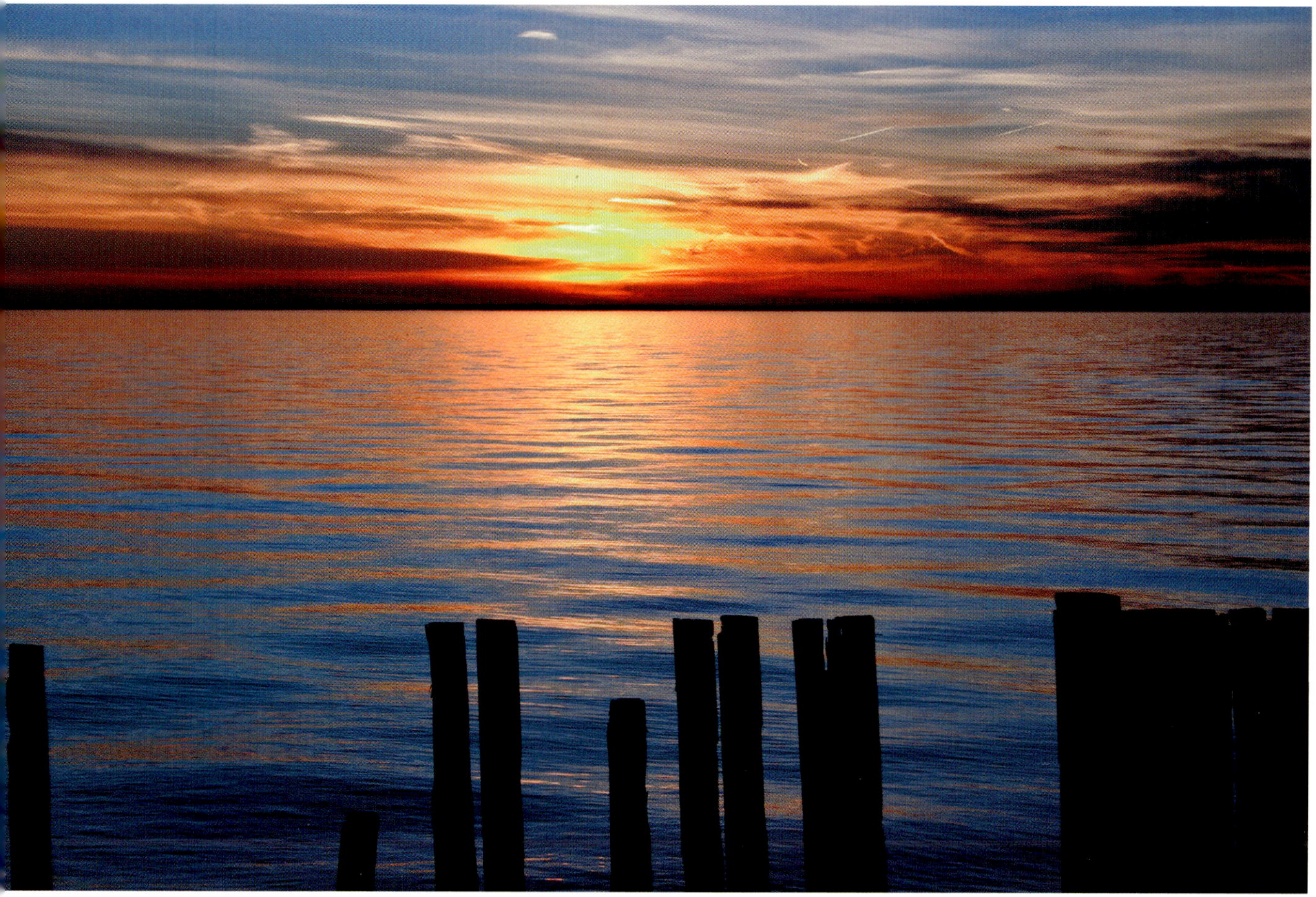

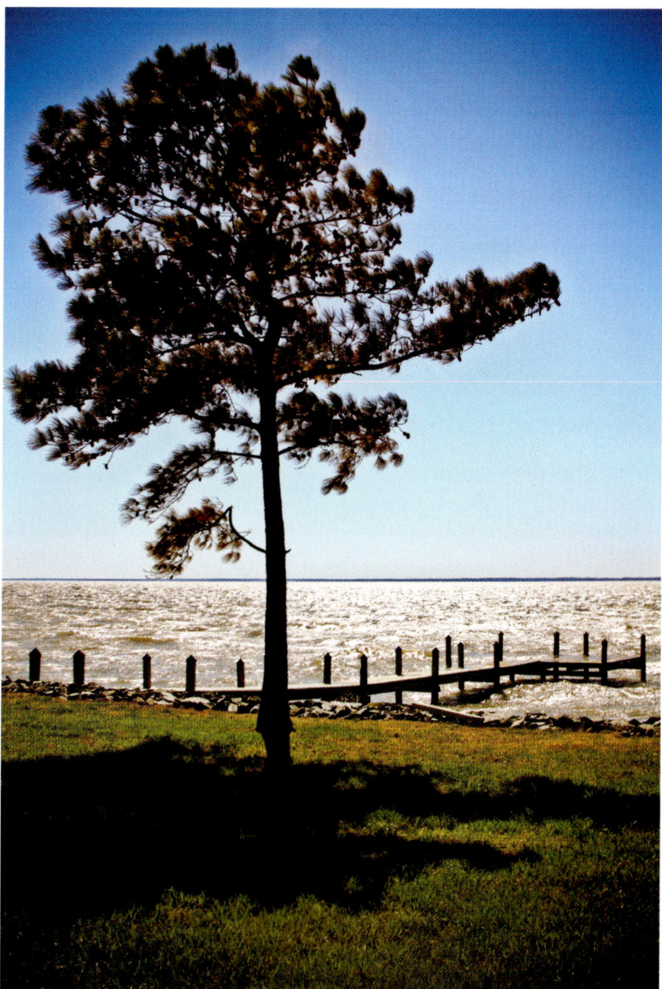

Paw Paw Cove, Tilghman, Maryland

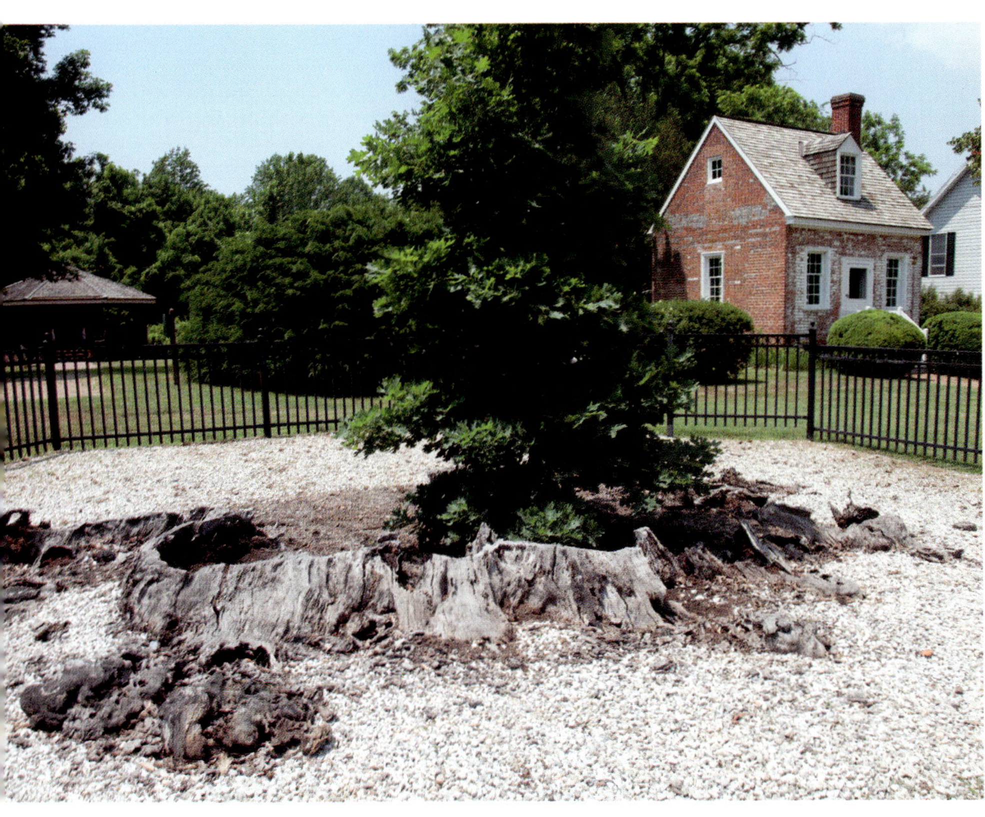

A new white oak sapling emerges from the remains of the Great Wye Oak.

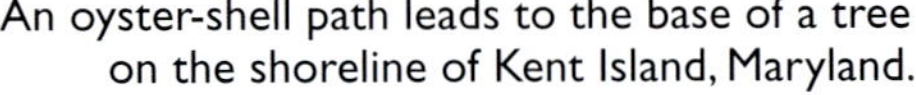

An oyster-shell path leads to the base of a tree on the shoreline of Kent Island, Maryland.

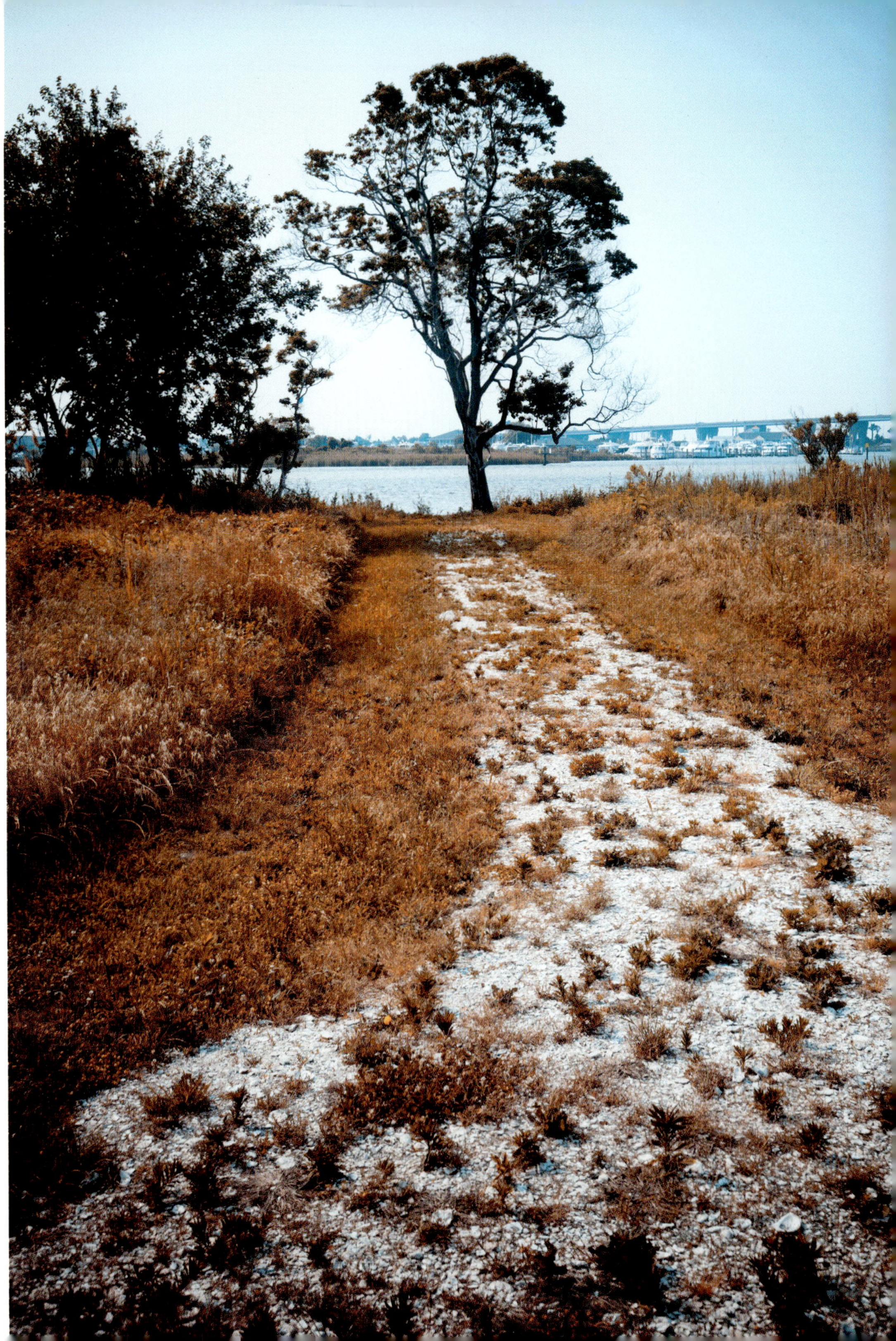

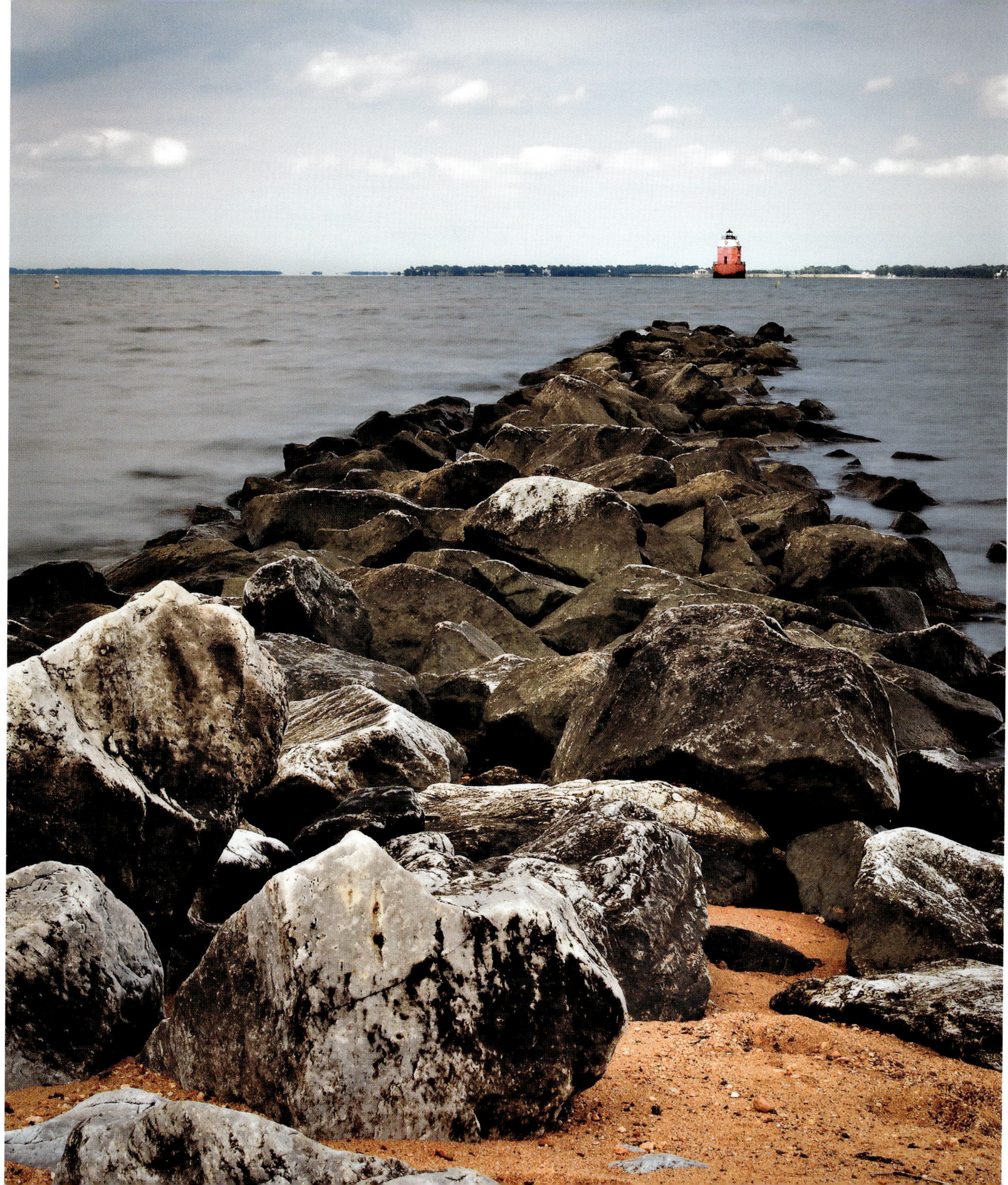

Sandy Point Lighthouse

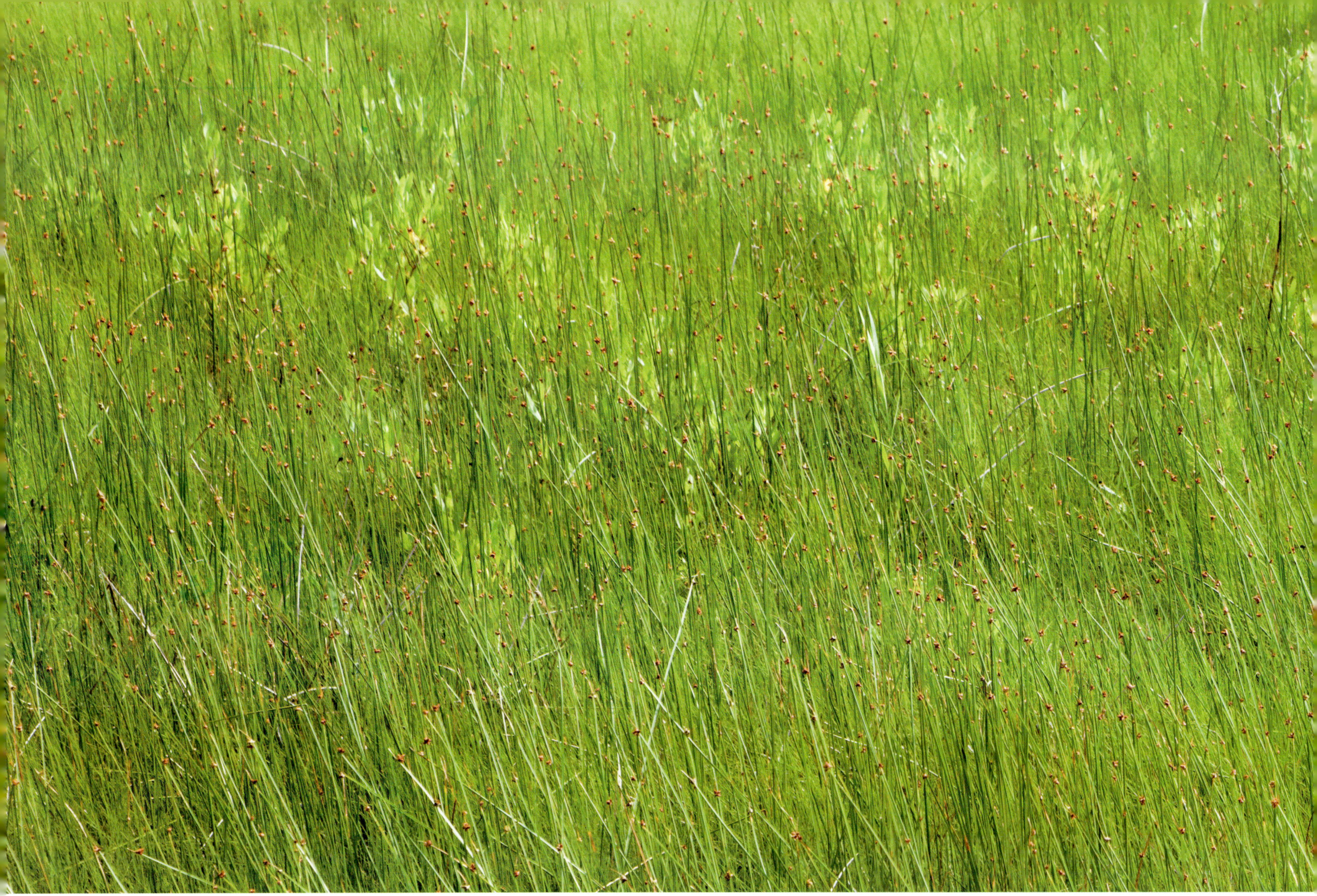

Marsh grass provides a rich habitat for many of the Bay's creatures.

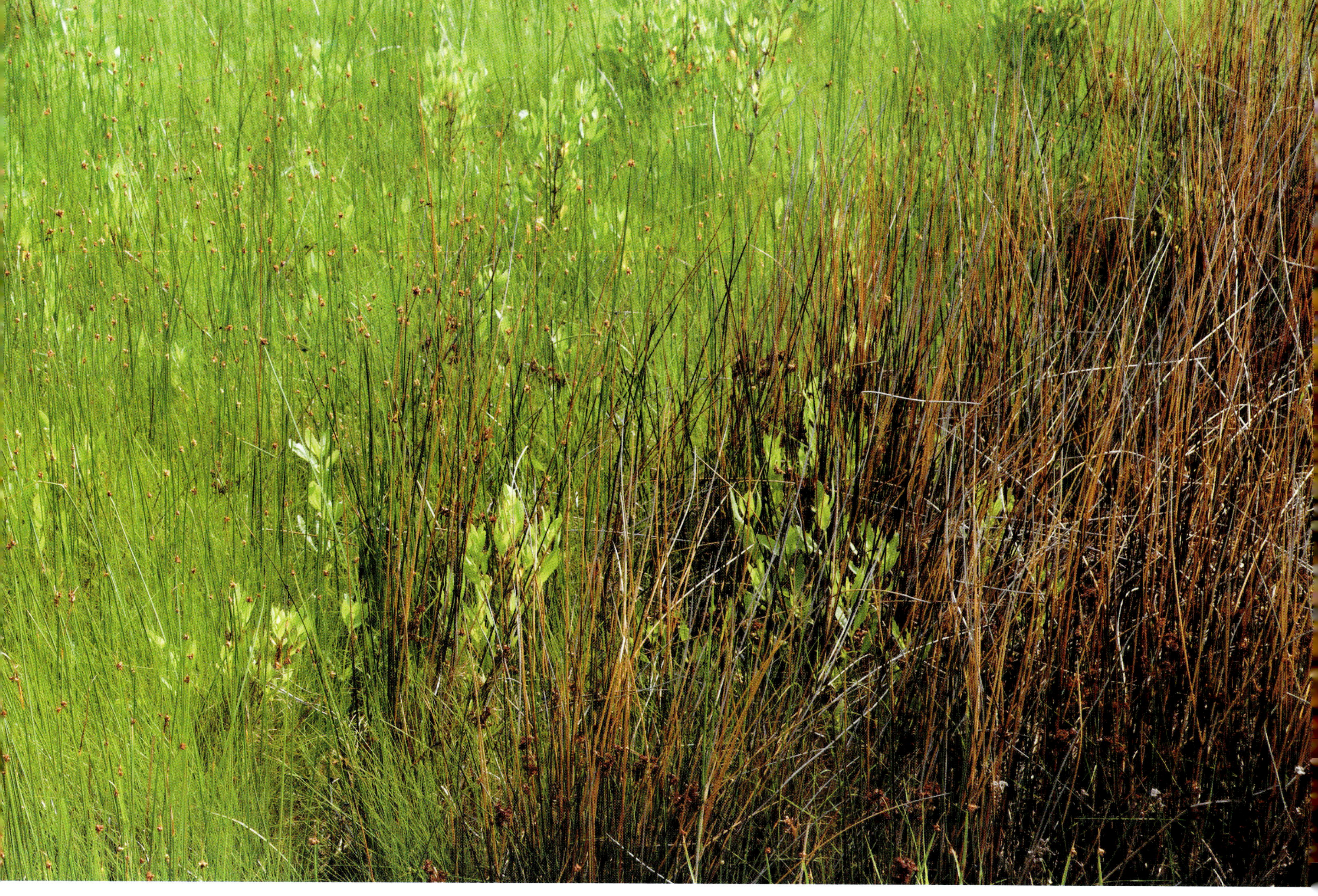

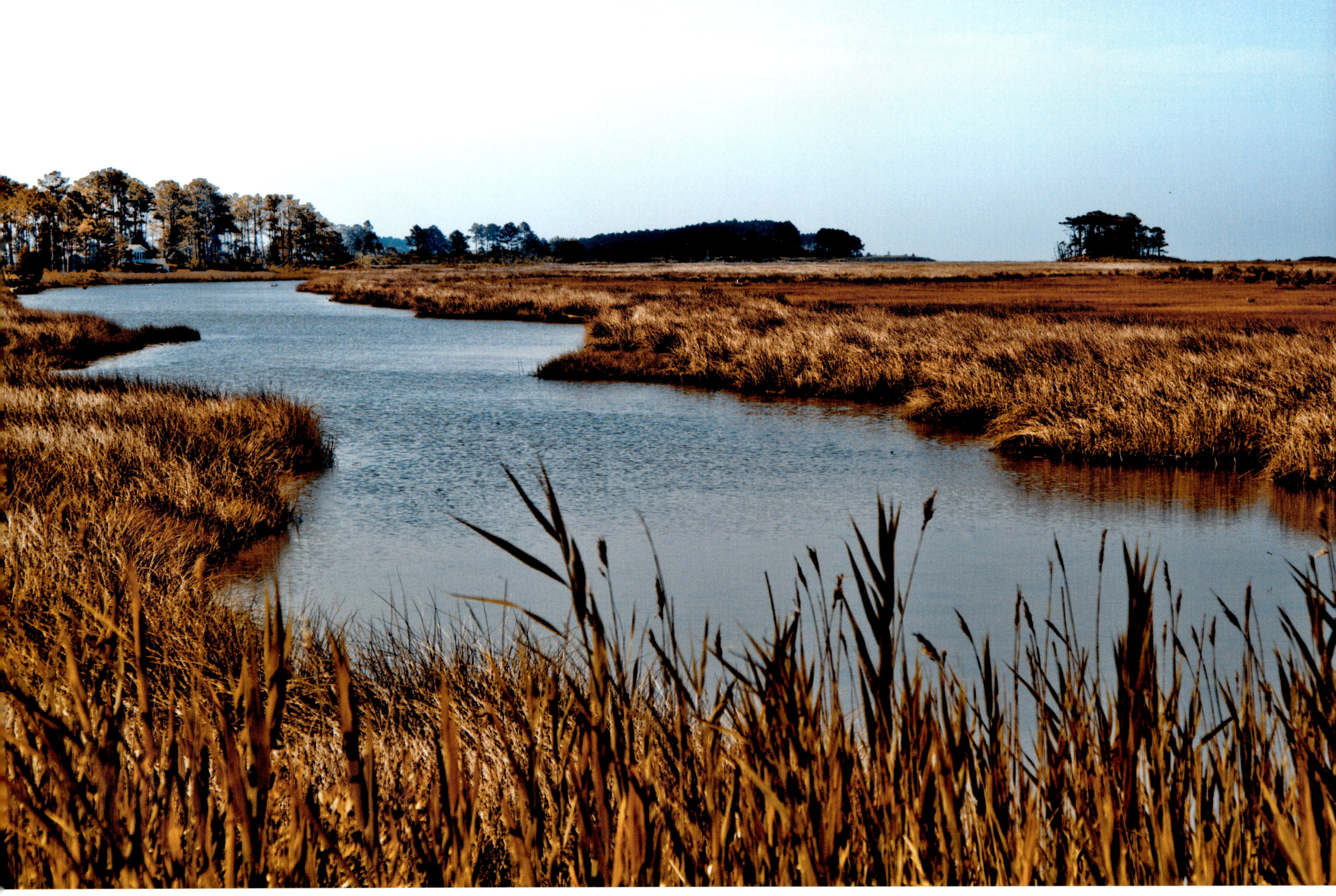

Hooper's Island, Maryland

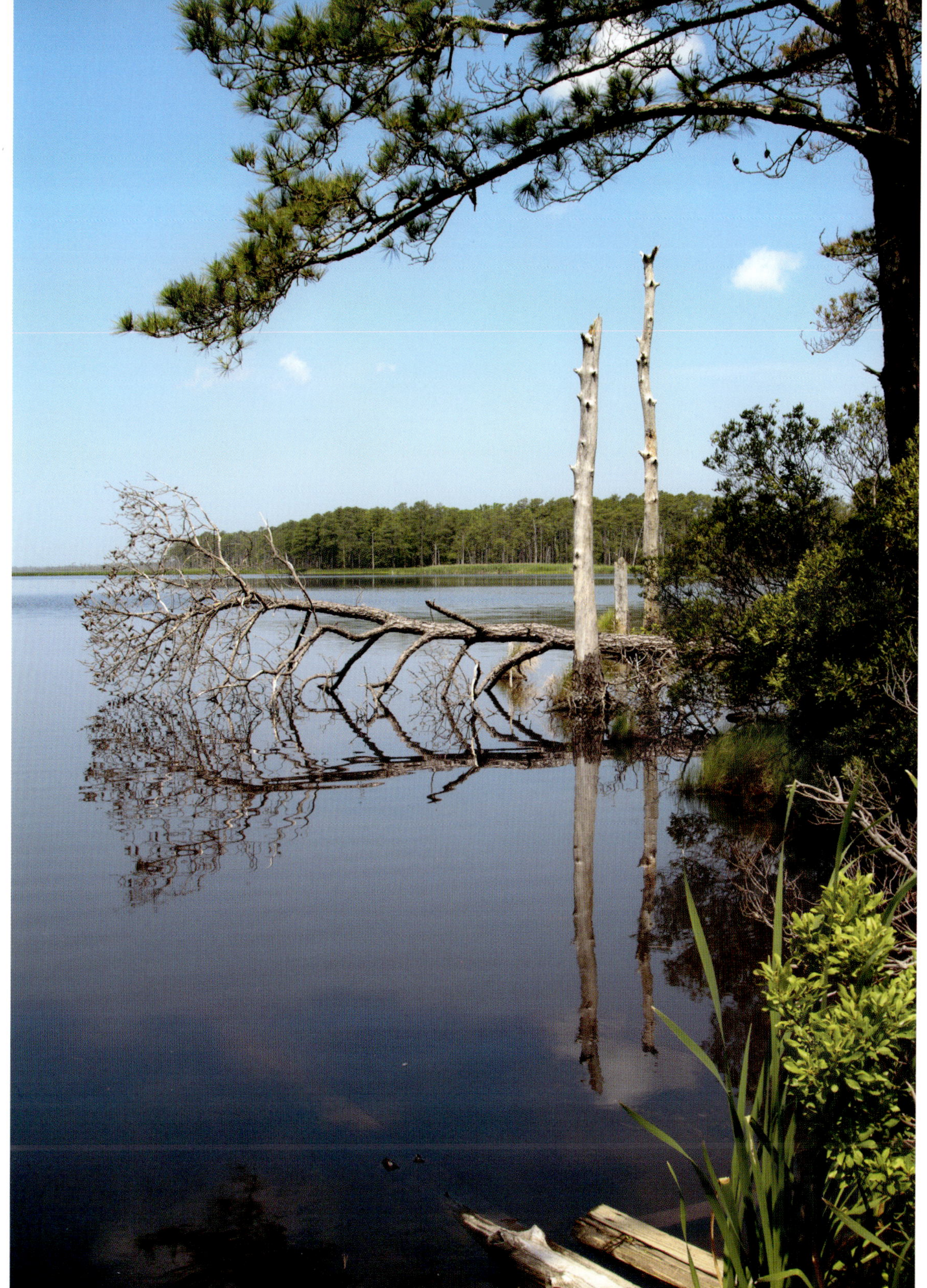

A fallen tree reflects in a mirror of calm water in Blackwater National Wildlife Refuge.

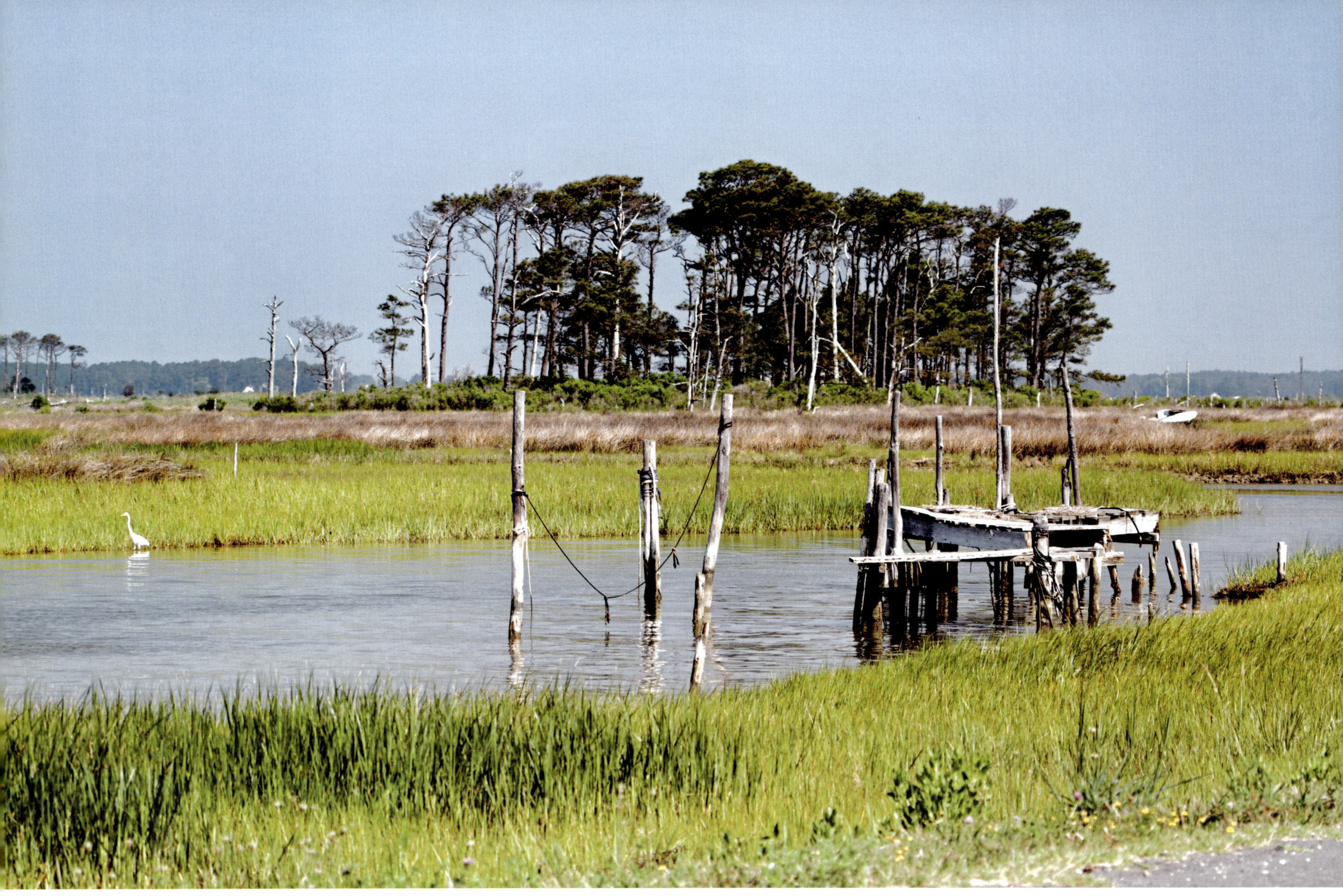

Blackwater National Wildlife Refuge

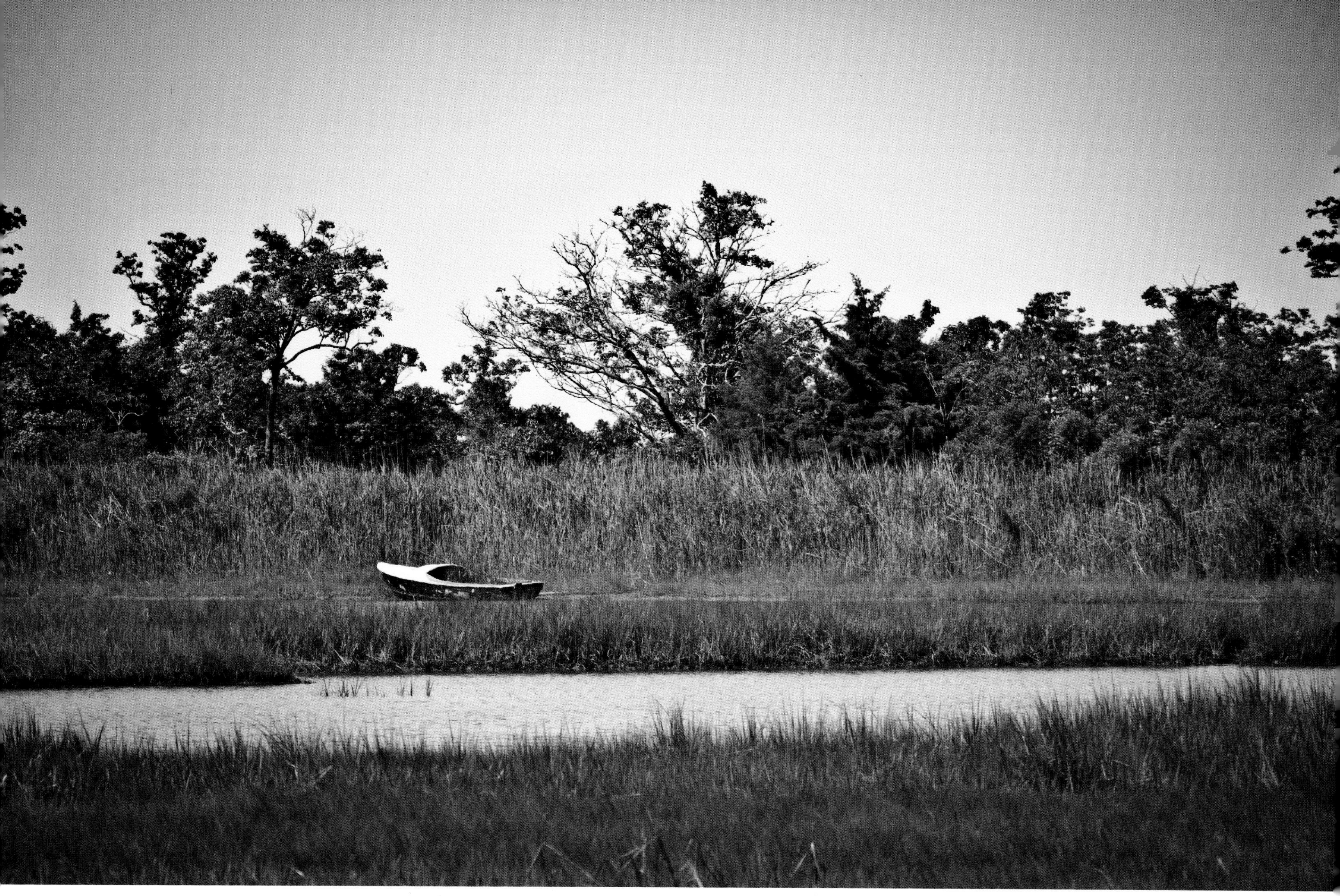

Grasses emerge from the hull of an abandoned boat on Hooper's Island.

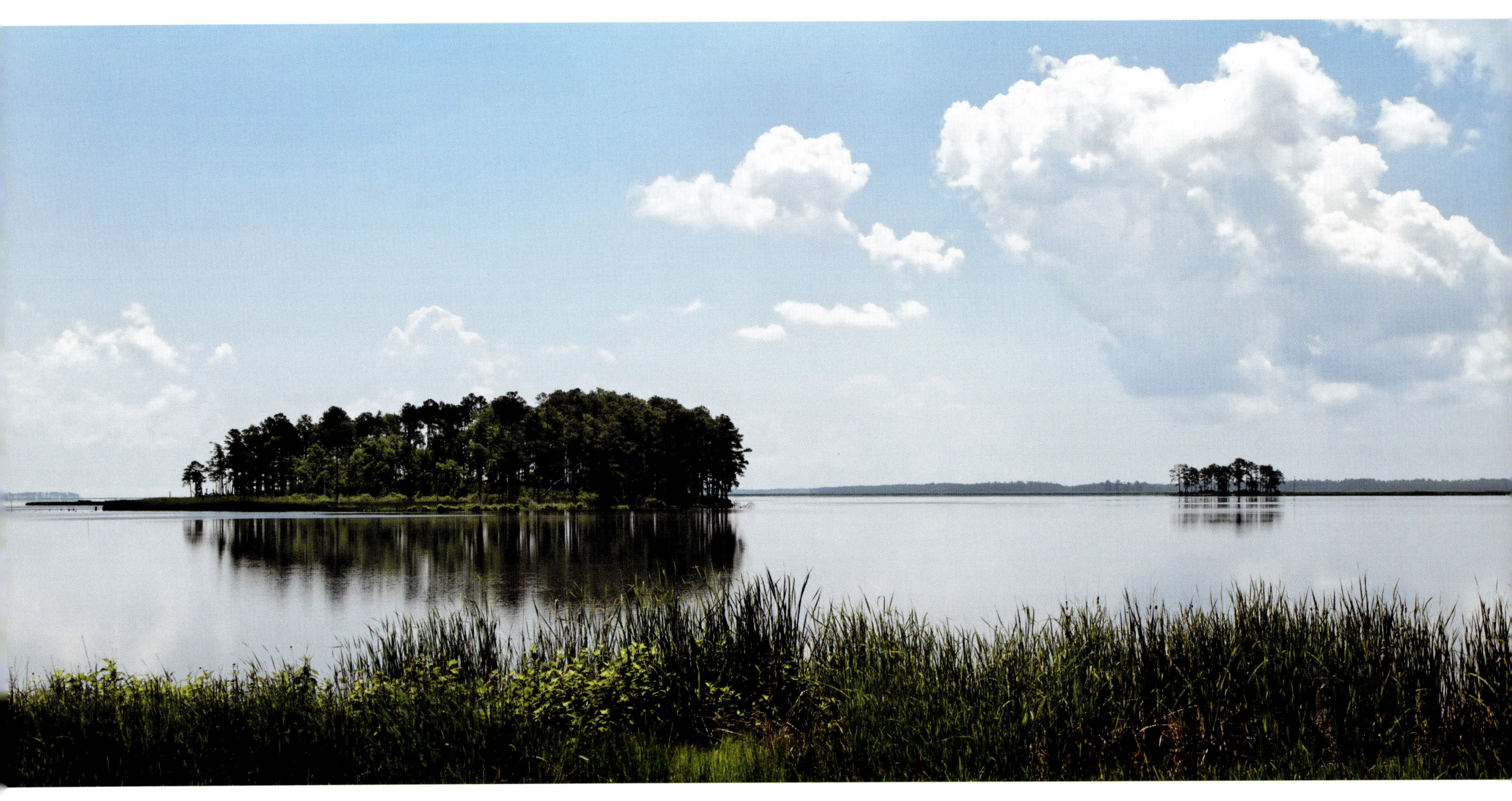

Blackwater National Wildlife Refuge

Cormorants adorn the tops of pier pilings for a decaying building near channel marker 16 on Smith Island.

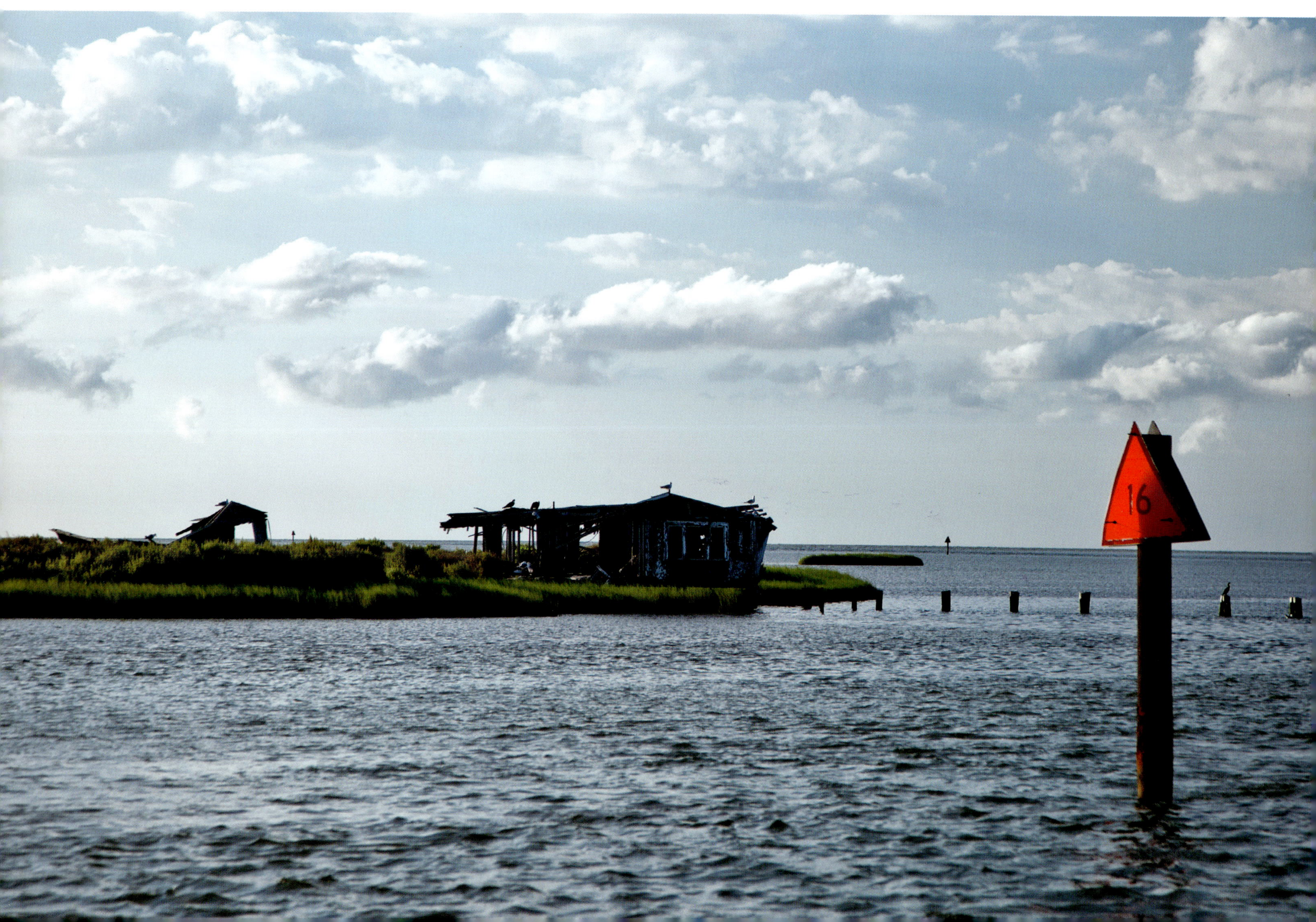
16

A stand-up paddle board waits for another journey around Smith Island.

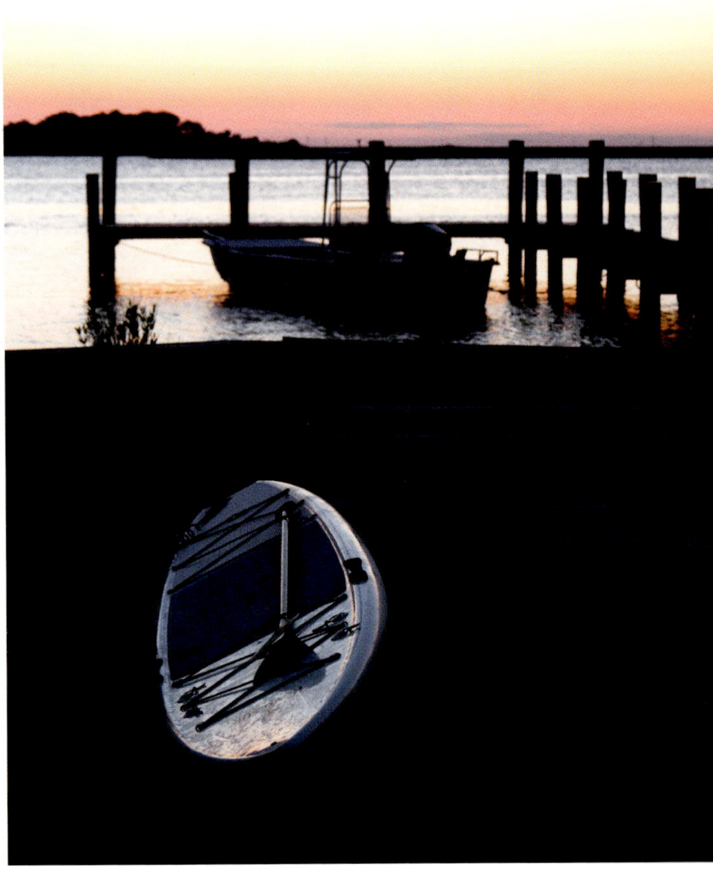

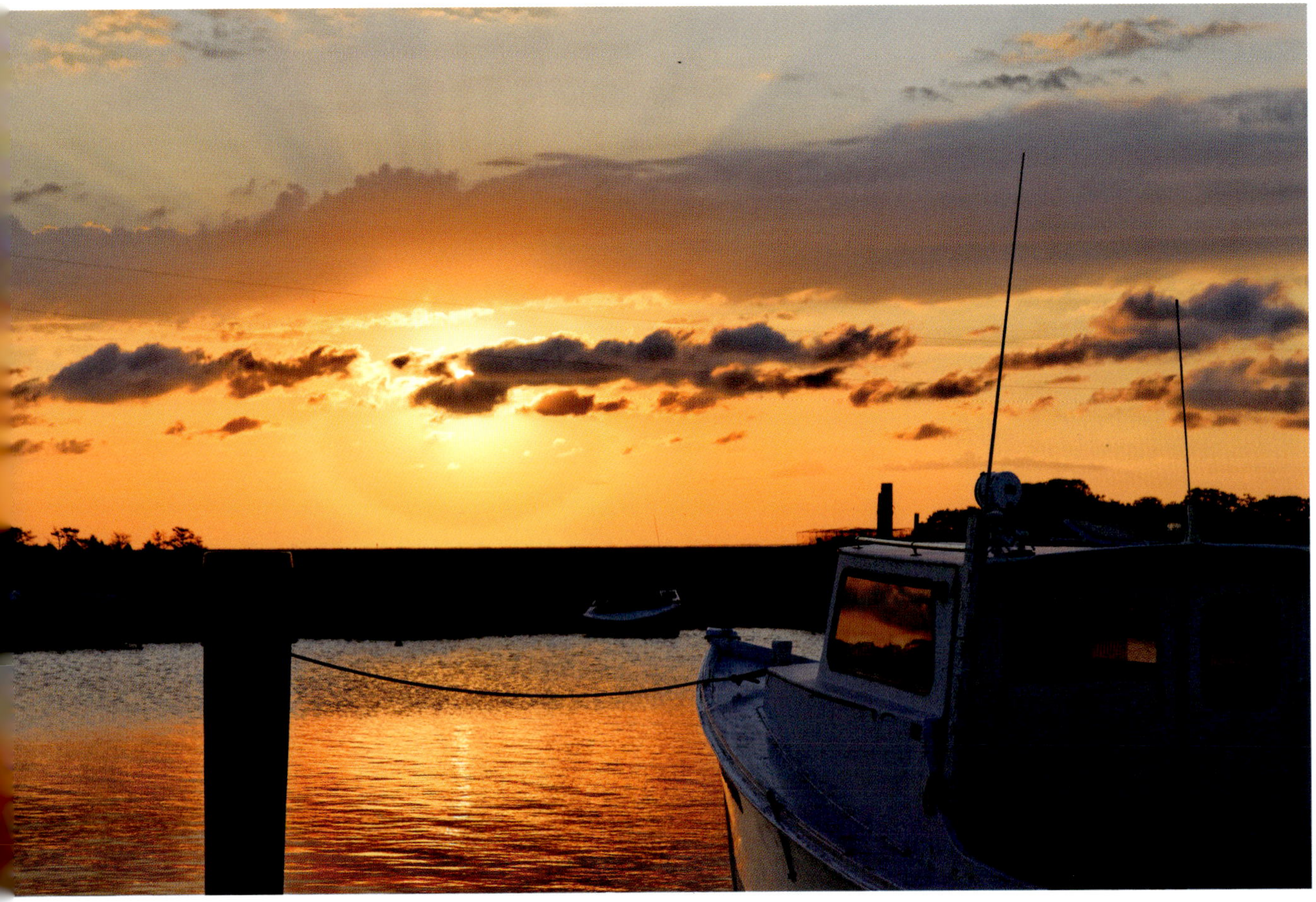

The sun rises in Tylerton, Smith Island.

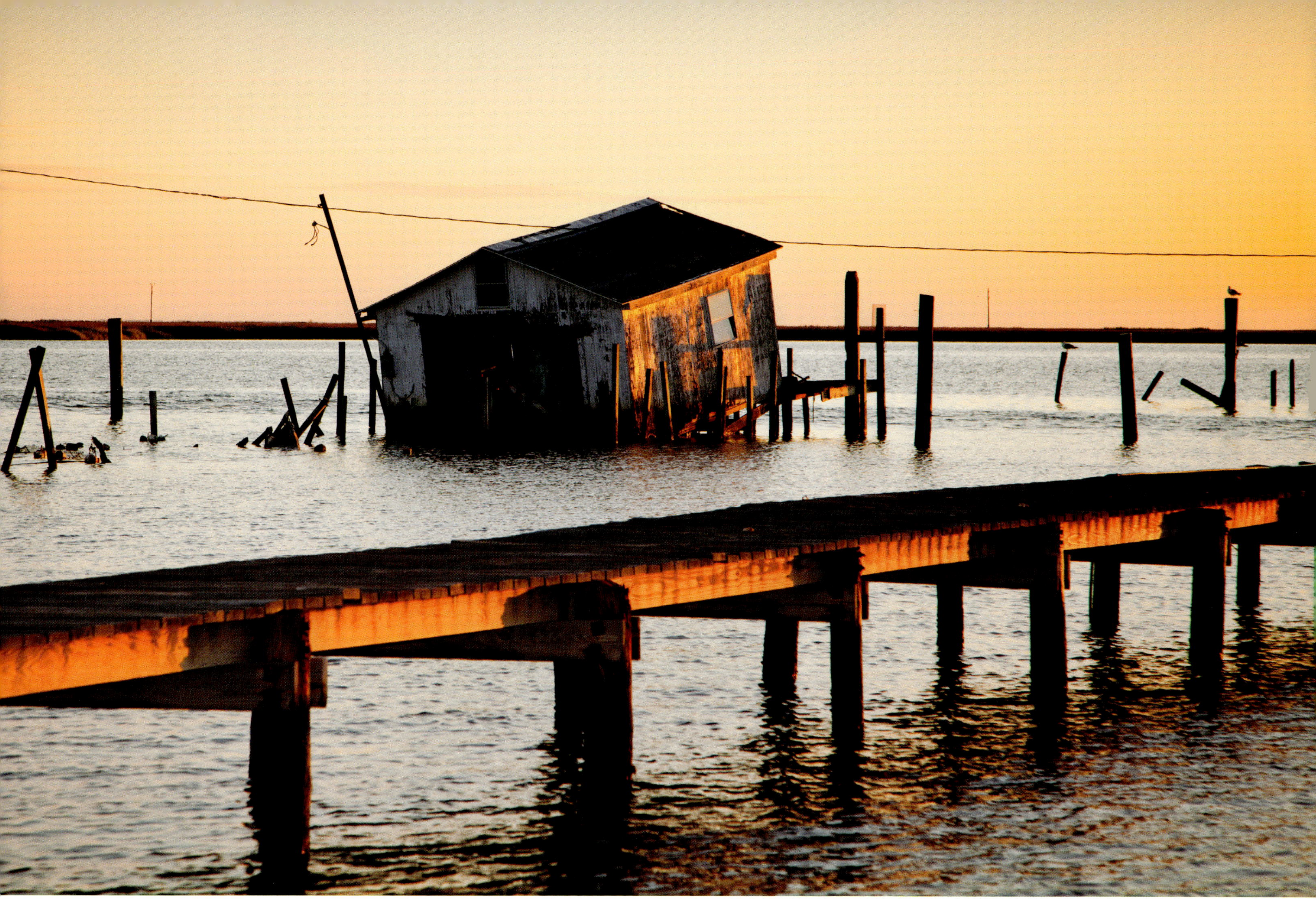

The Bay begins to claim a Crab Shanty on Tylerton, Smith Island.

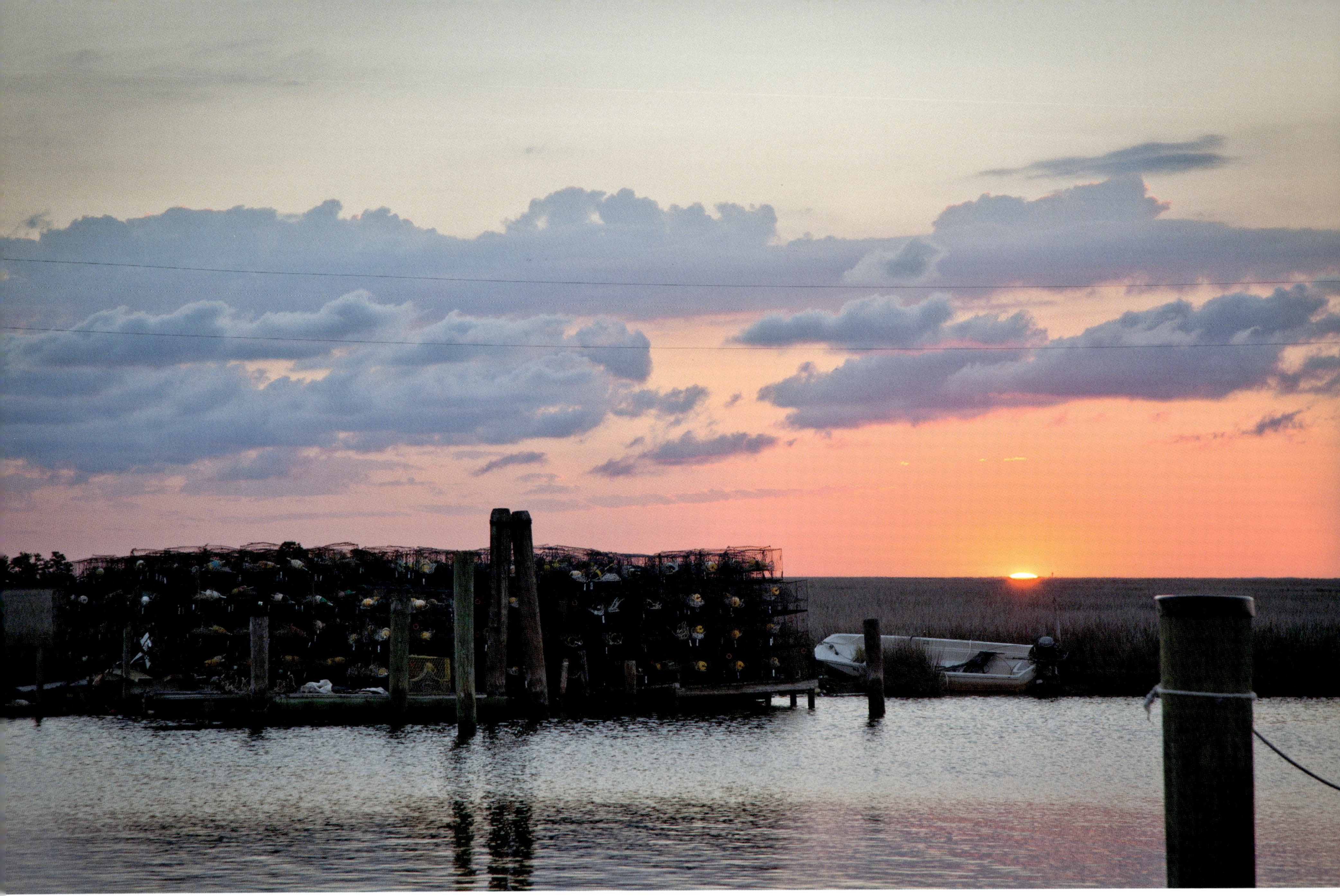

An orange and pink sky at 6:00 A.M. over Smith Island.

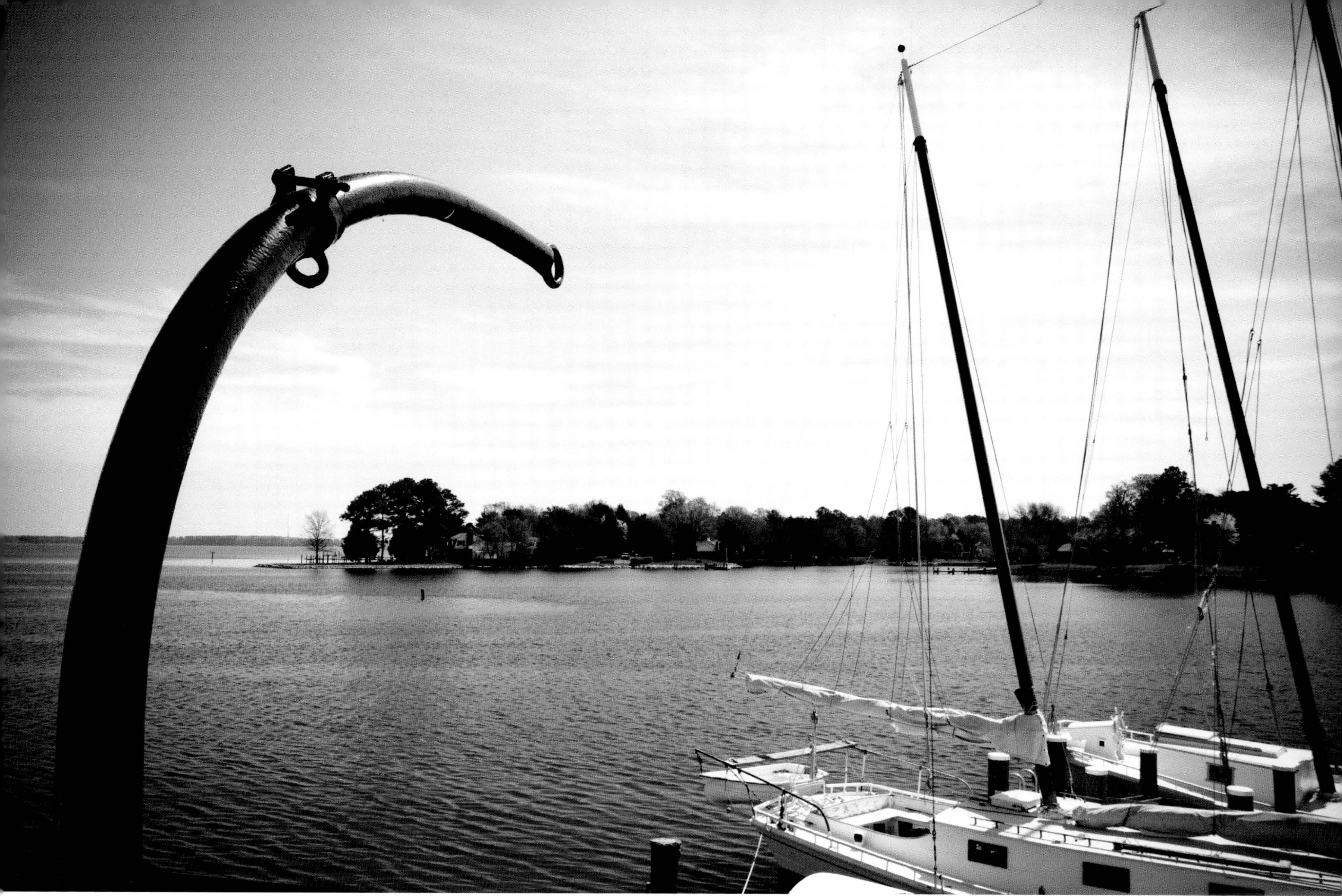

The view over St. Michaels Harbor from the Hooper Strait Lighthouse exhibit at the Chesapeake Bay Maritime Museum.

# The Wild Things

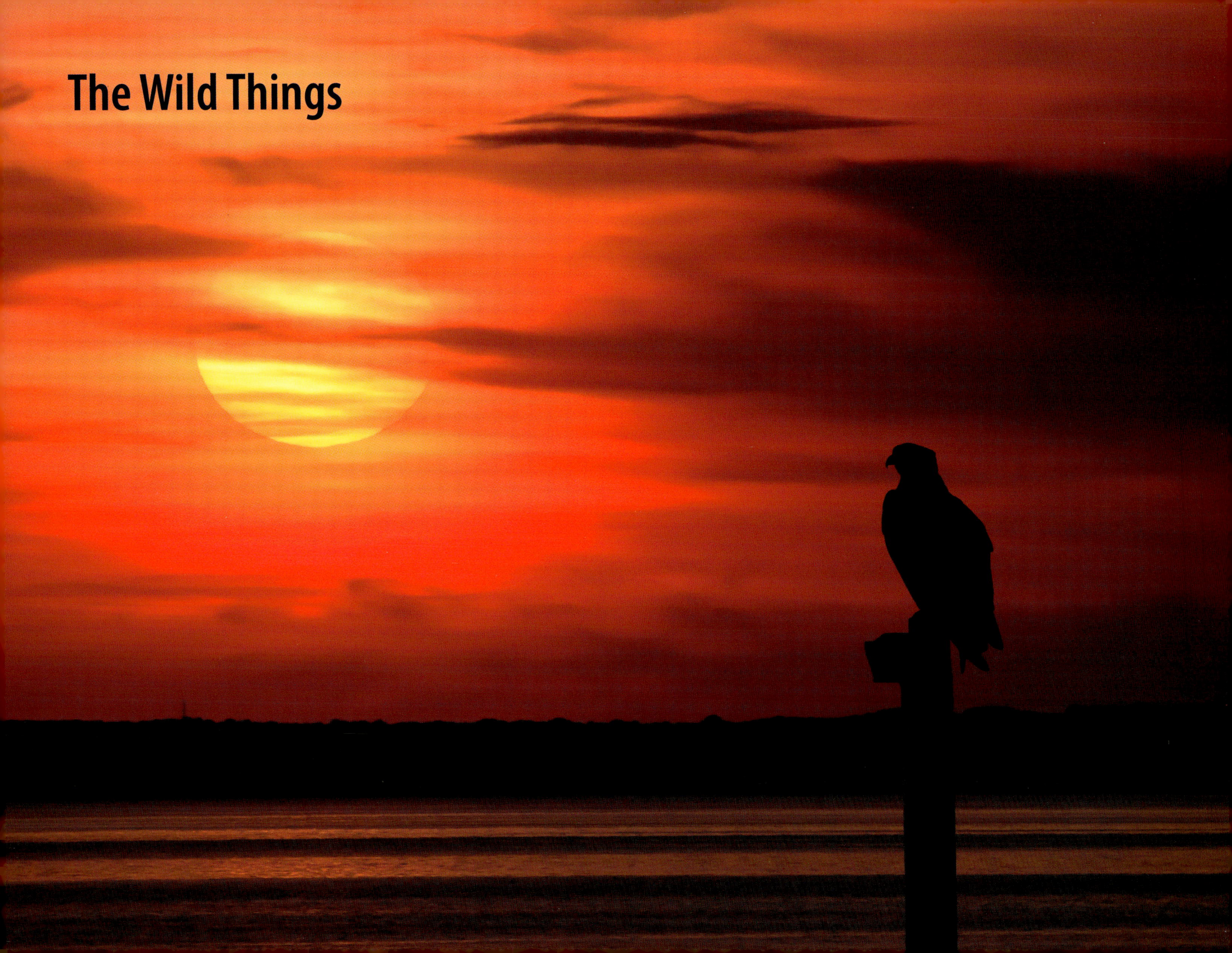

A busted peeler crab beginning the molting process.

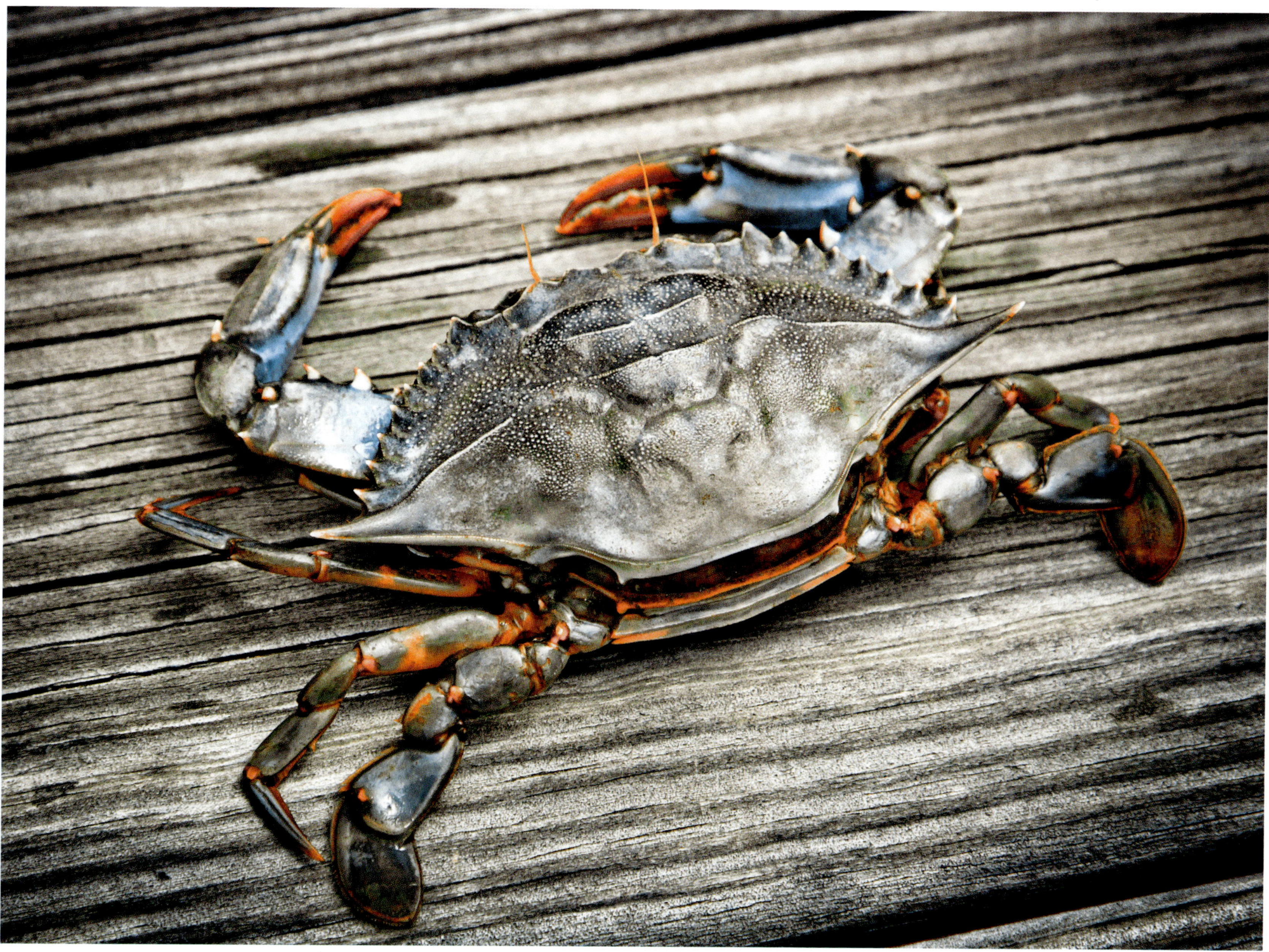

An osprey retreats from the nest to his favorite pole most nights at sunset on Tilghman Island.

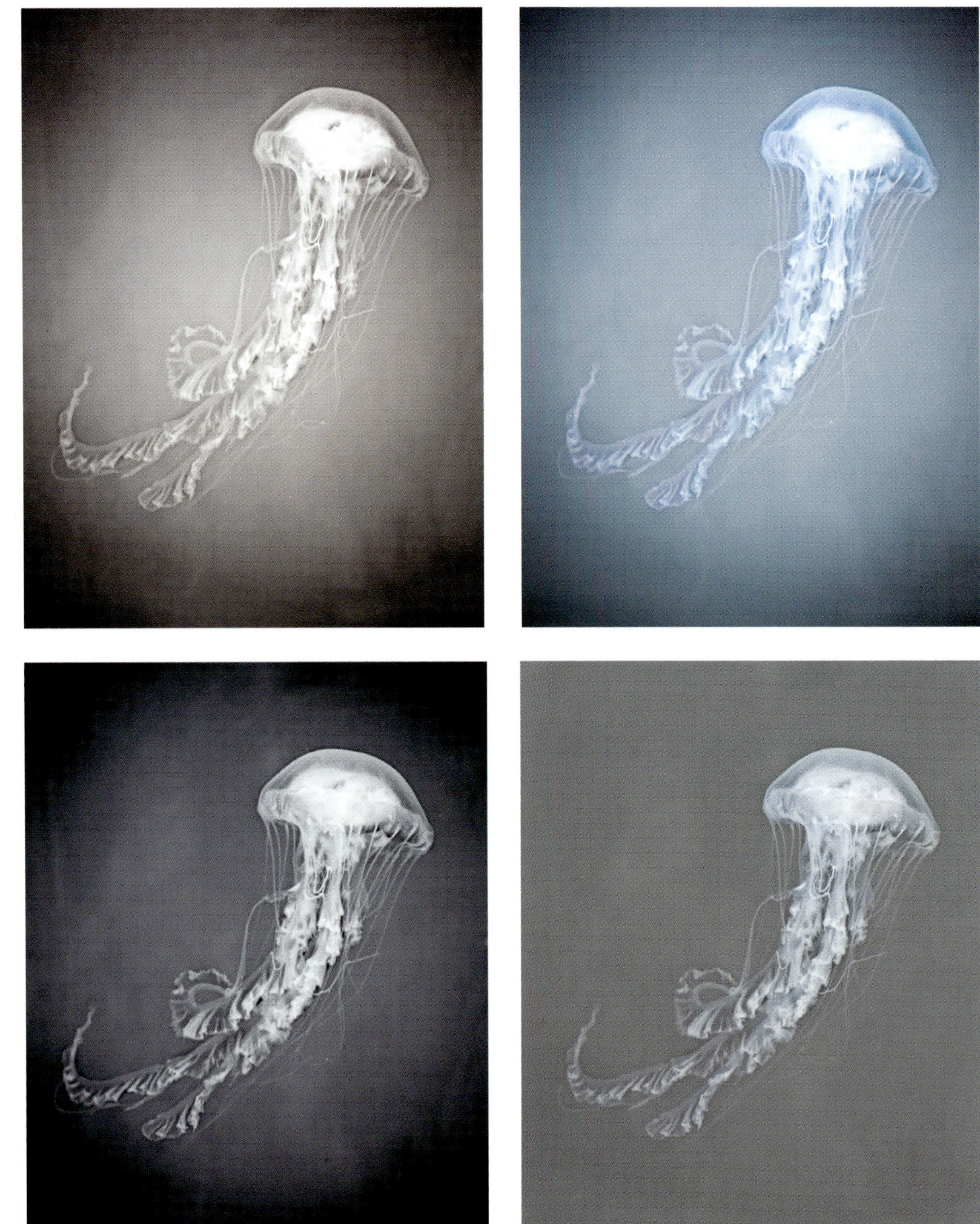

A sea nettle makes its way just below the surface of the Bay.

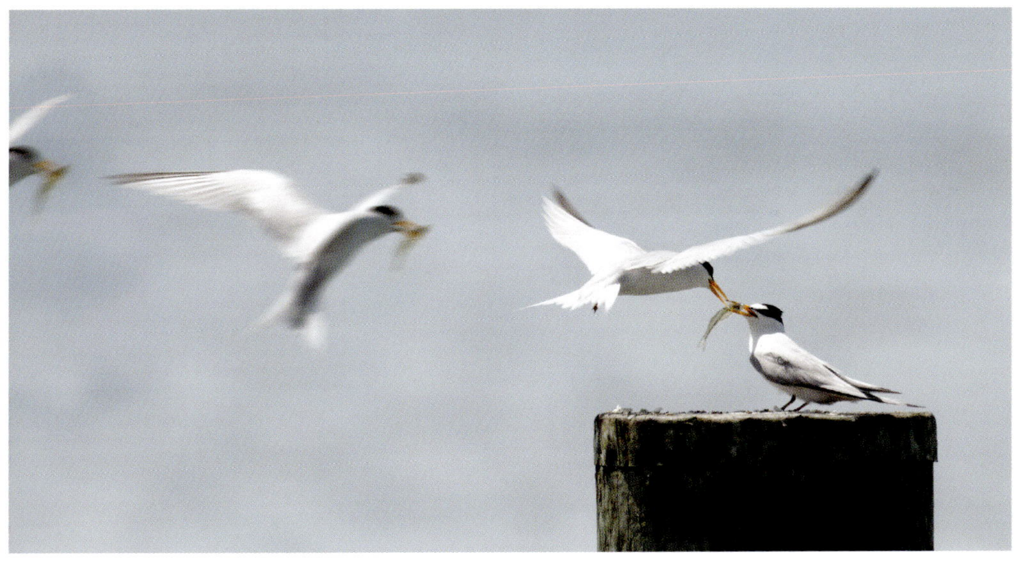

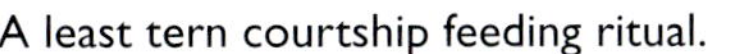

A least tern courtship feeding ritual.

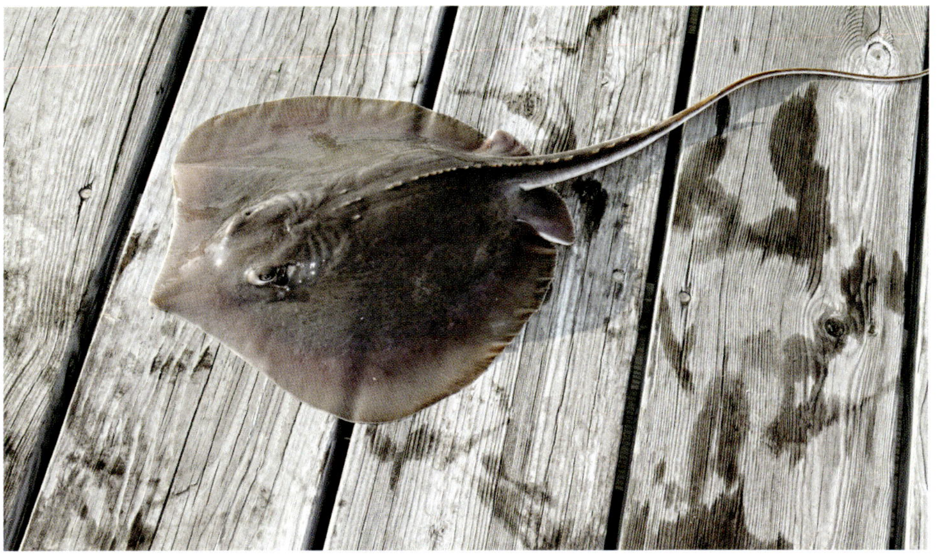

A skate lies on the pier after being removed from a fish hook.

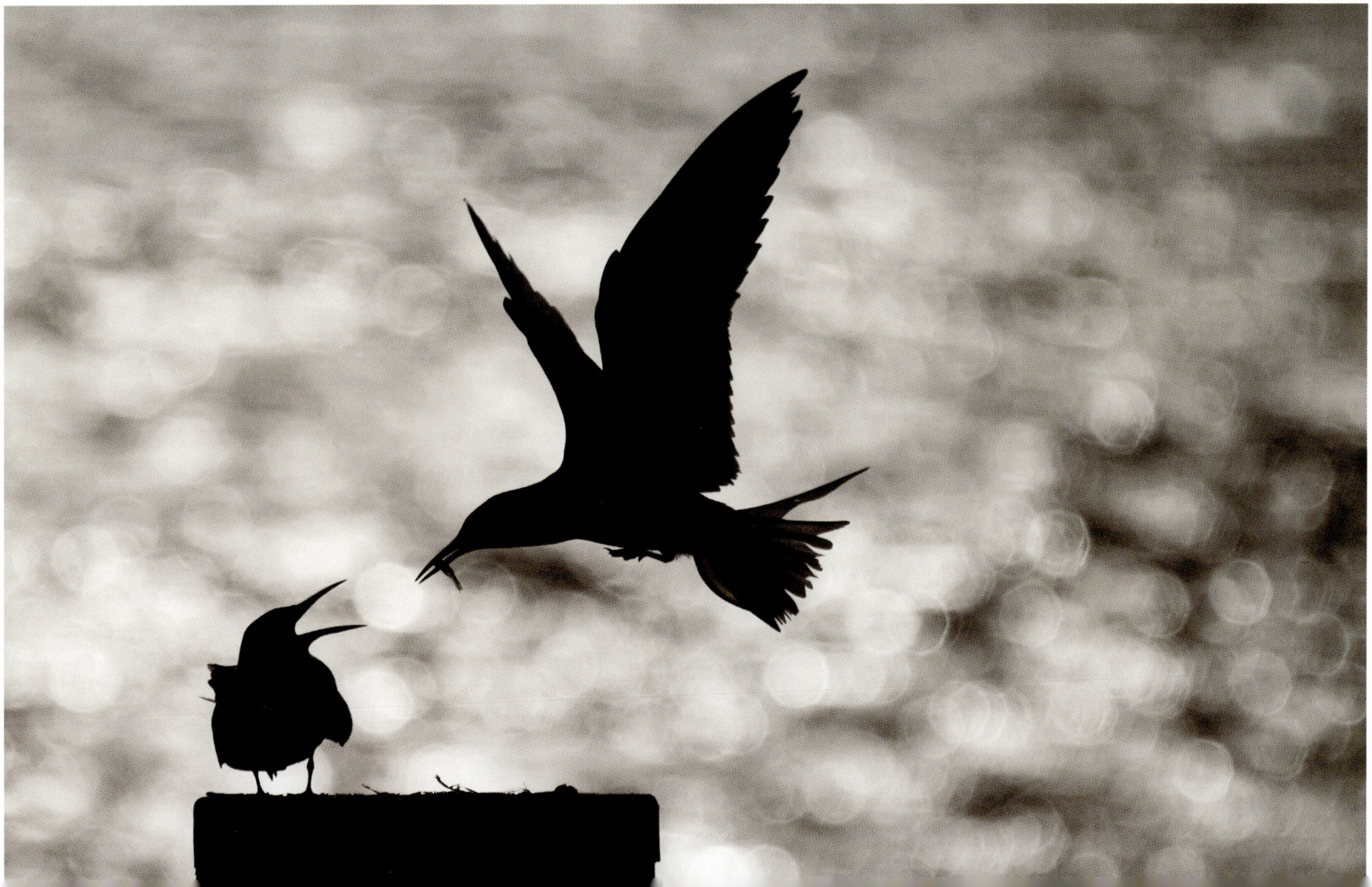

A tern courtship feeding ritual.

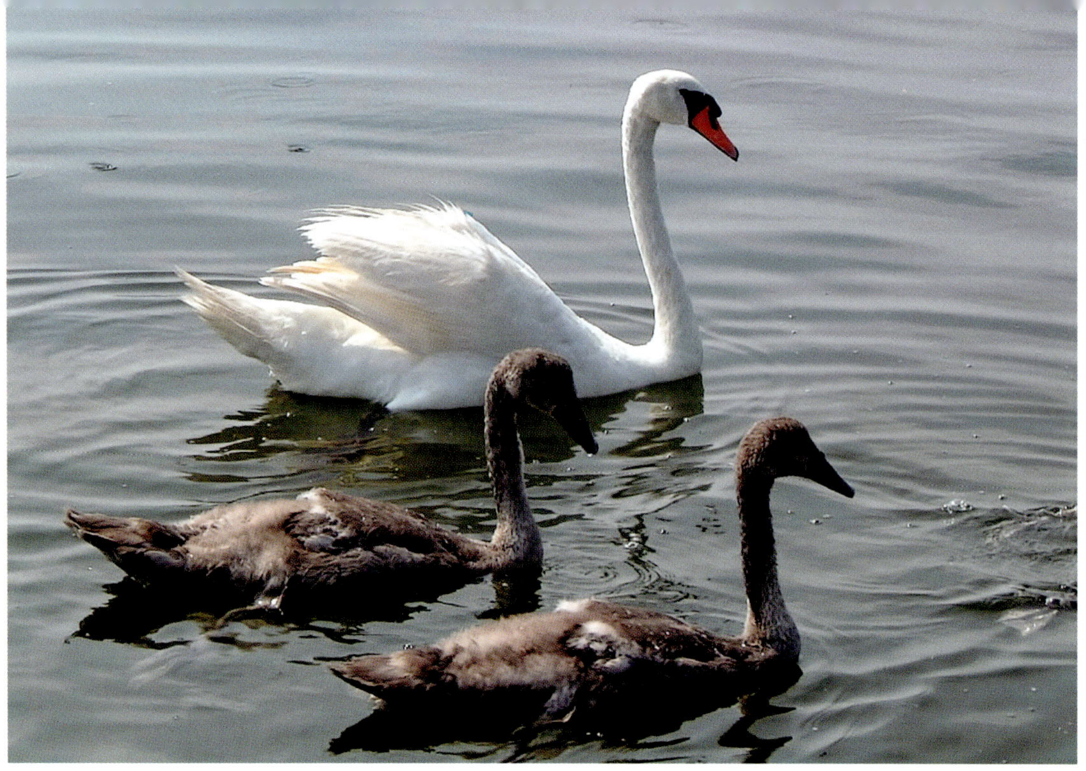

A mother mute swan and two of her cygnets.

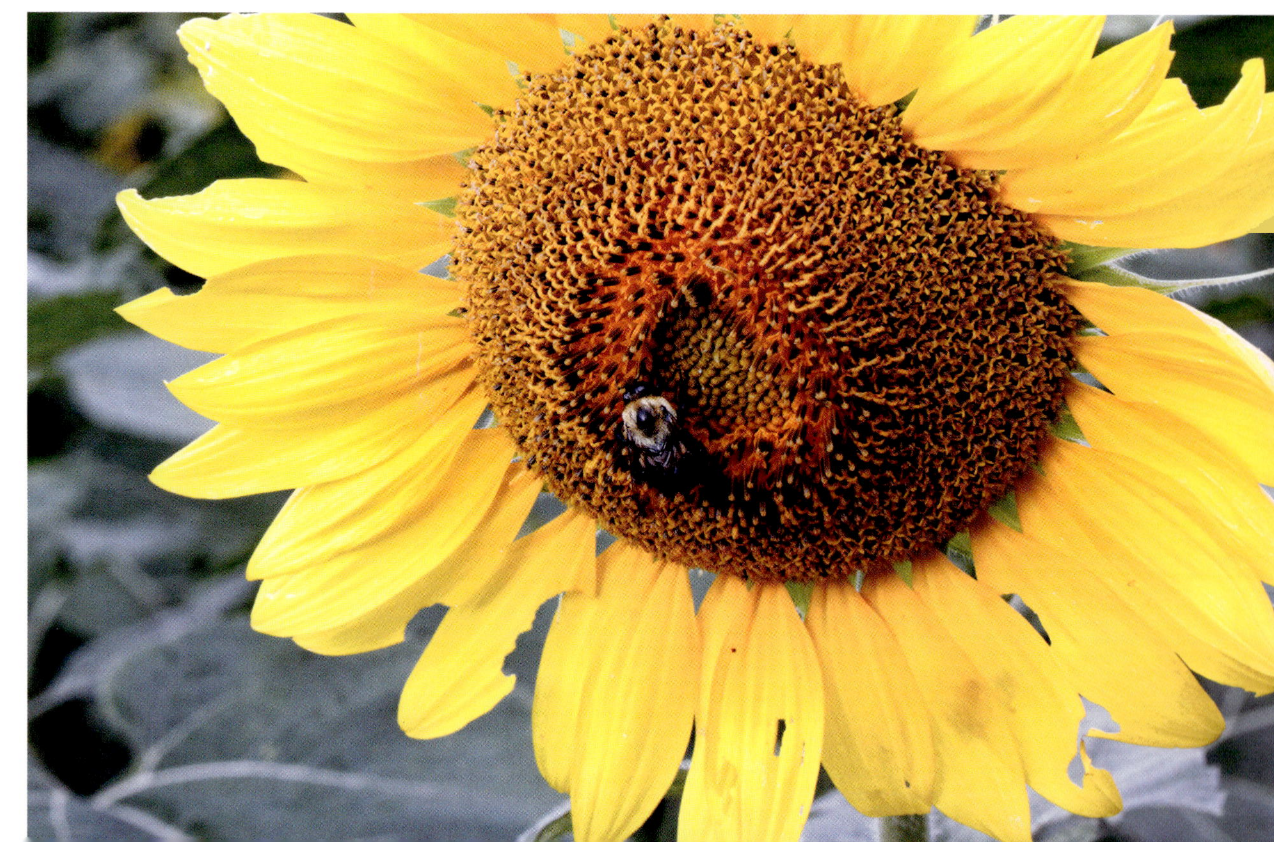

Sunflowers are a common sight in the fields of the Chesapeake Bay watershed.

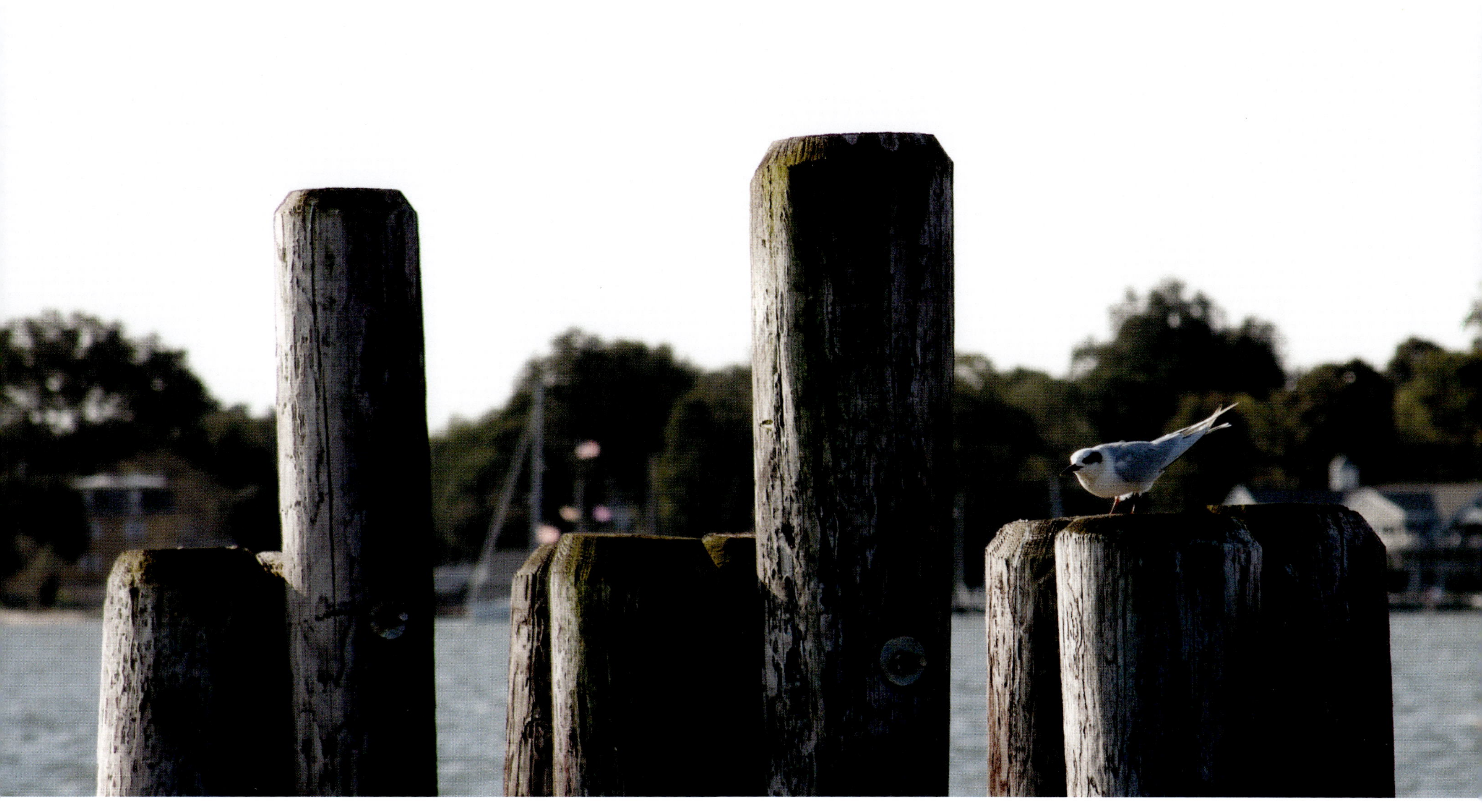

A Forster's tern greets visitors to the ferry landing at Oxford, Maryland.

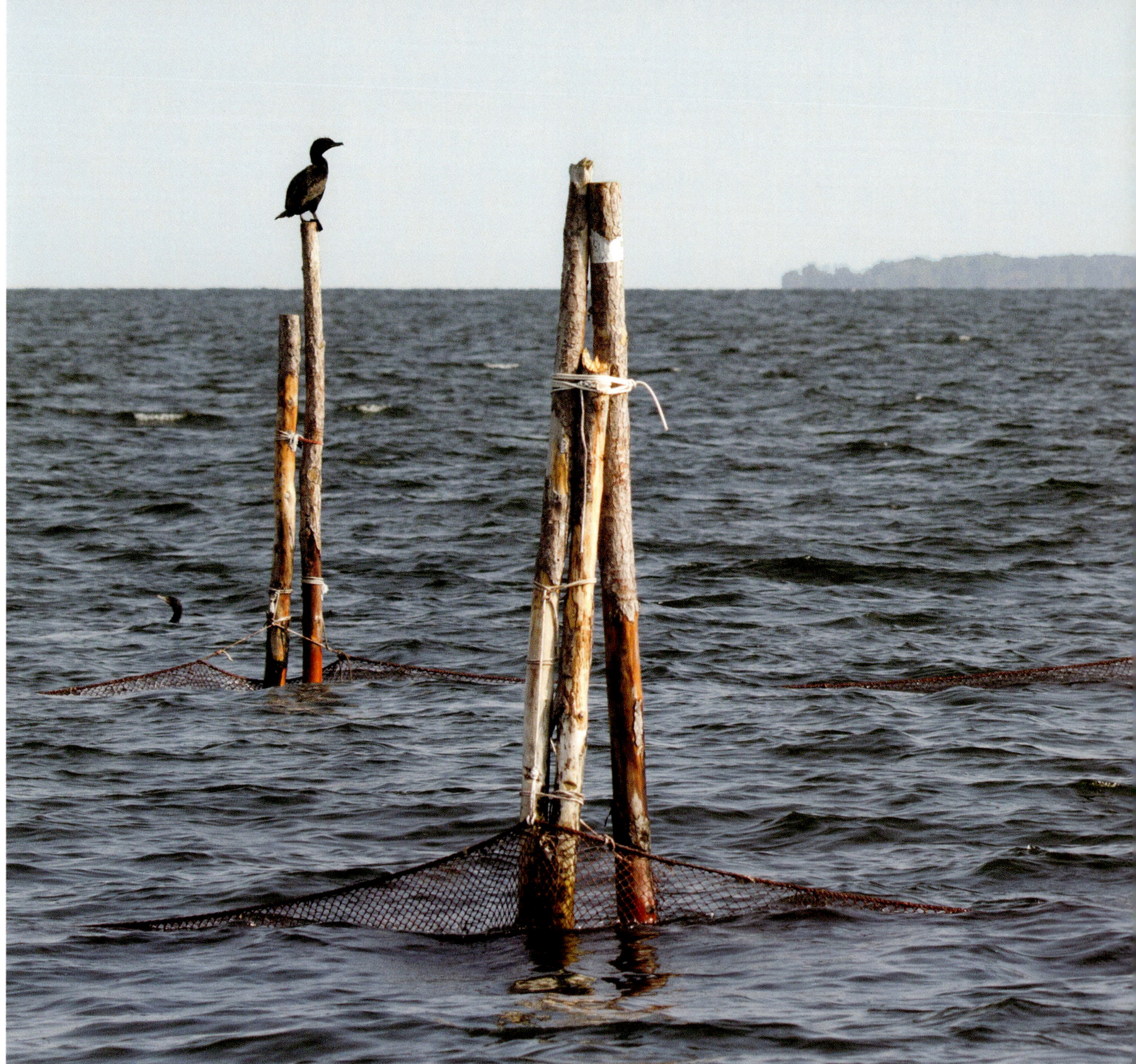

An easy meal can be found at the pound nets.

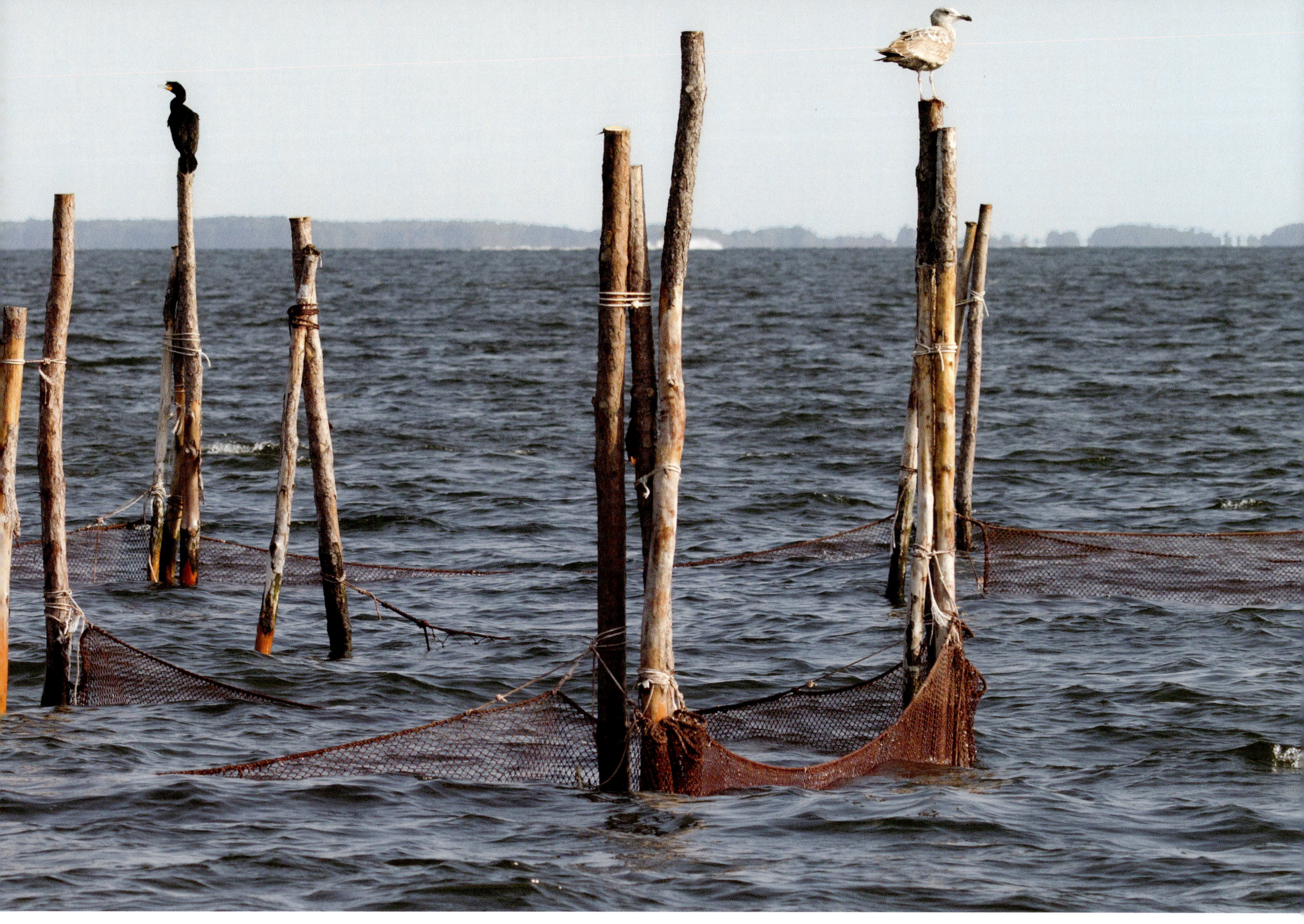

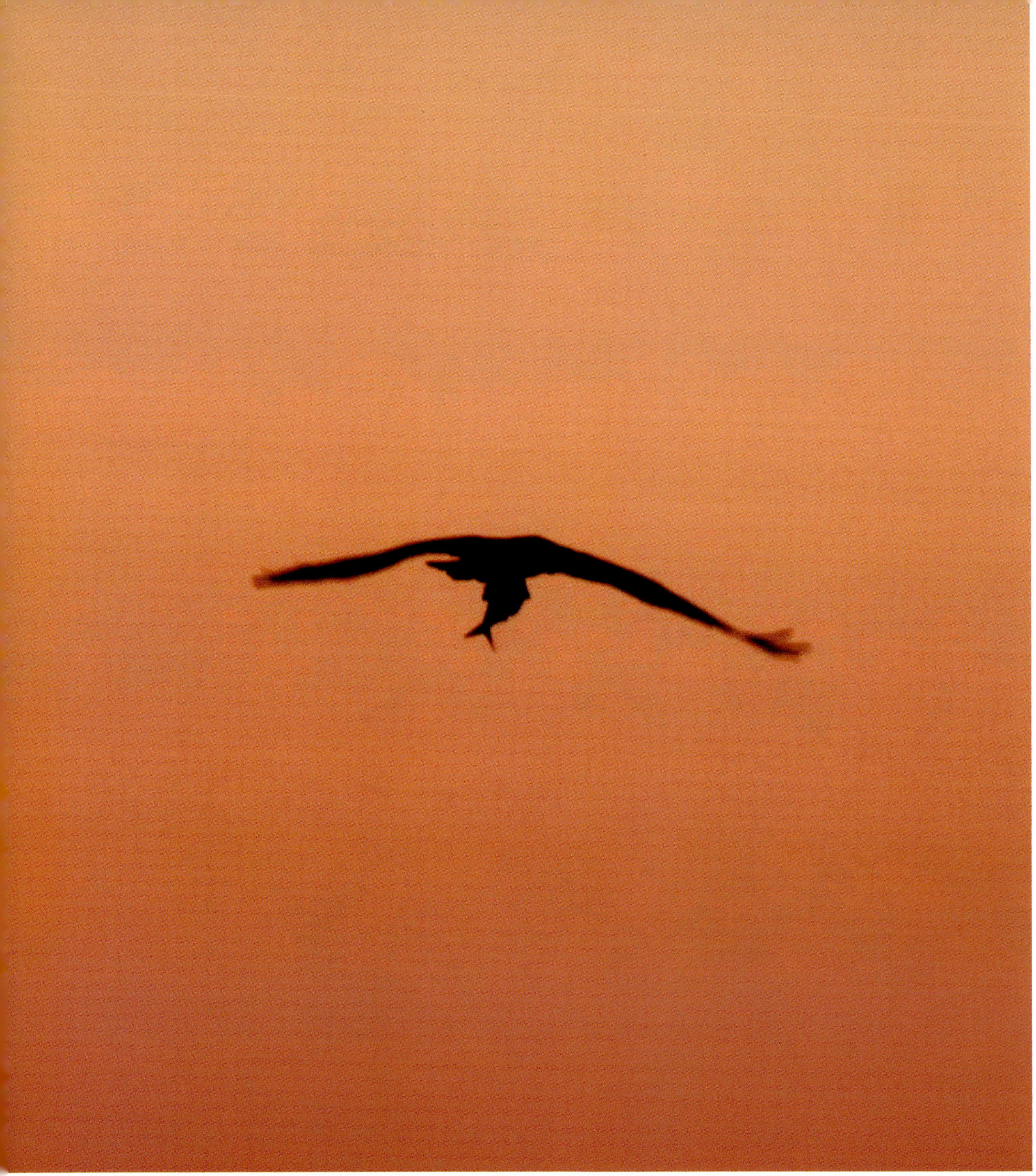

An osprey flies into the sunset with his dinner.

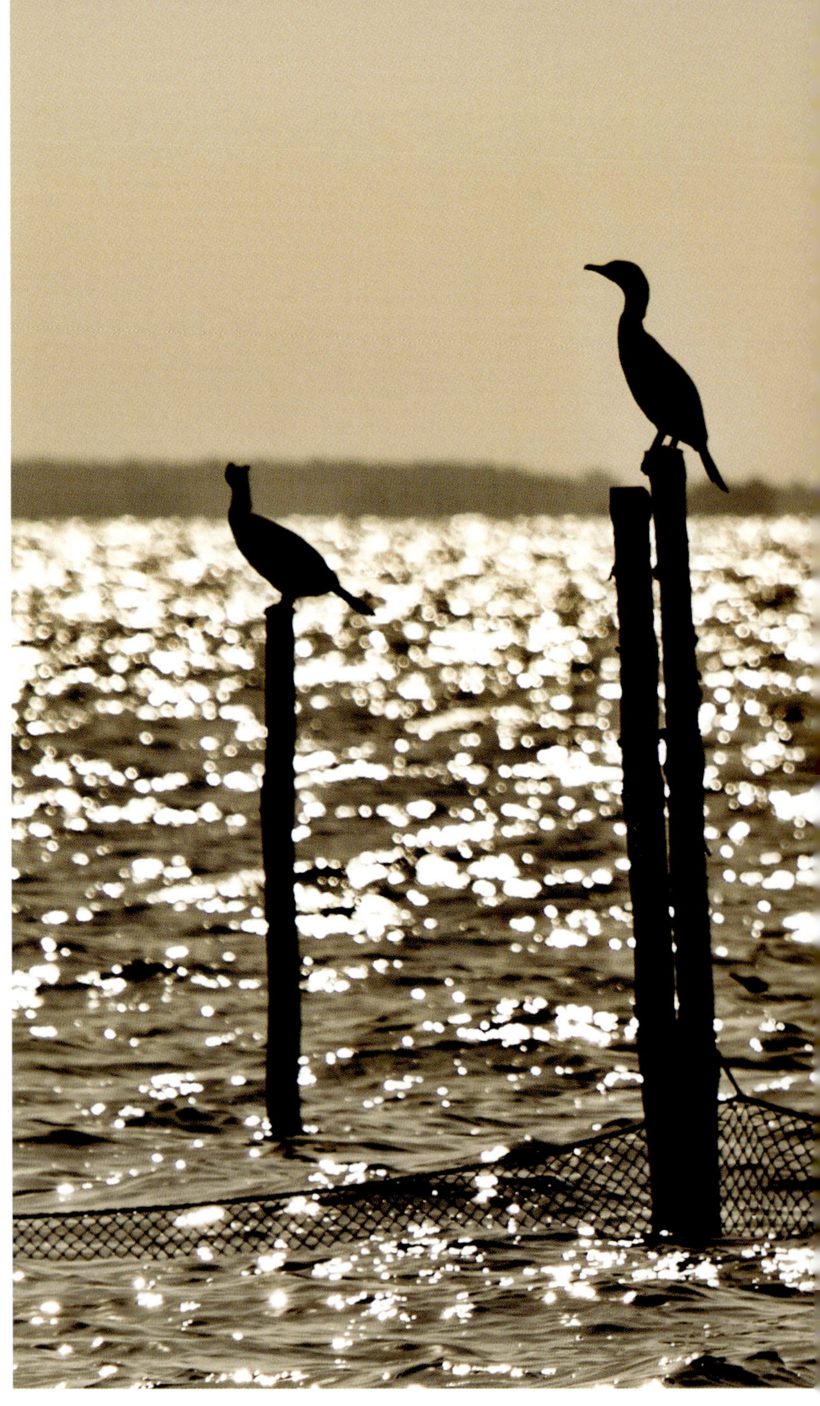

Cormorants at the pound nets, some so laden with fish that they cannot fly.

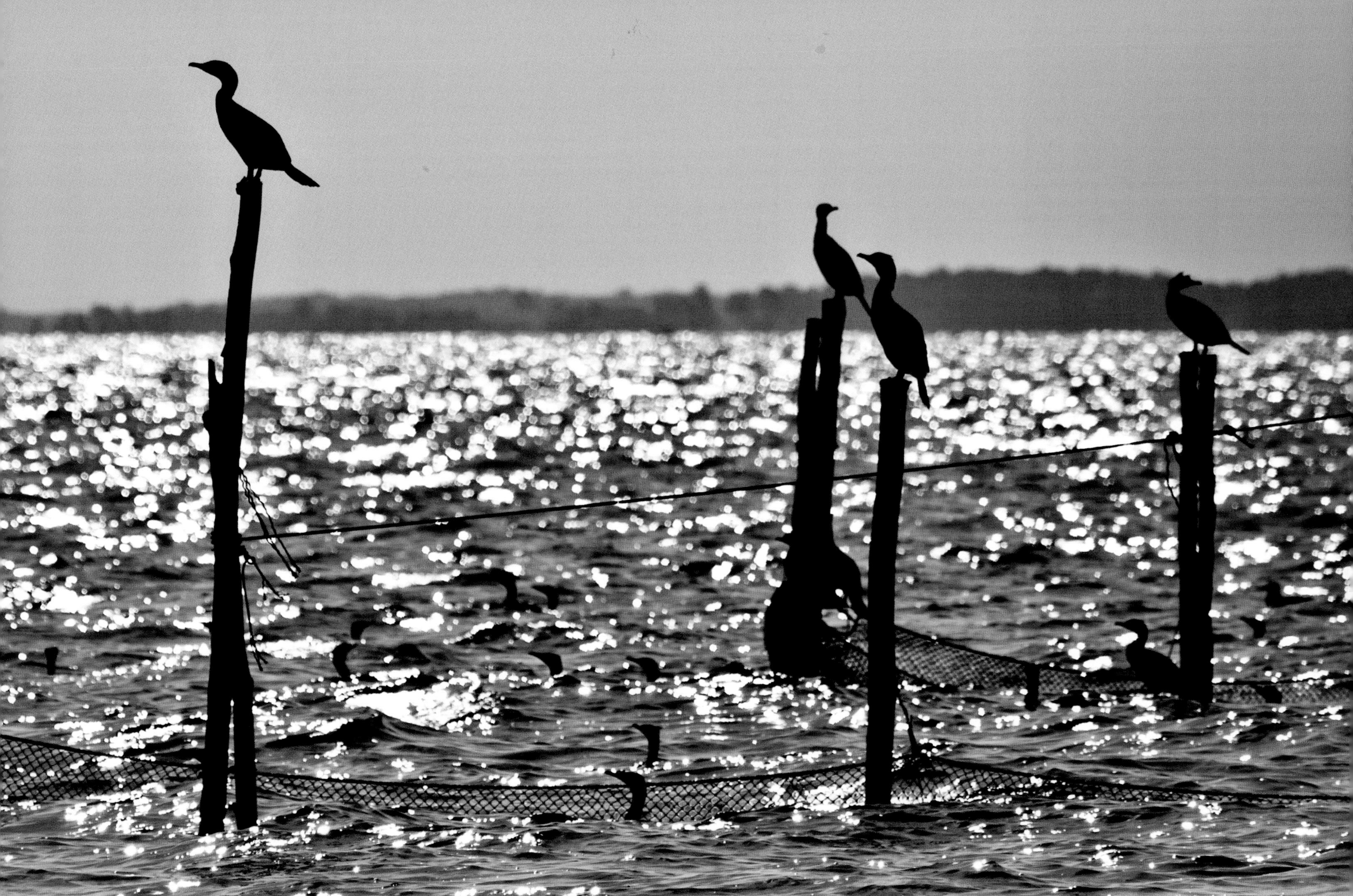

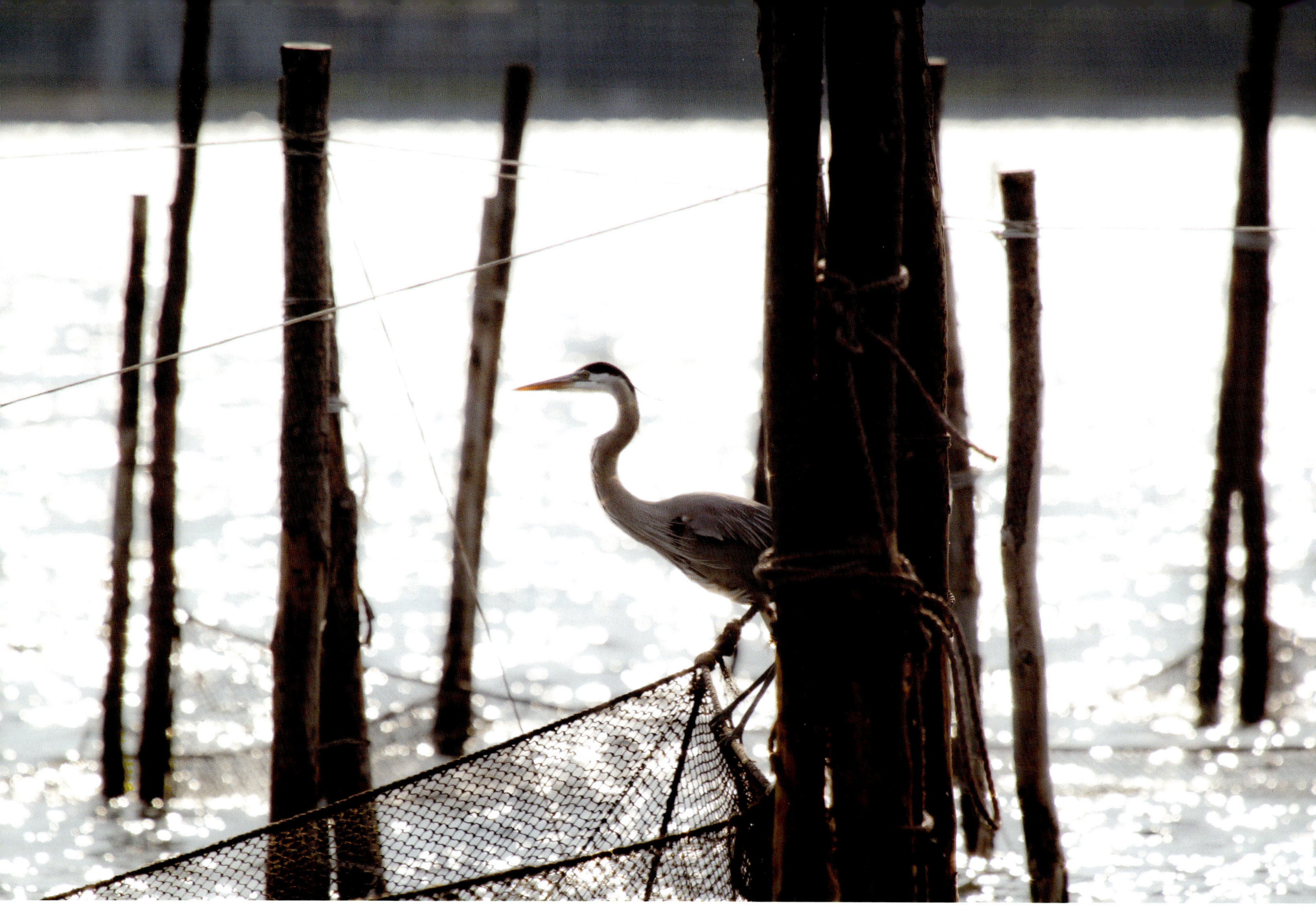

Great blue heron at the pound nets off Tilghman, Maryland.

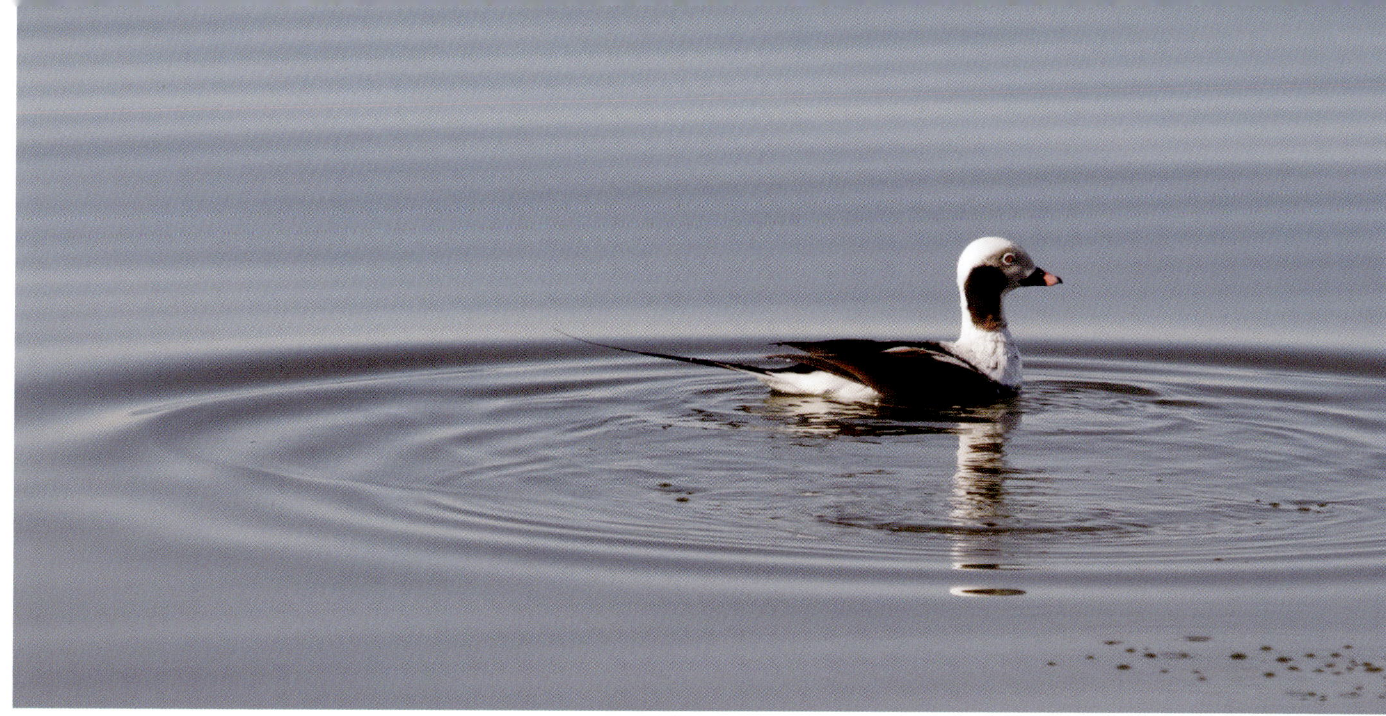

Long-tailed duck

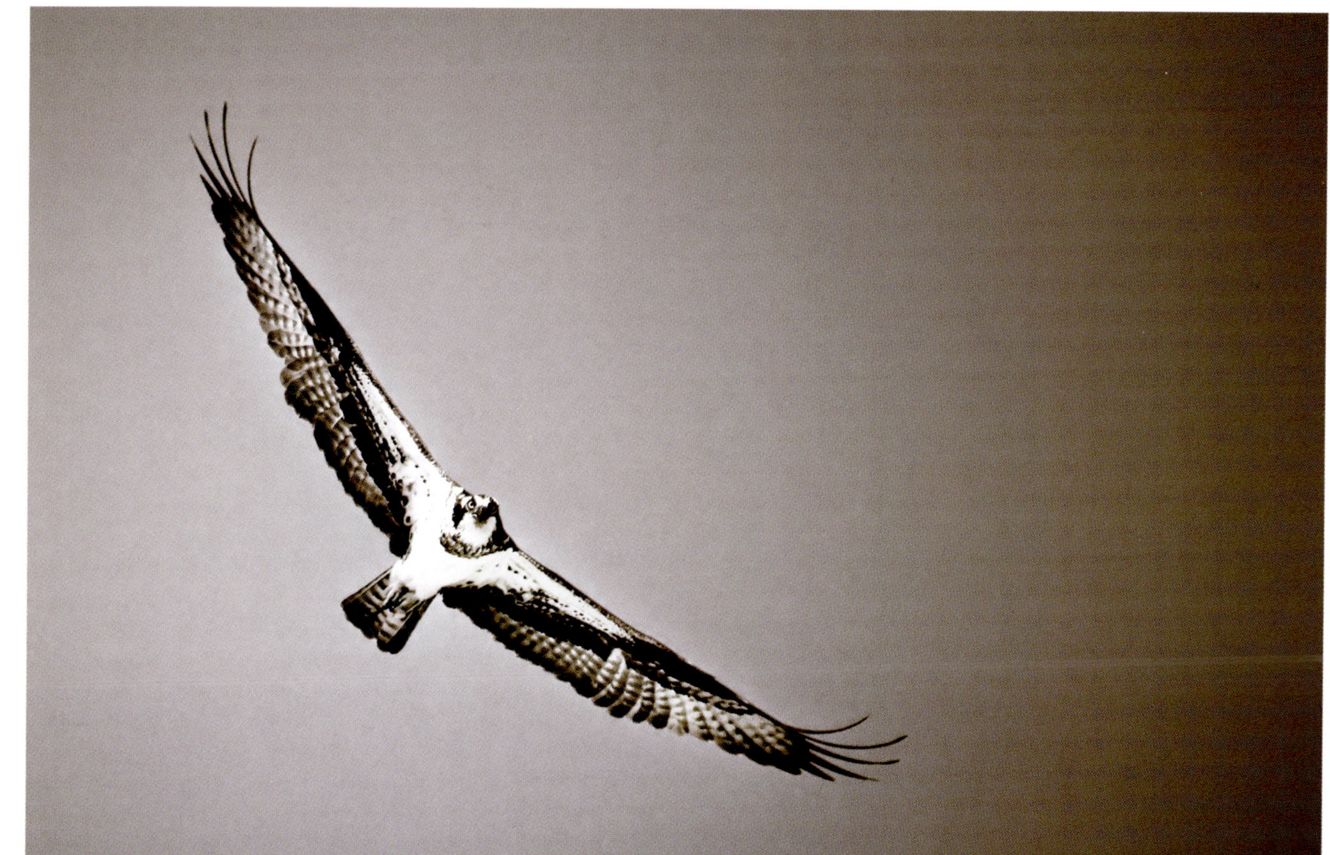

An osprey protecting the nest.

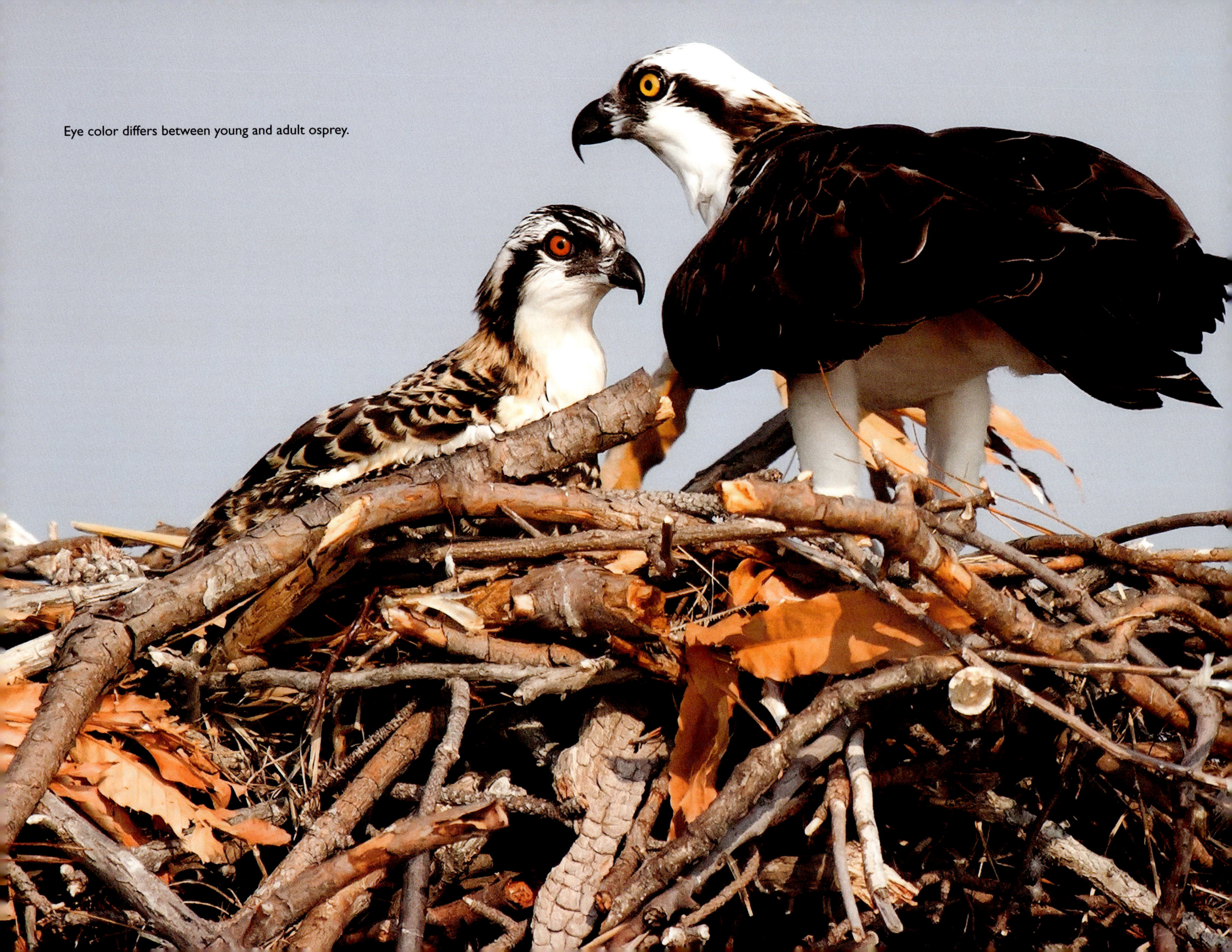
Eye color differs between young and adult osprey.

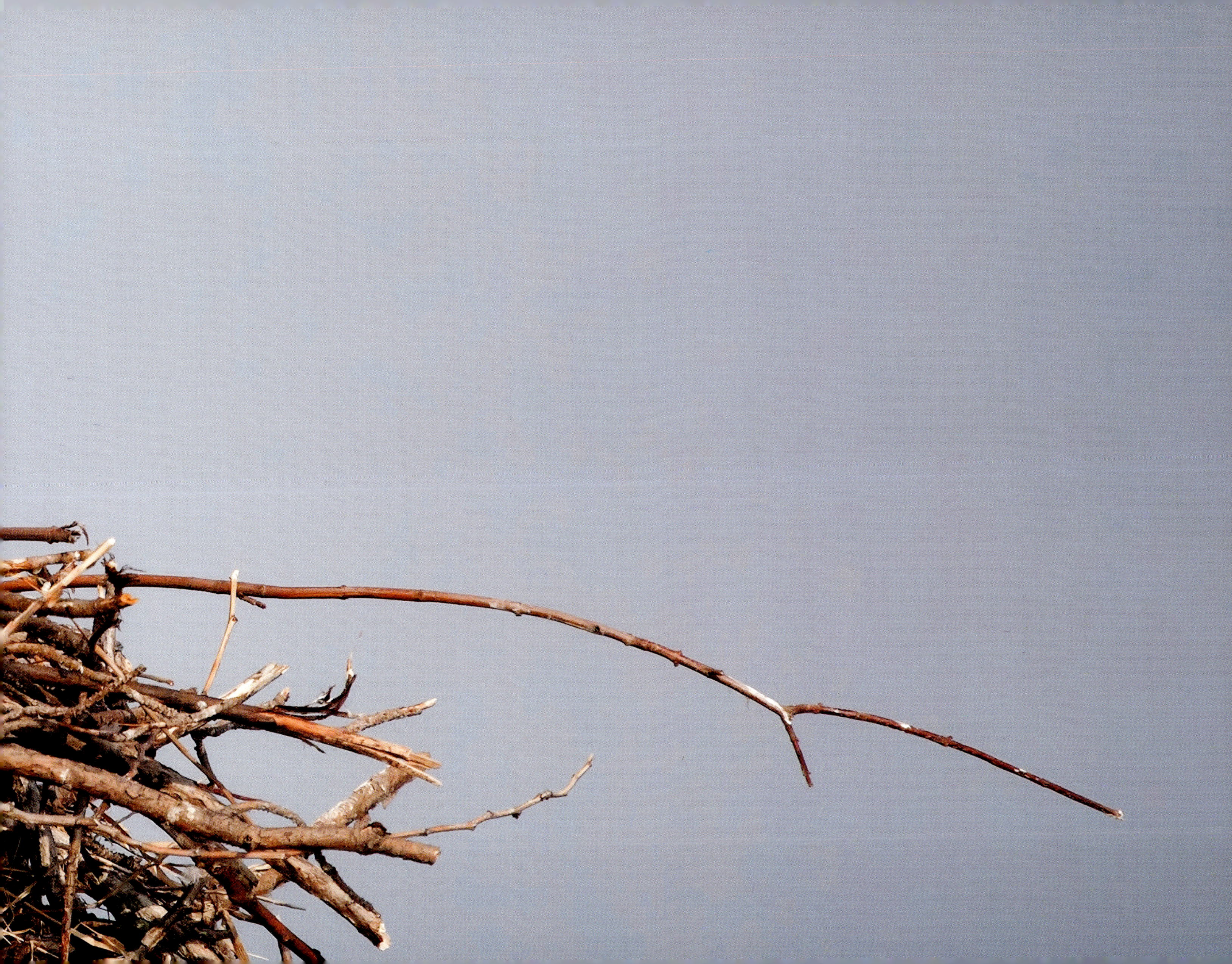

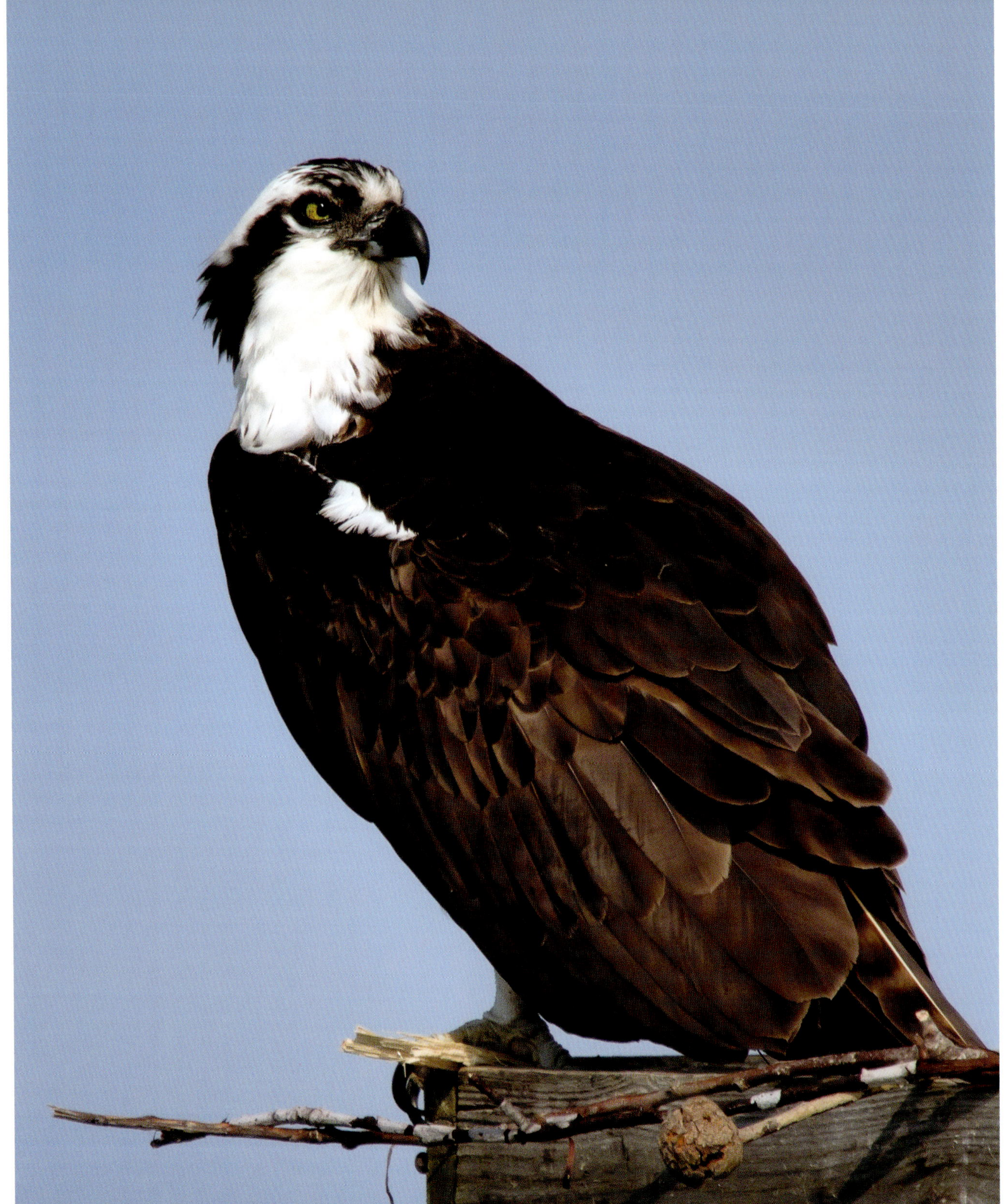

An osprey hasn't made much progress on its nesting box.

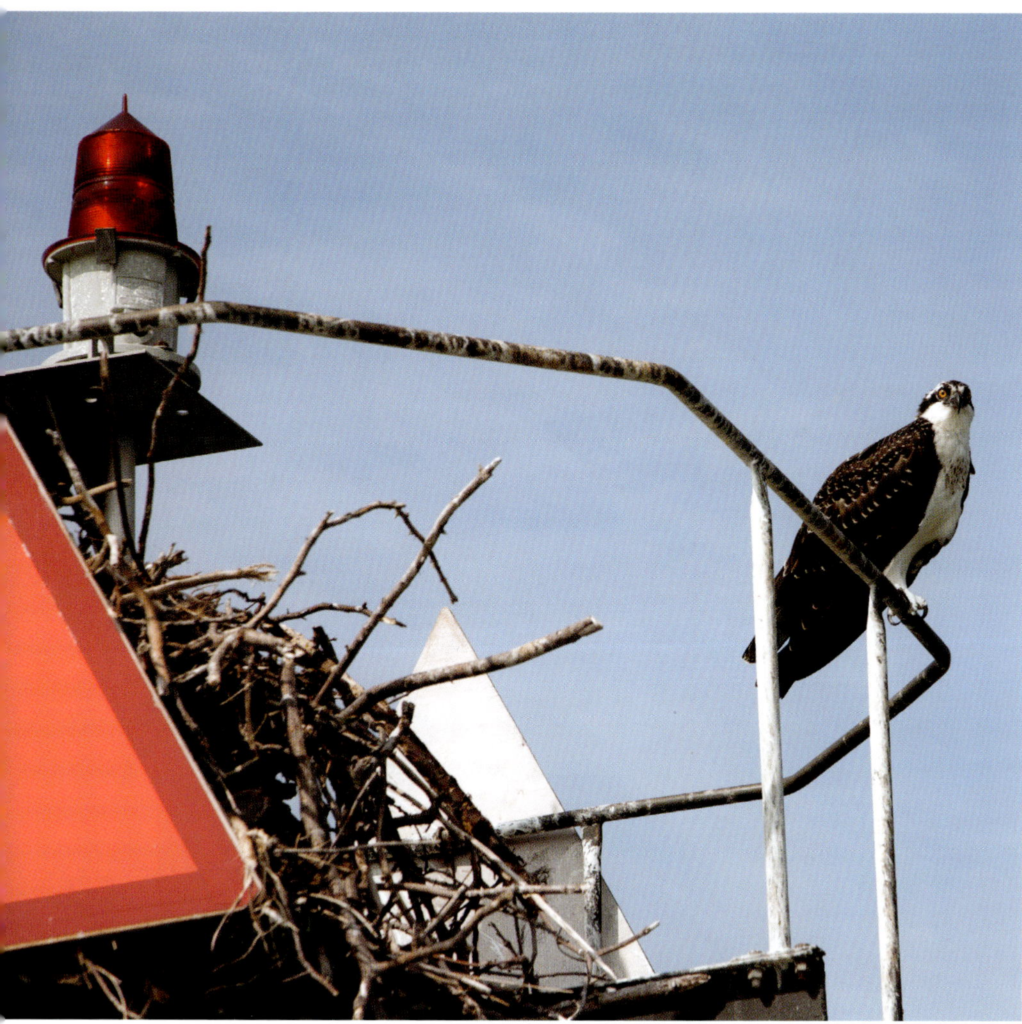

Large nests can be constructed within the channel marker structures.

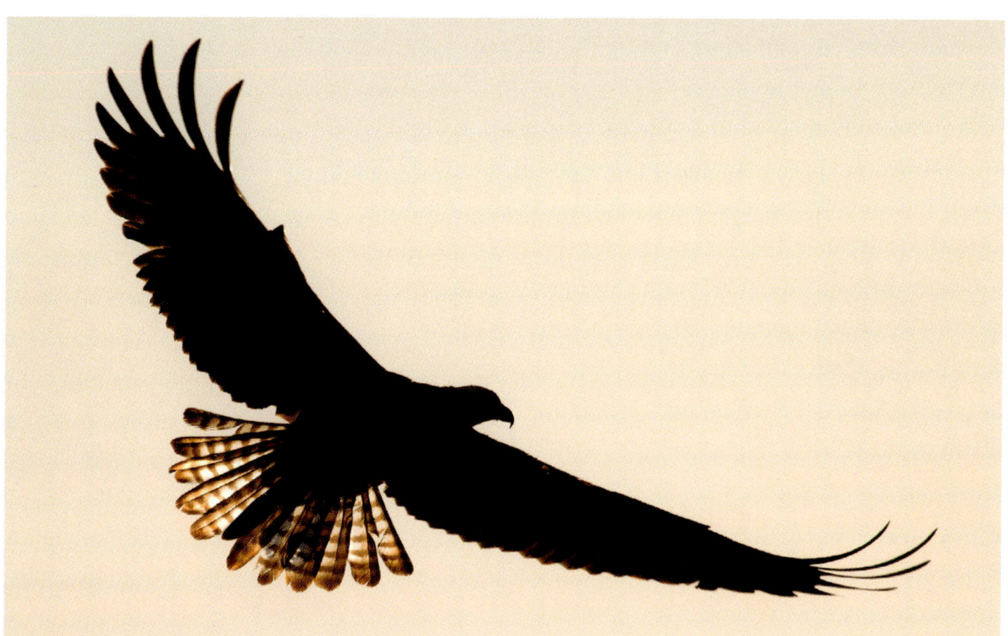

Tail feathers glow as they allow the sun's light through at the end of the day.

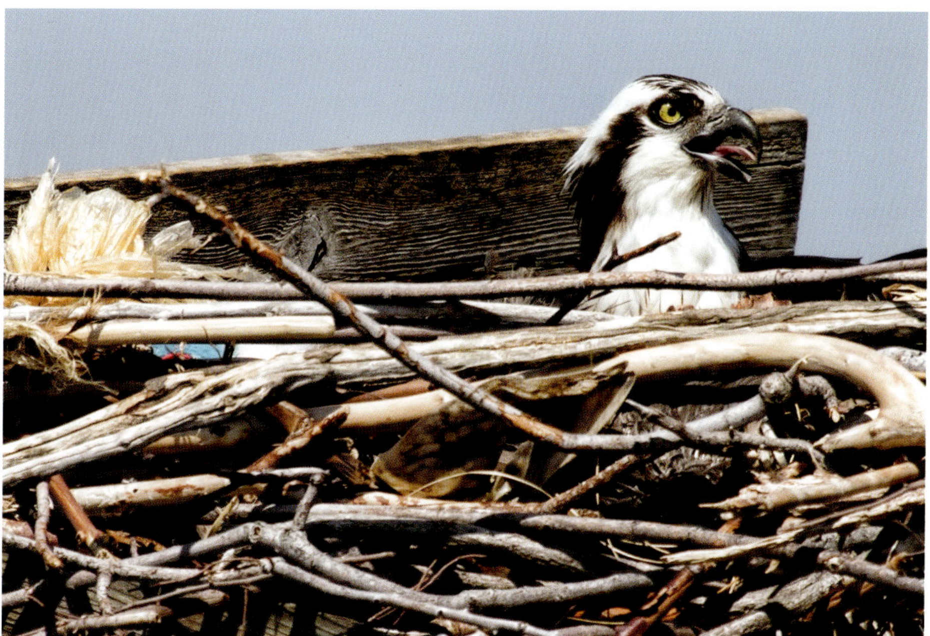

Waiting on the eggs.

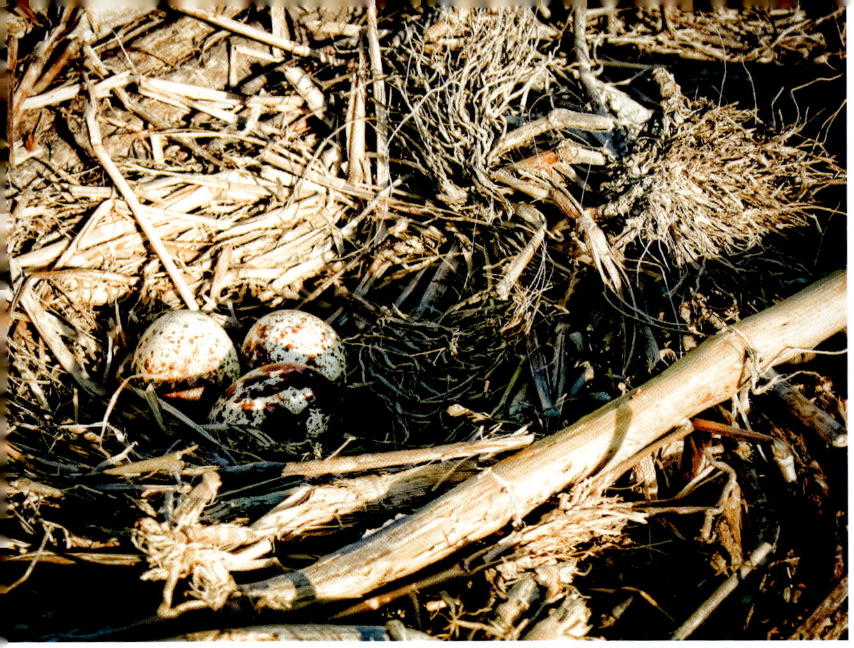

Two of these three osprey eggs would later hatch and I was fortunate enough to observe their development from hatchling to successful flight.

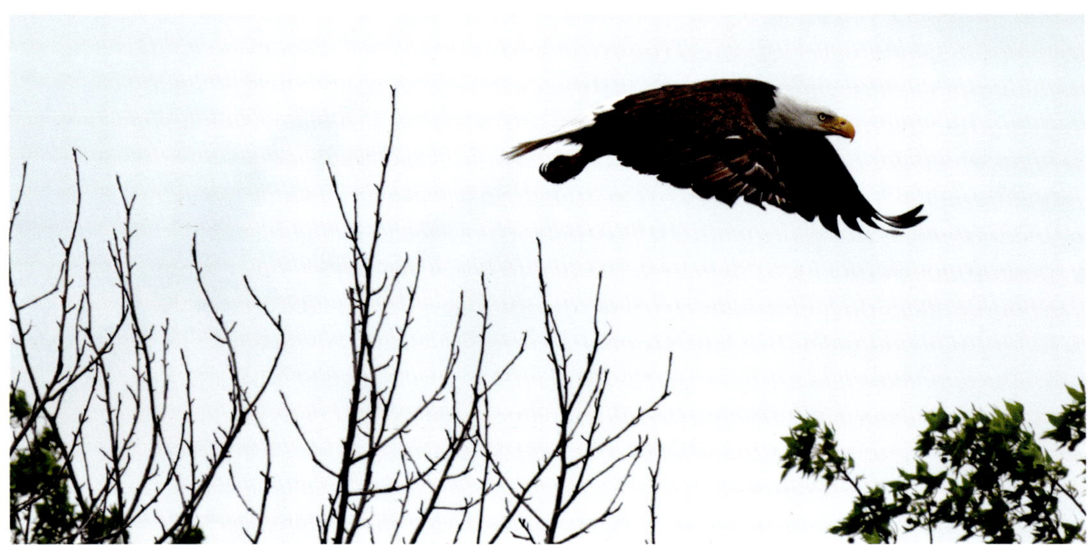

Bald eagle at Blackwater National Wildlife Refuge (*above and below*)

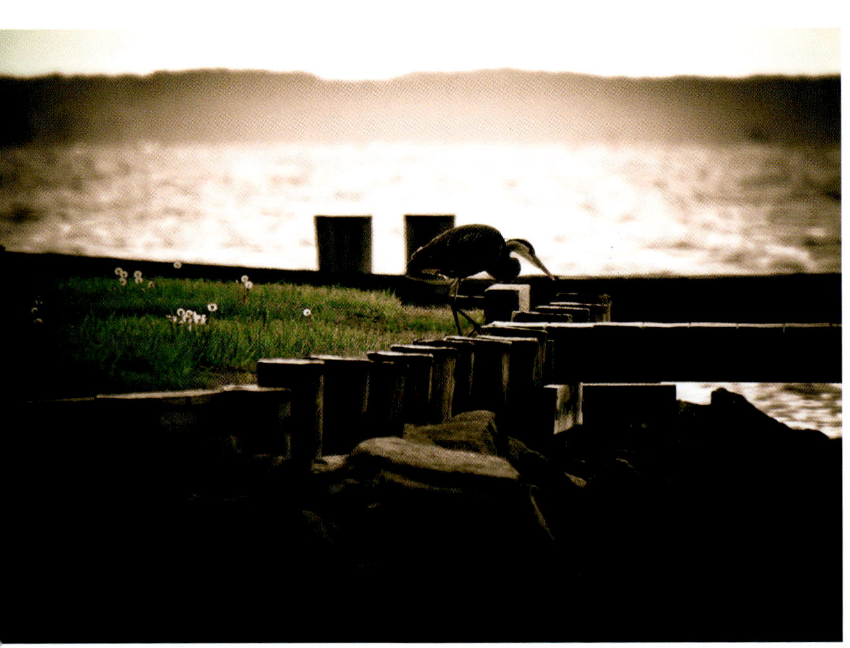

A great blue heron hunts along Knapp's Narrows.

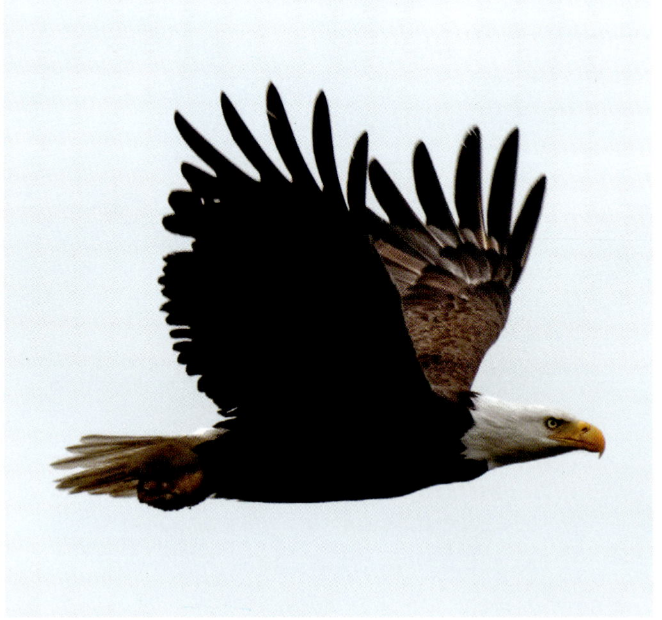

Osprey, Tilghman Island

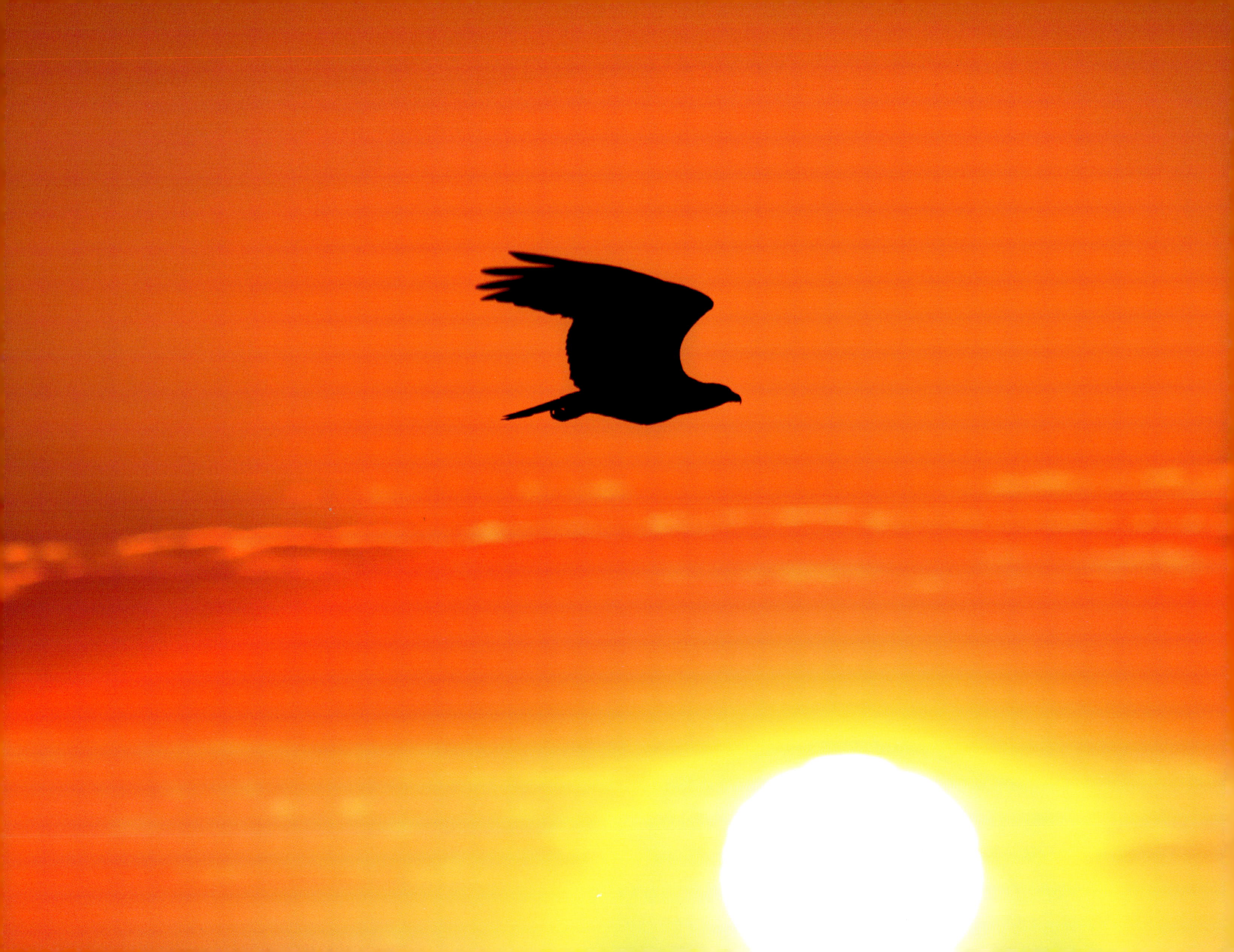

Blue heron, Blackwater National Wildlife Refuge

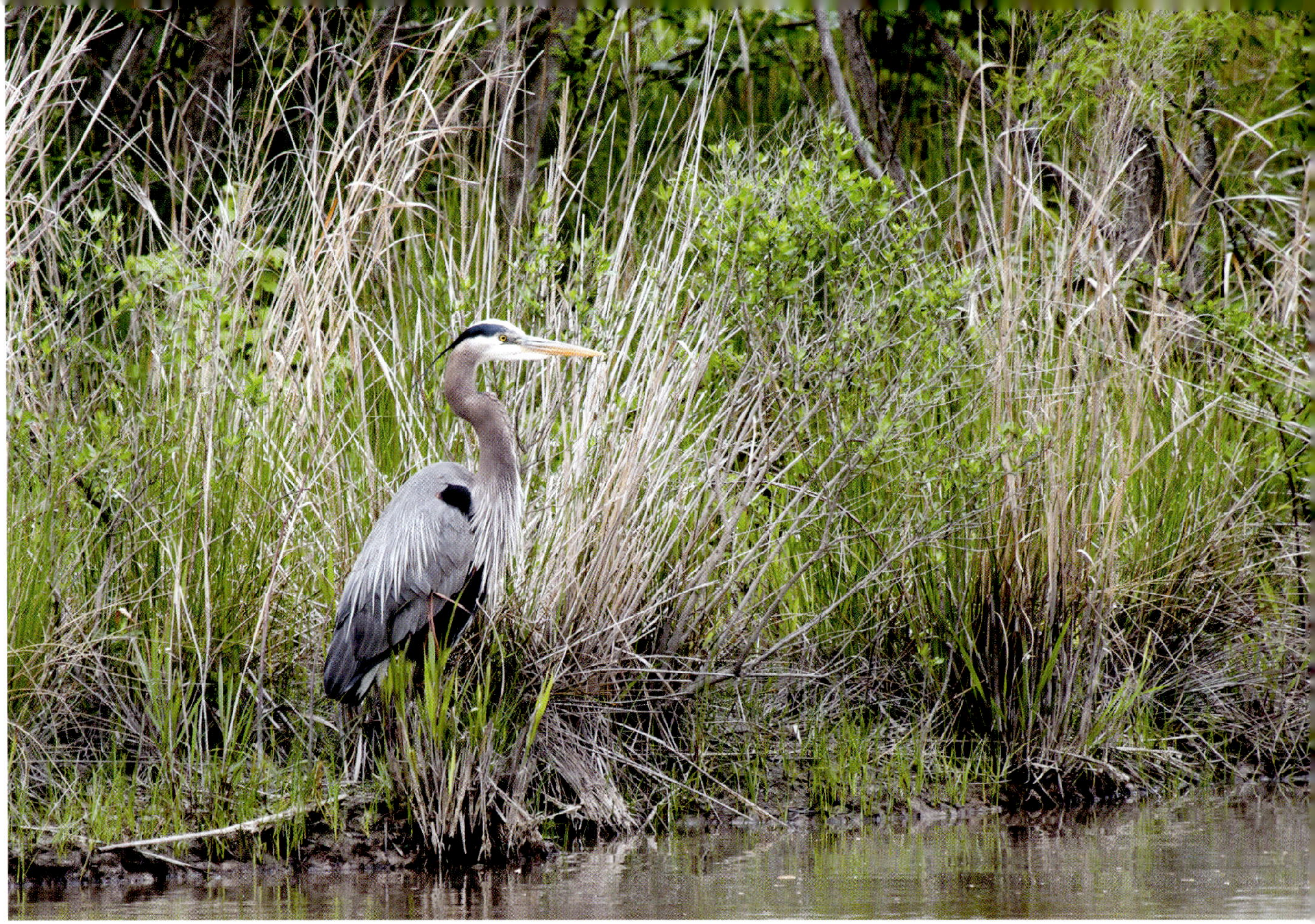

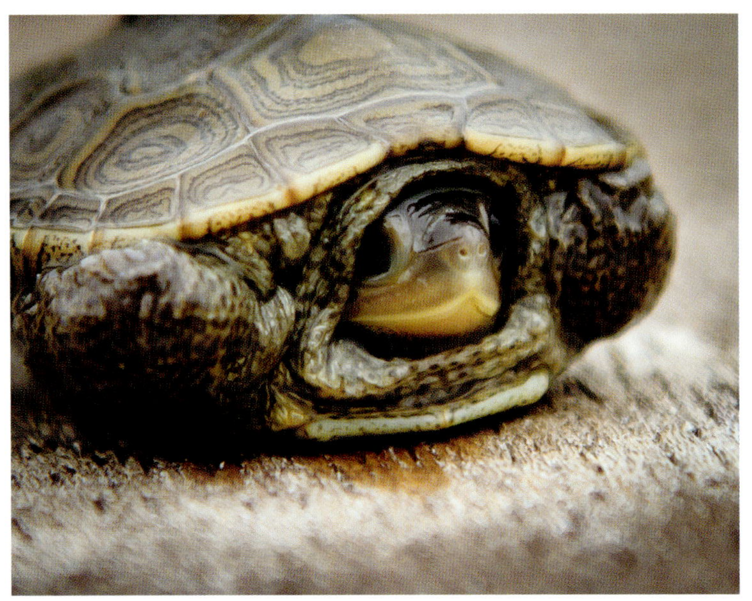

A quarter-sized baby terrapin.

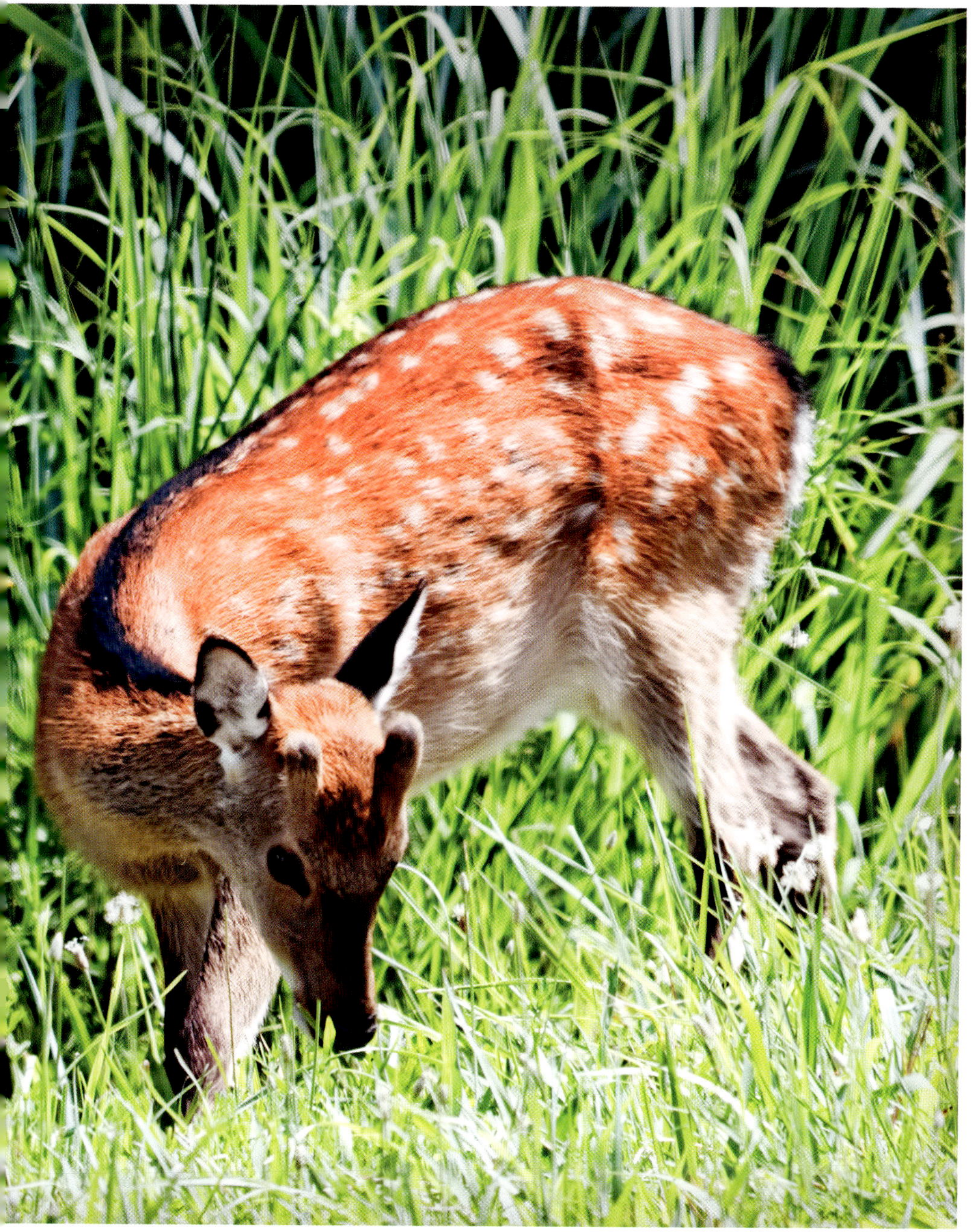

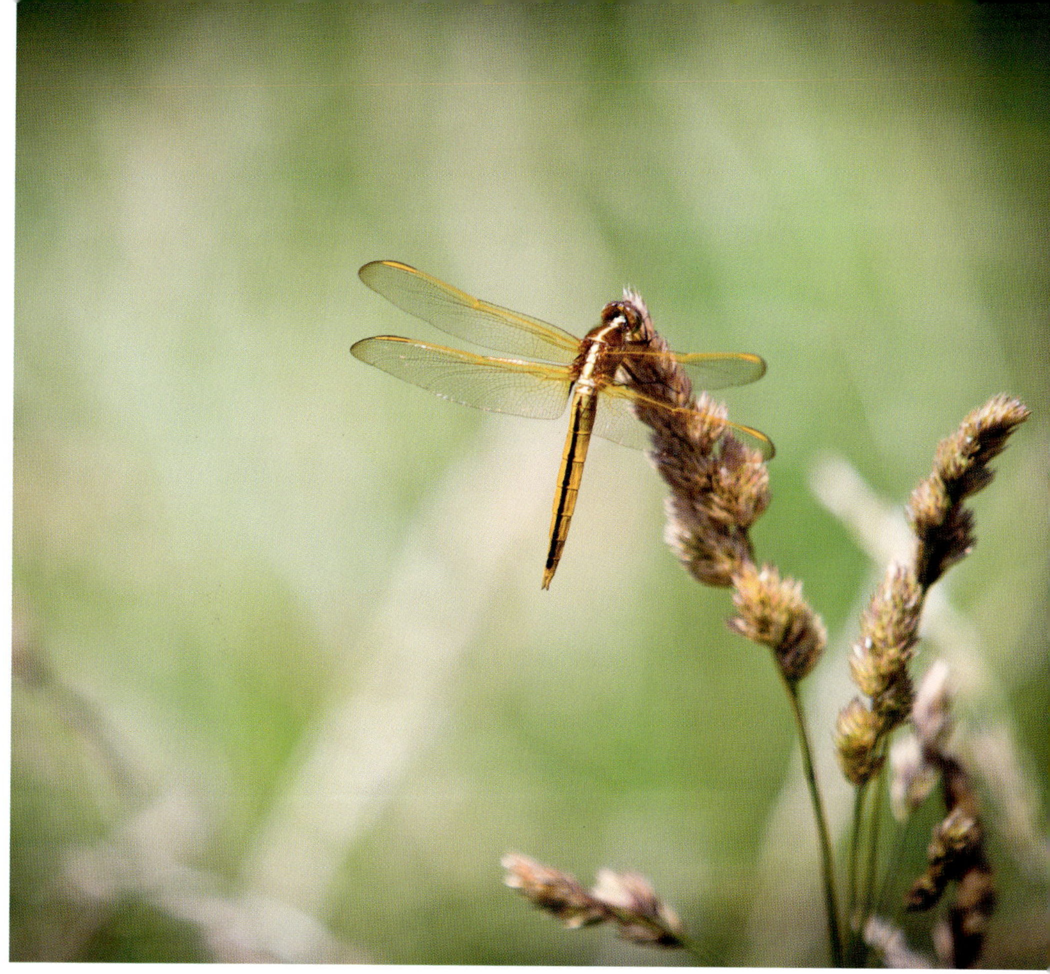

Dragonfly, Blackwater National Wildlife Refuge

A young male deer feeding by the road
in Dorchester County, Maryland.

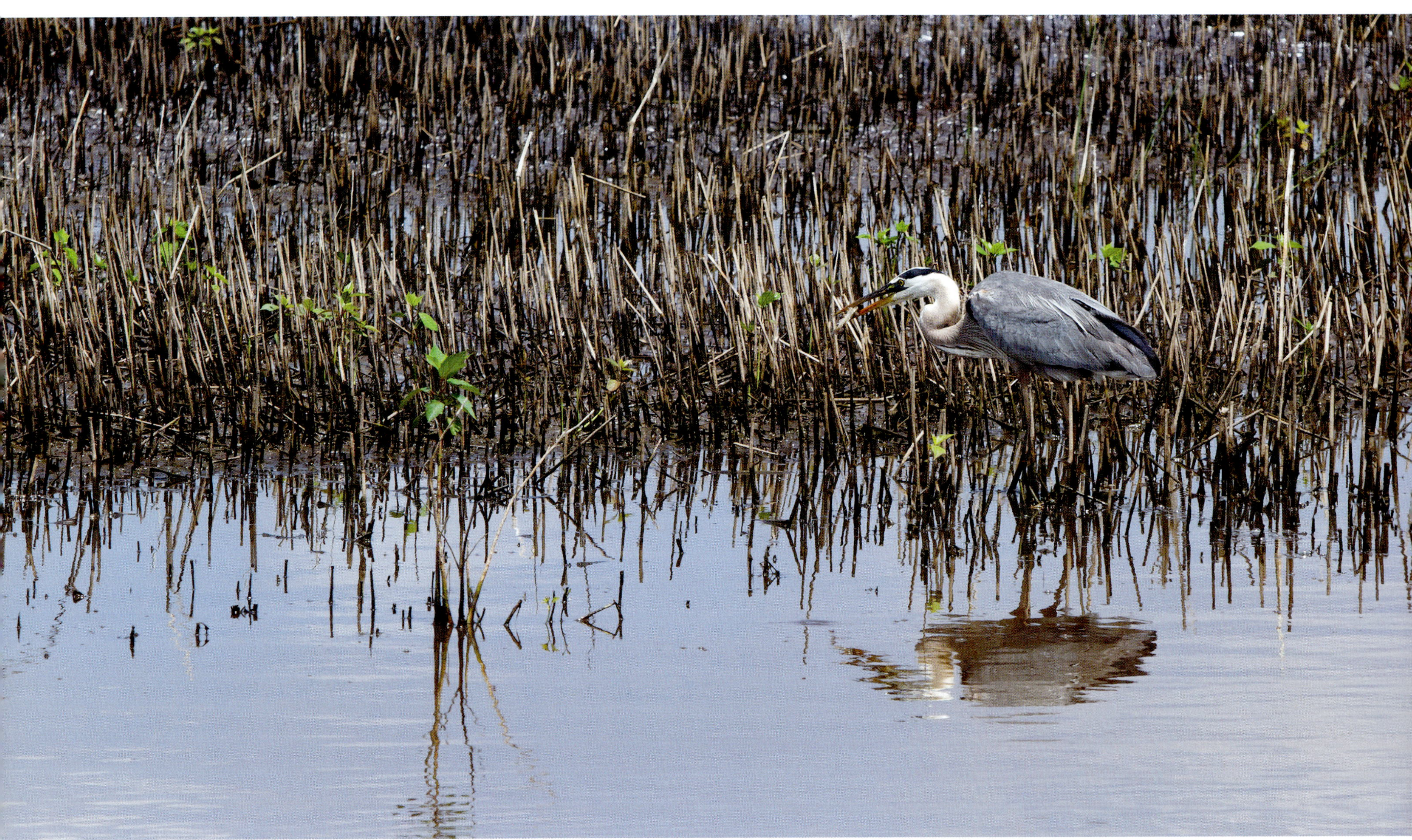
Great blue heron and lunch, Blackwater National Wildlife Refuge

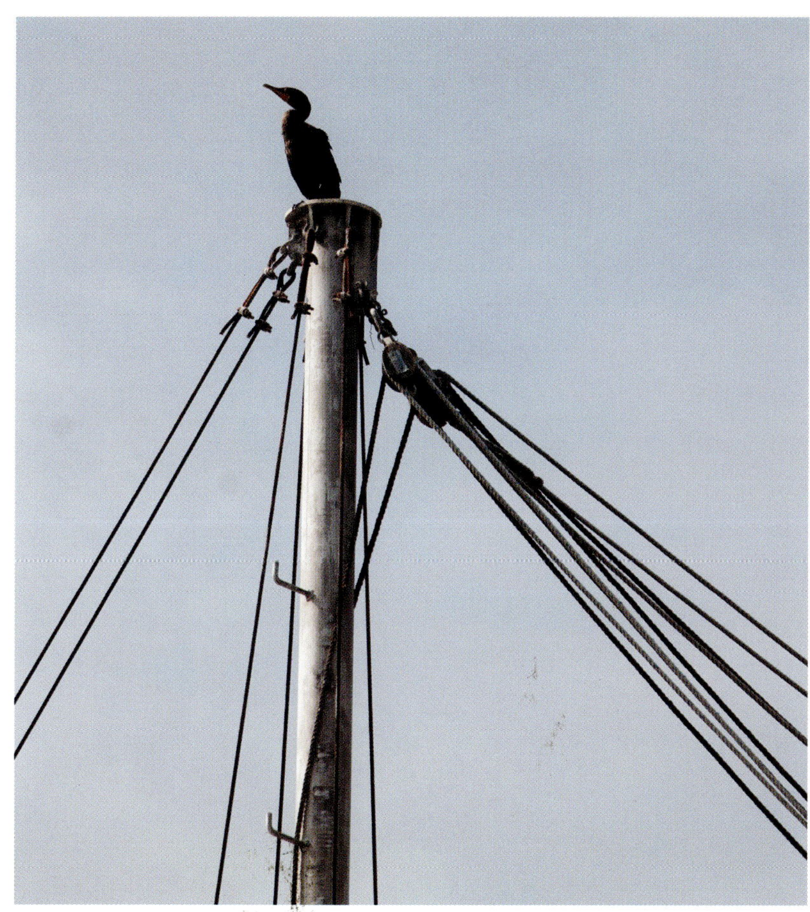

A cormorant watches over Knapp's Narrows on Tilghman Island.

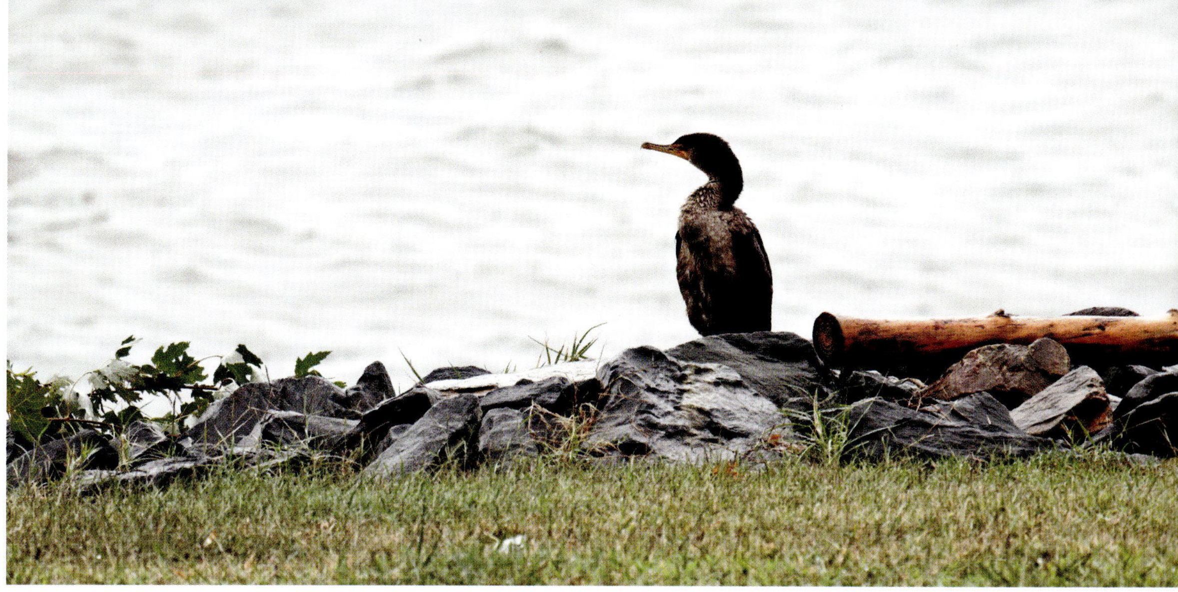

After a storm with high-speed winds, this cormorant seems a bit dazed and out-of-place.

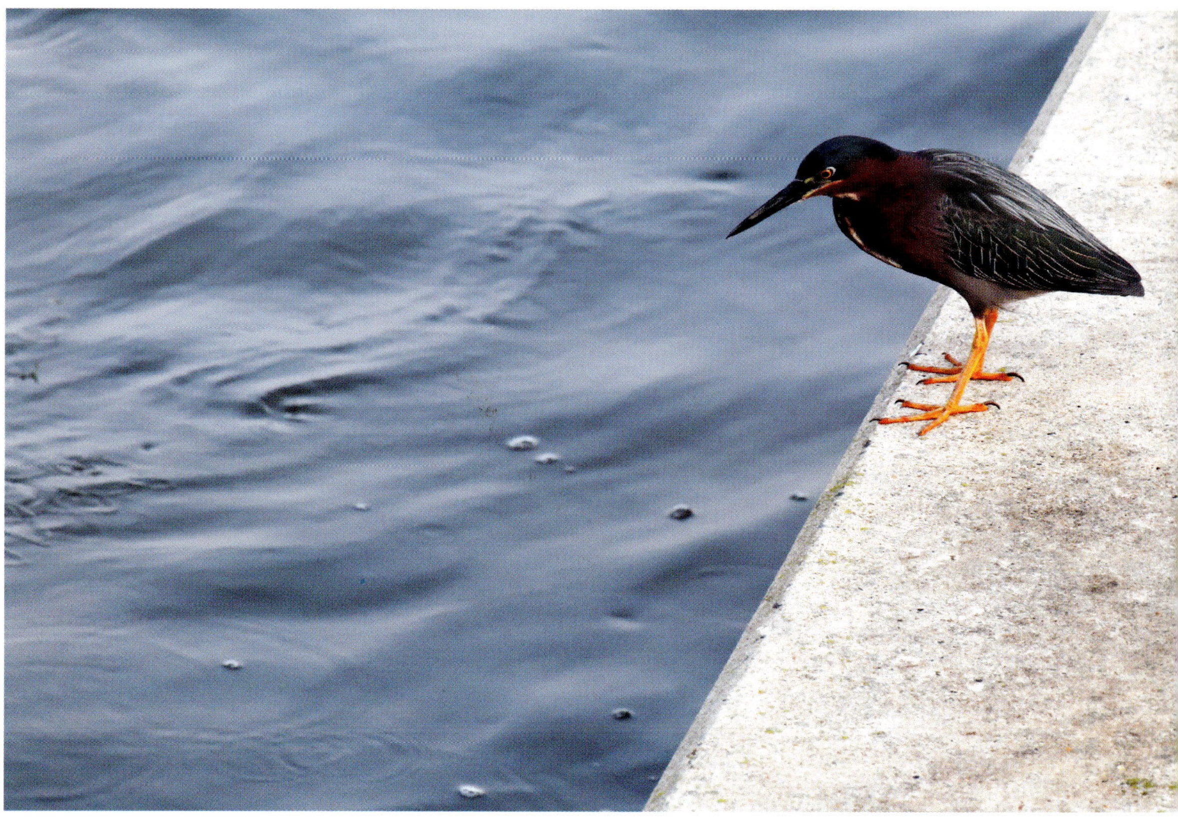

Green heron, Tilghman Island

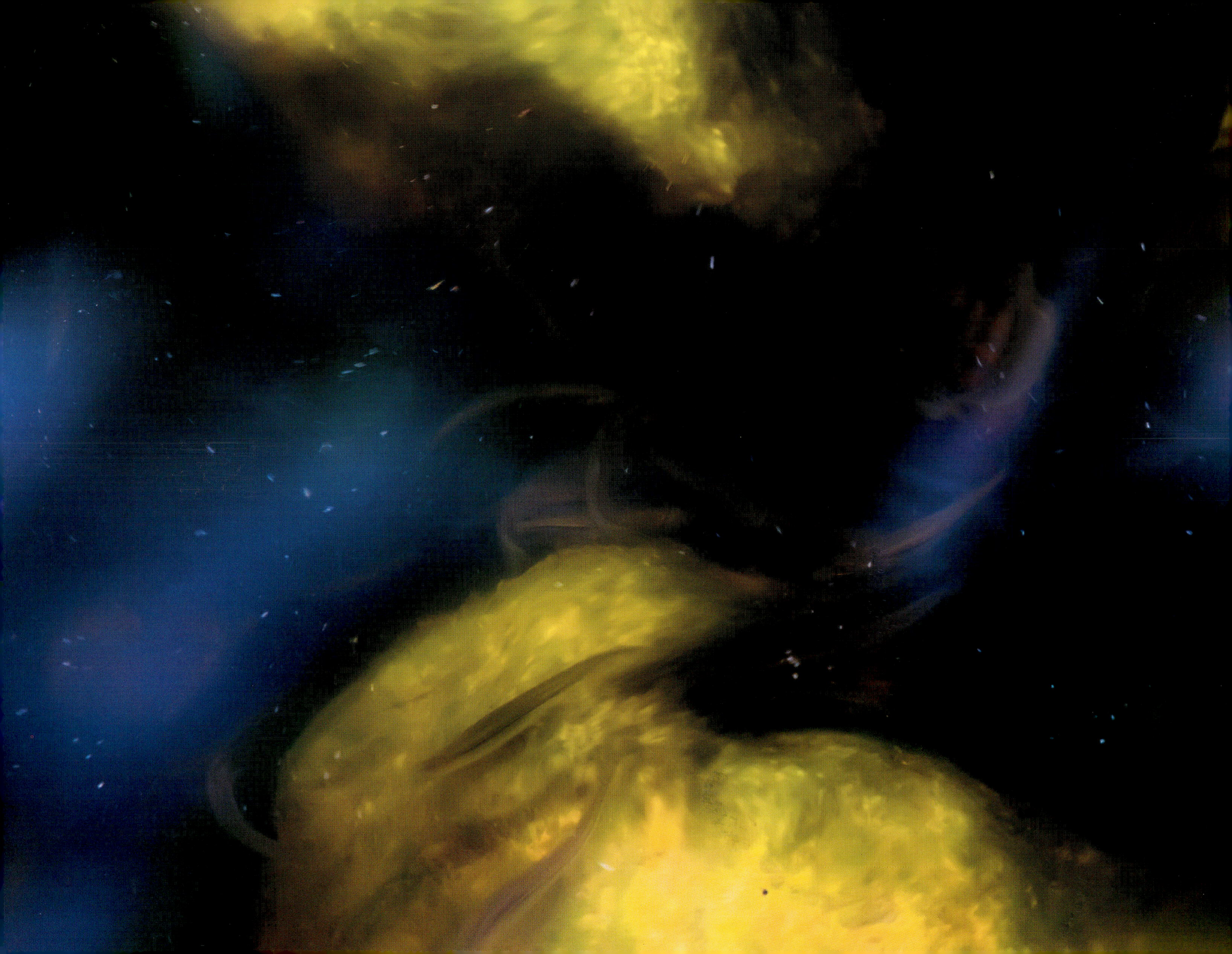

Three mallard ducks have a meeting on Kent Island, Maryland.

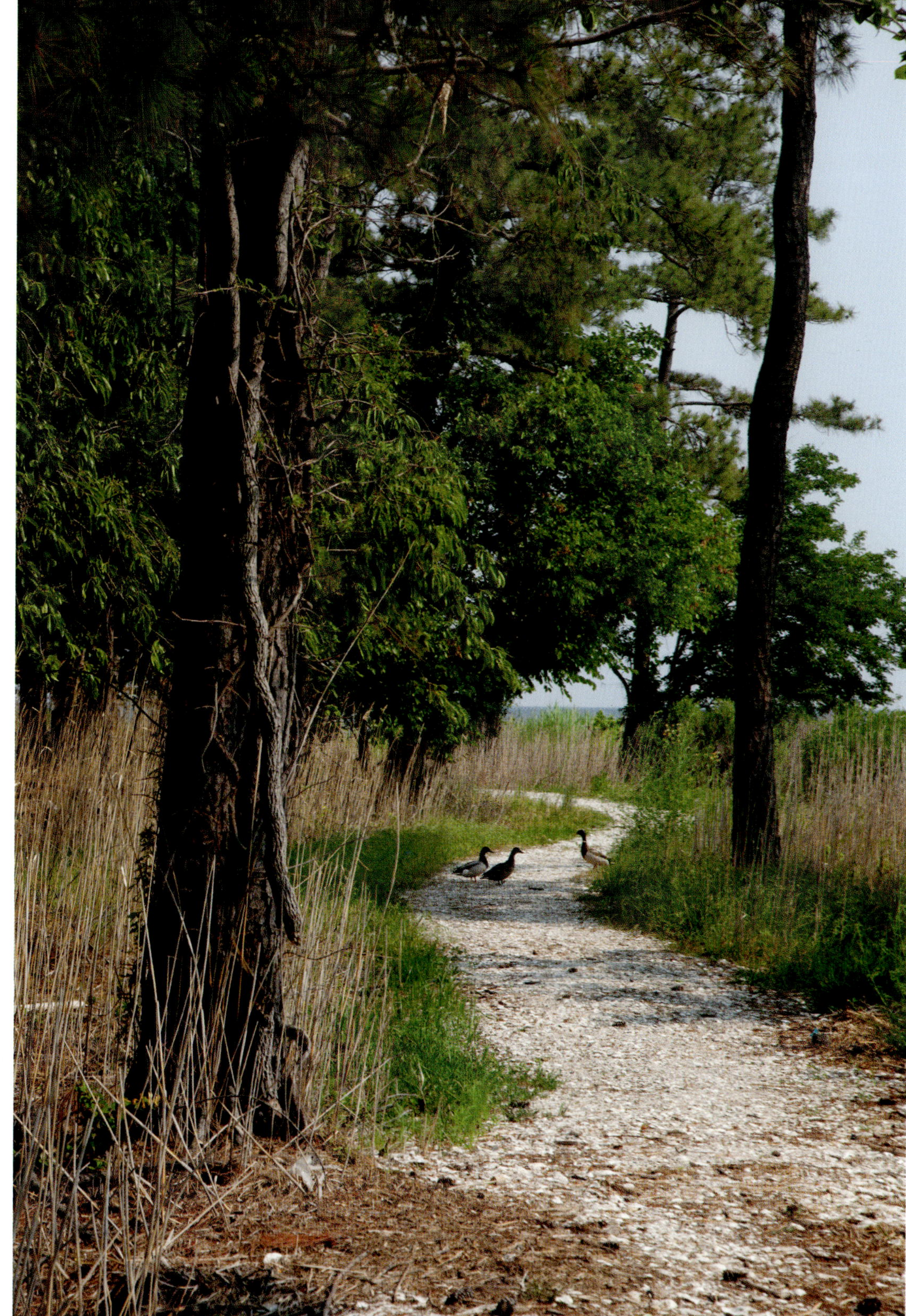

Small fish swim amongst the rocks at the edge of the shoreline.

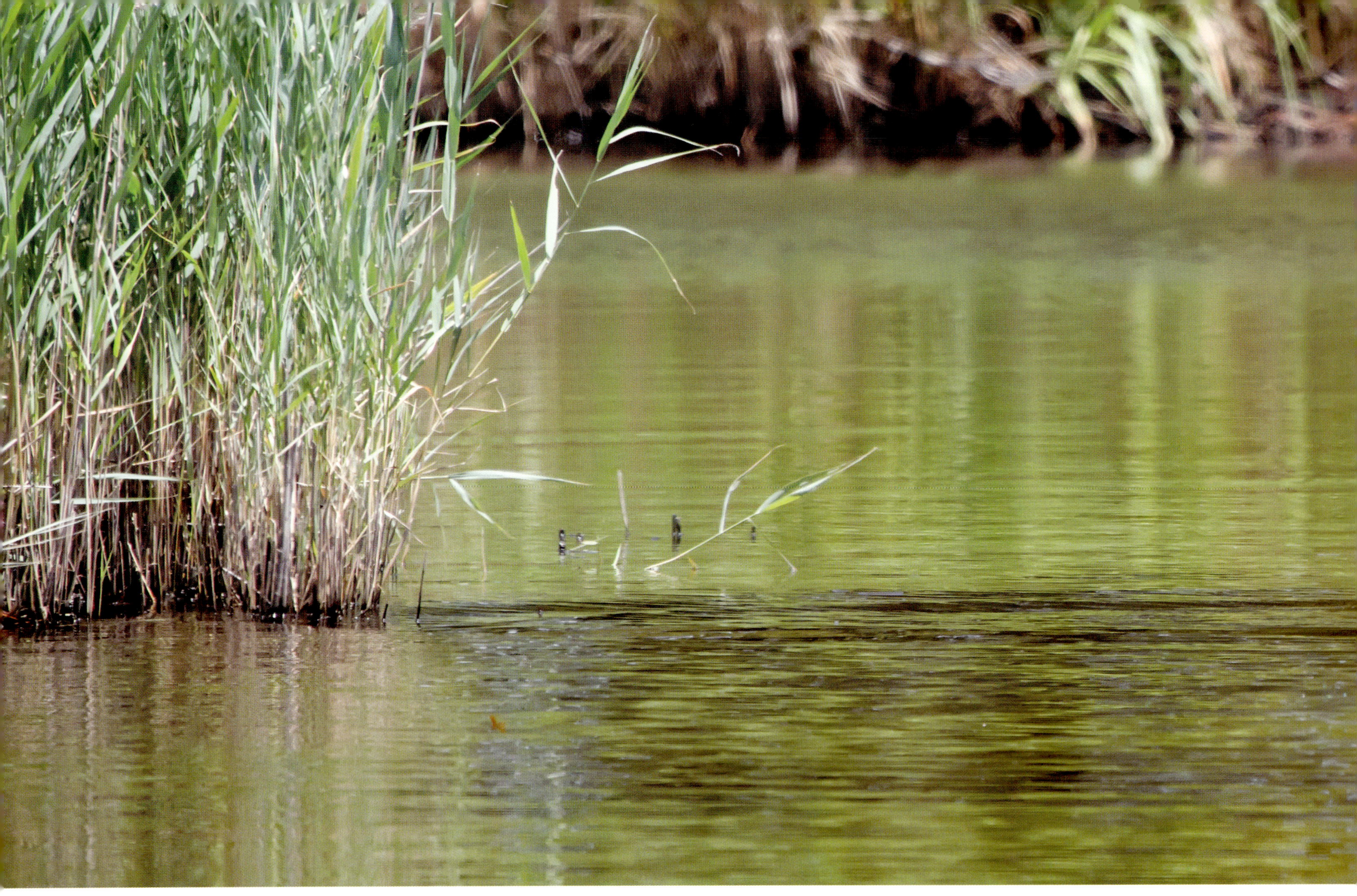

A great egret fishes at the Blackwater National Wildlife Refuge.

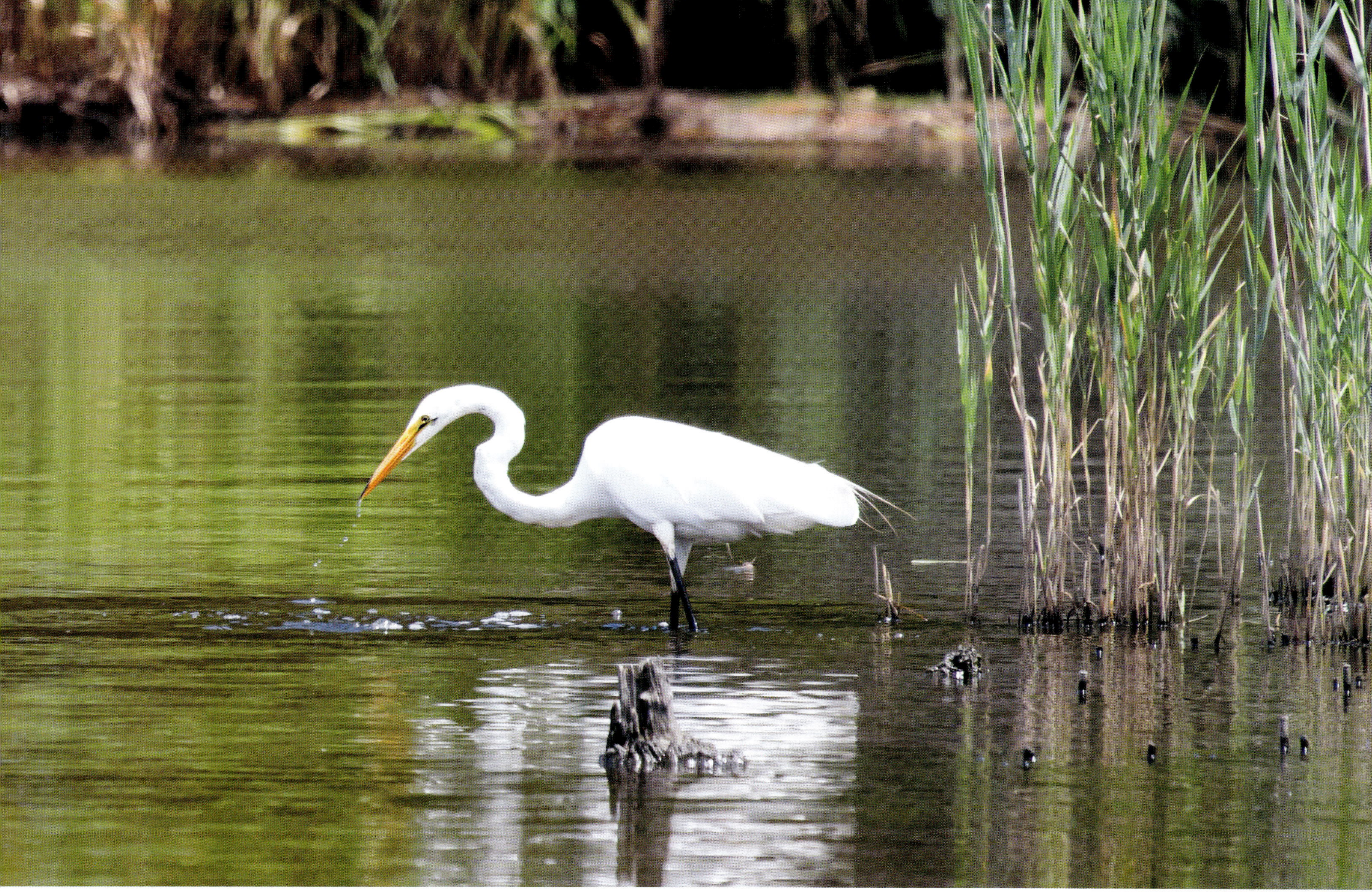

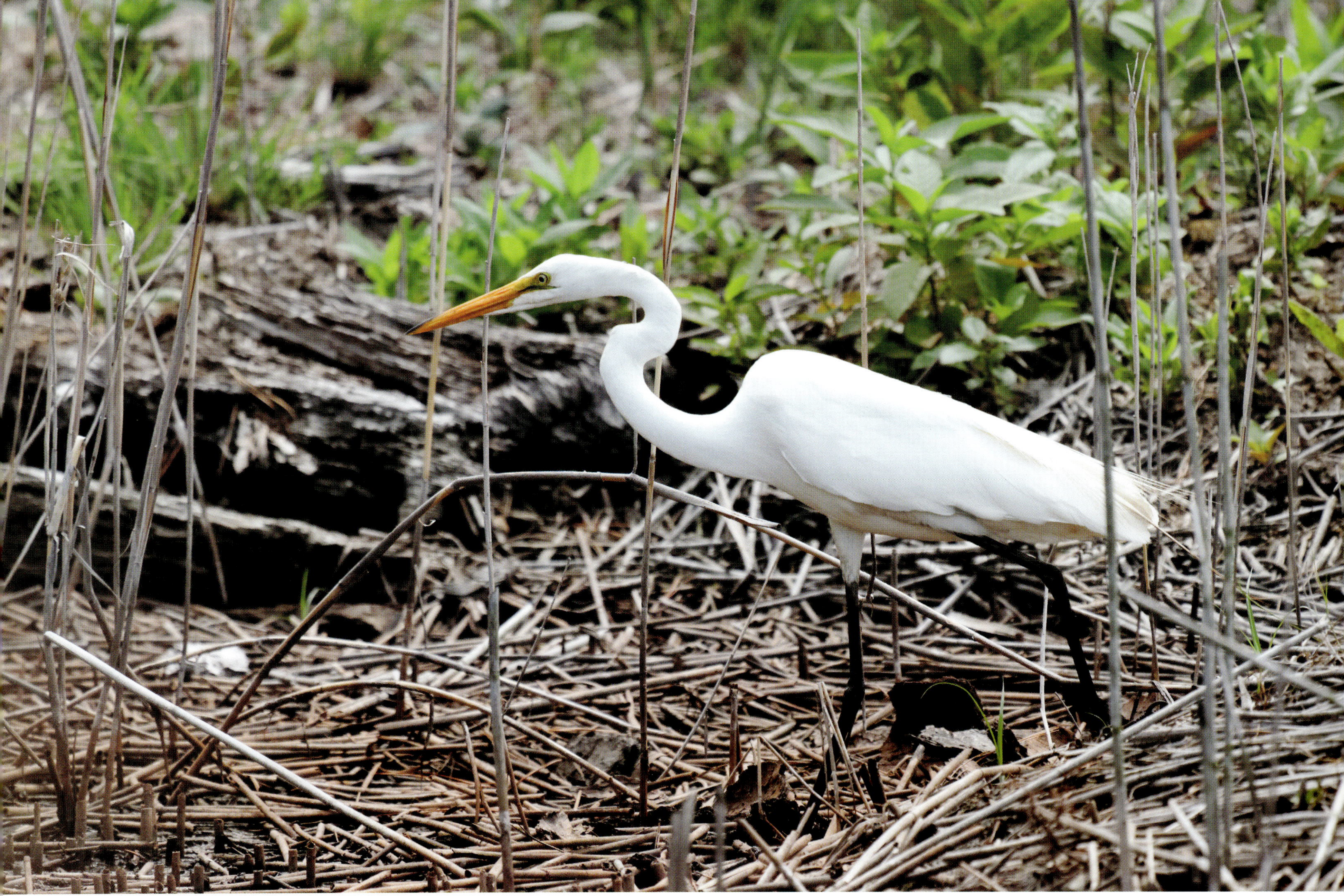

Great egret, Blackwater National Wildlife Refuge

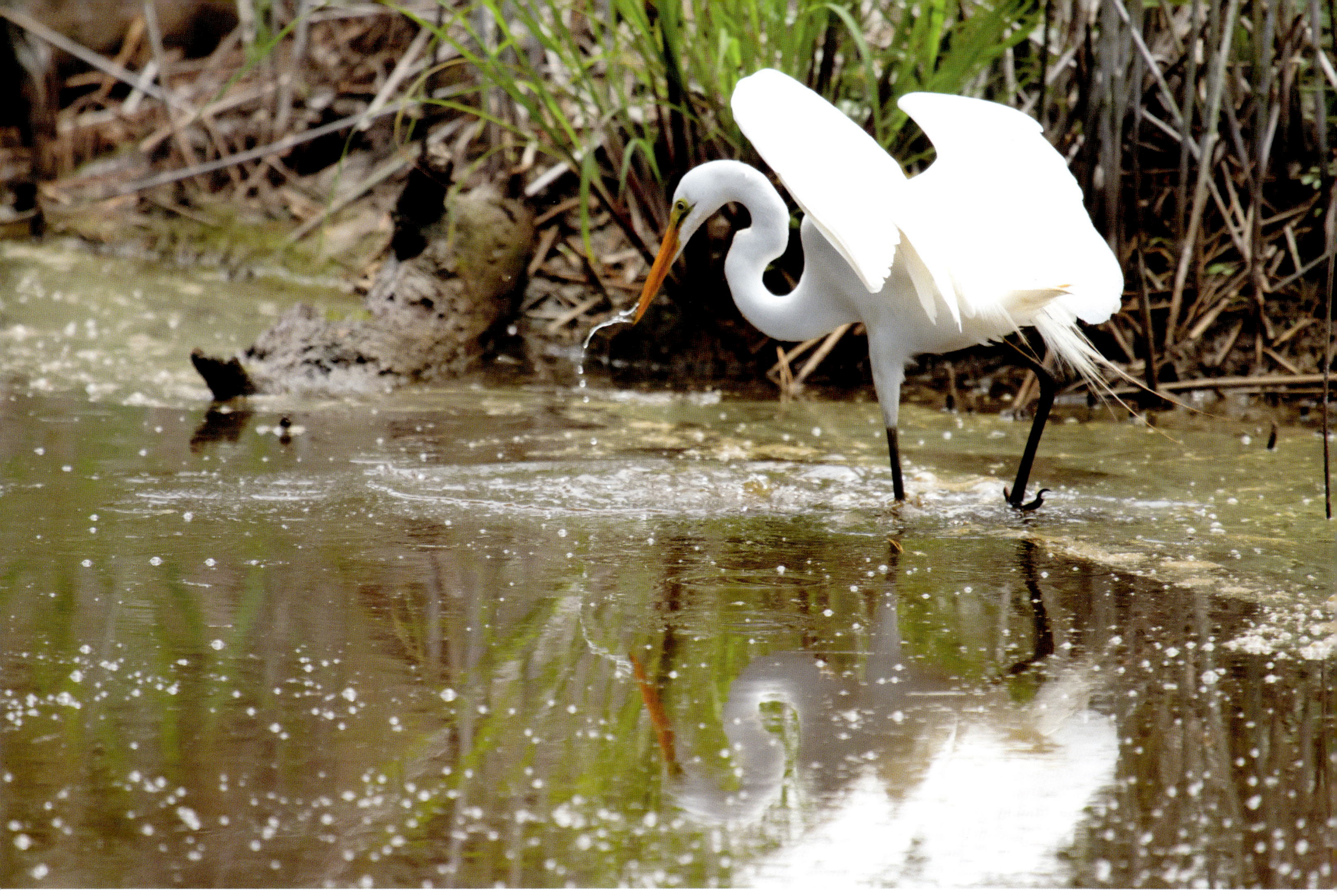

Great egret, Blackwater National Wildlife Refuge

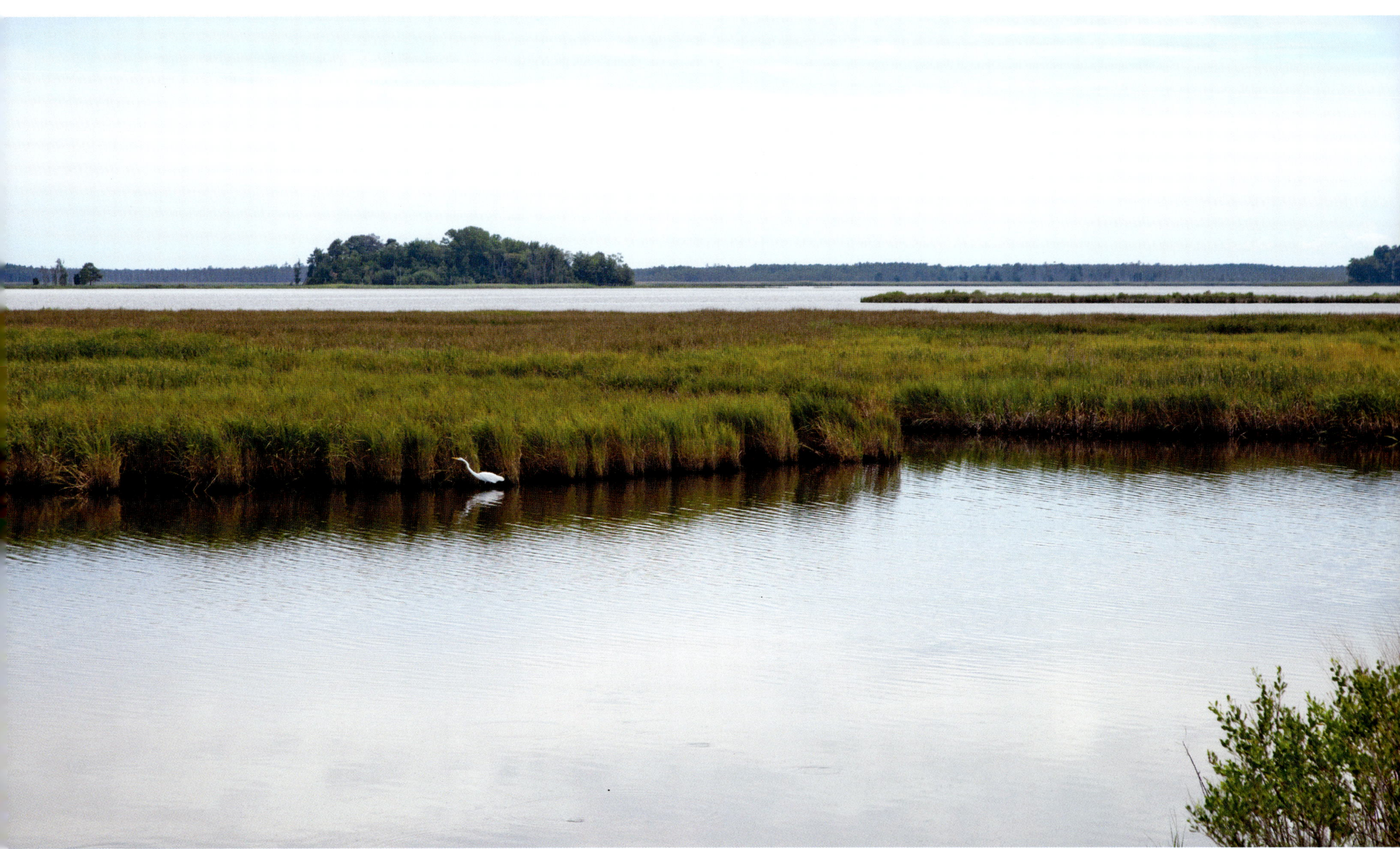

Great egret, Blackwater National Wildlife Refuge

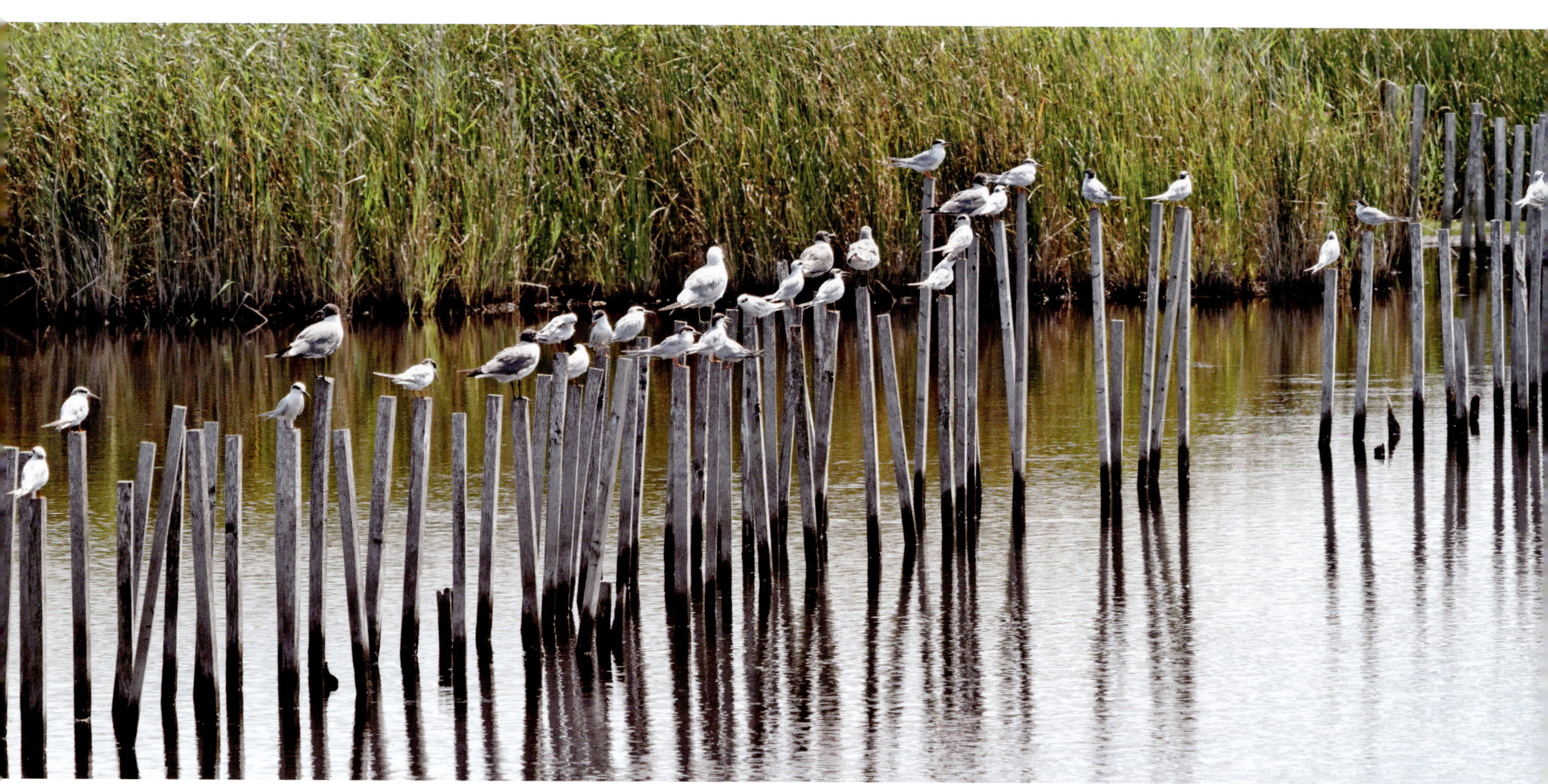

At the Blackwater National Wildlife Refuge, terns sit atop stakes installed to prohibit the passage of paddlers.

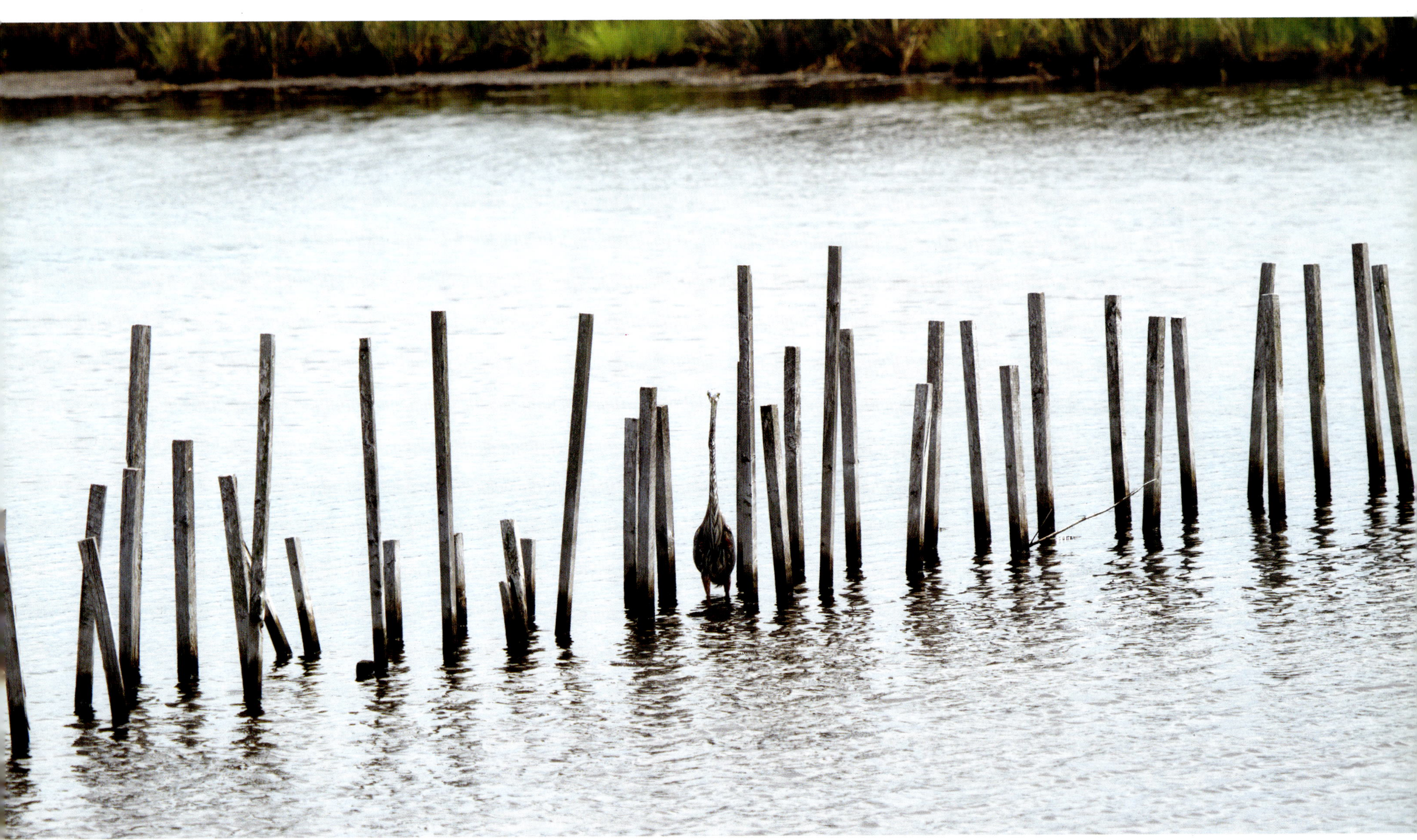

A heron does a successful job of blending in at the Blackwater National Wildlife Refuge.

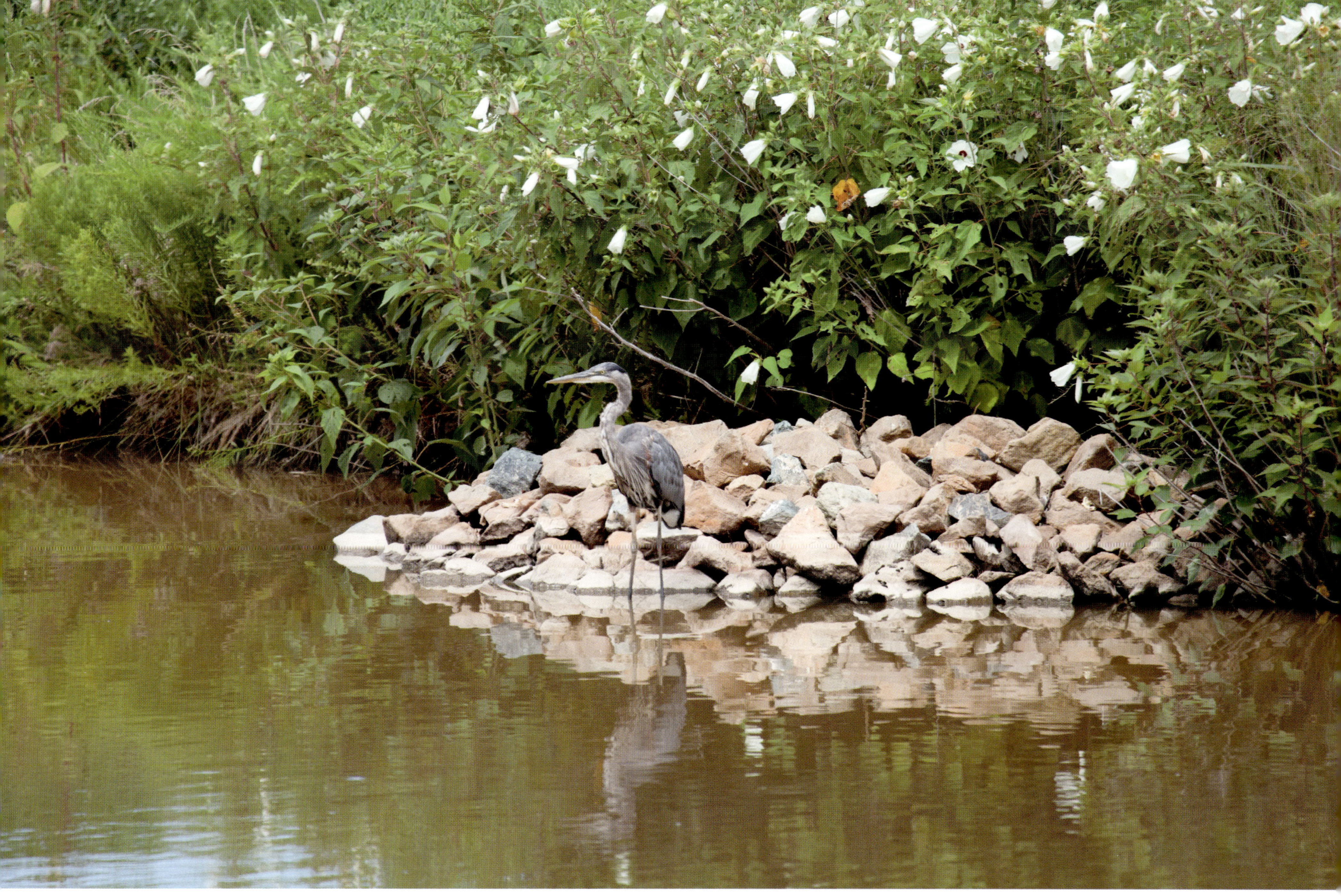

A great blue heron picks a picturesque location to grab a meal.

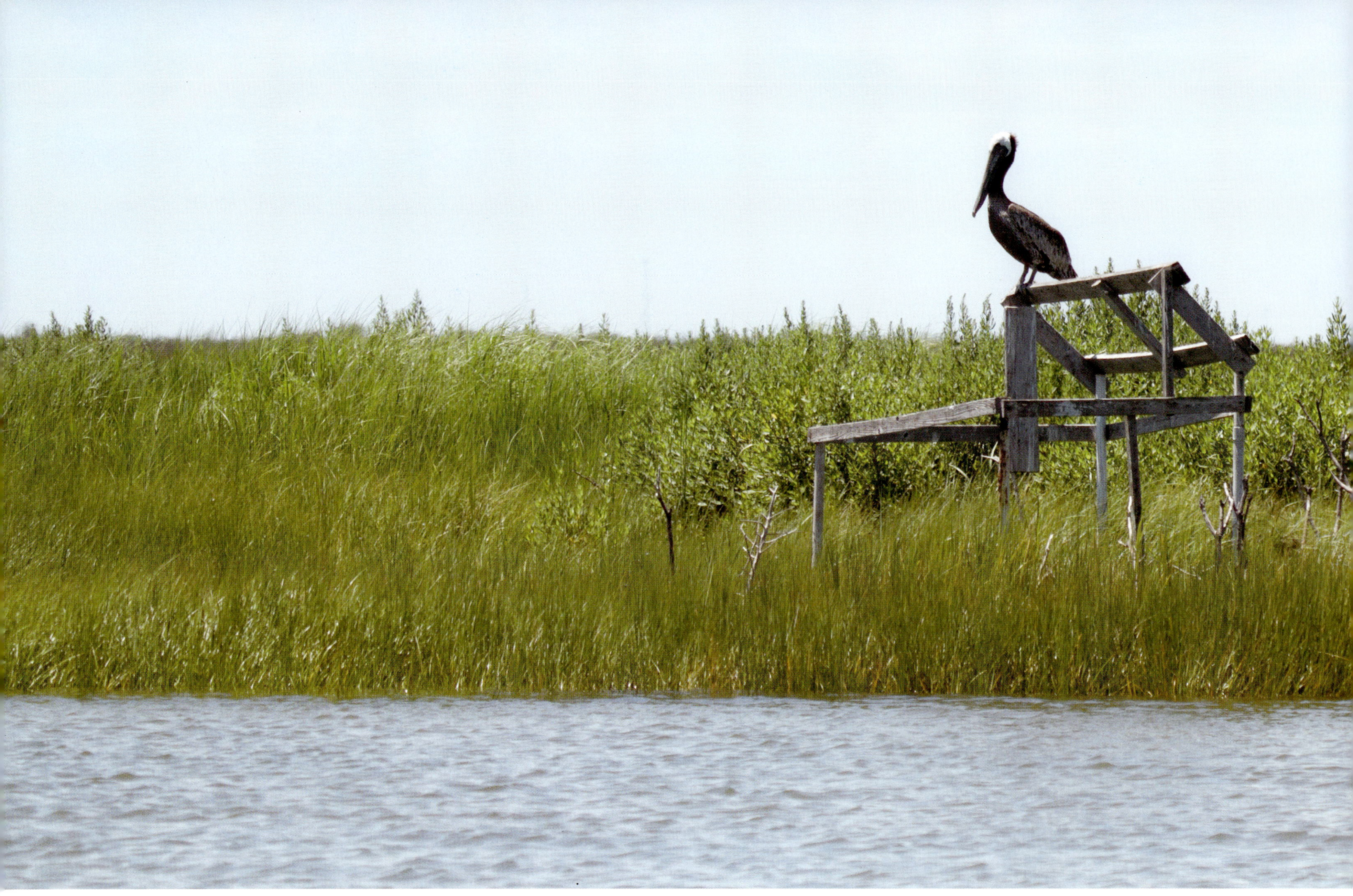

One brave pelican makes his presence known, but behind the grasses are hundreds of others, as evidenced by the one on the far right.

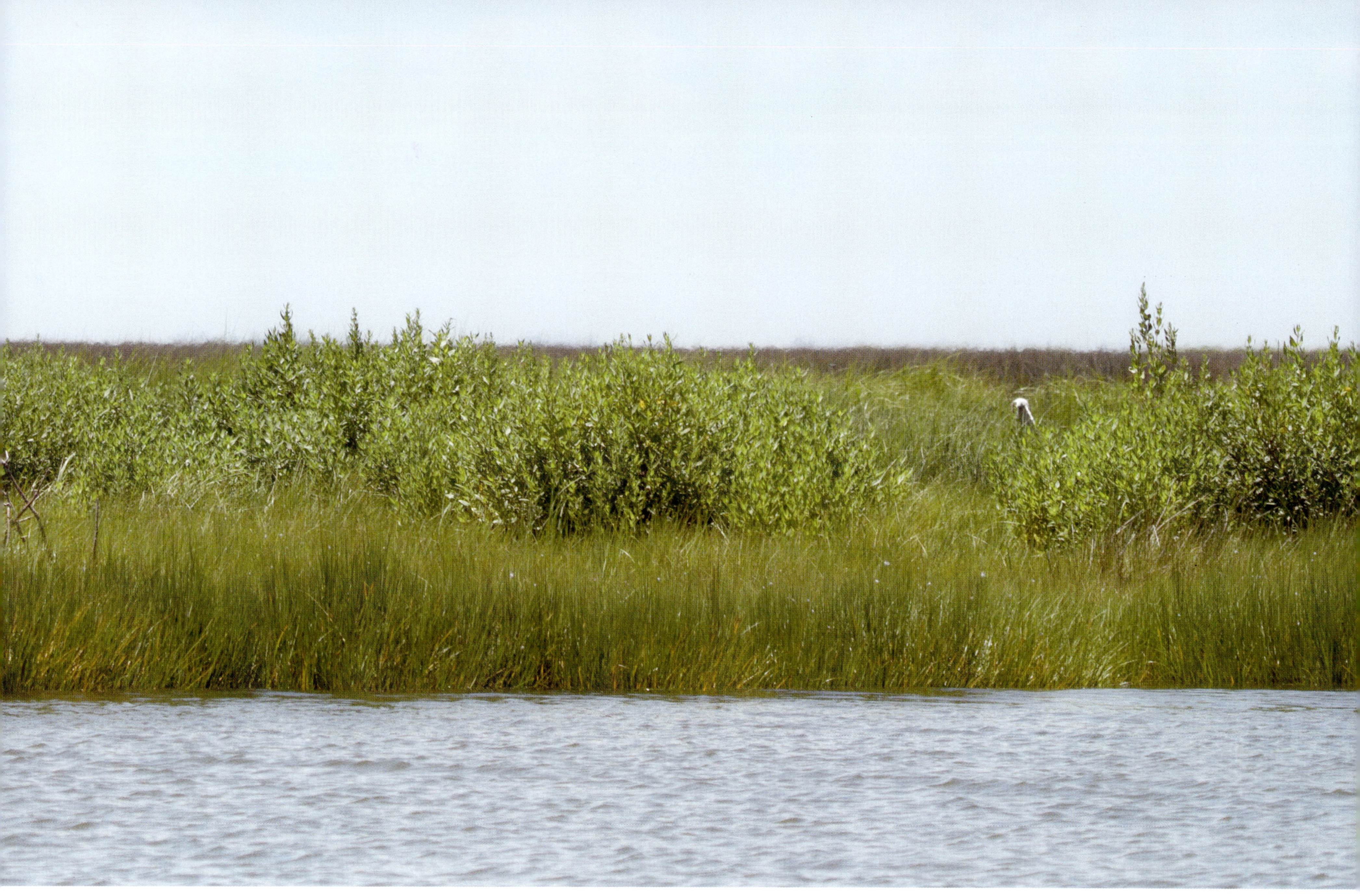

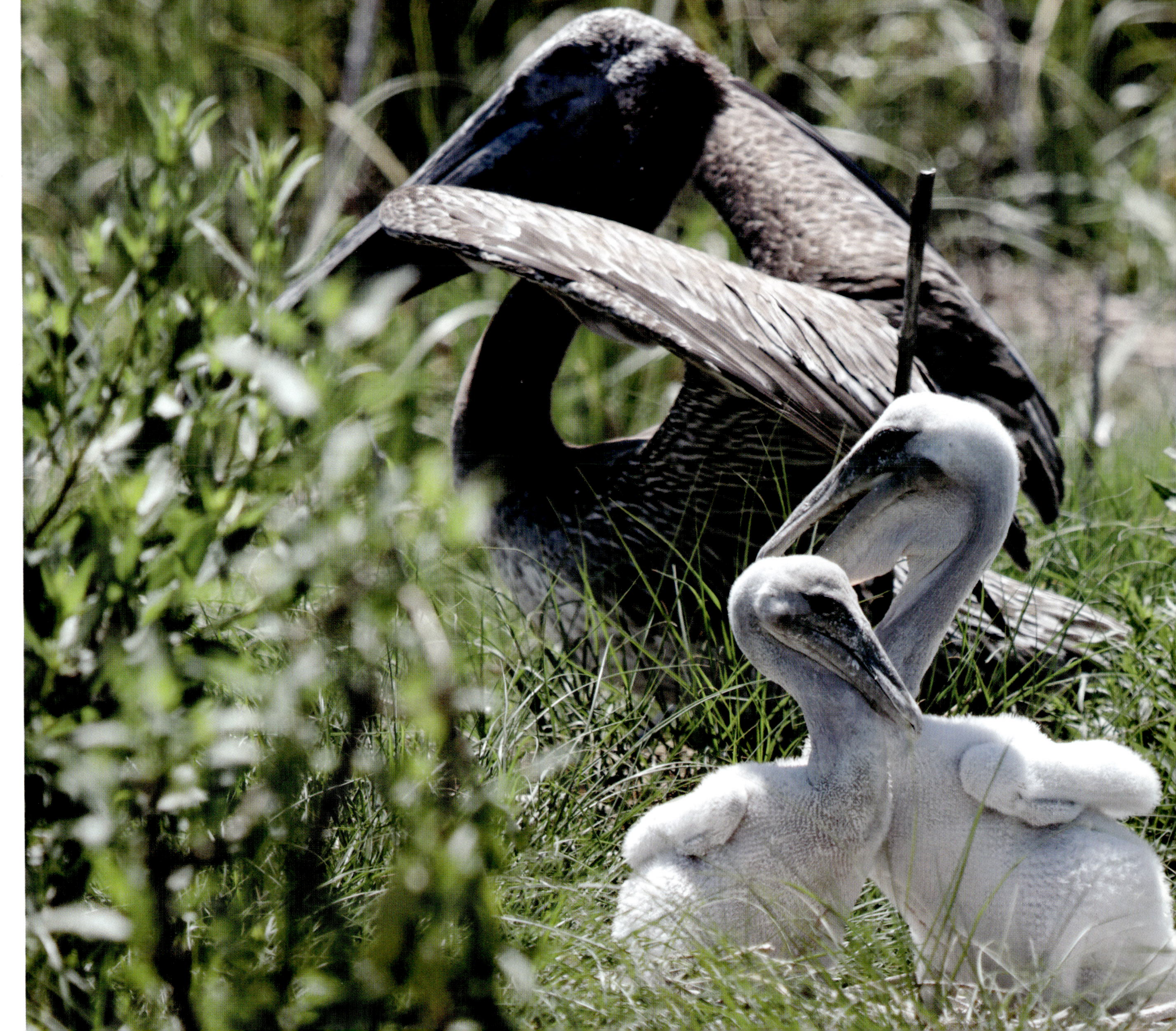

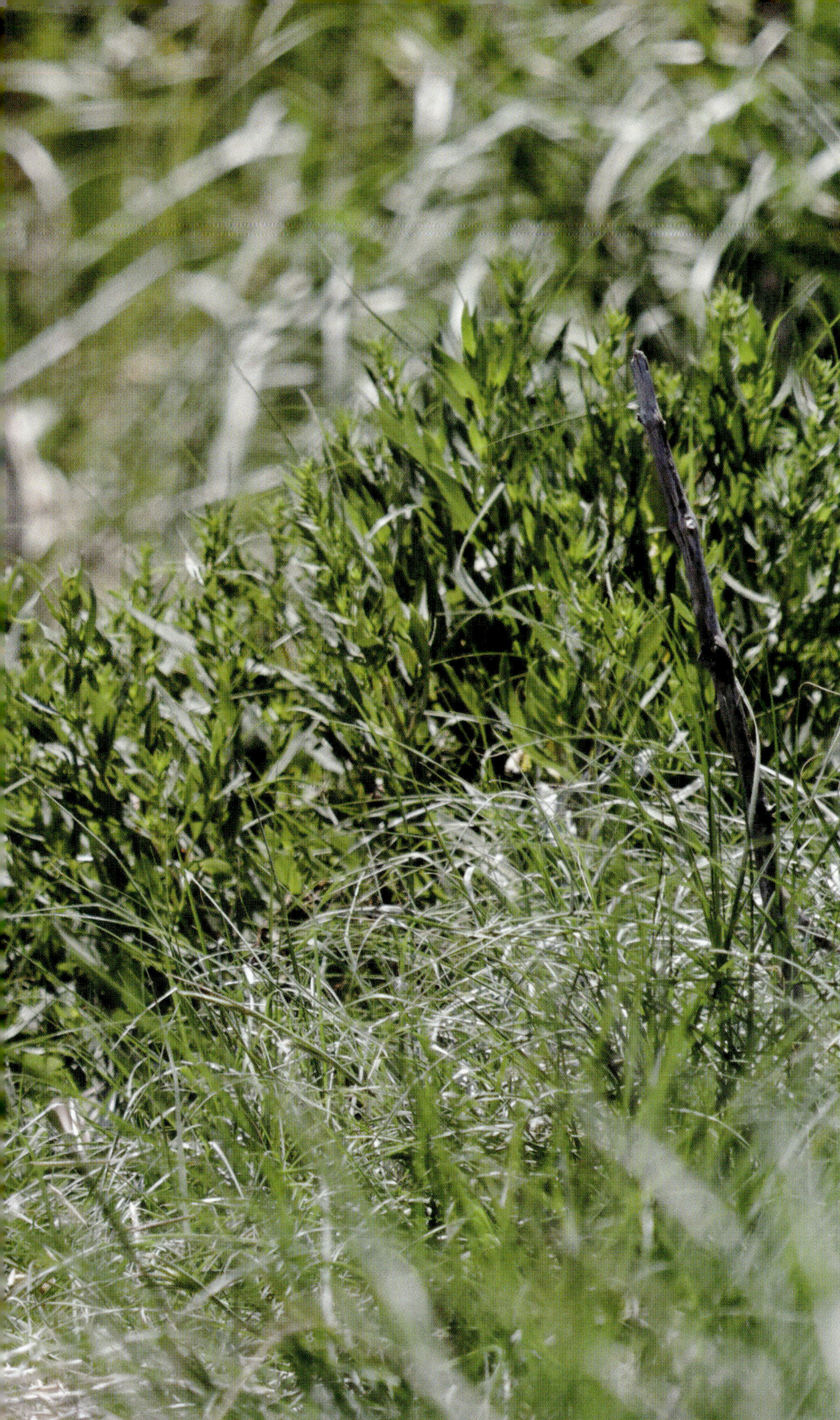

A pair of pelican siblings stick close together.

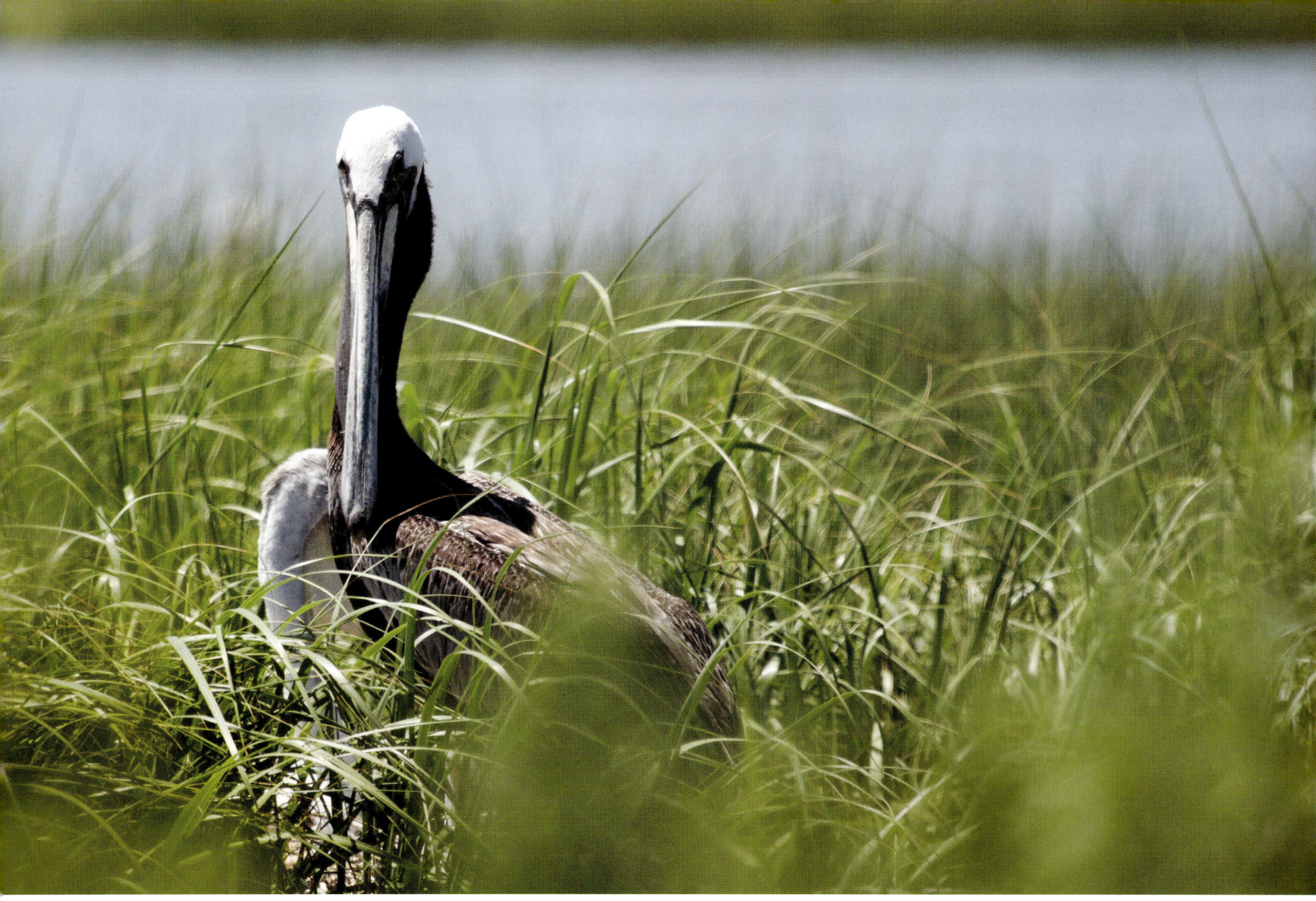

A pelican on Smith Island watching our boat, warily.

Taking temporary flight until the humans leave the vicinity of the rookery.

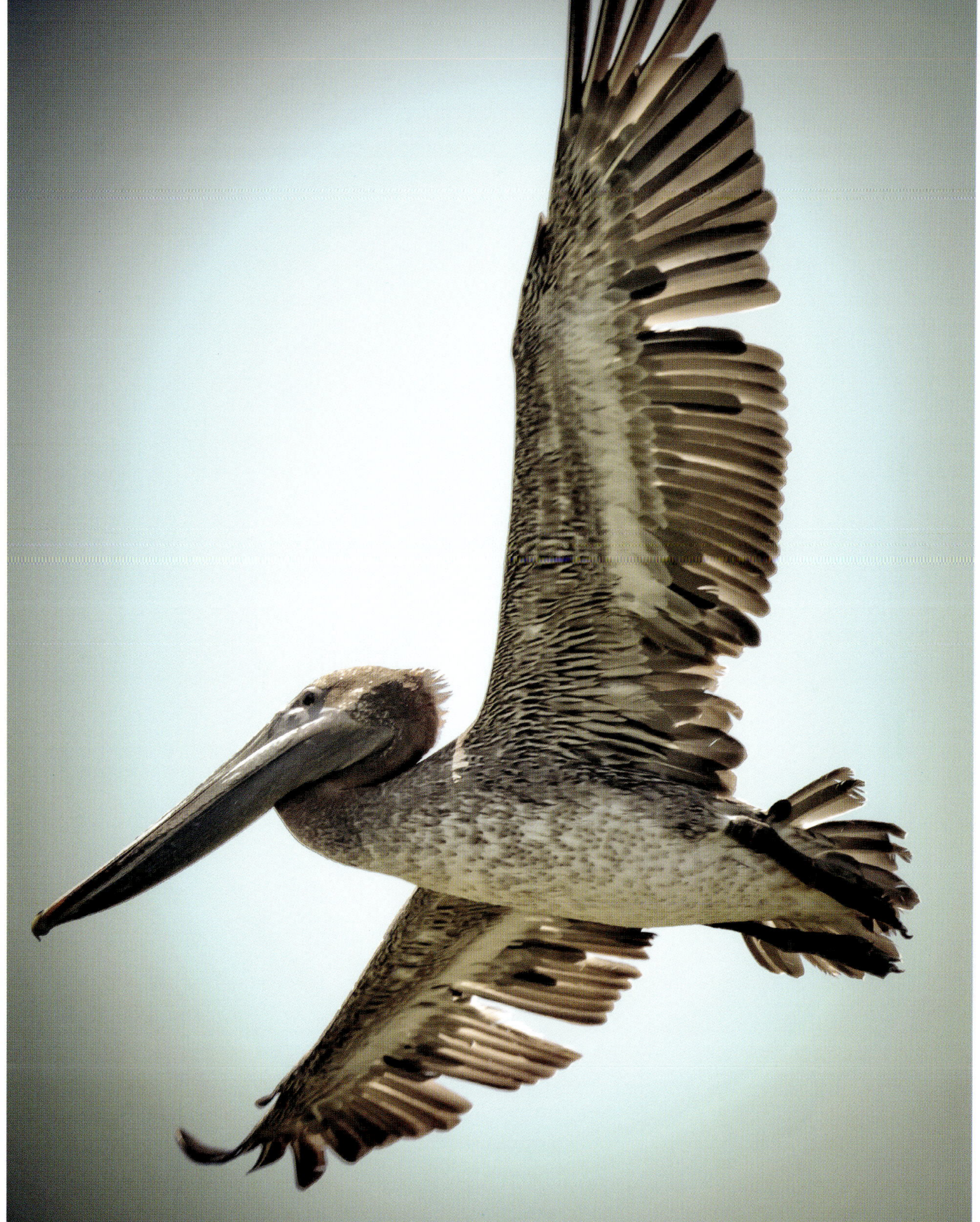

A great egret makes the evening trek home.

# Watermen

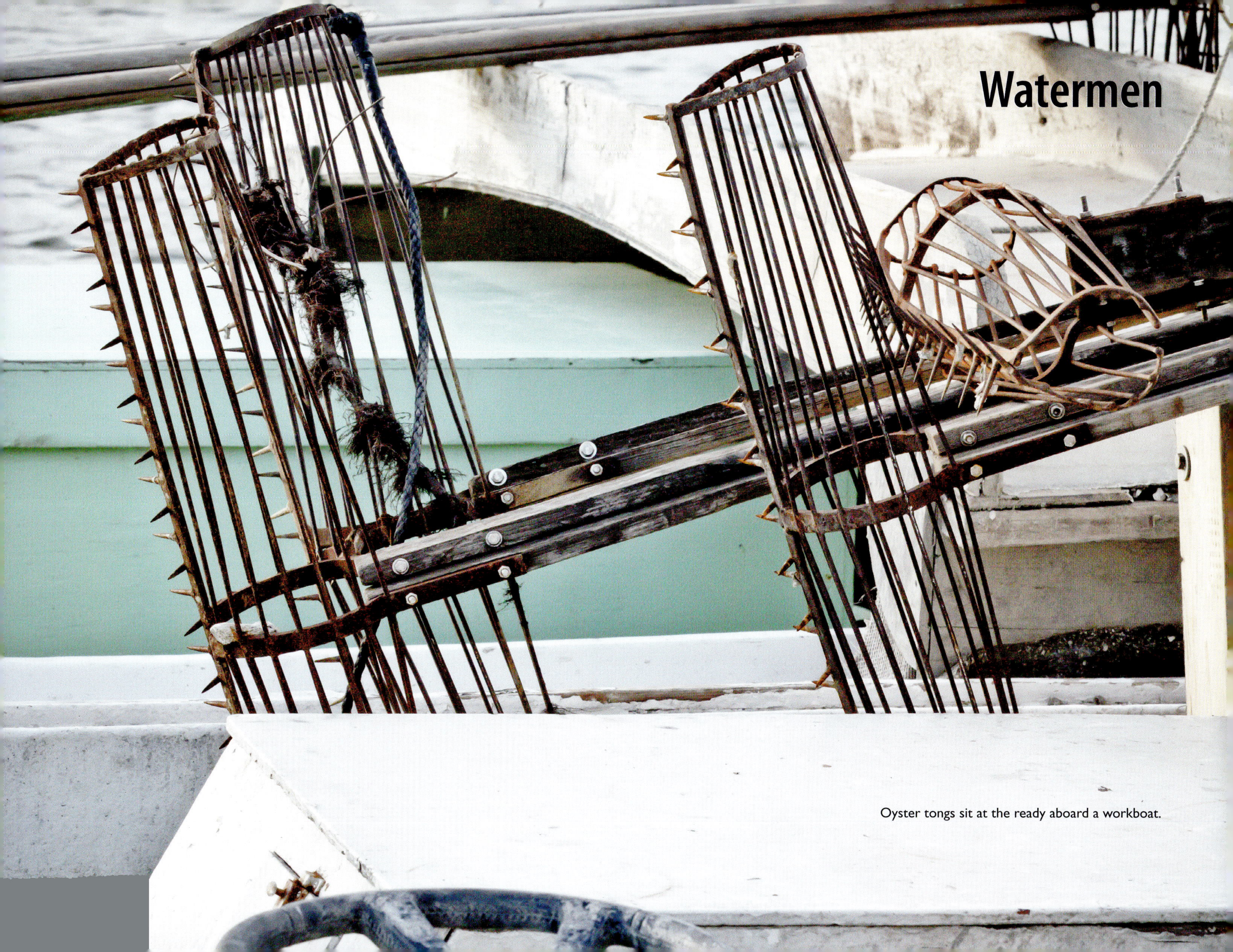

Oyster tongs sit at the ready aboard a workboat.

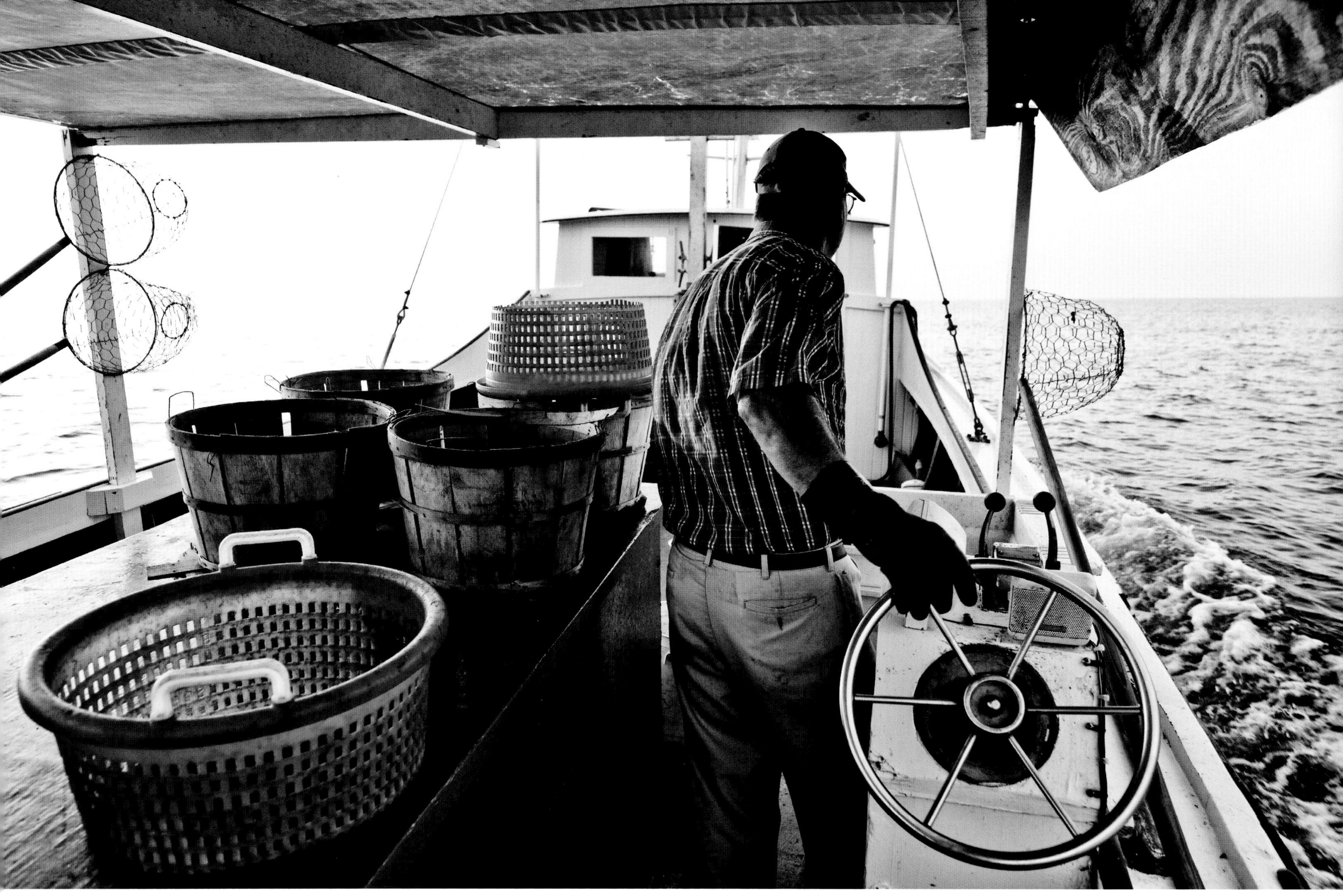

Bunky Chance pilots his boat during a day of trotlining for crabs.

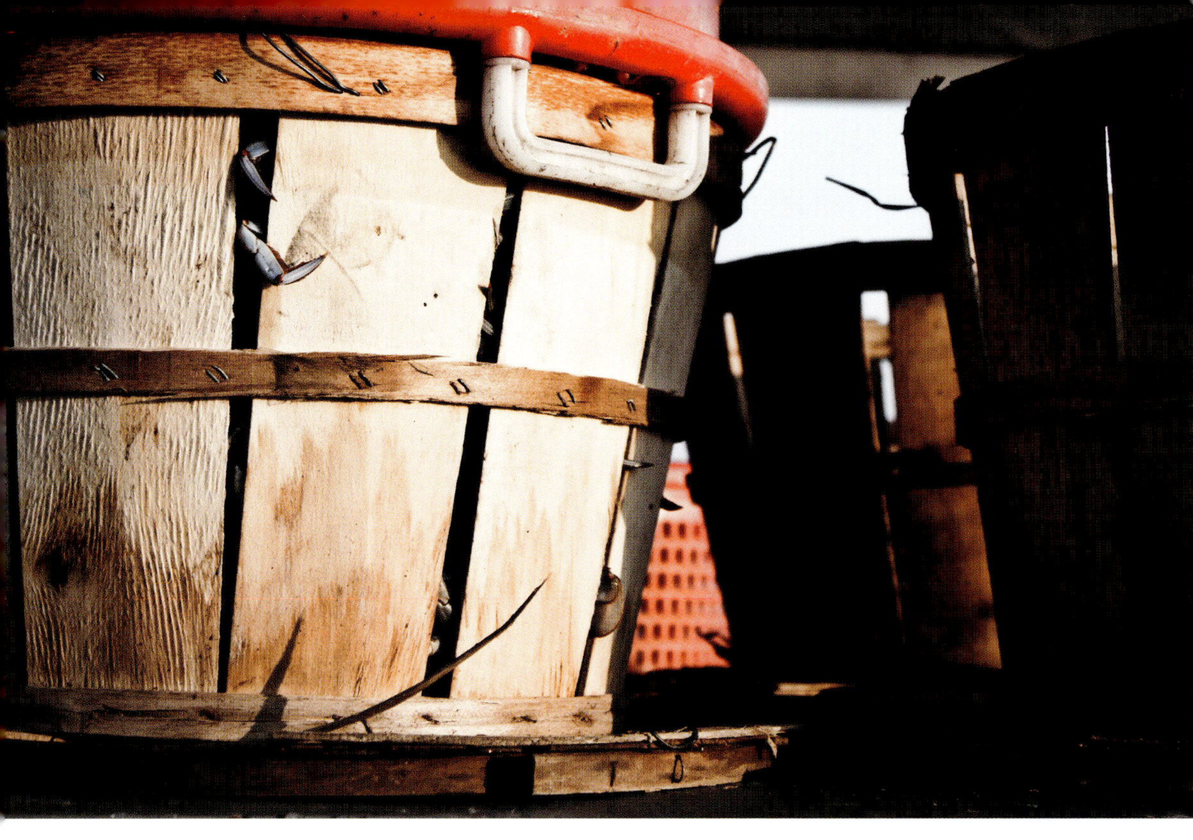

A nearly full bushel of keepers.

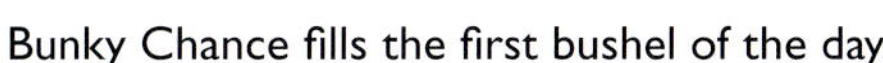

Bunky Chance fills the first bushel of the day.

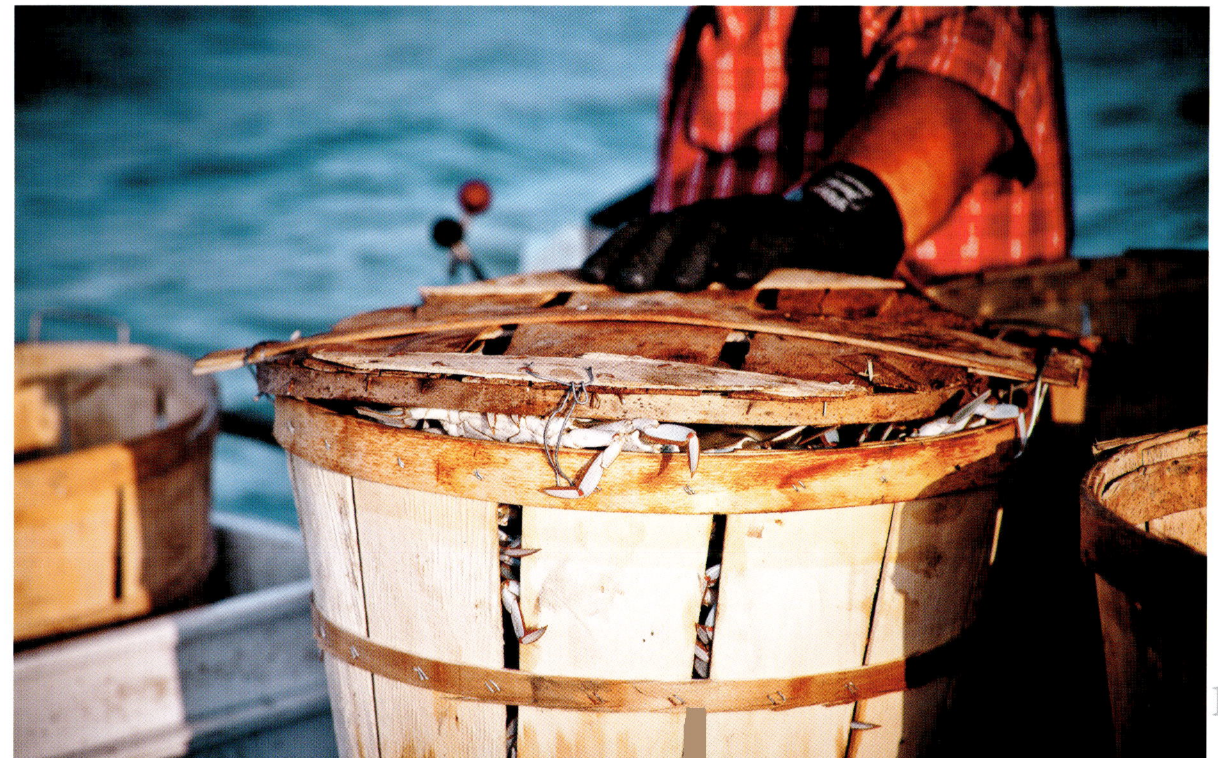

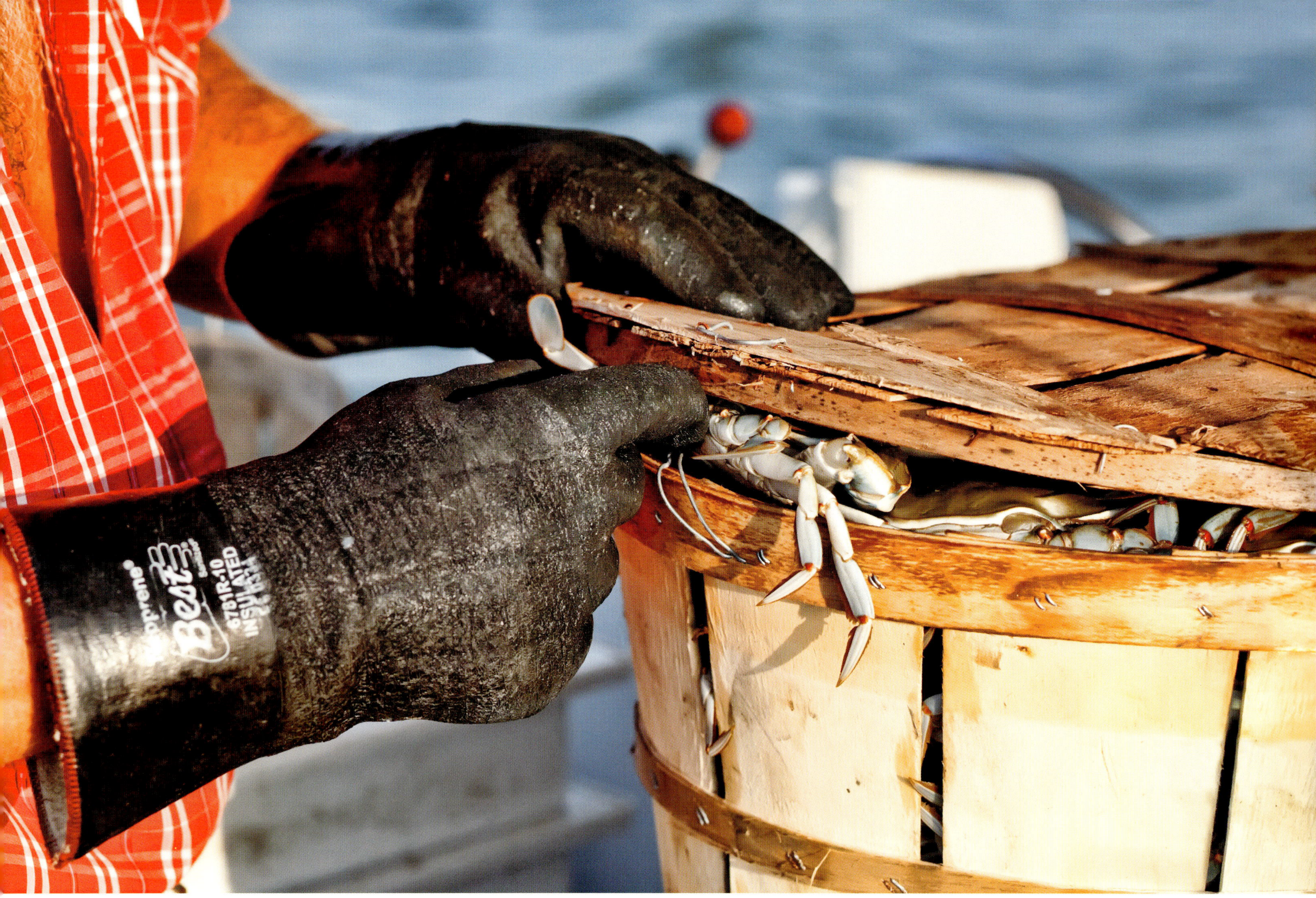


The last one squeezes in.

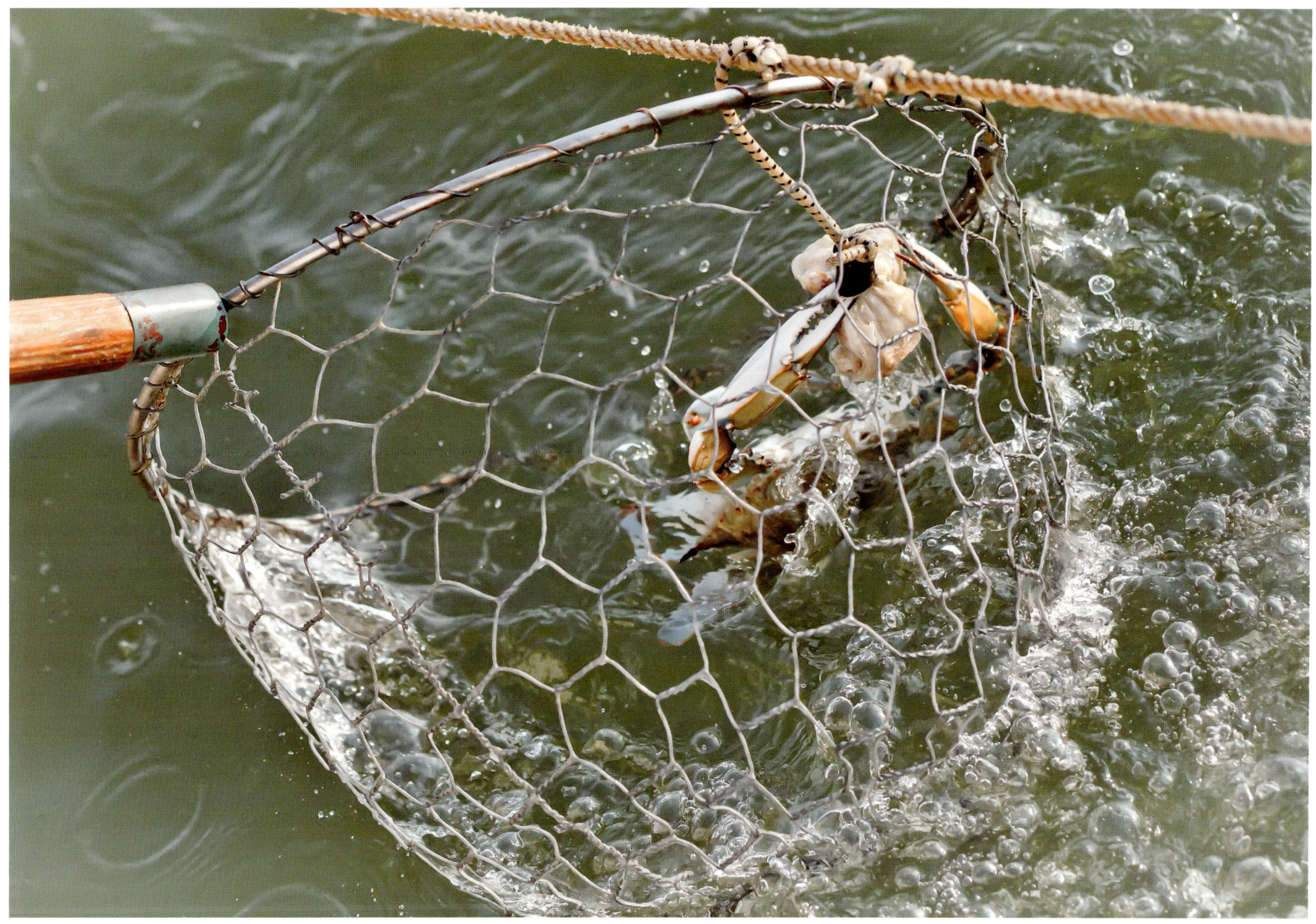

Crabs can't resist bull lips.

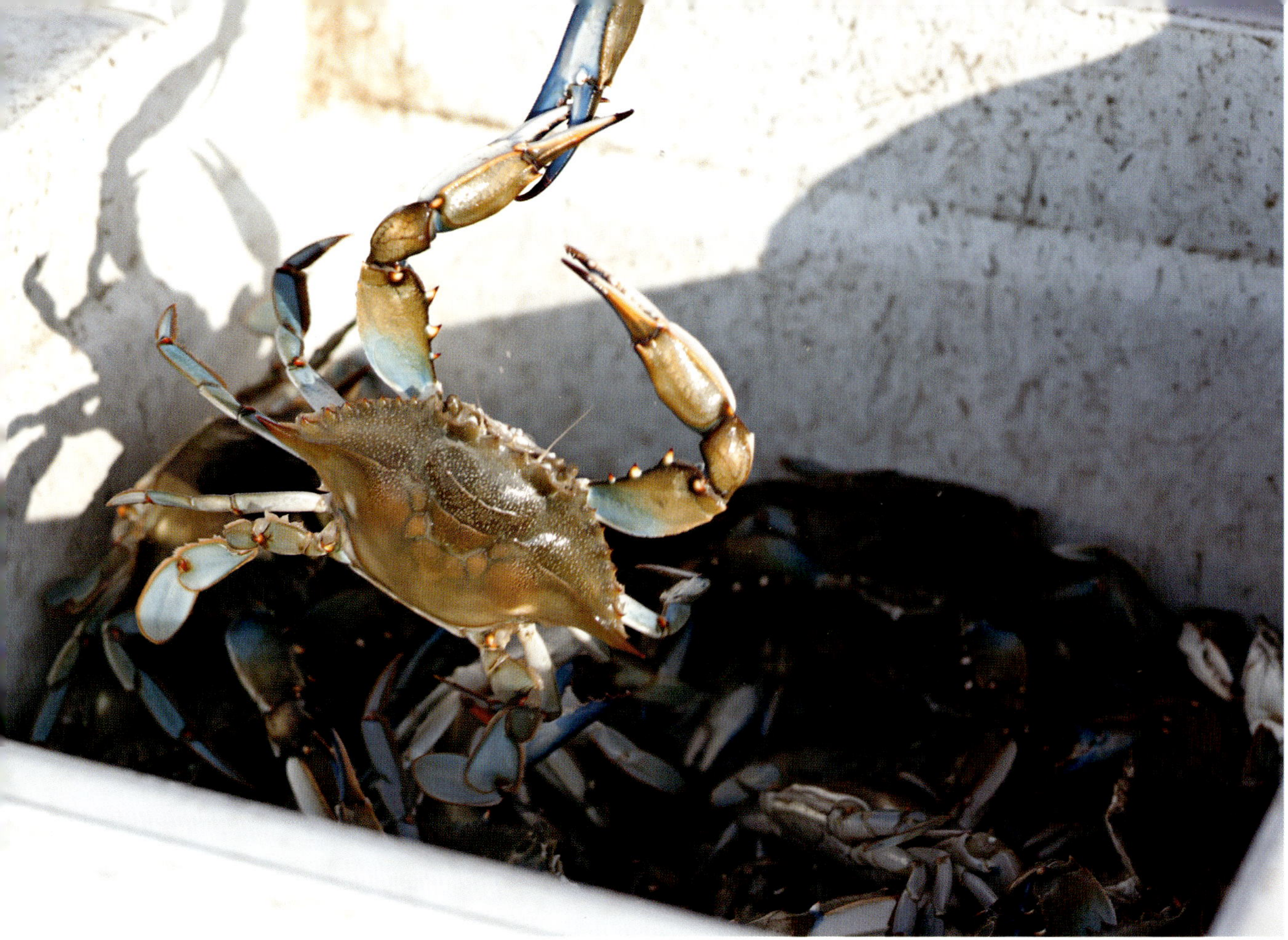

A male crab is lowered into a sink for sorting with some help from a friend.

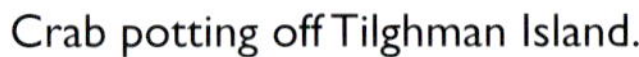

Crab potting off Tilghman Island.

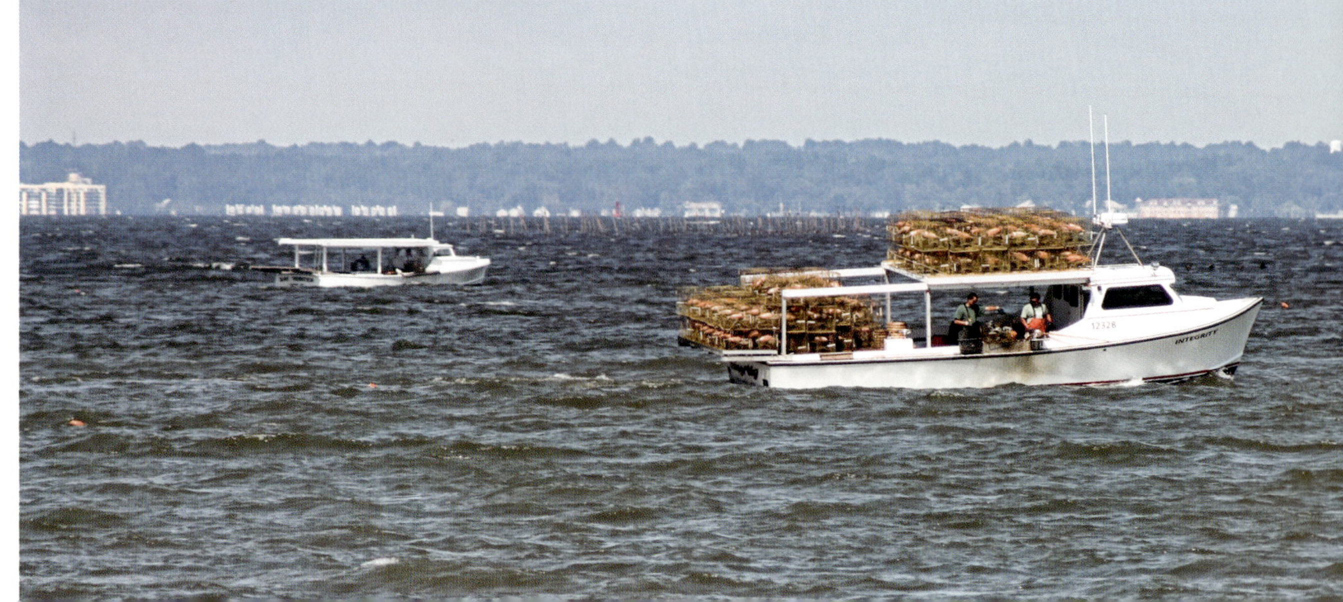

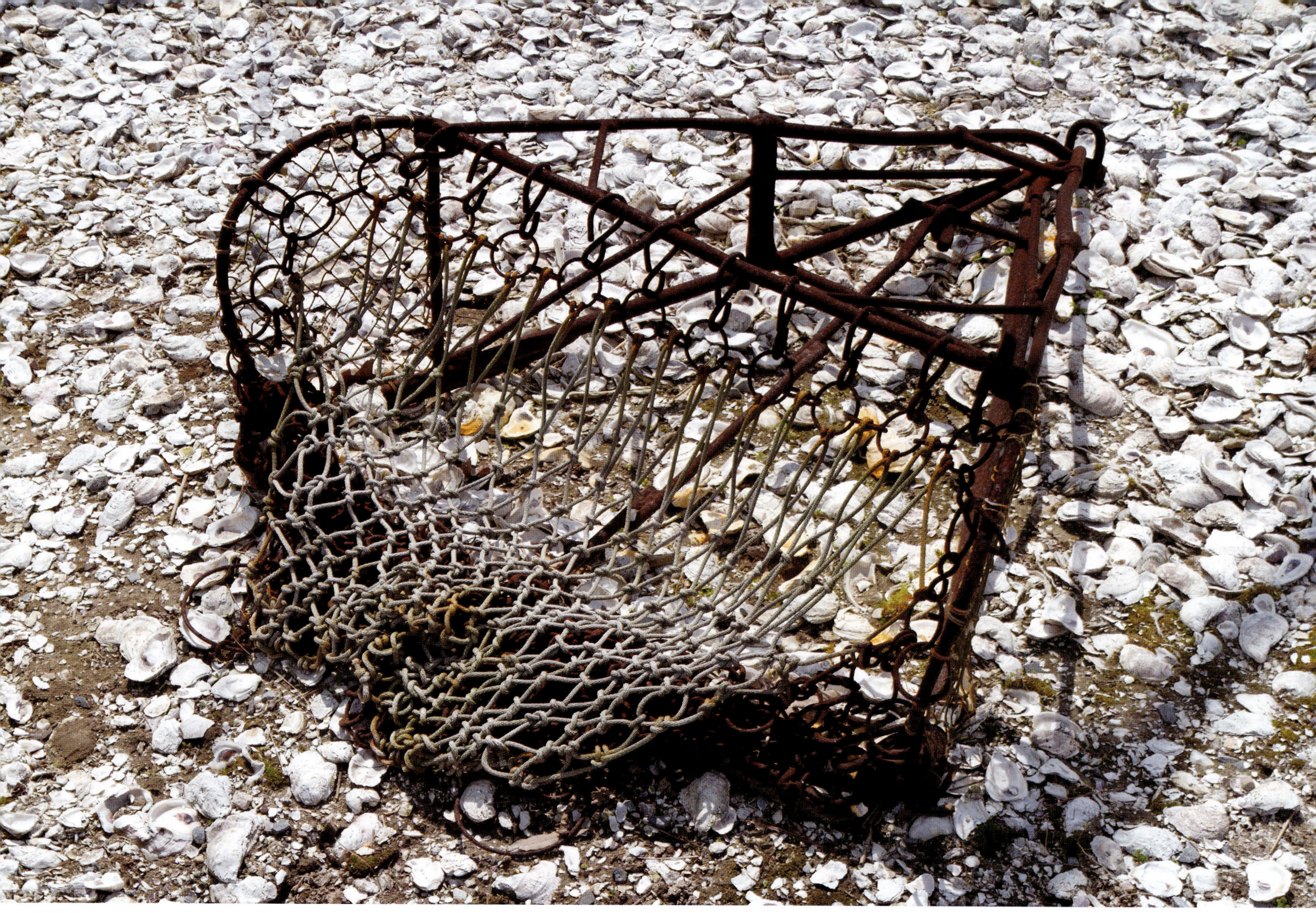

An oyster dredge sits in an outdoor museum display.

Barry Bruce, a member of the dwindling numbers of Smith Island watermen.

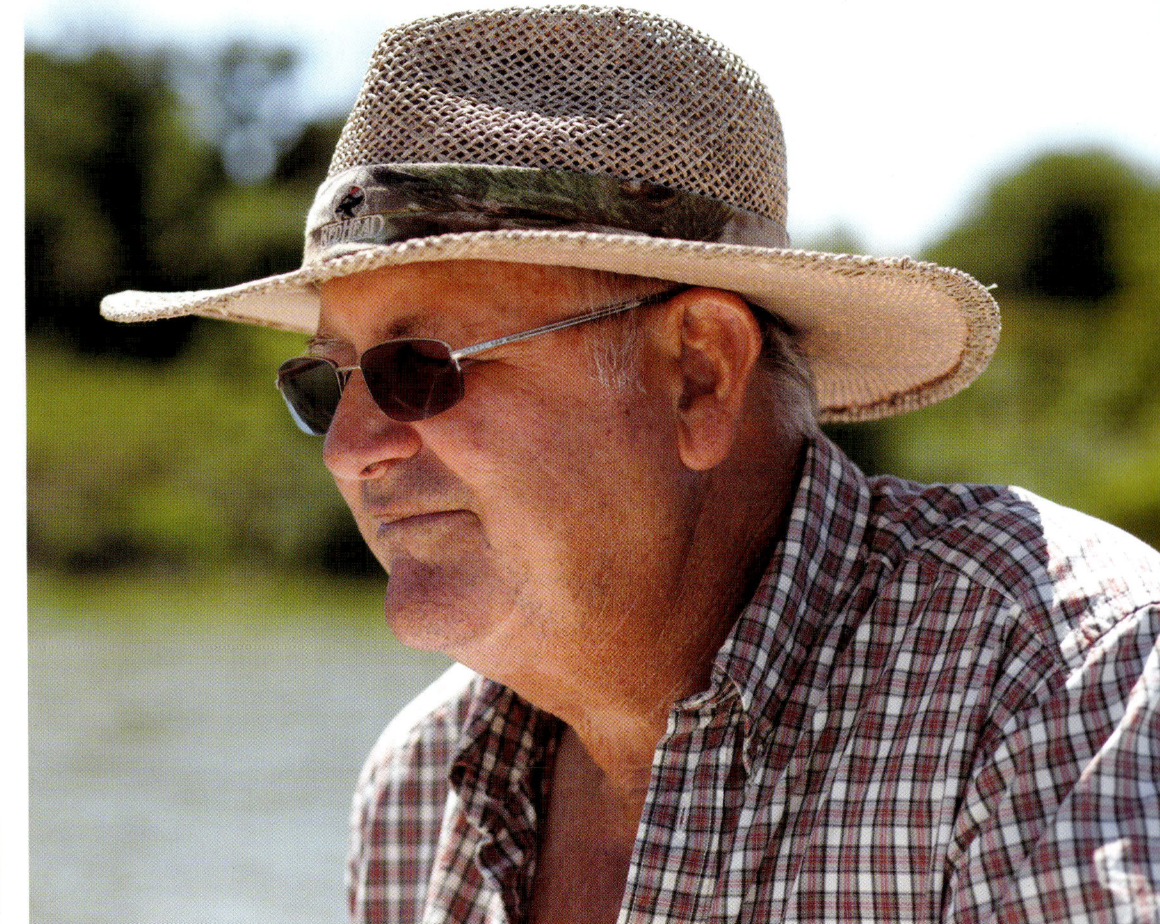

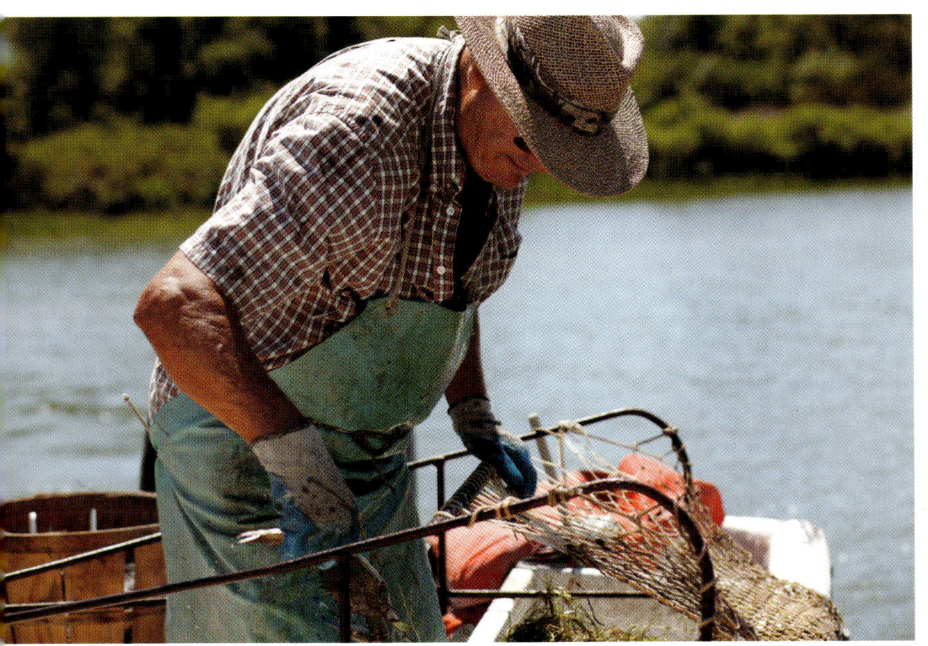

Barry prepares the crab scrape.

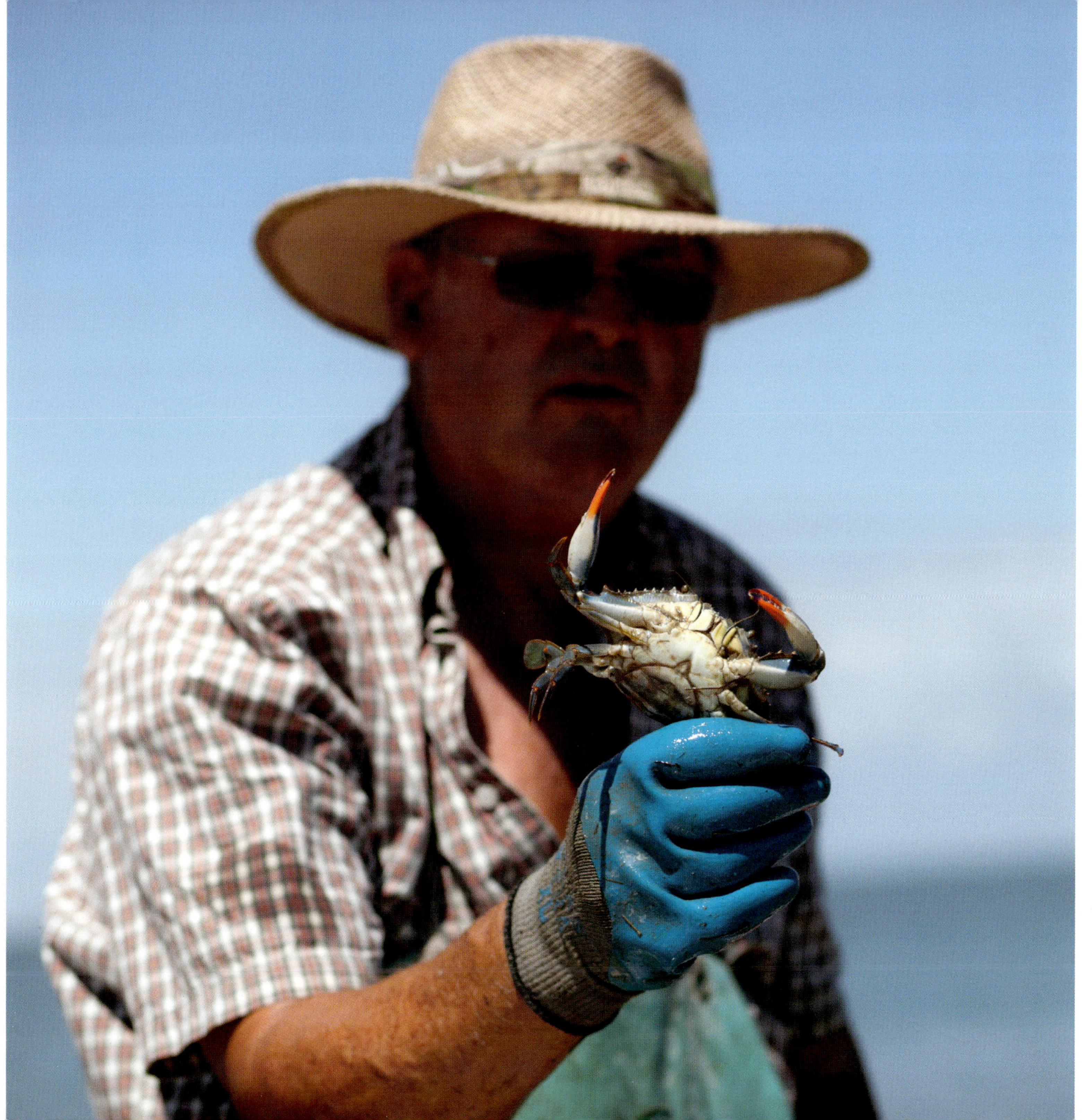

Barry examines a female blue crab caught in his crab scrape.

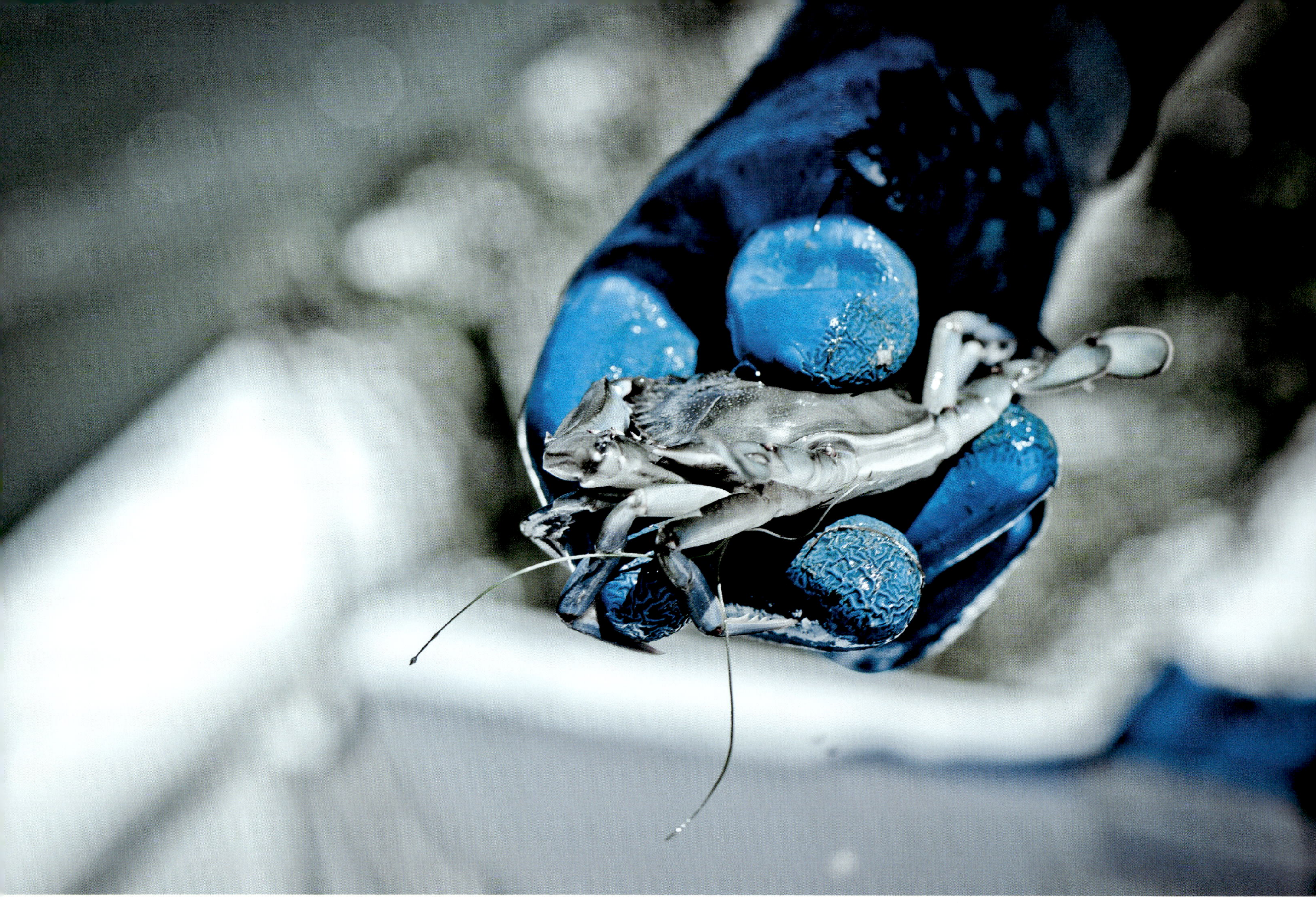

Barry checks a softcrab for hardness.

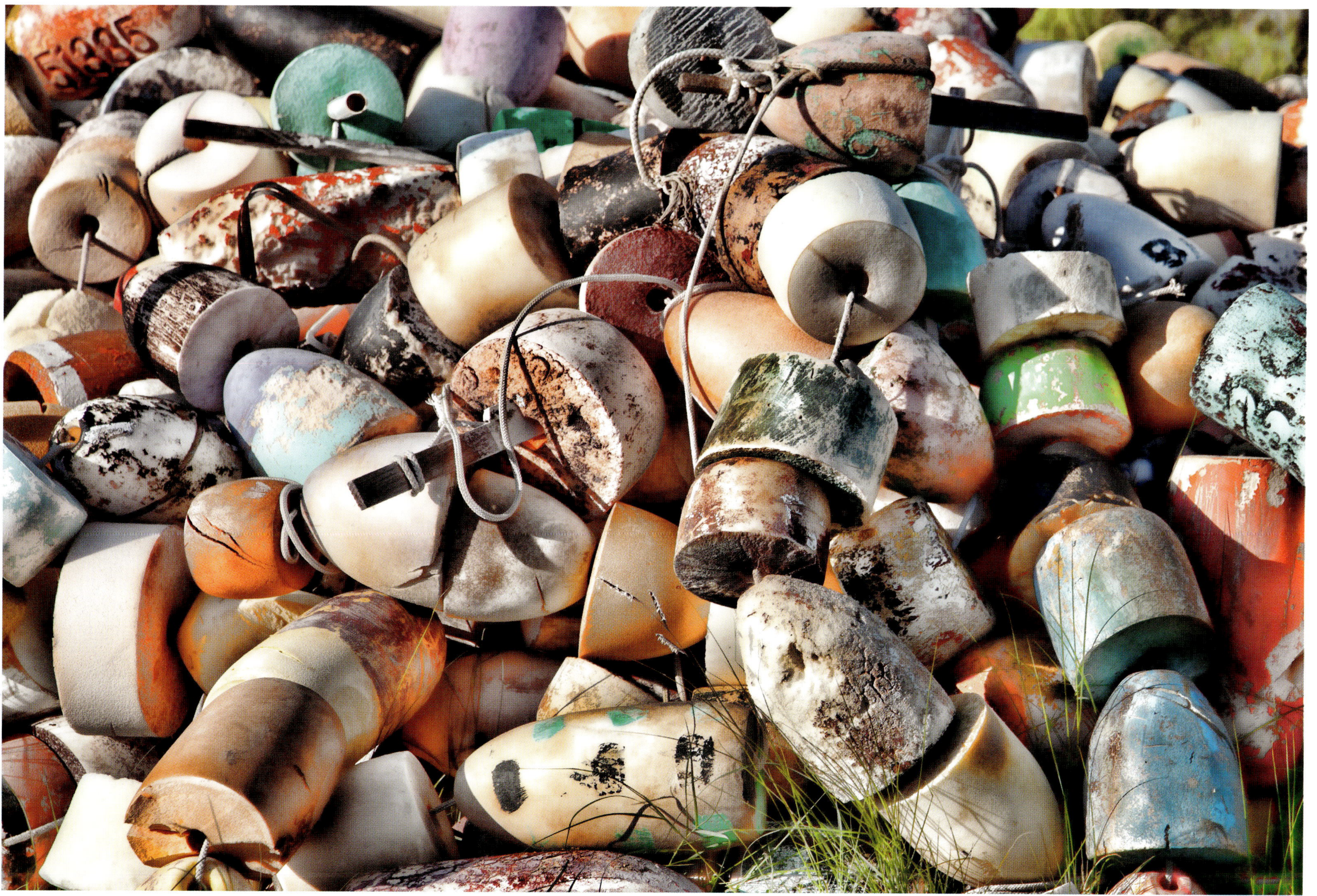

Hundreds of crab floats in a pile at Ewell, Maryland, Smith Island.

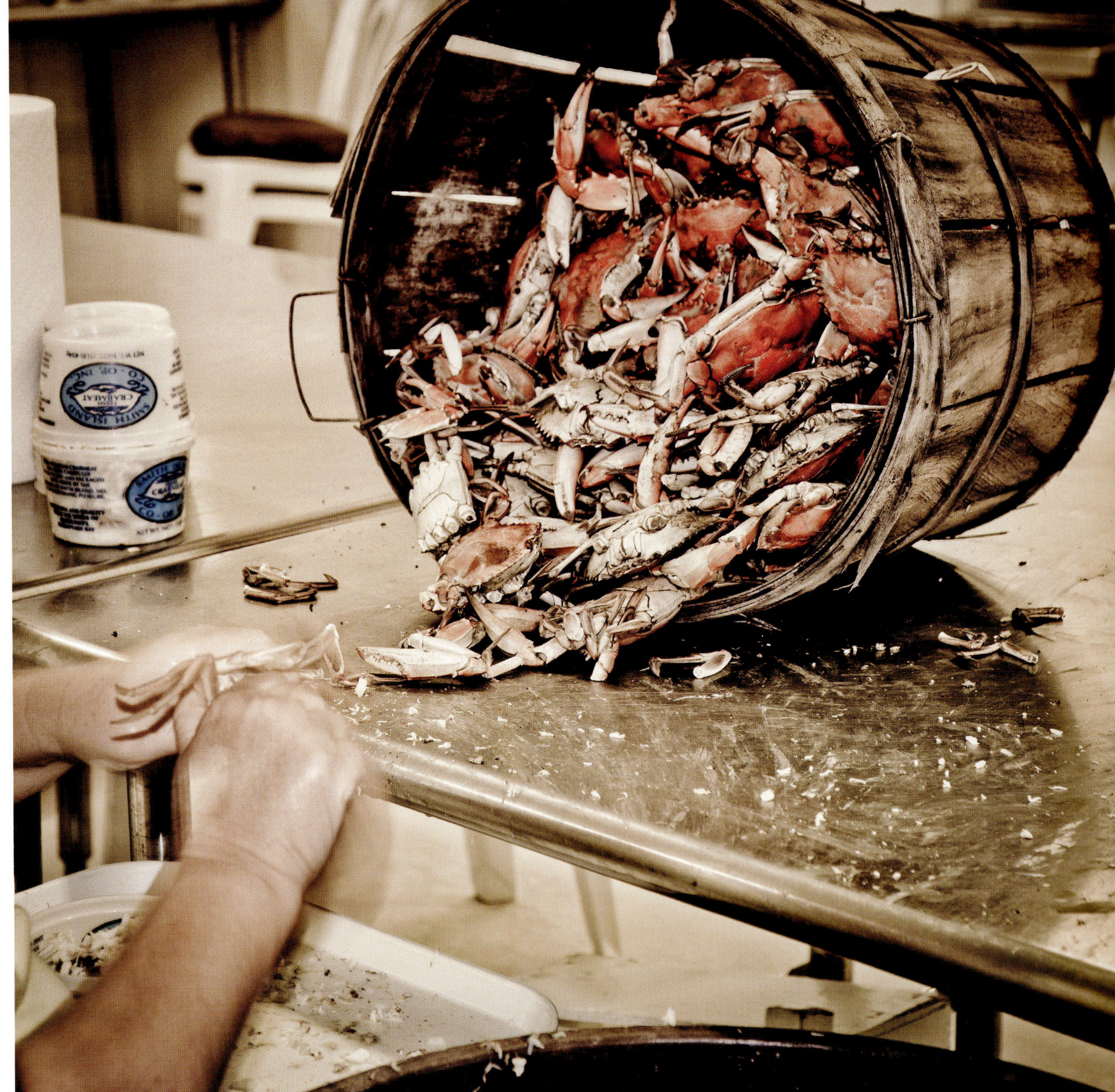

Picking crabs by the bushel at the Co-op on Smith Island.

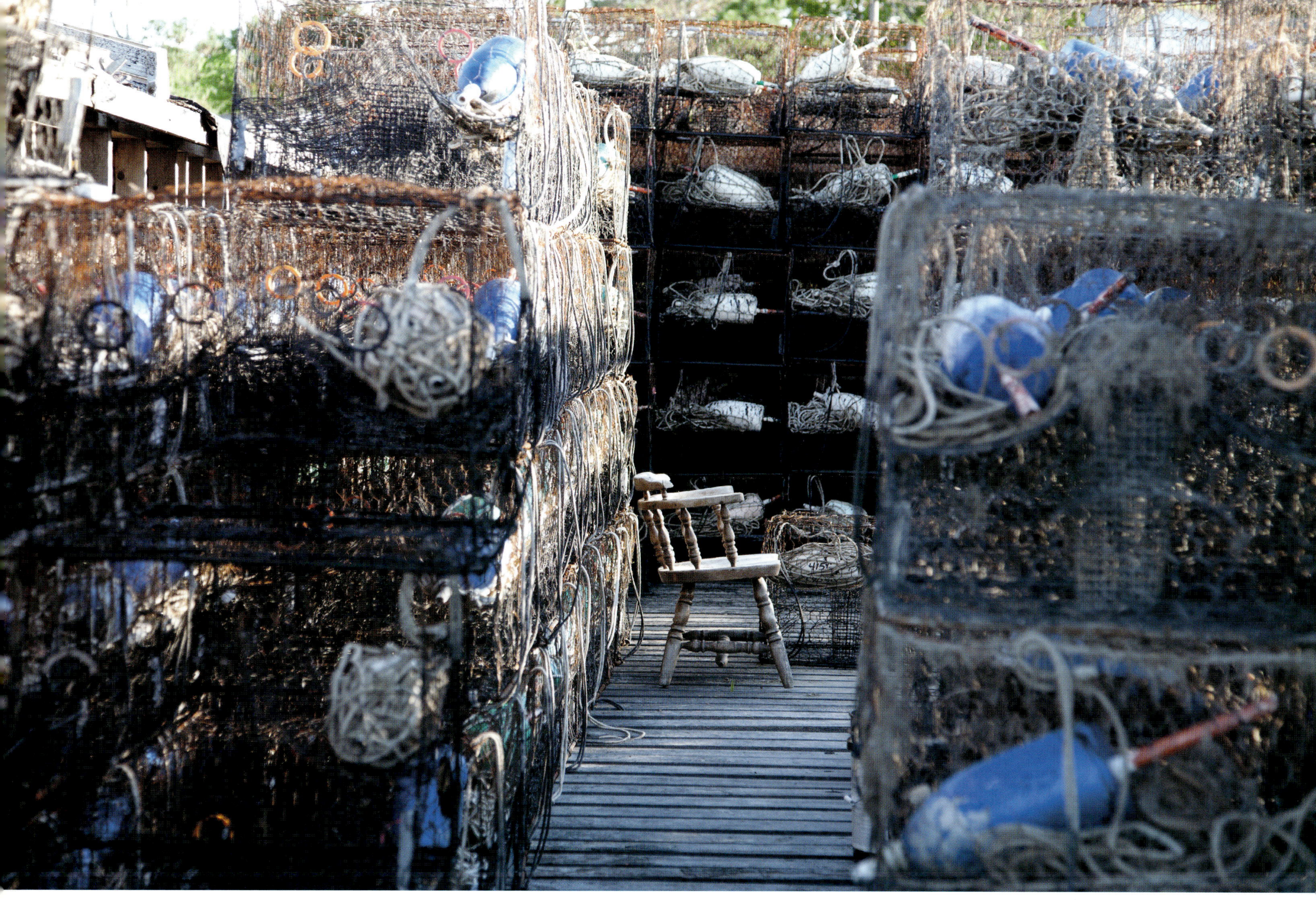

A chair in a shanty alleyway lined with crab pots.

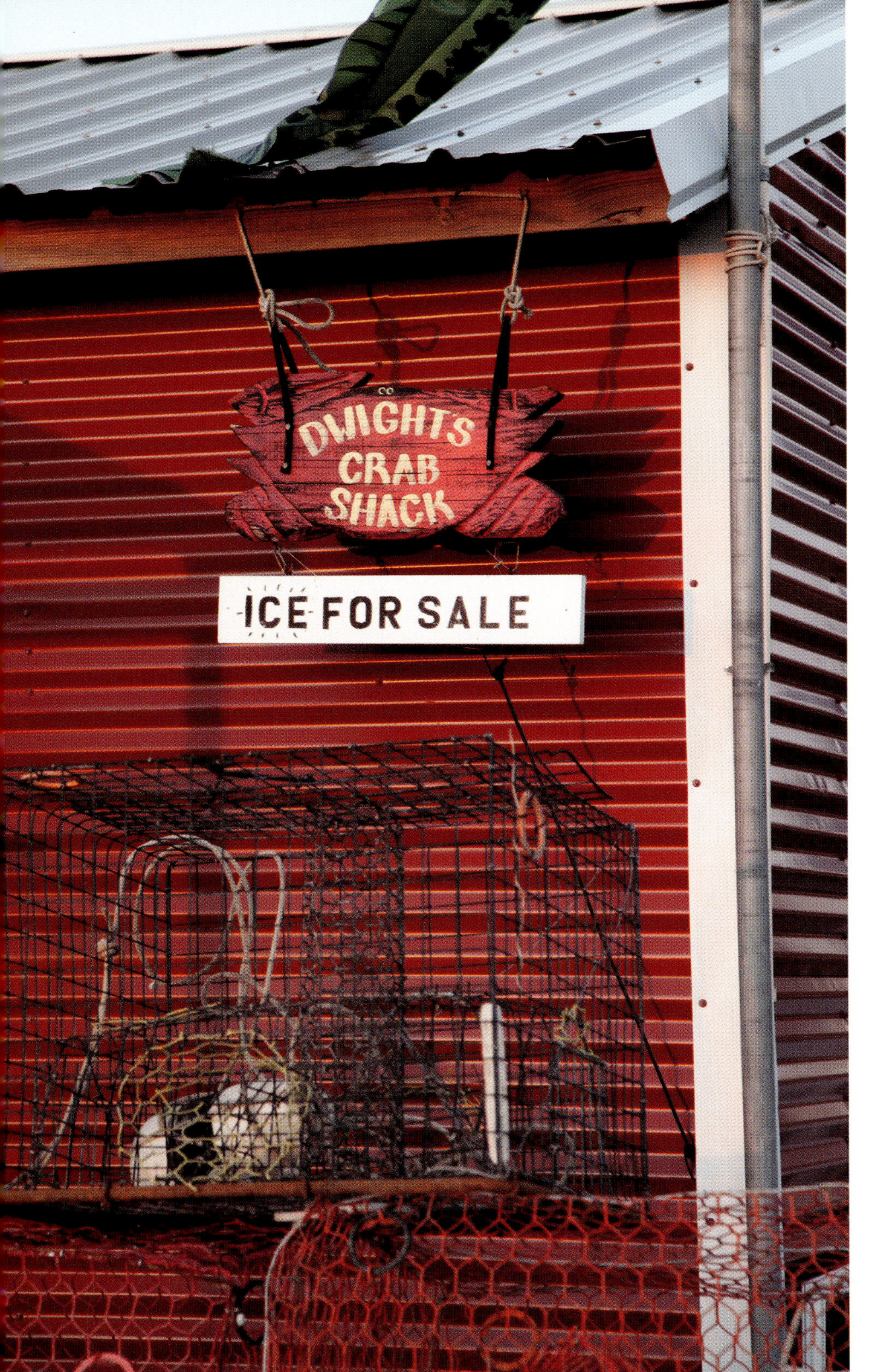


Dwight Marshall's Crab Shack in Tylerton.

A crab shanty at Tylerton, Smith Island, reflects the early morning sun.

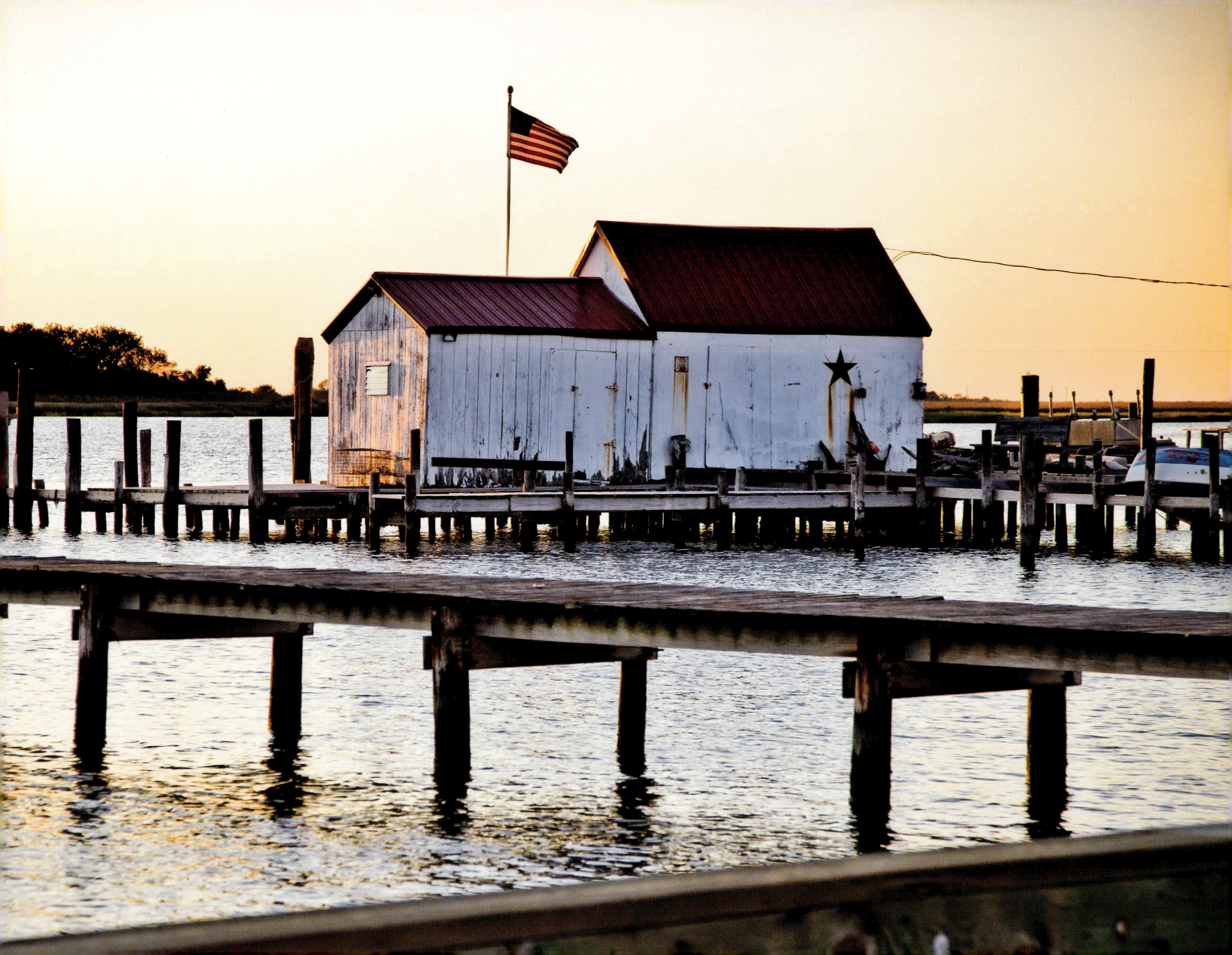

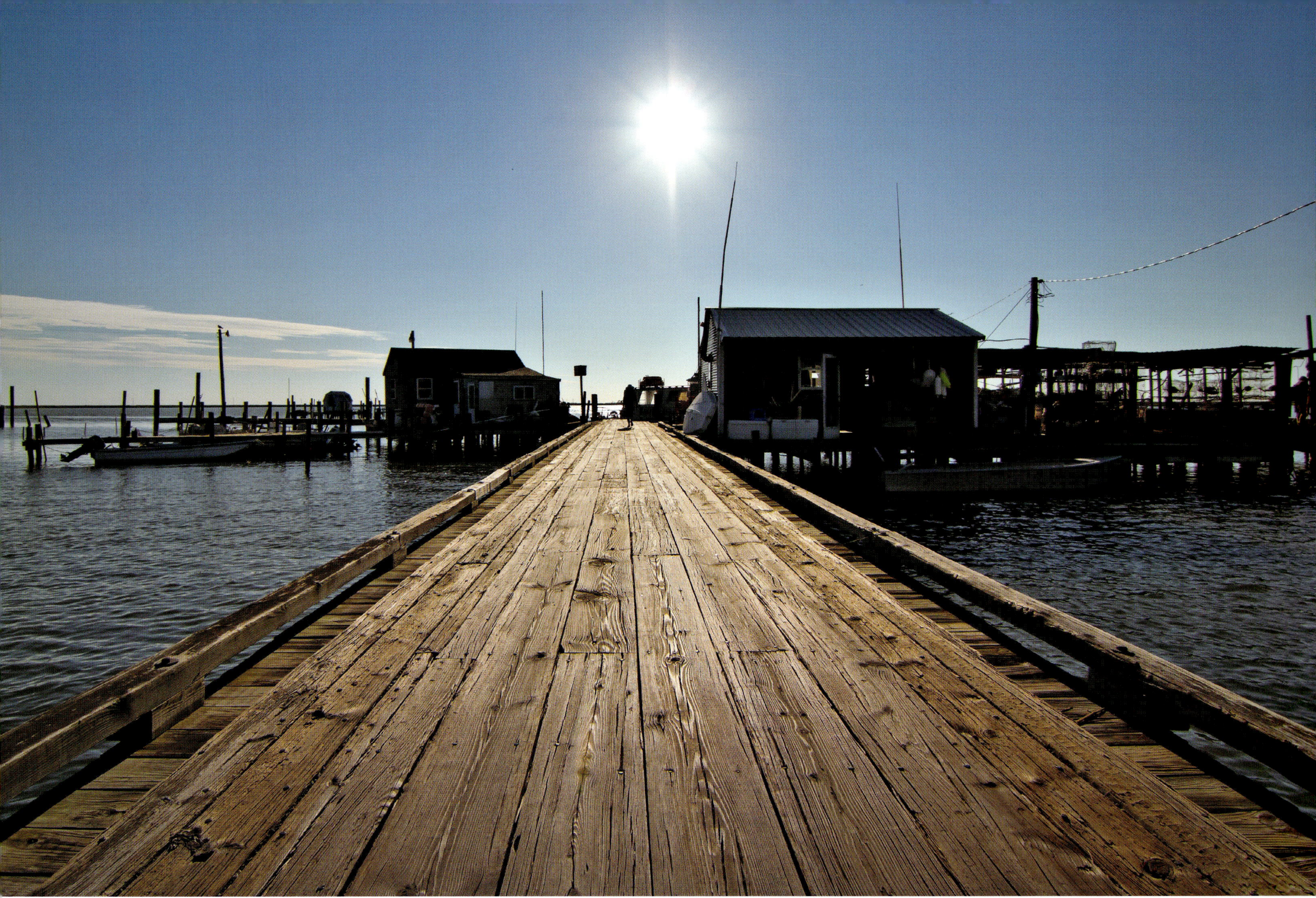

The ferry pier at Tylerton.

A deteriorating pier points to Rhodes Point off in the distance.

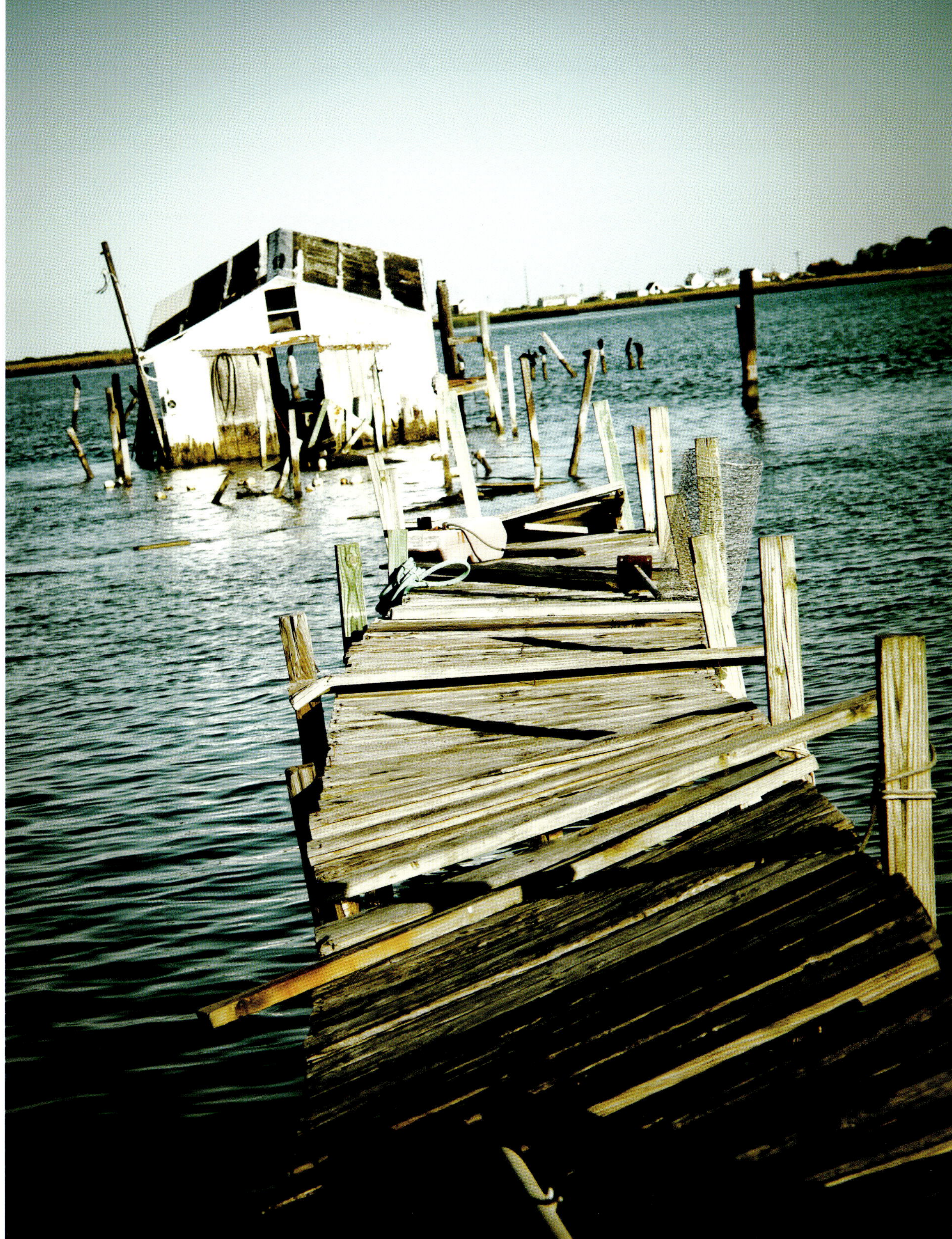

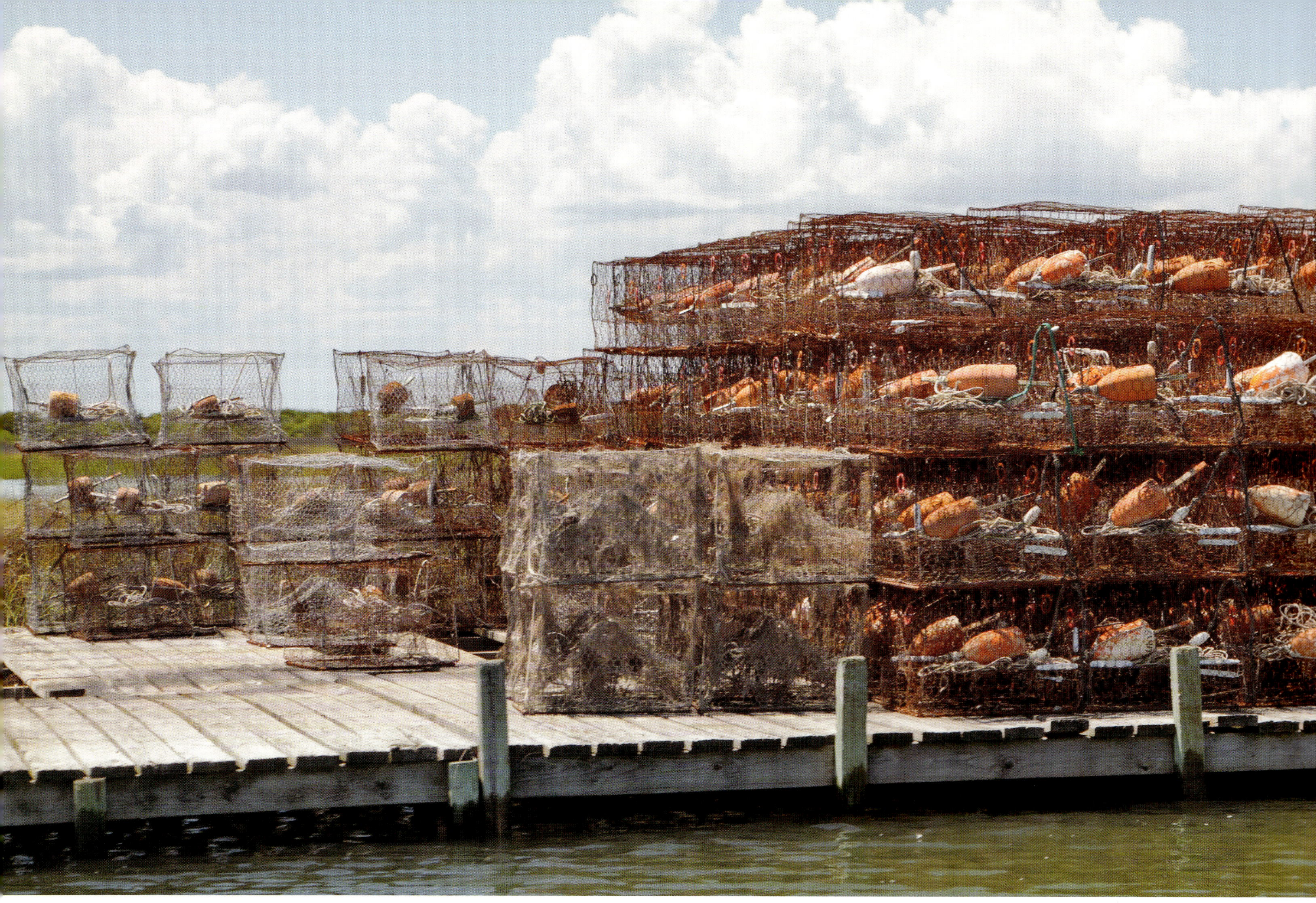

Hundreds of crab pots, ready to be deployed.

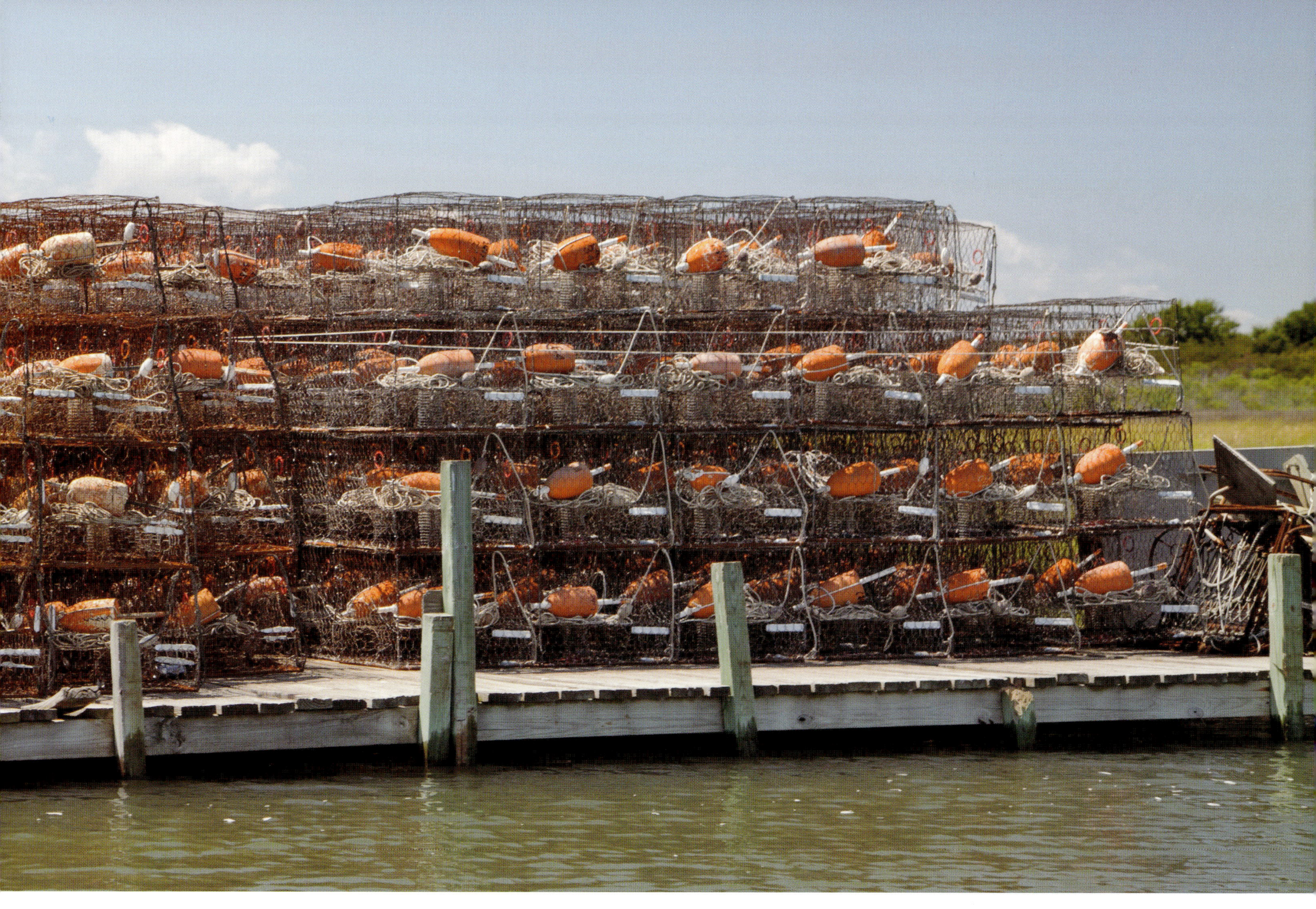

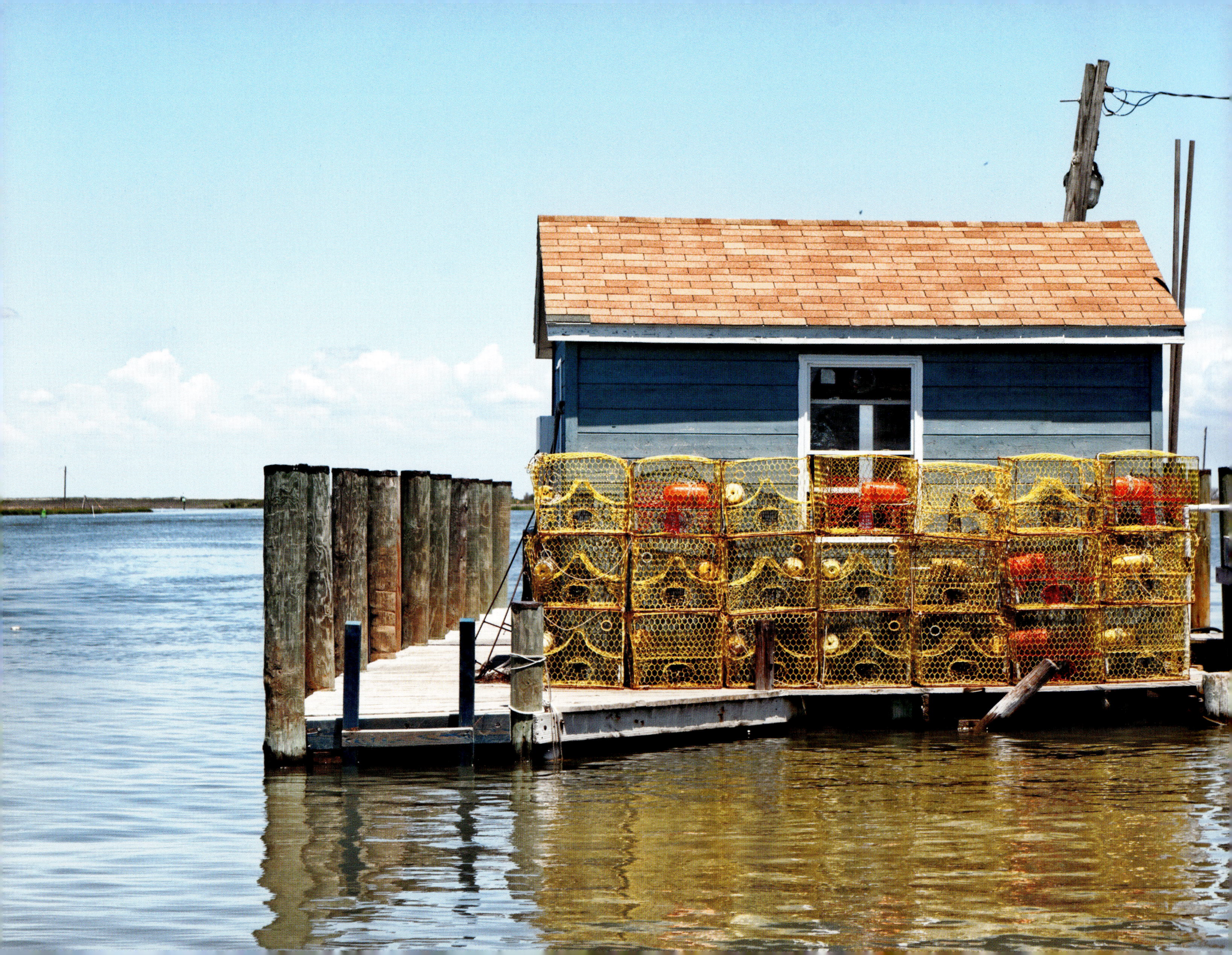

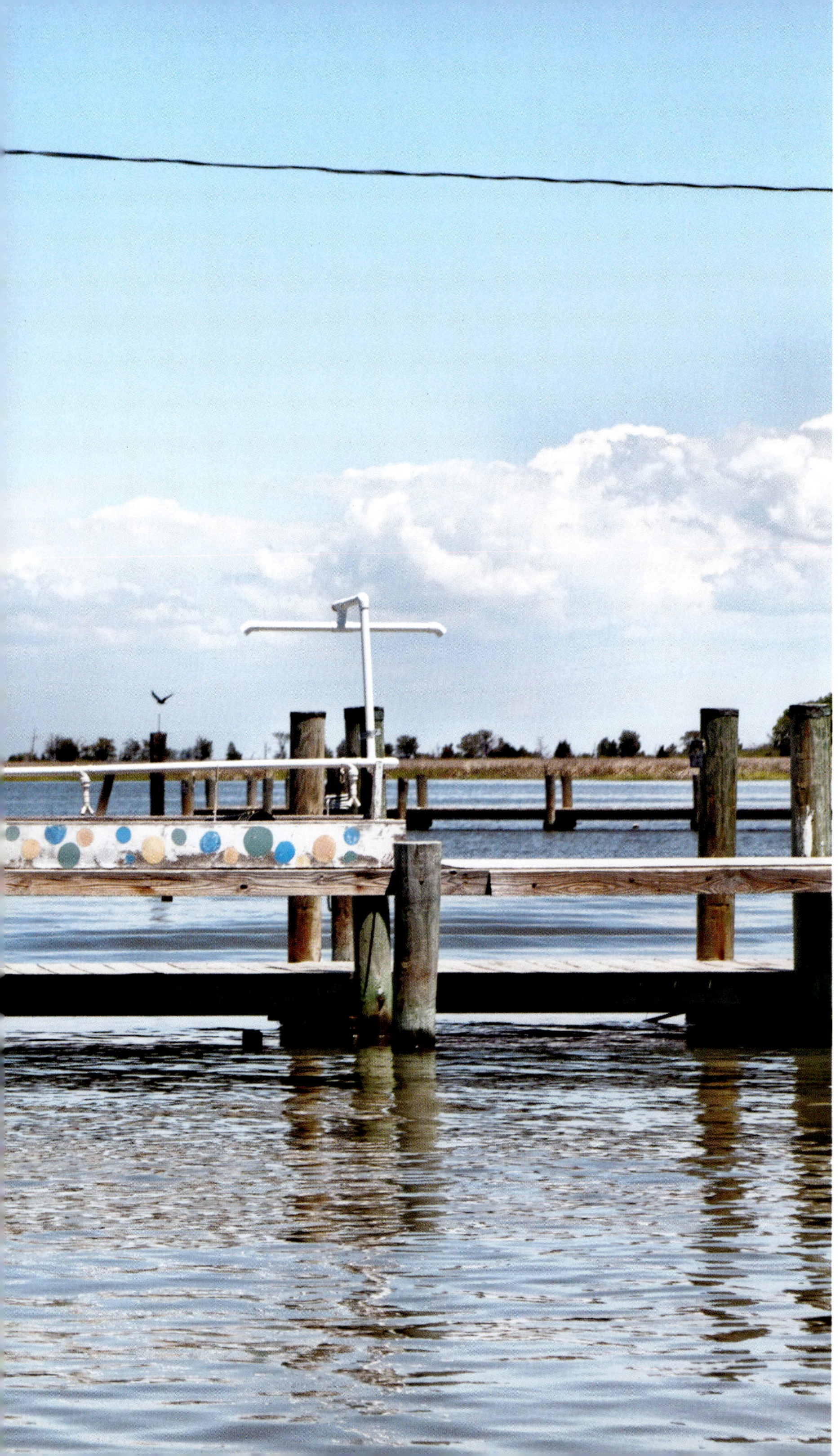

Crab pots standing by beside a crab shanty in Tylerton.

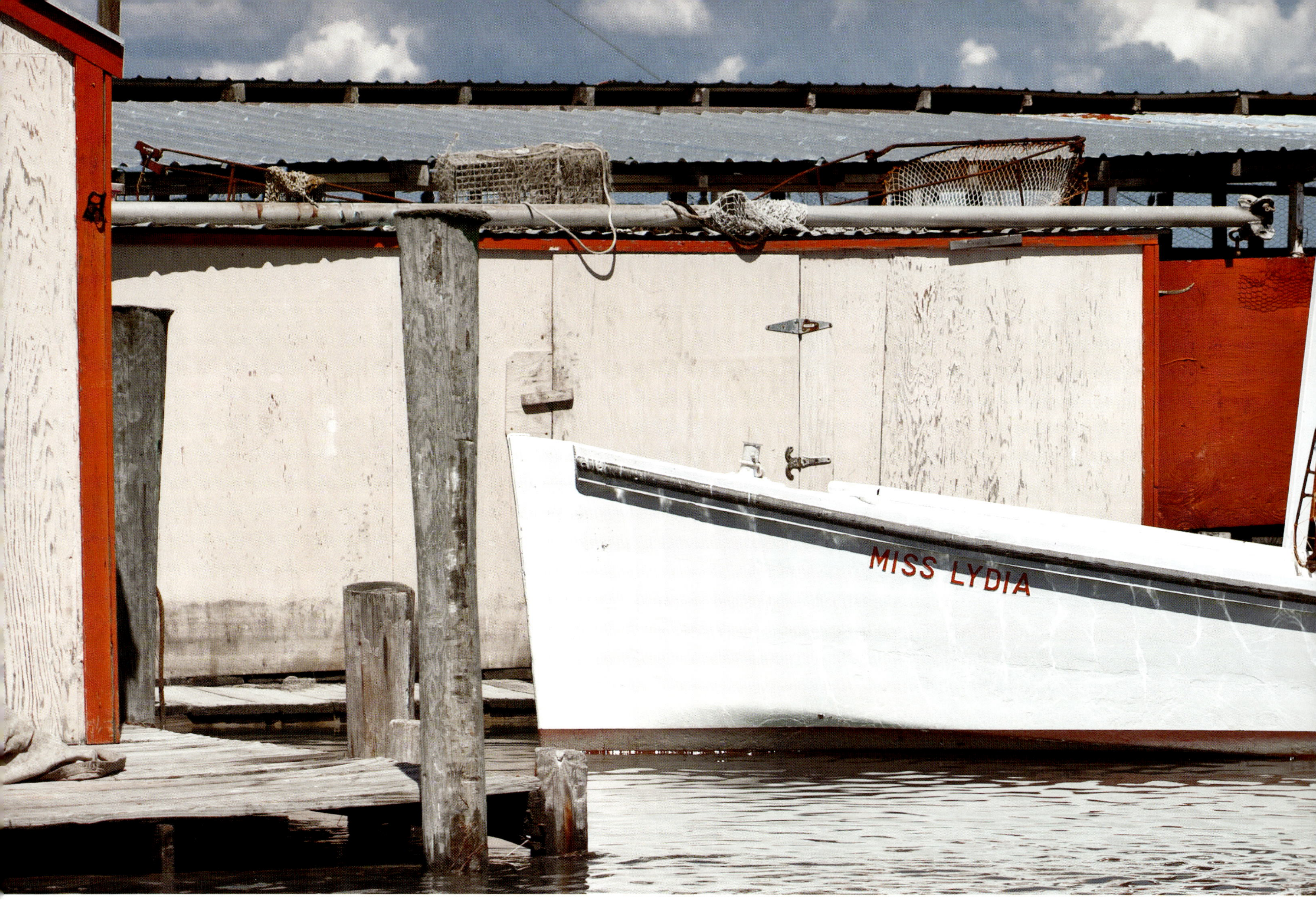


Shedding tanks for peeler crabs reside behind the docked *Miss Lydia*.

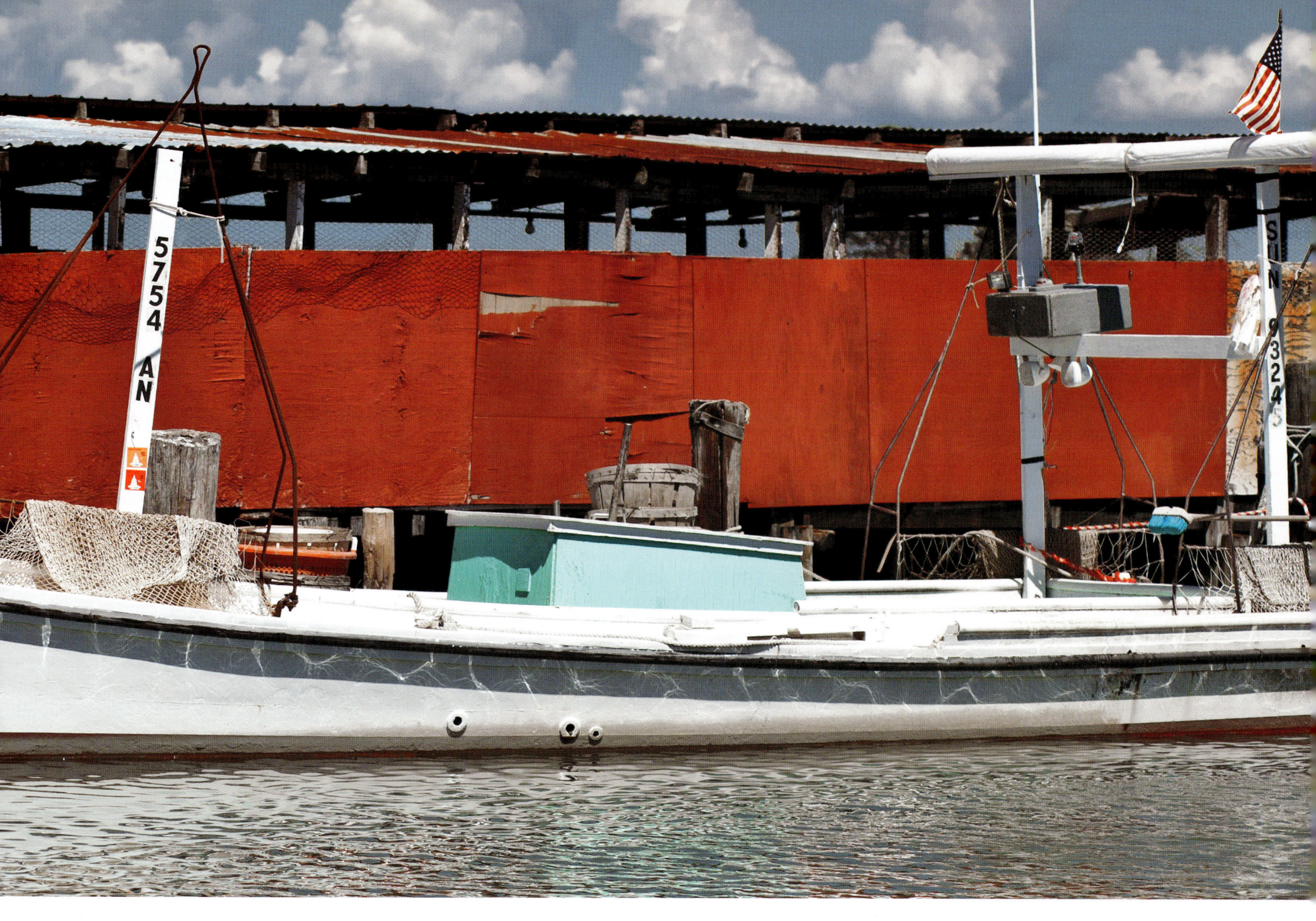
5754 AN

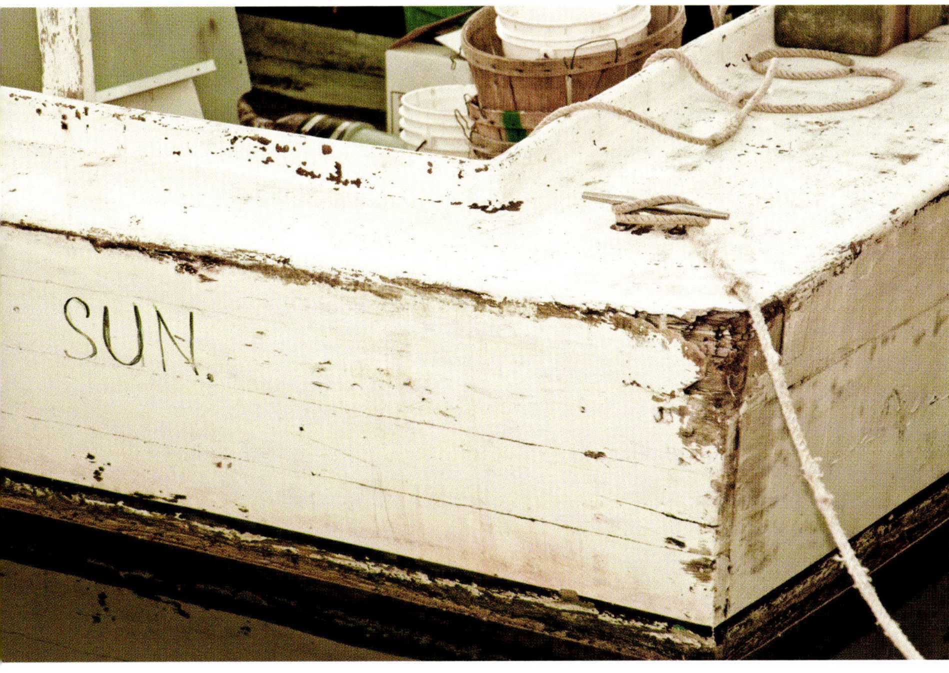


A waterman's day off is documented on the side of his boat.

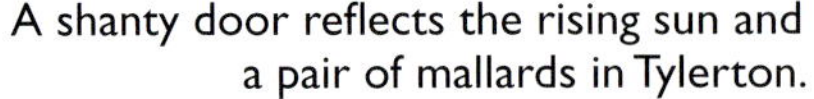

A shanty door reflects the rising sun and a pair of mallards in Tylerton.

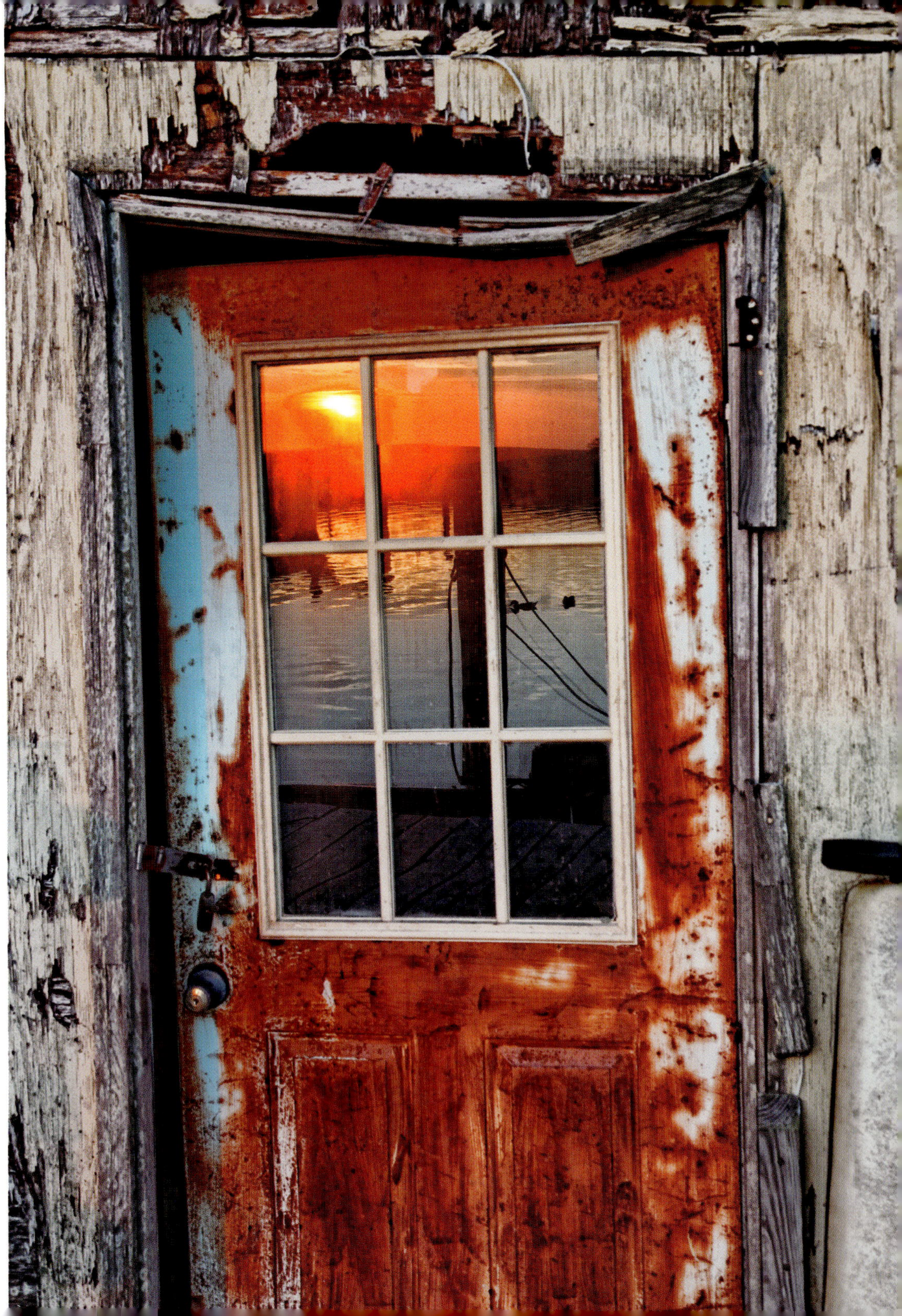

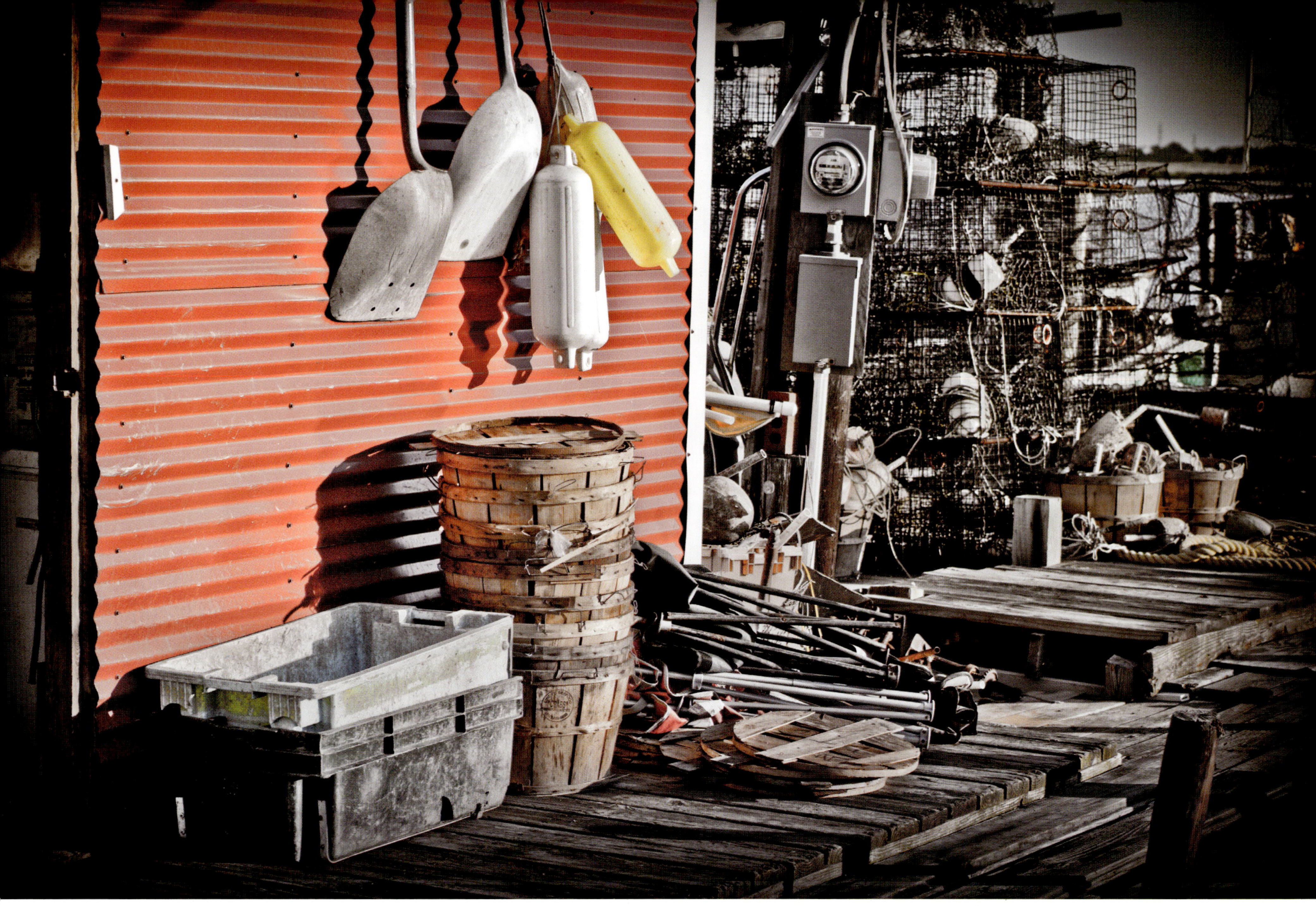

The tools of the trade.

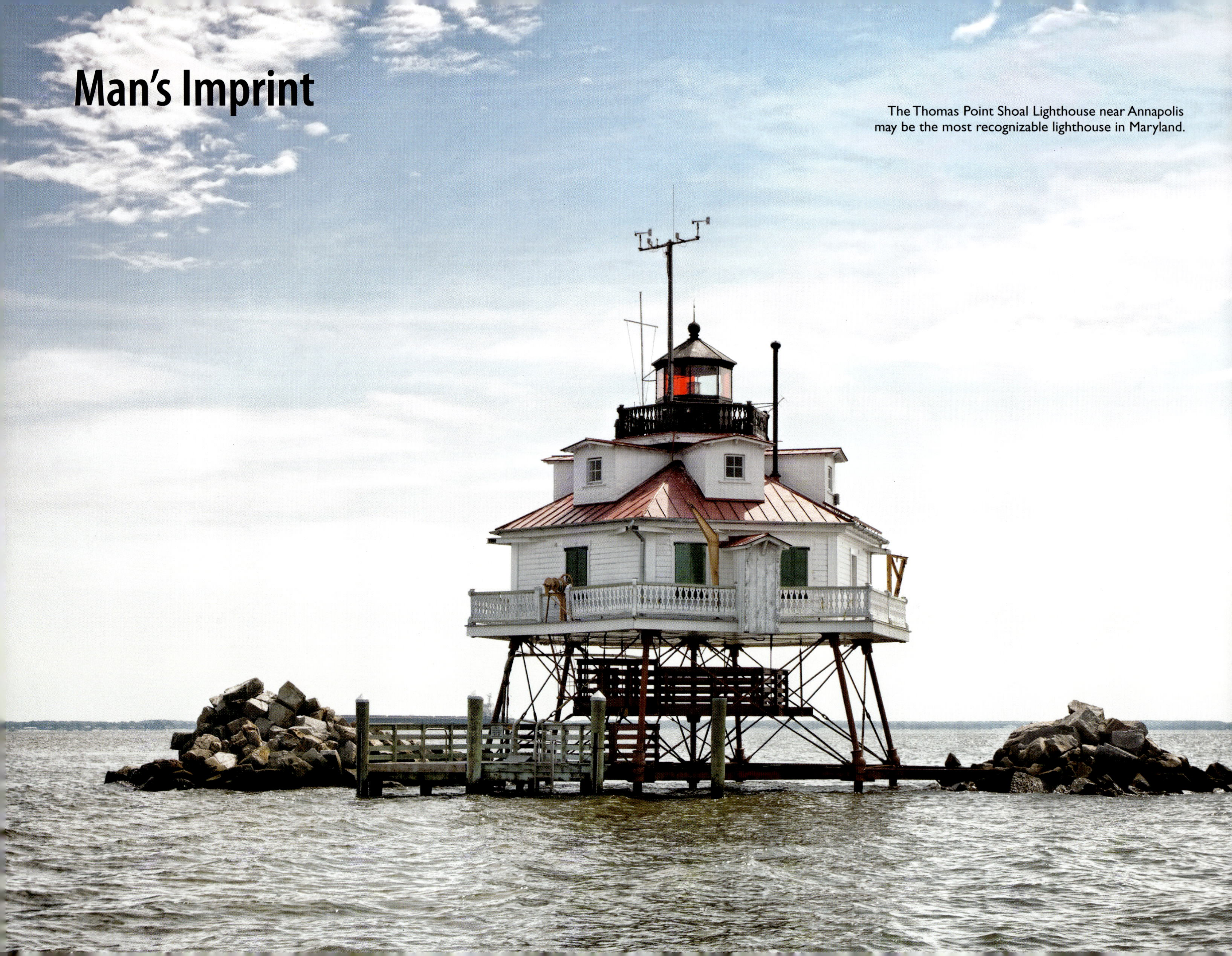

# Man's Imprint

The Thomas Point Shoal Lighthouse near Annapolis may be the most recognizable lighthouse in Maryland.

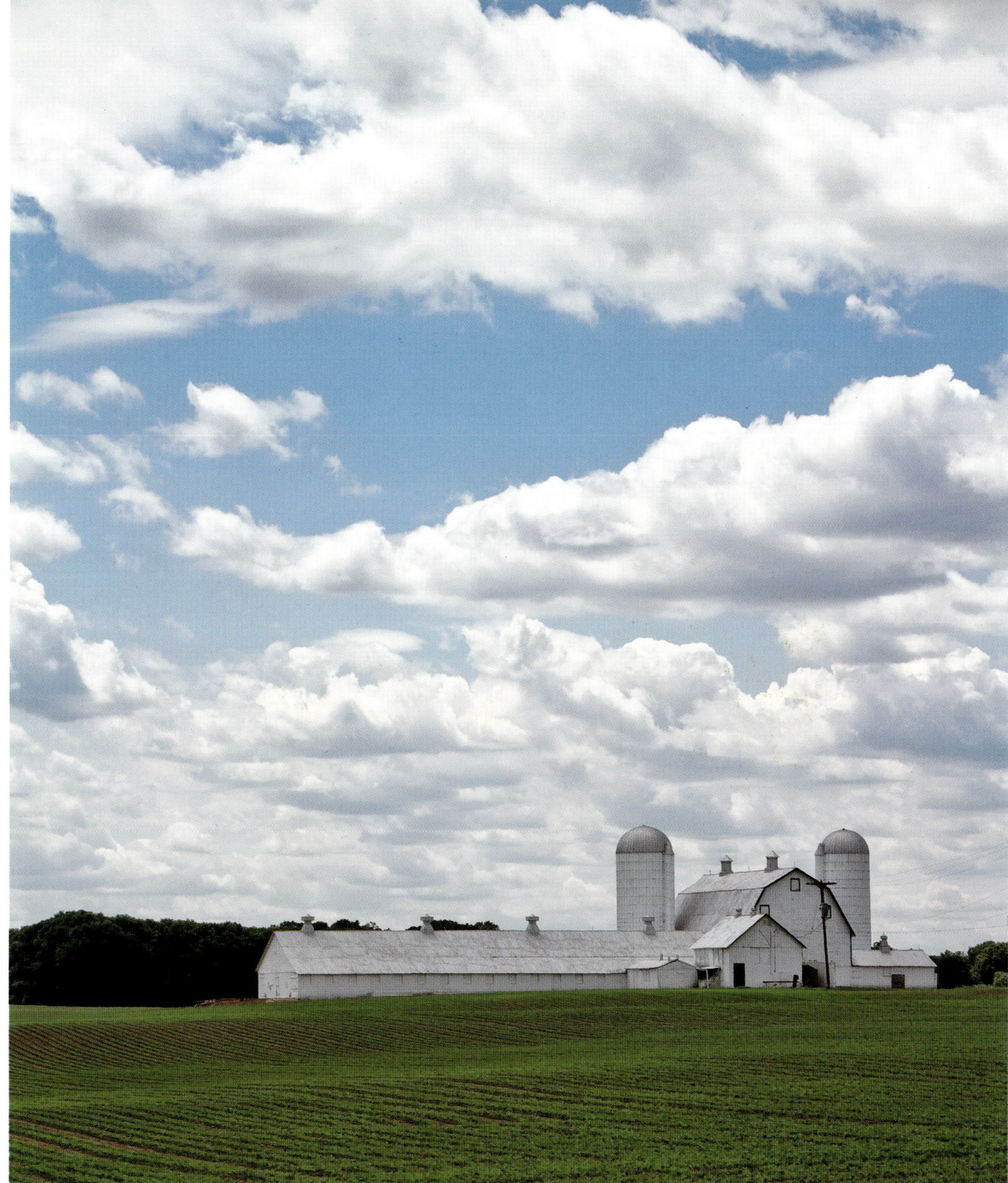

White farm buildings point to a dramatic sky.

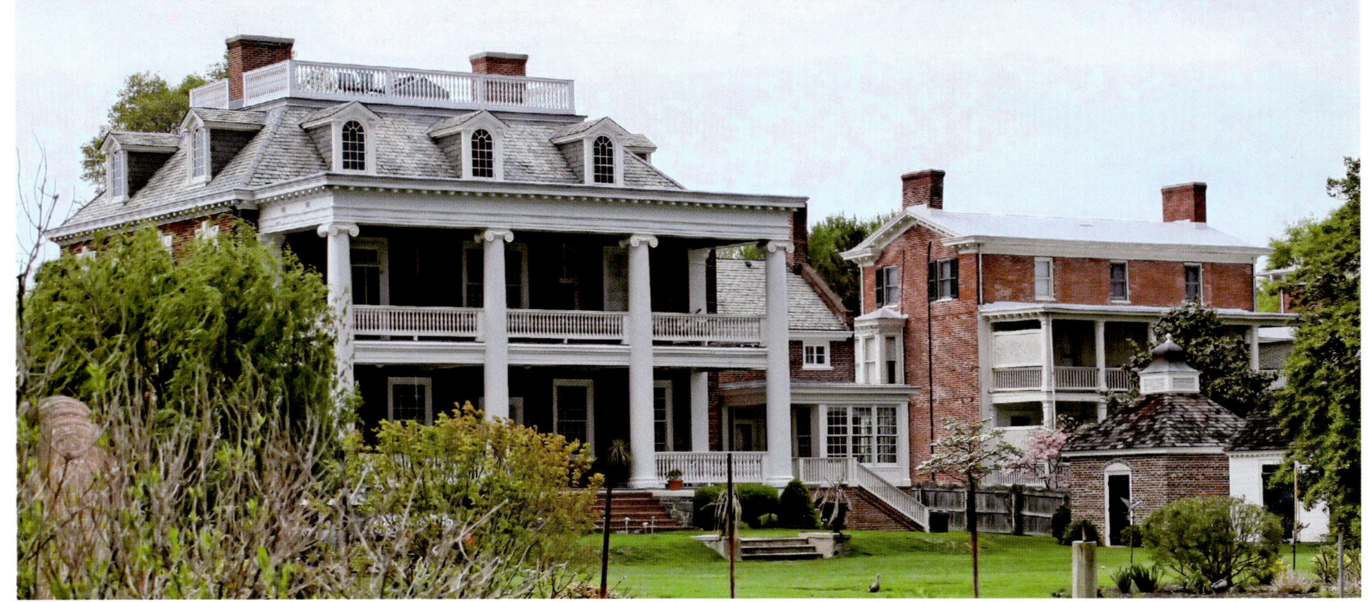

Widehall, as seen from the waterside in Chestertown, Maryland.

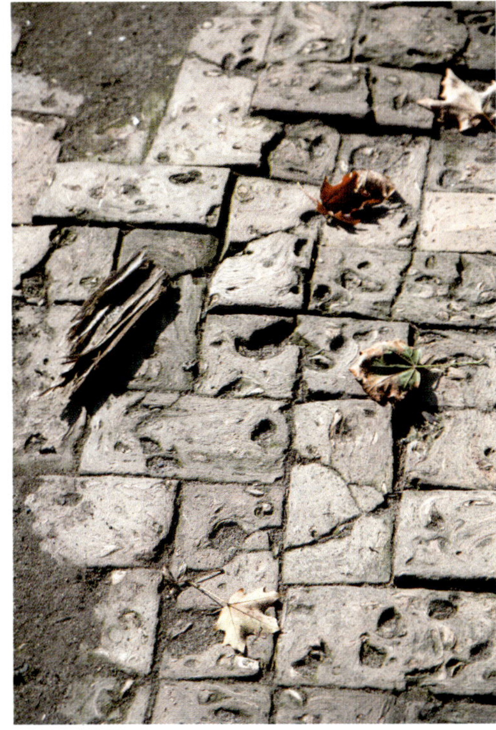

A brick sidewalk in Oxford, Maryland.

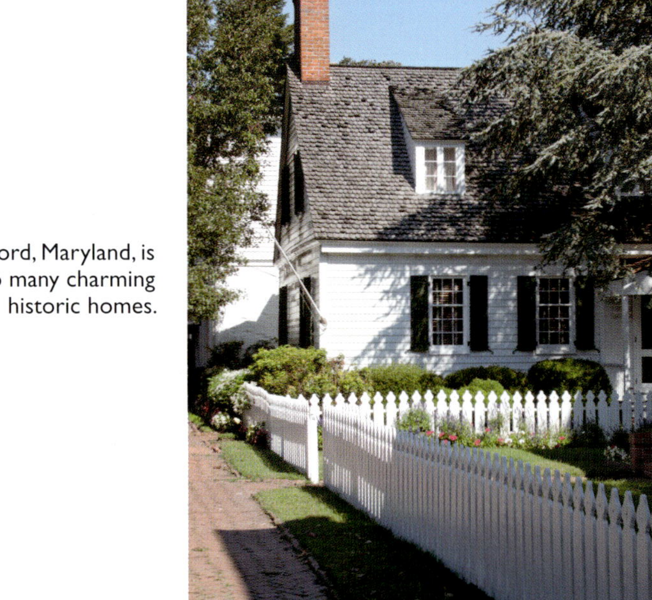

Oxford, Maryland, is home to many charming historic homes.

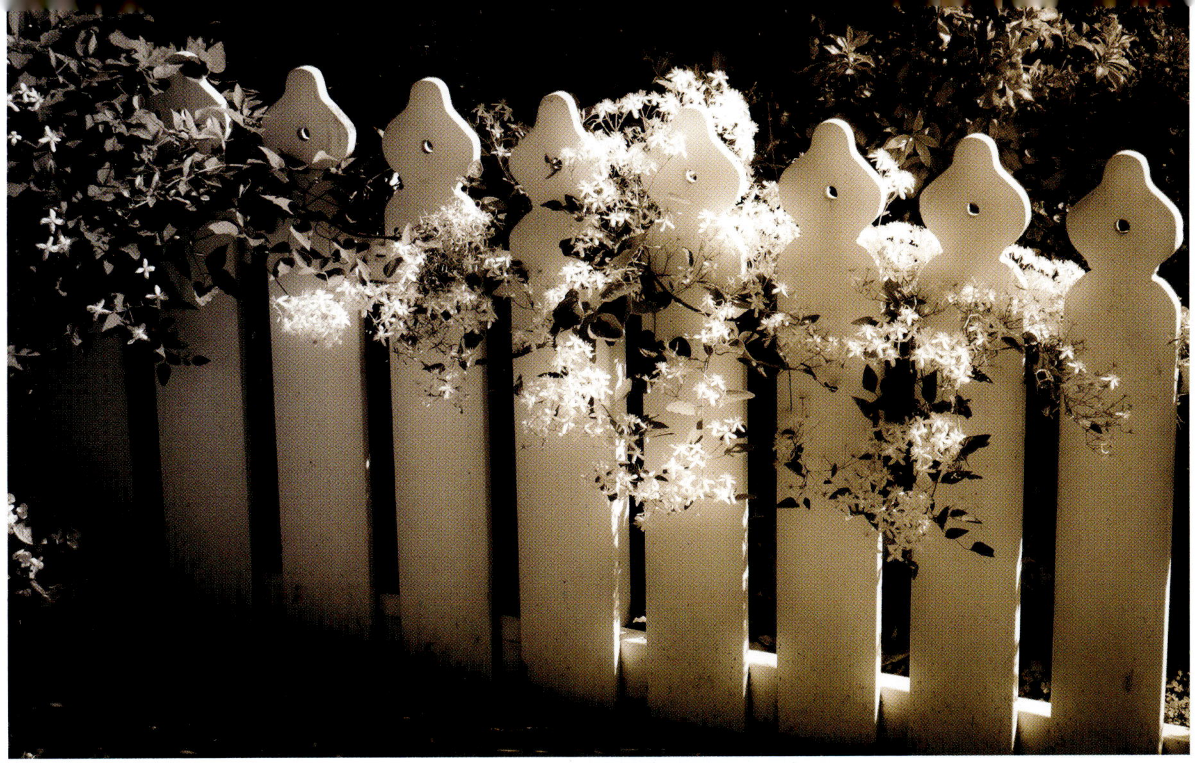

The signature picket fences of Oxford, Maryland.

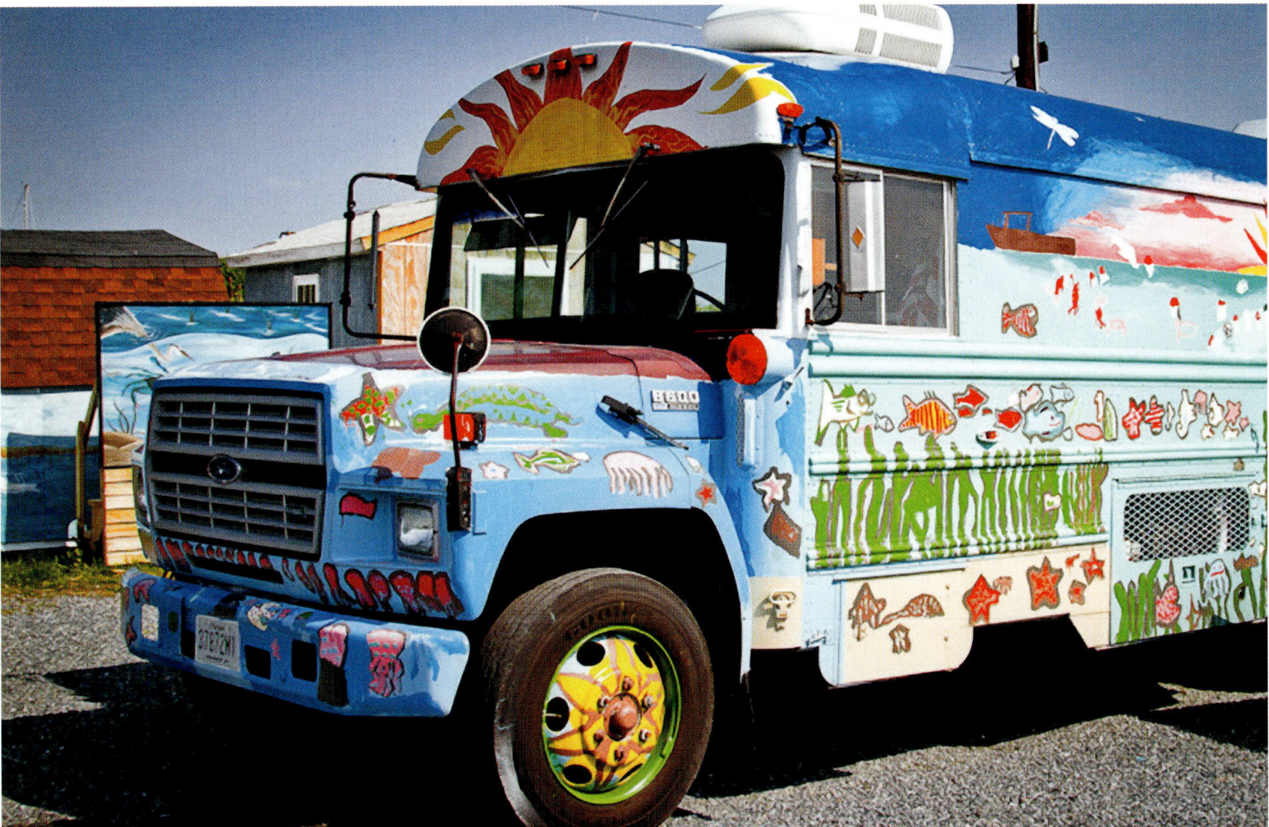

The Phillips Wharf Environmental Center's "Fishmobile" waits for another group of children to educate about the Bay.

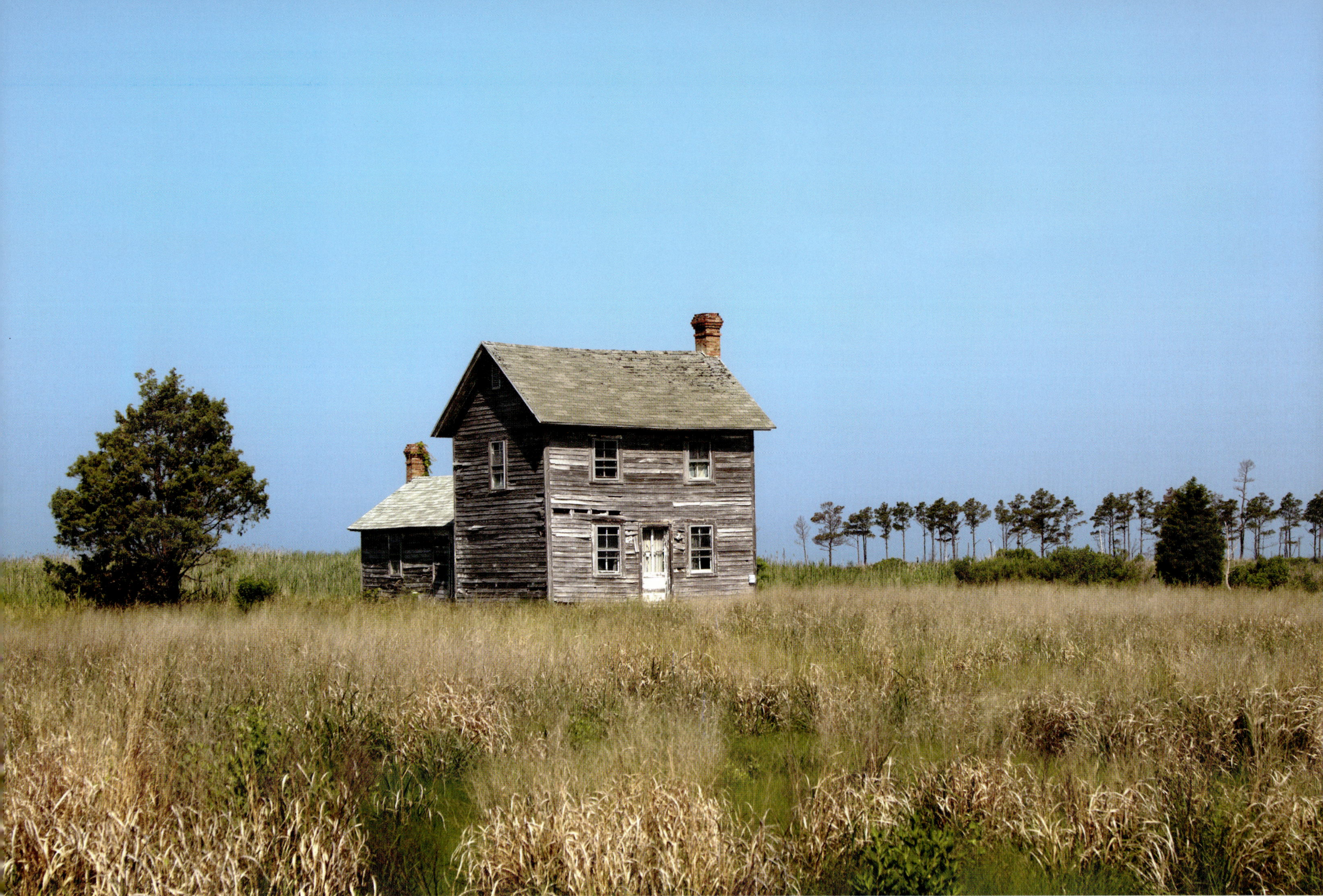

An abandoned home on Hooper's Island.

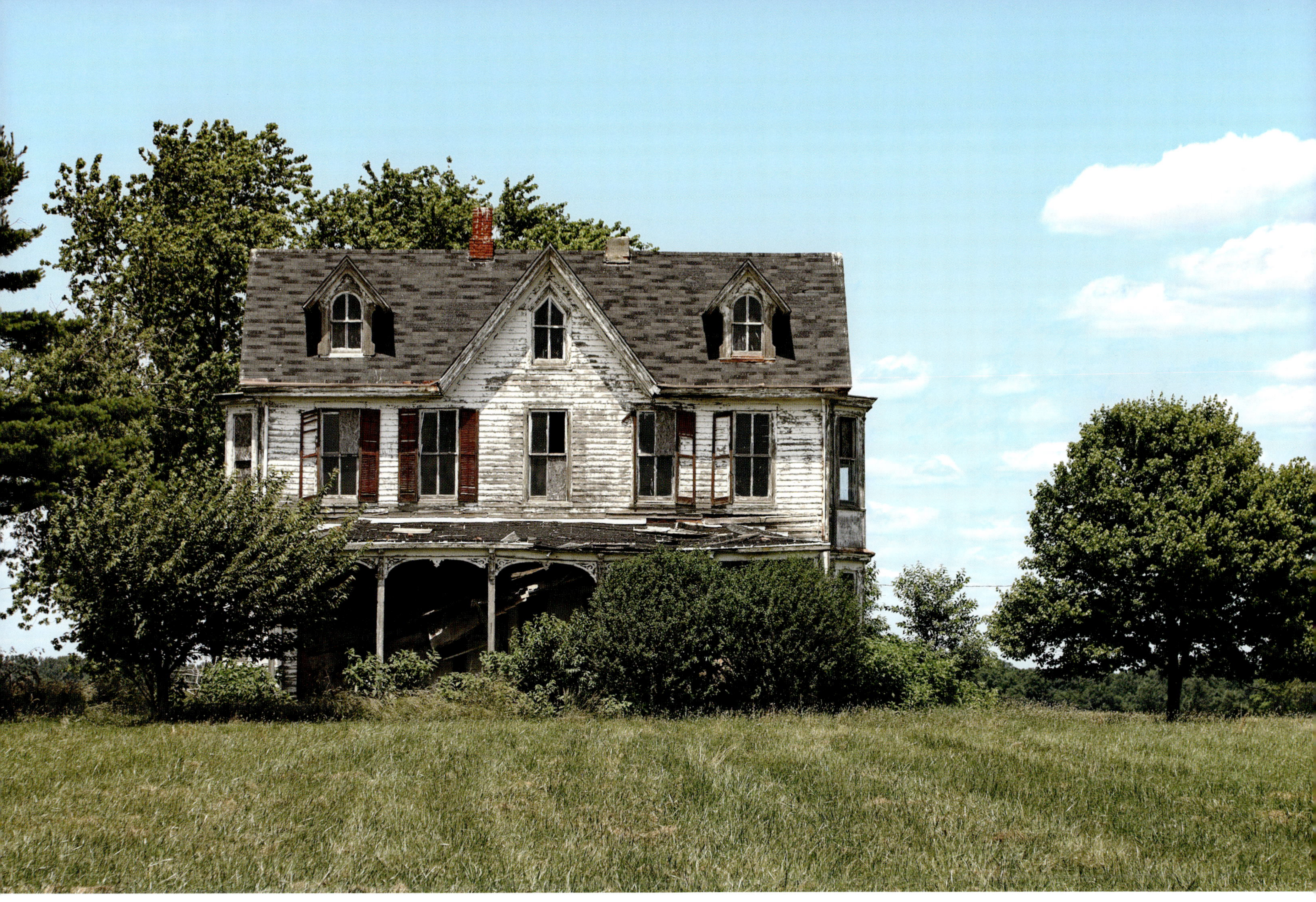

Time is not kind to the Bay watershed's wooden structures.

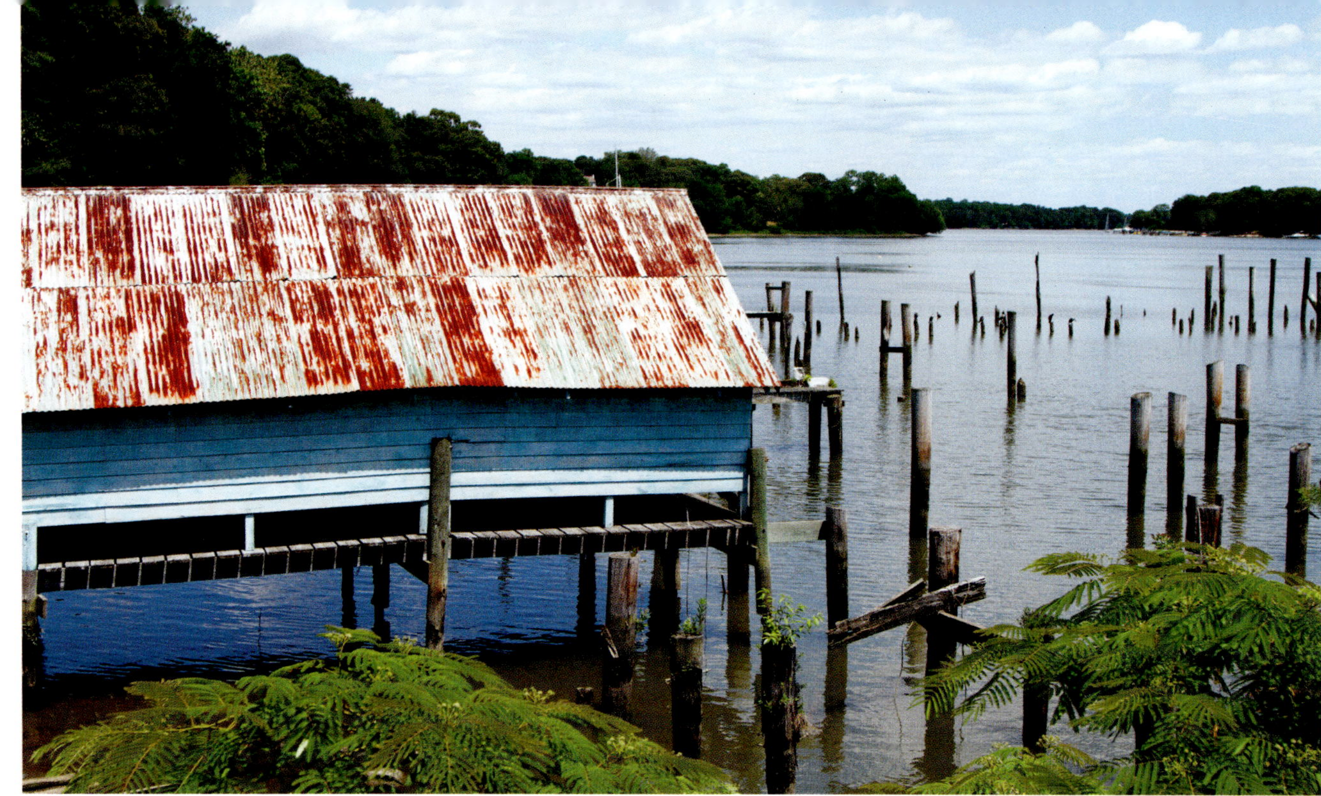

A boathouse on the Sassafras River near Georgetown, Maryland.

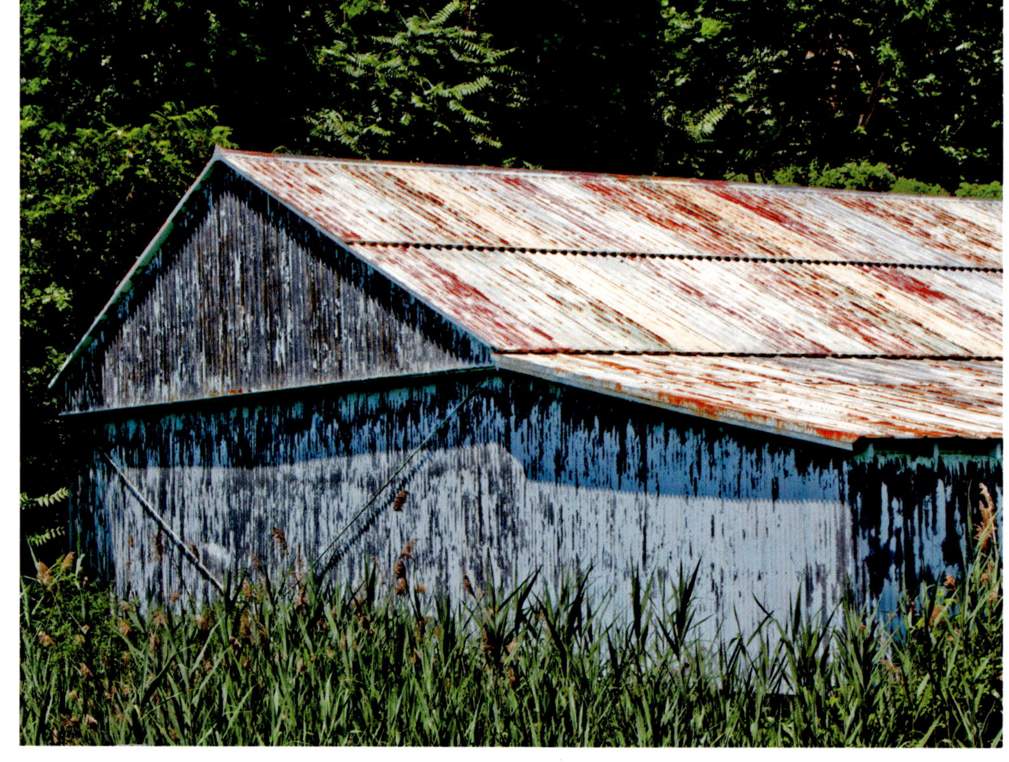

Sassafras River, Georgetown, Maryland

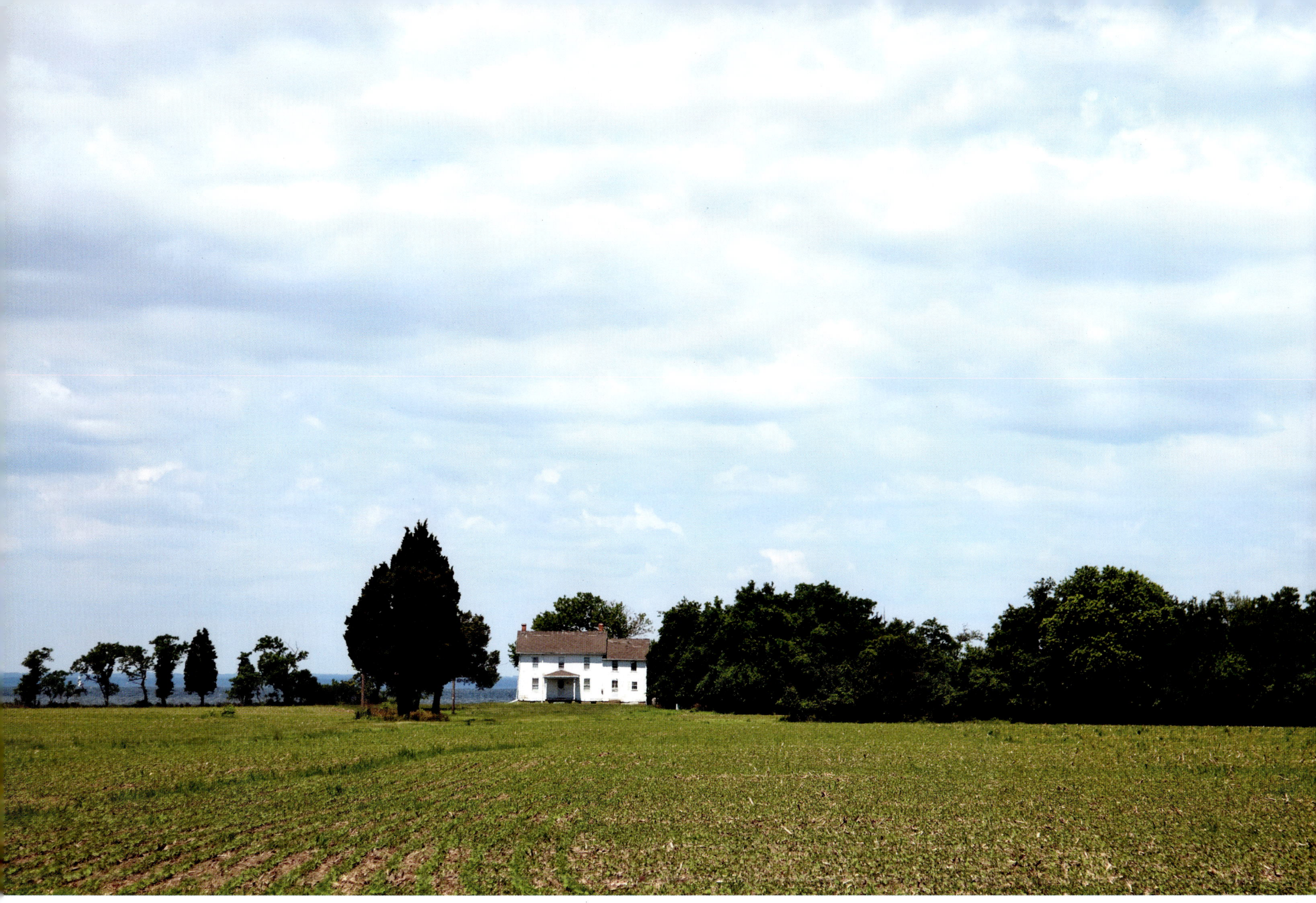

A lonely farmhouse on Maryland's Eastern Shore.

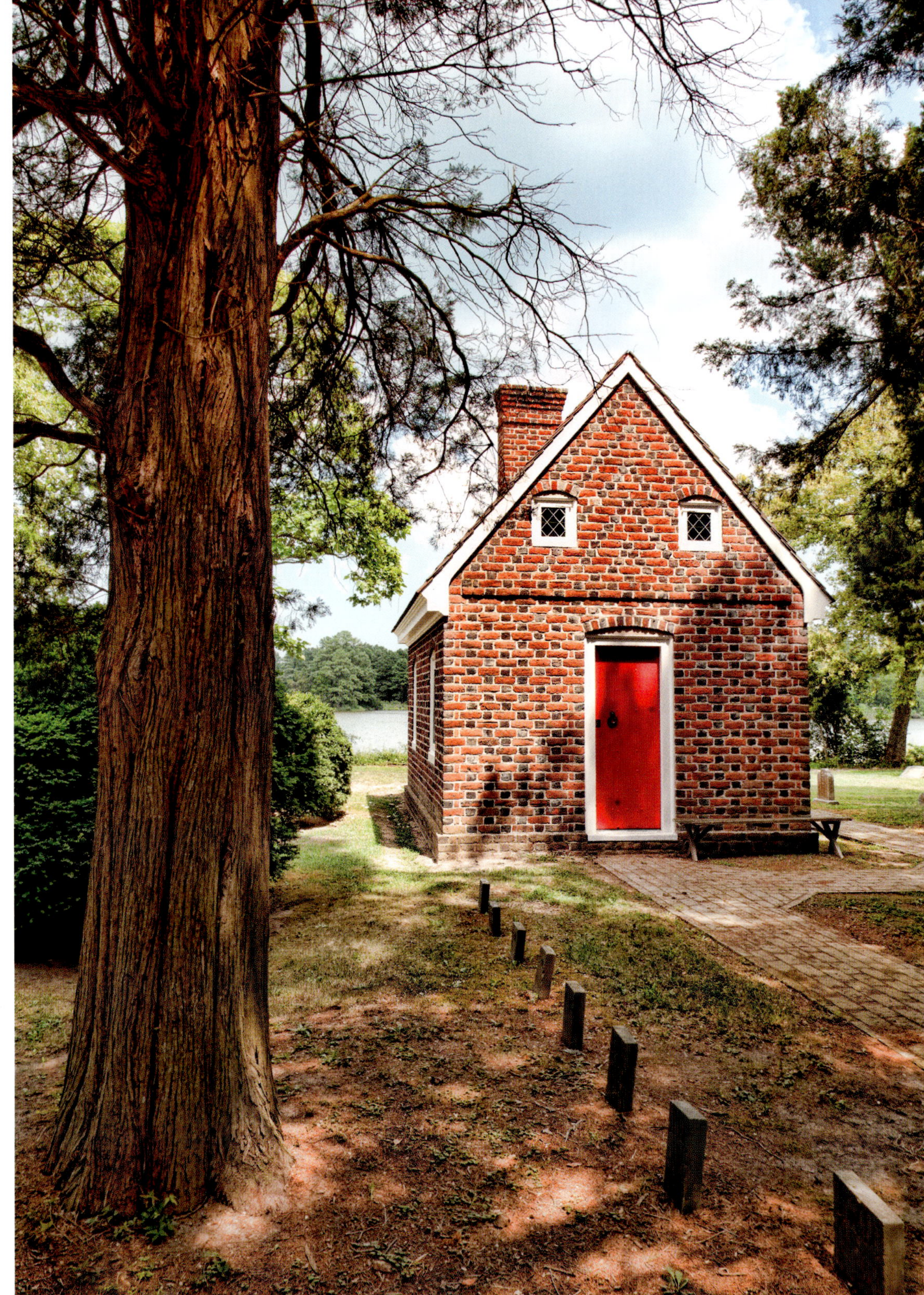

A waterside building on Old Trinity Church property in Church Creek, Maryland.

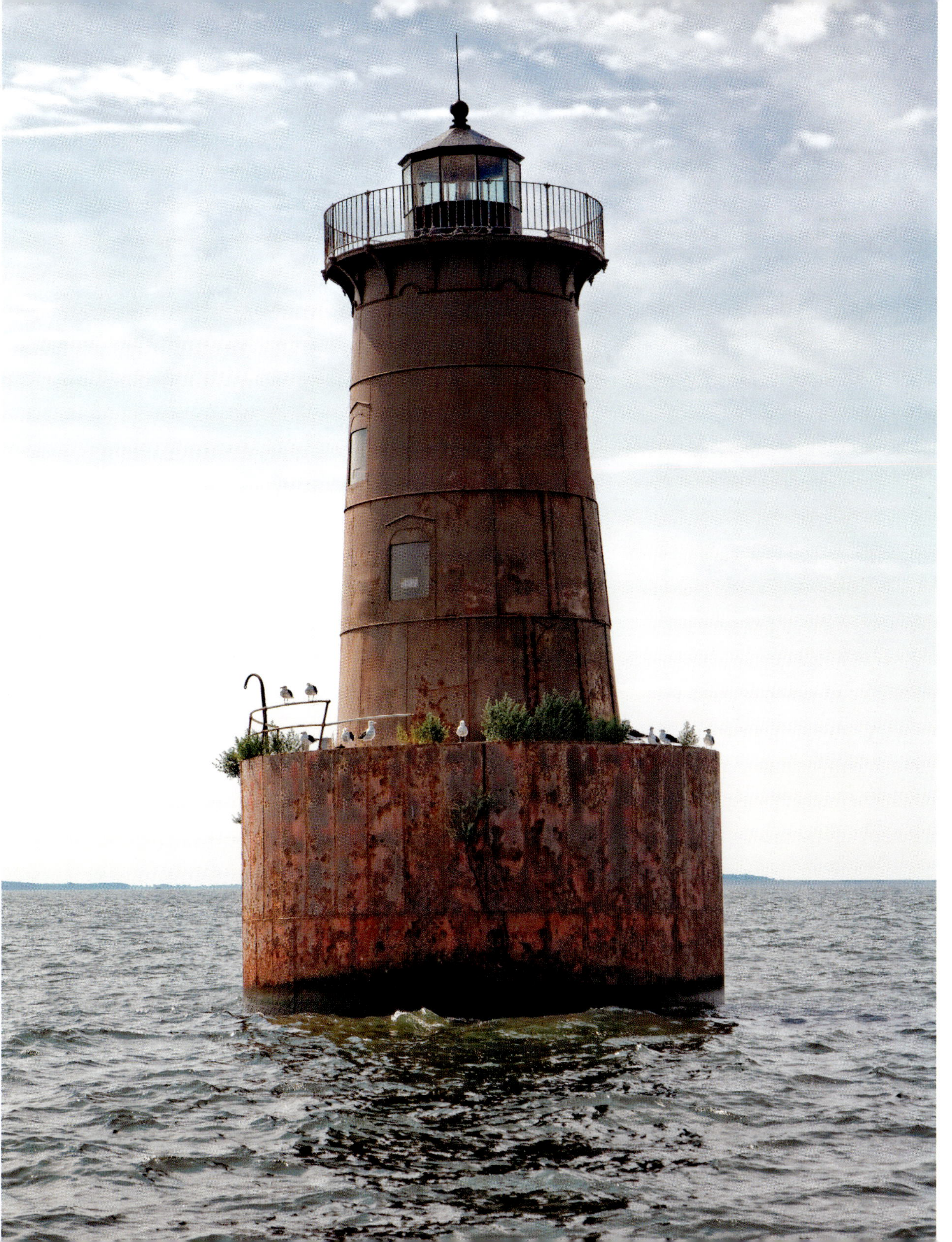

Bloody Point Bar Lighthouse near the southern tip of Kent Island.

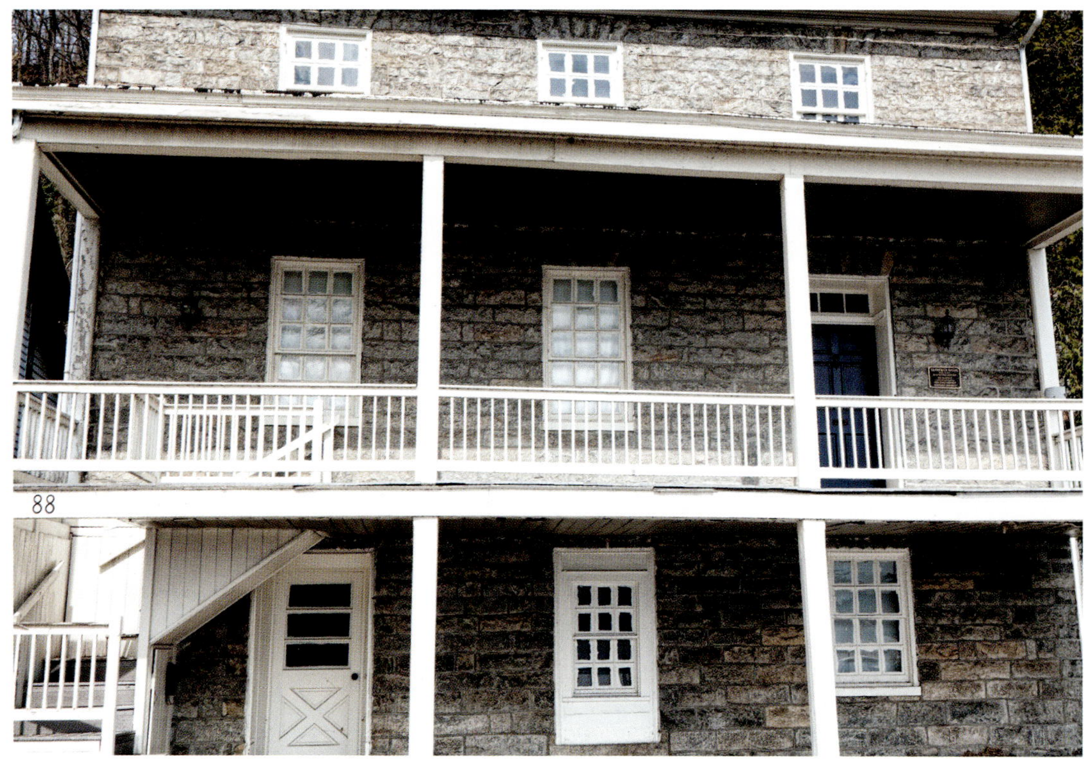



The Vanneman House in Port Deposit, Maryland, was built around 1814.

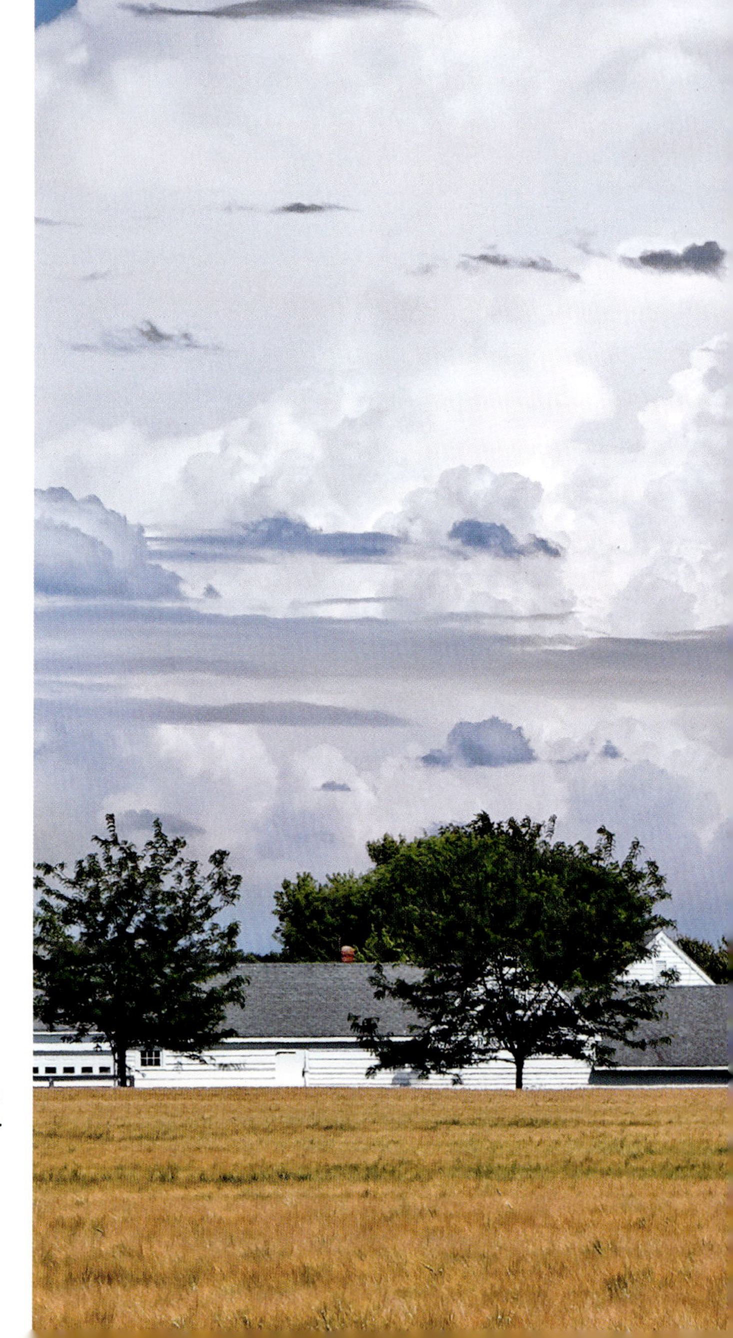

The Langdon Farm in Sherwood, Maryland.

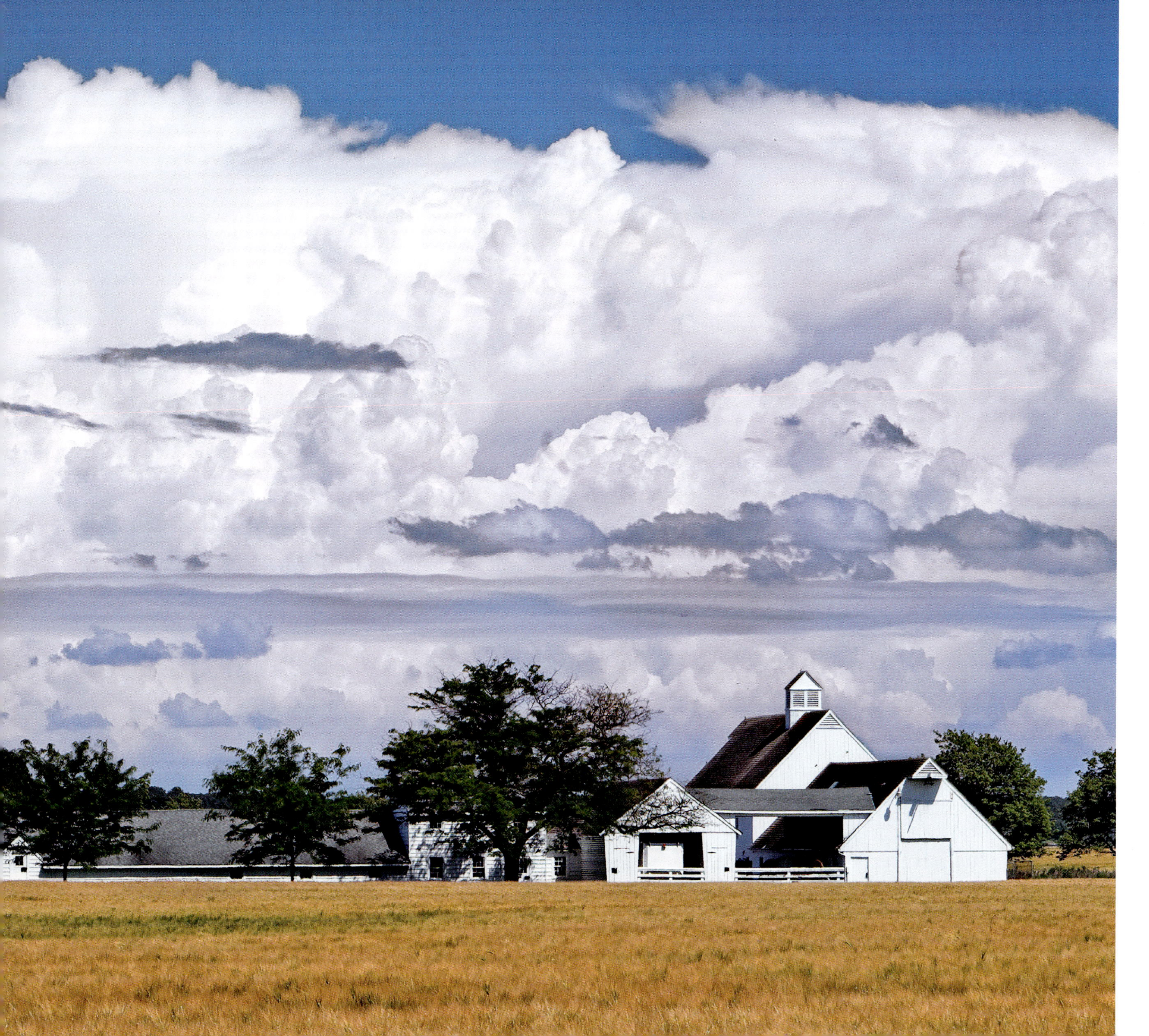

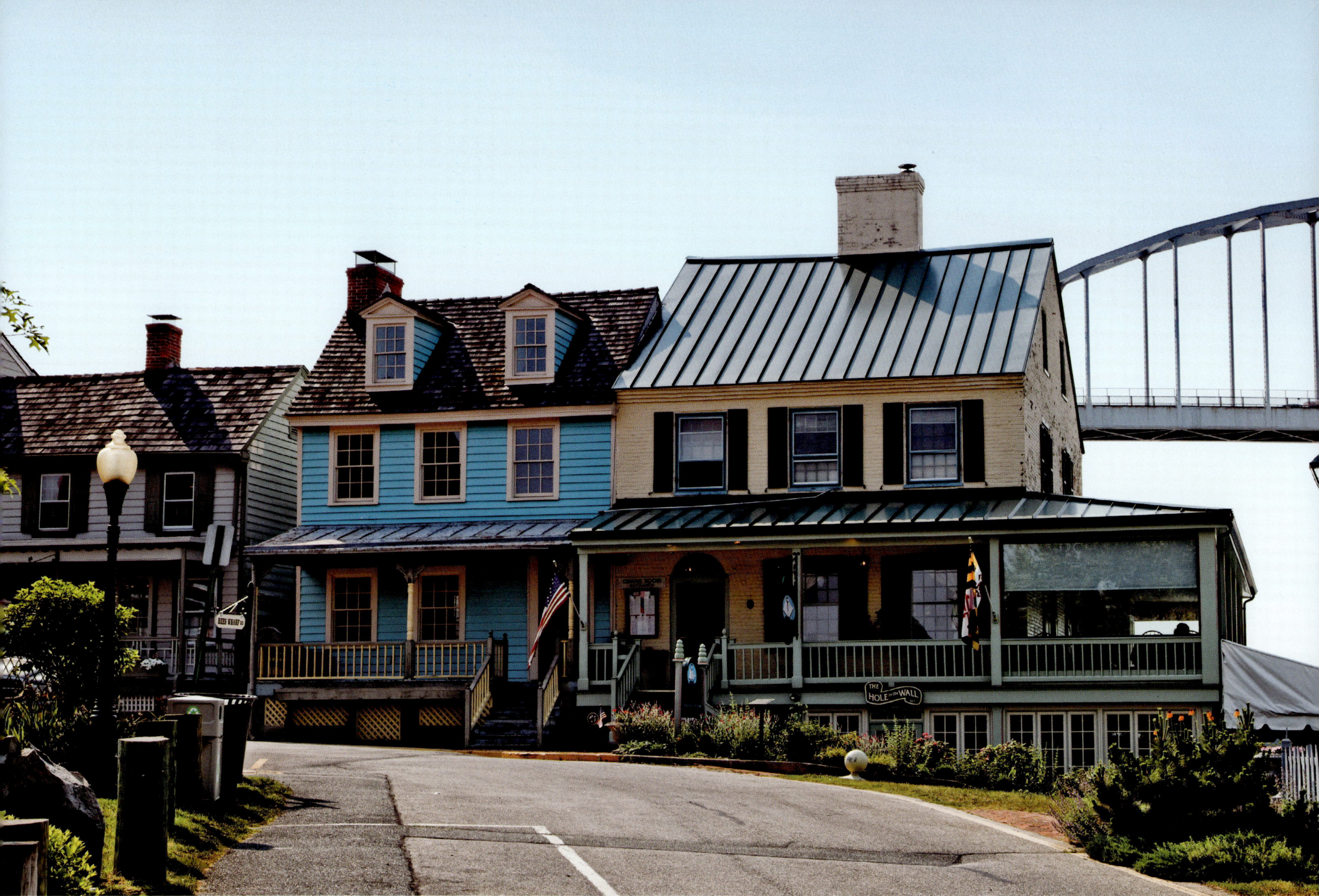


The Bayard House on the banks of the Chesapeake and Delaware Canal in historic Chesapeake City, Maryland.

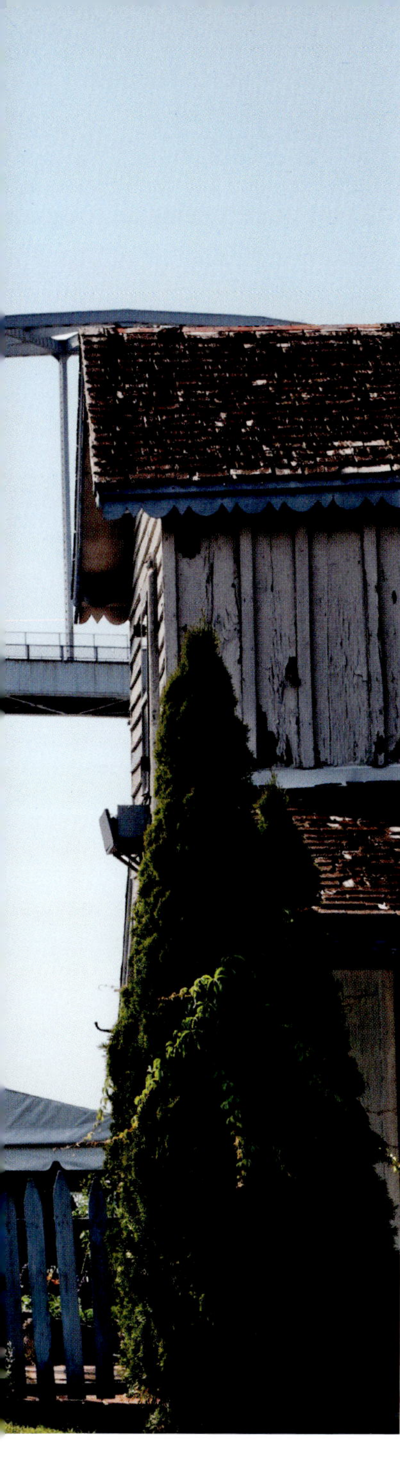

State Circle,
Annapolis, Maryland

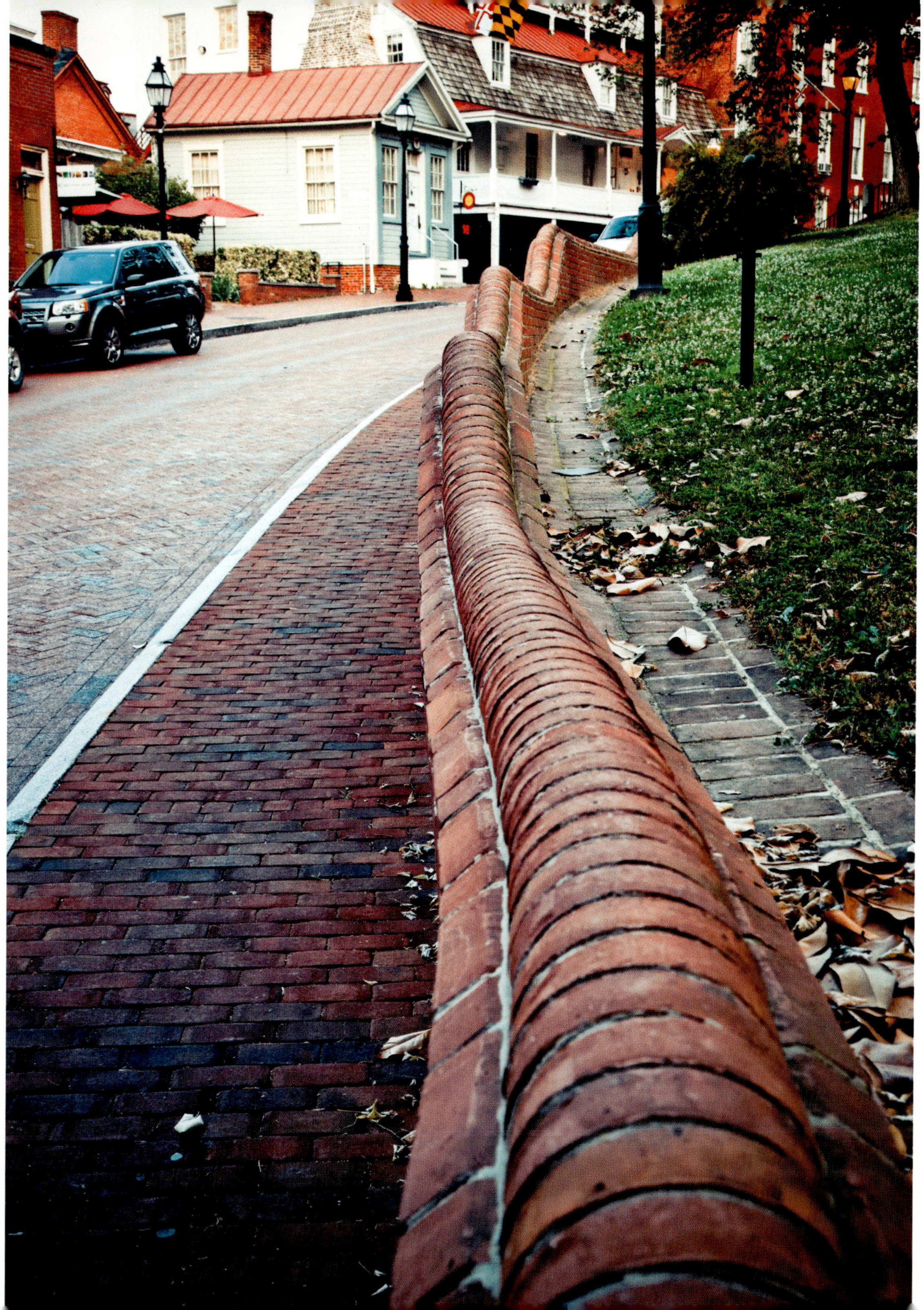

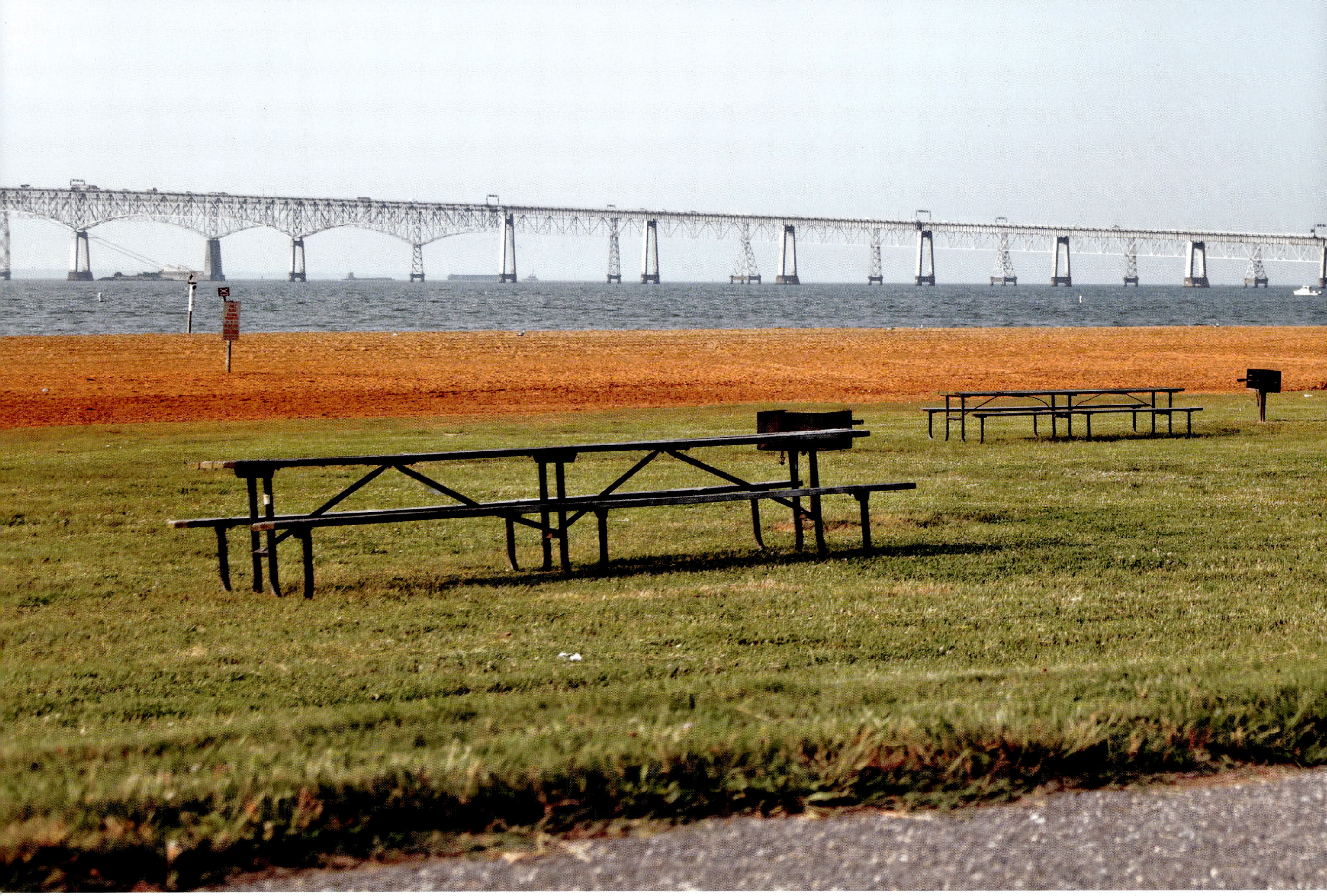

A view of the Bay Bridge from Sandy Point State Park.

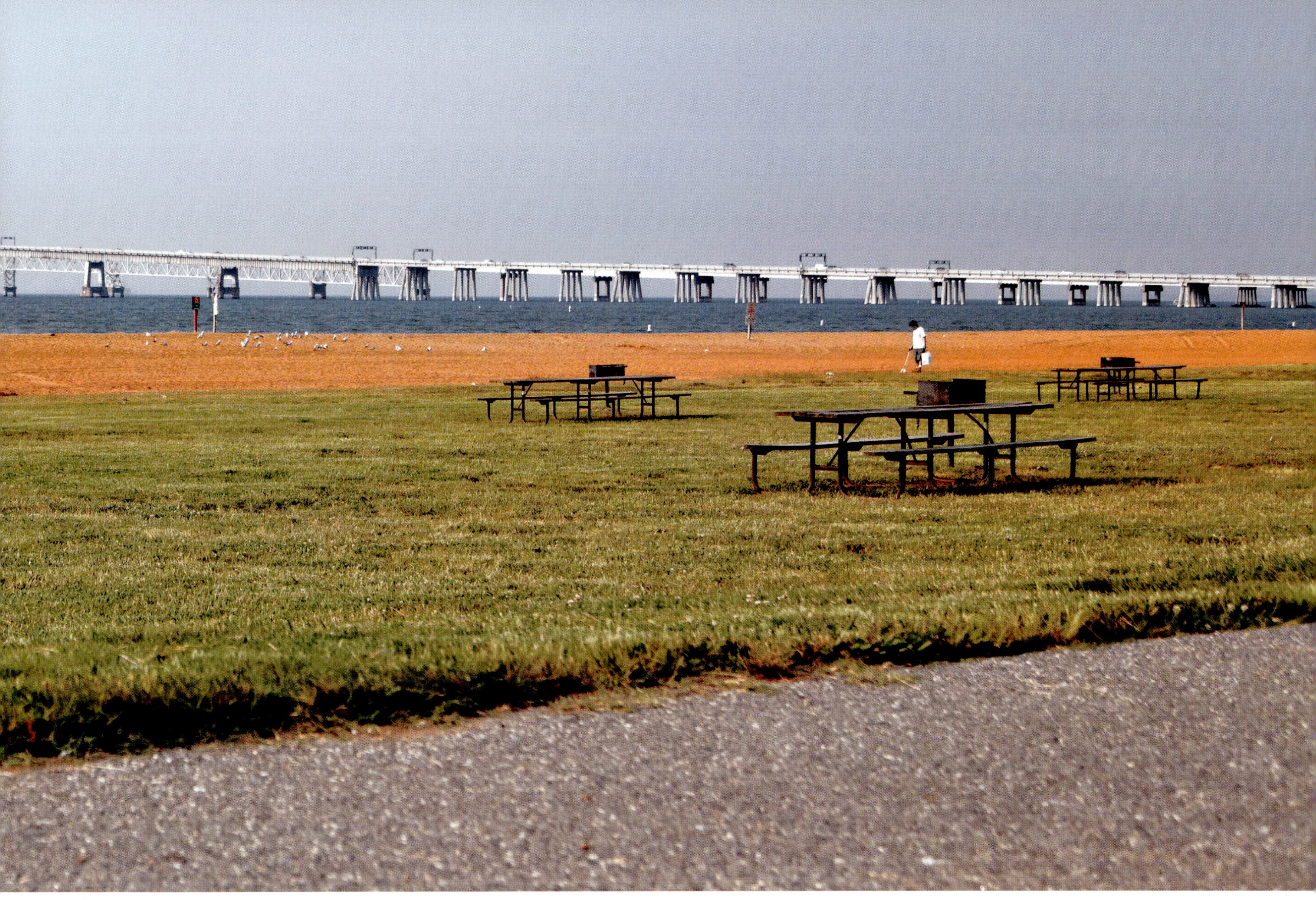

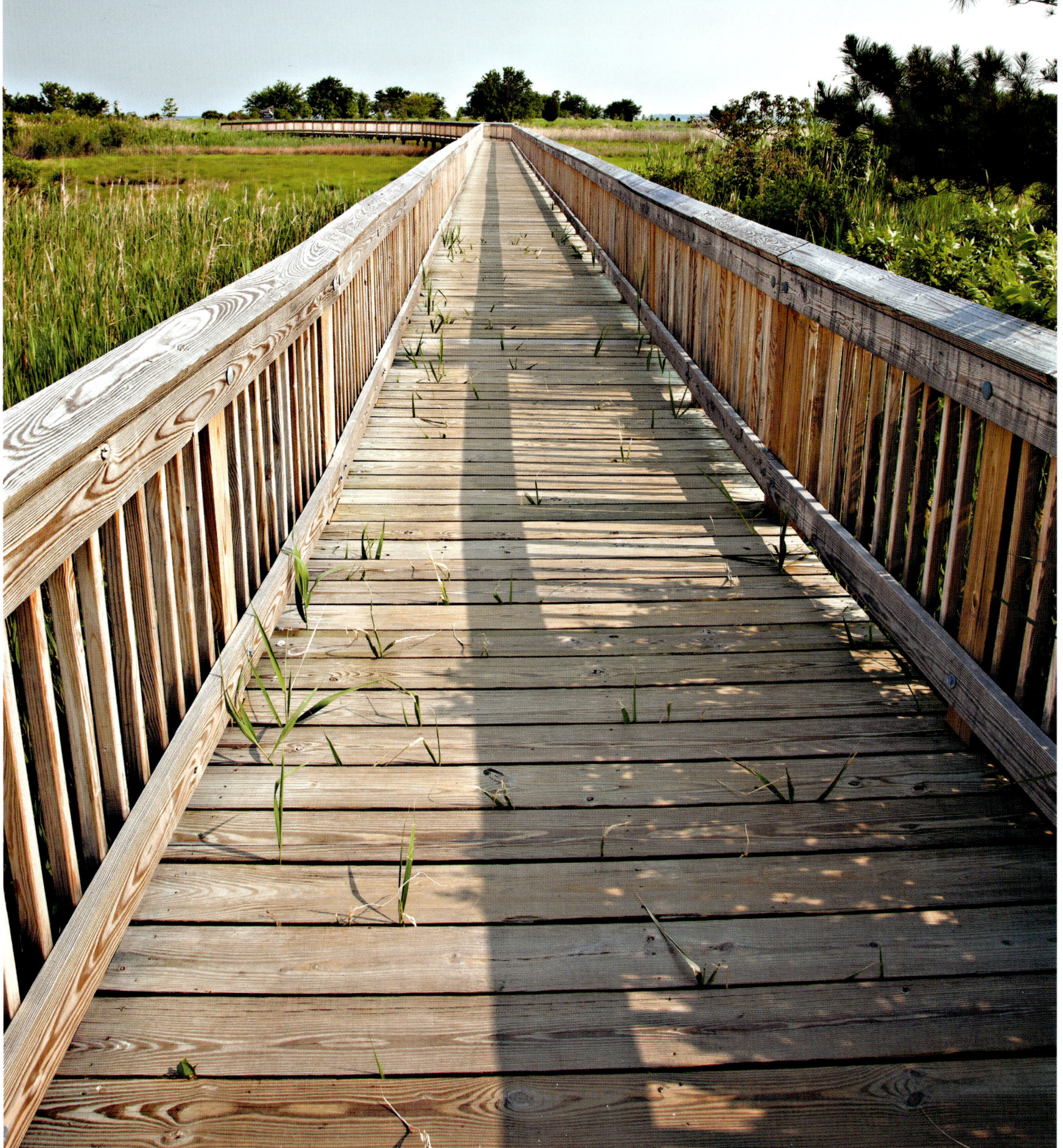

A boardwalk over the marsh at the Chesapeake Exploration Center on Kent Island.

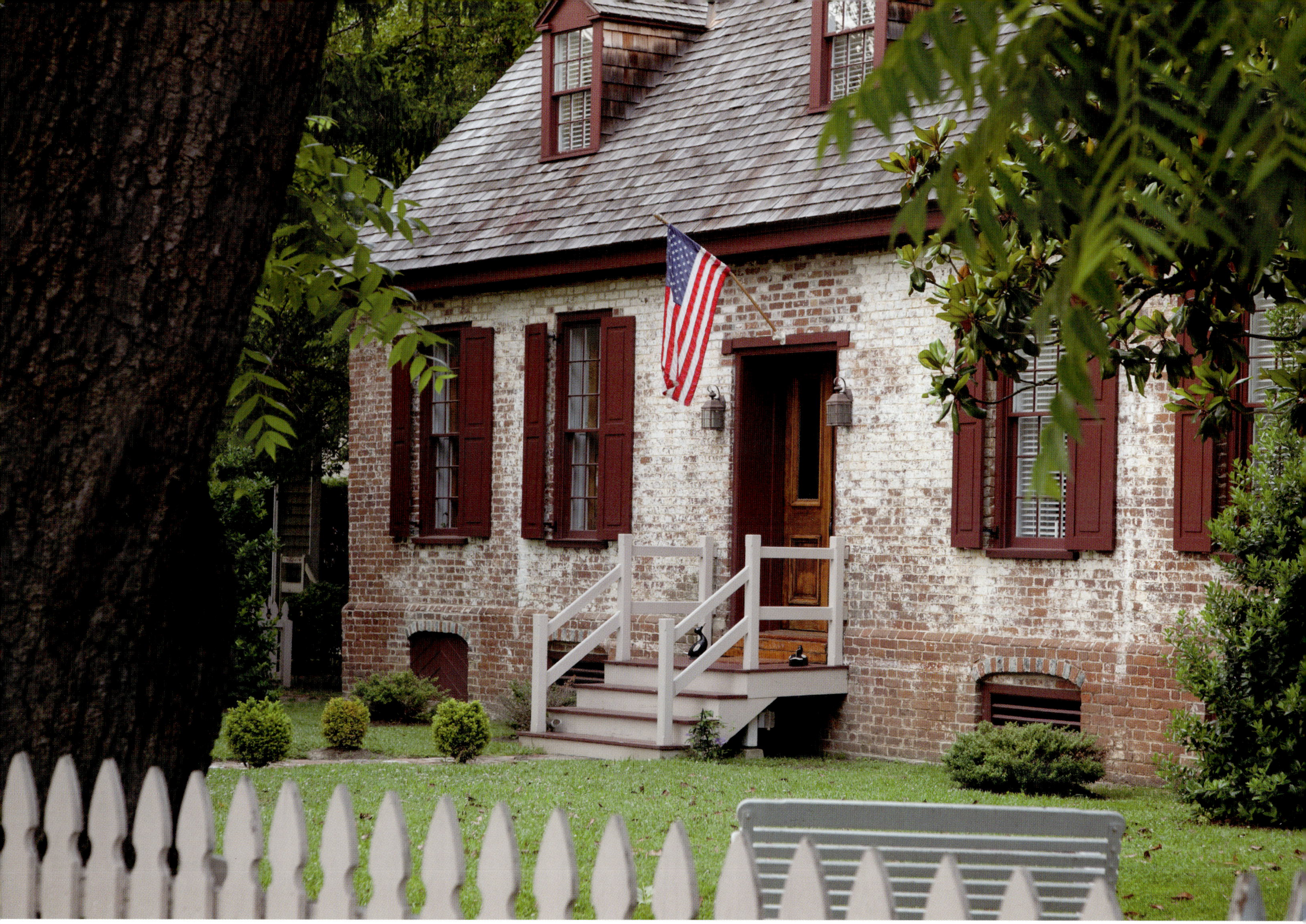

Locust Street in St. Michaels, Maryland.

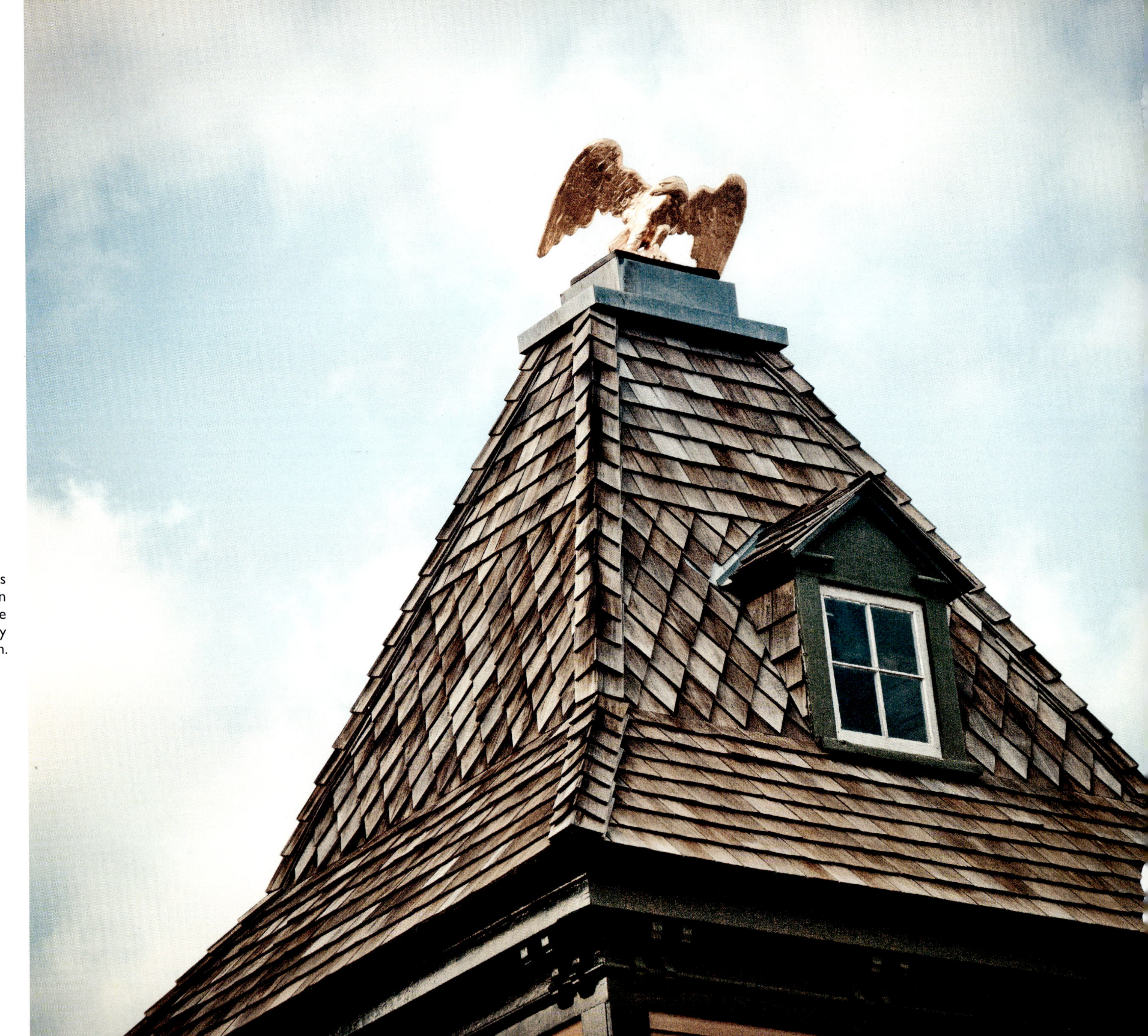

A golden eagle sits atop an administration building at the Chesapeake Bay Maritime Museum.

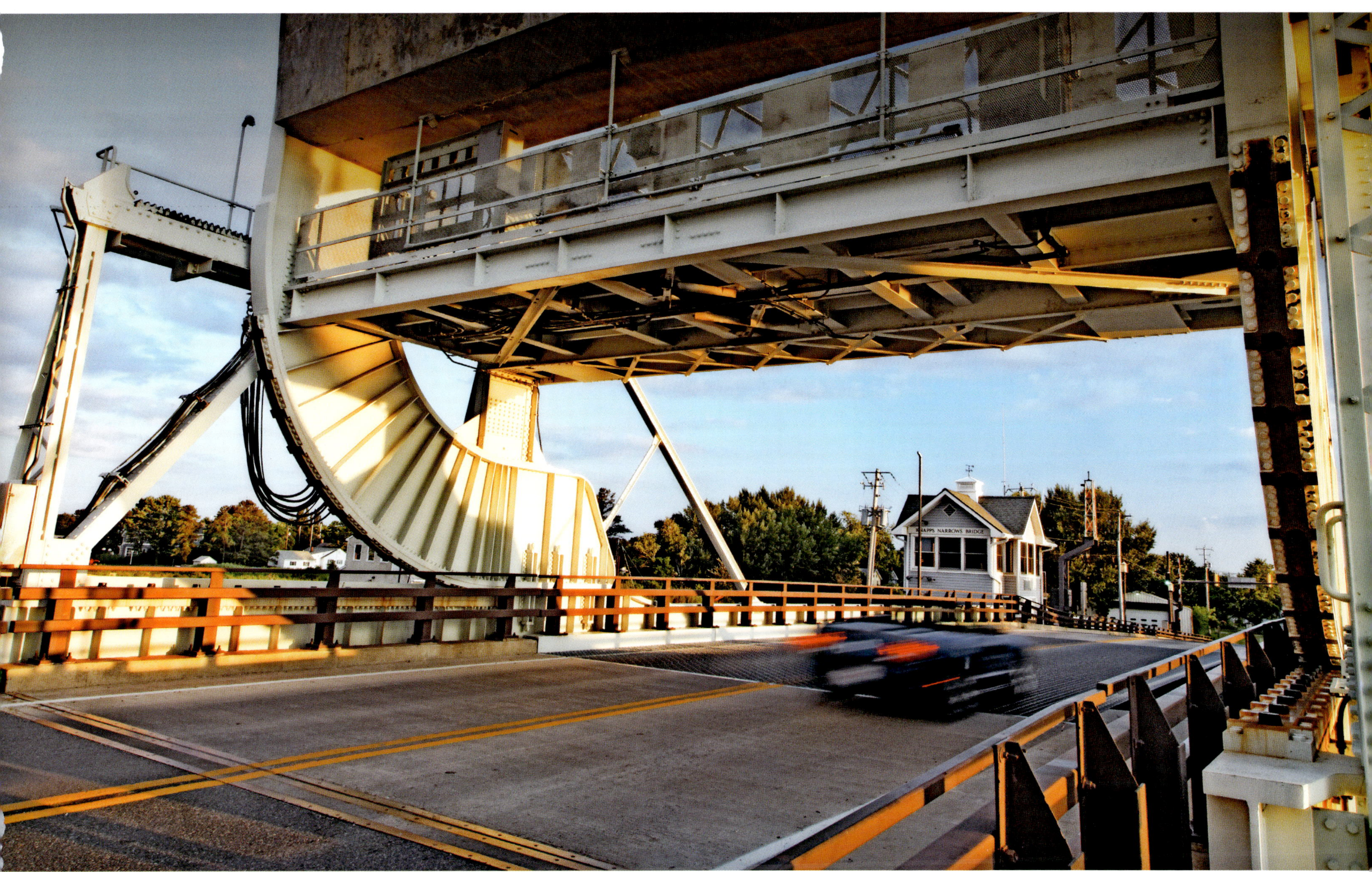


The bascule bridge over Knapp's Narrows, Tilghman, Maryland.

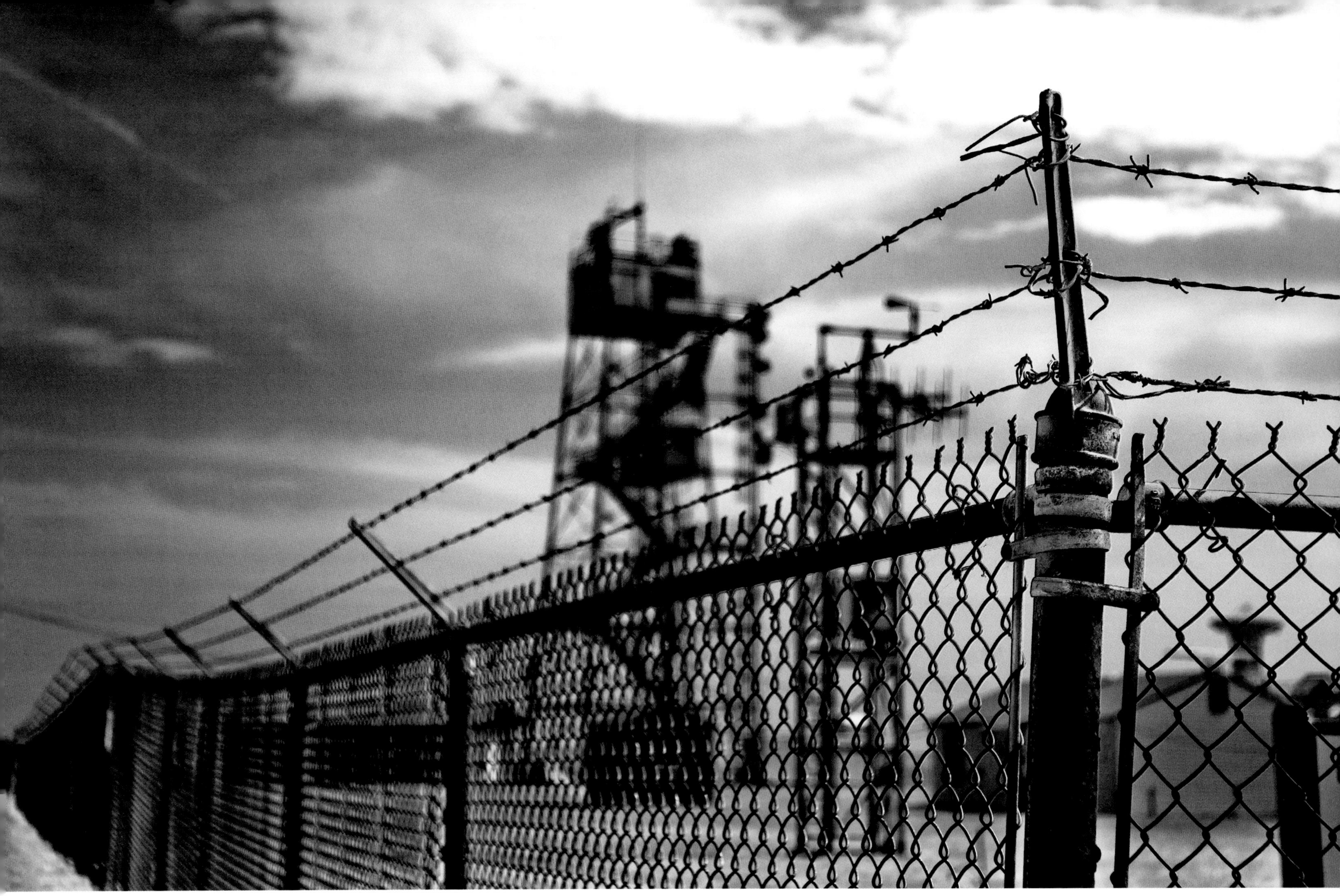

The Naval Research Laboratory near the end of Tilghman Island has been used since 1941 to reflect radar and laser signals across the Bay.

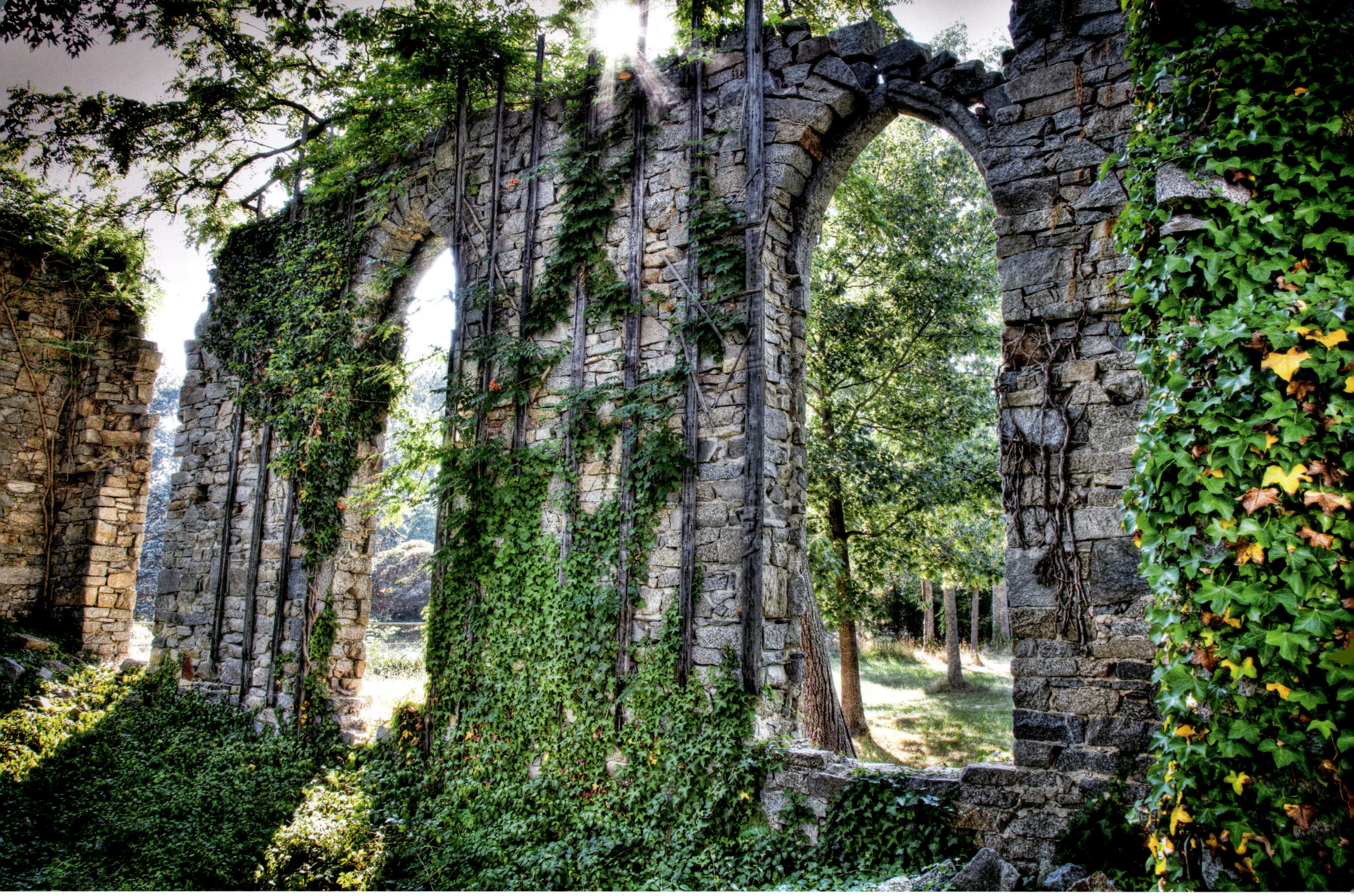

Located too close to the water, this 1830s-era church continues to crumble.

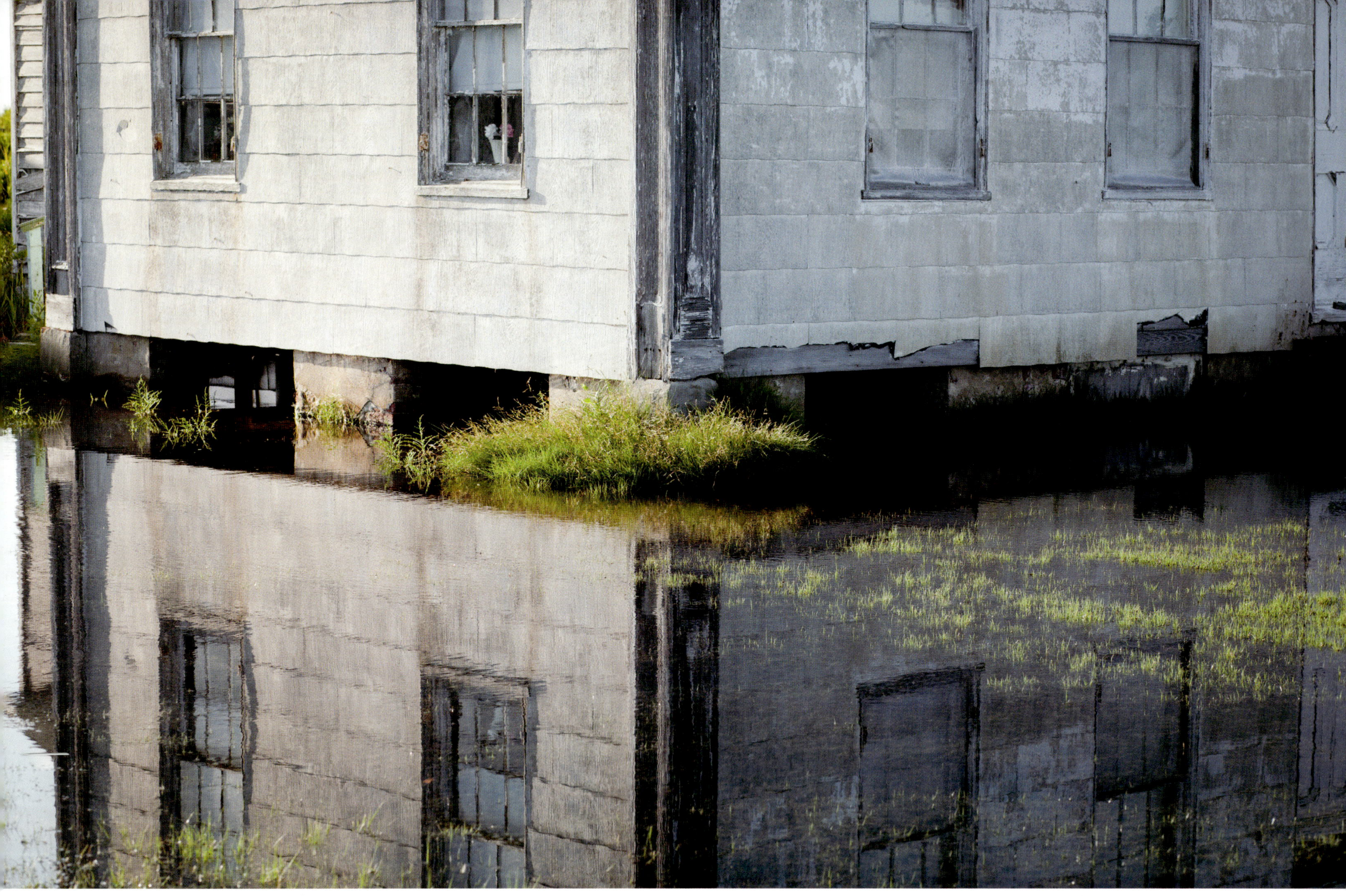

Many home yards near the edges of Smith Island are no stranger to encroachment by the Bay.

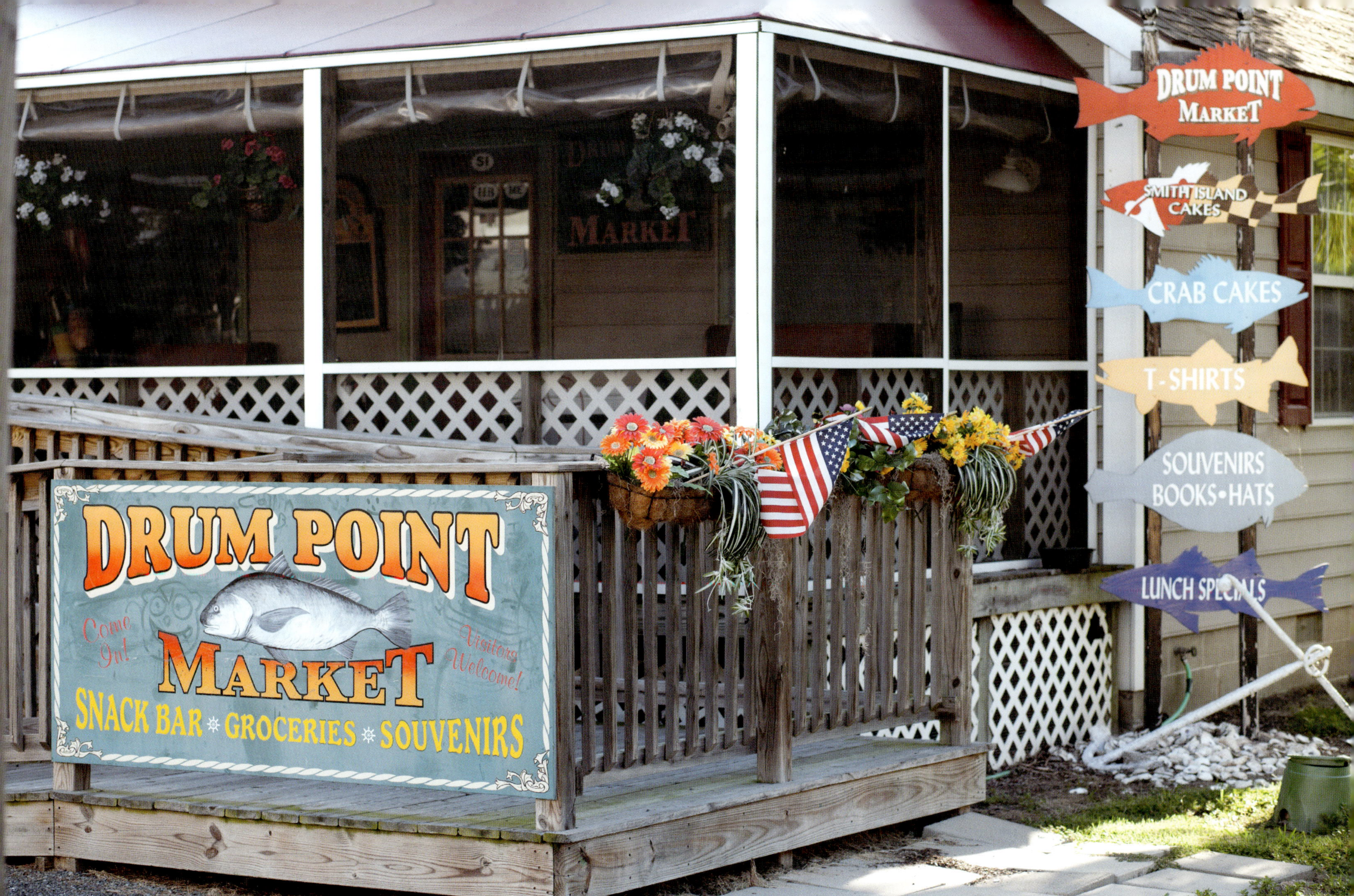


Tasty crabcakes can be had at Drum Point Market in Tylerton.

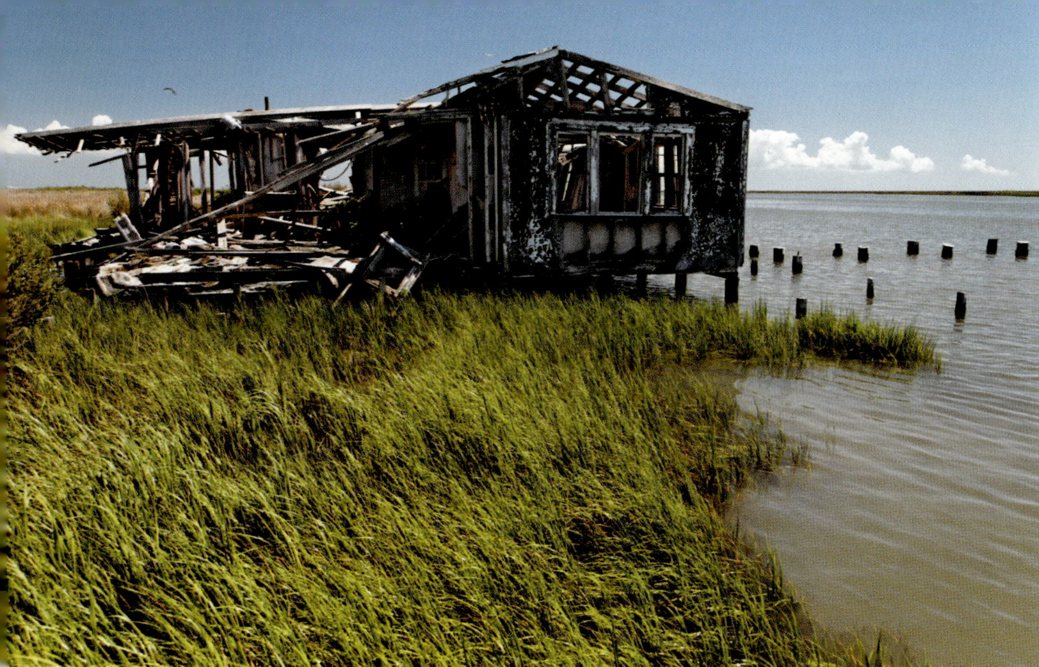

An abandoned lodge on Smith Island.

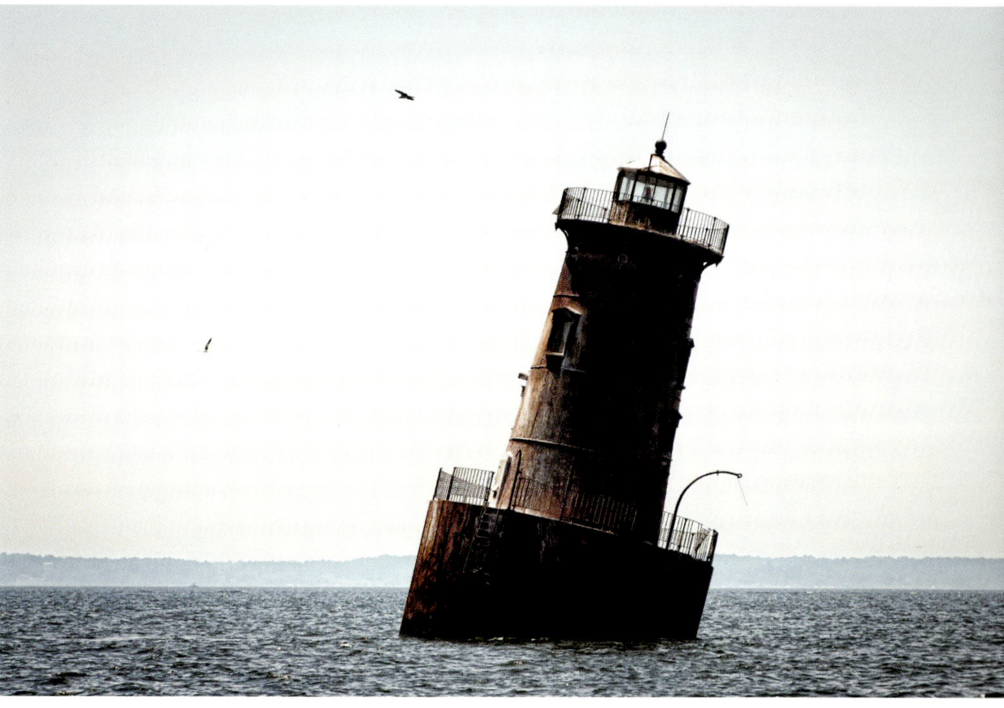

At the mouth of the Choptank River, Sharps Island Lighthouse has been leaning 15 degrees to the north since the Bay ice pushed it over in 1978.

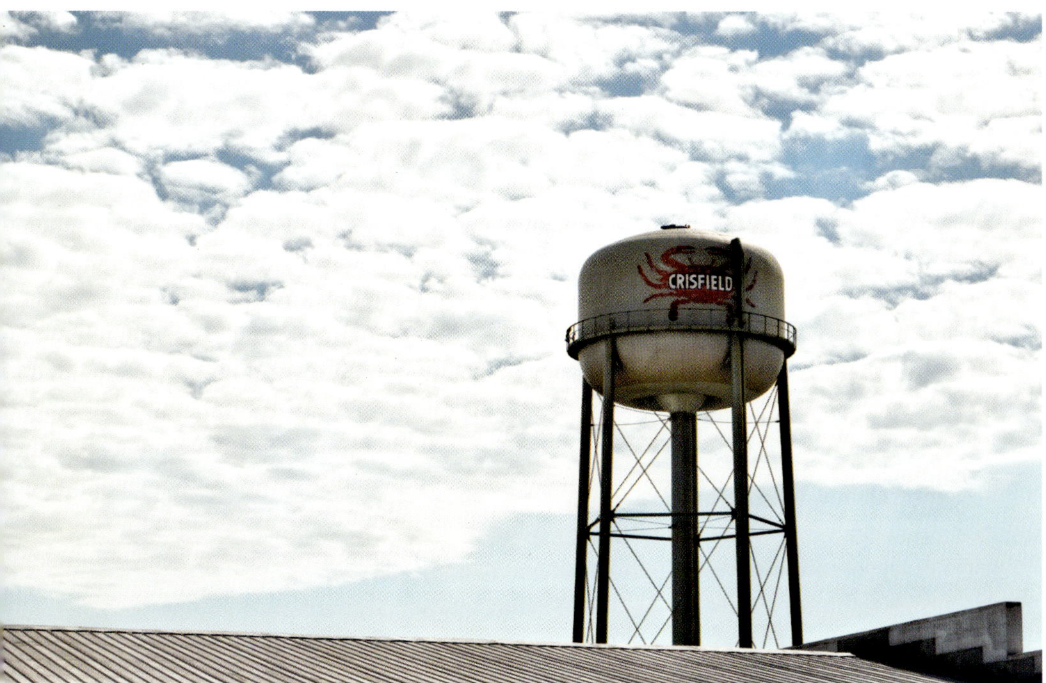


The water tower in Crisfield, Maryland.

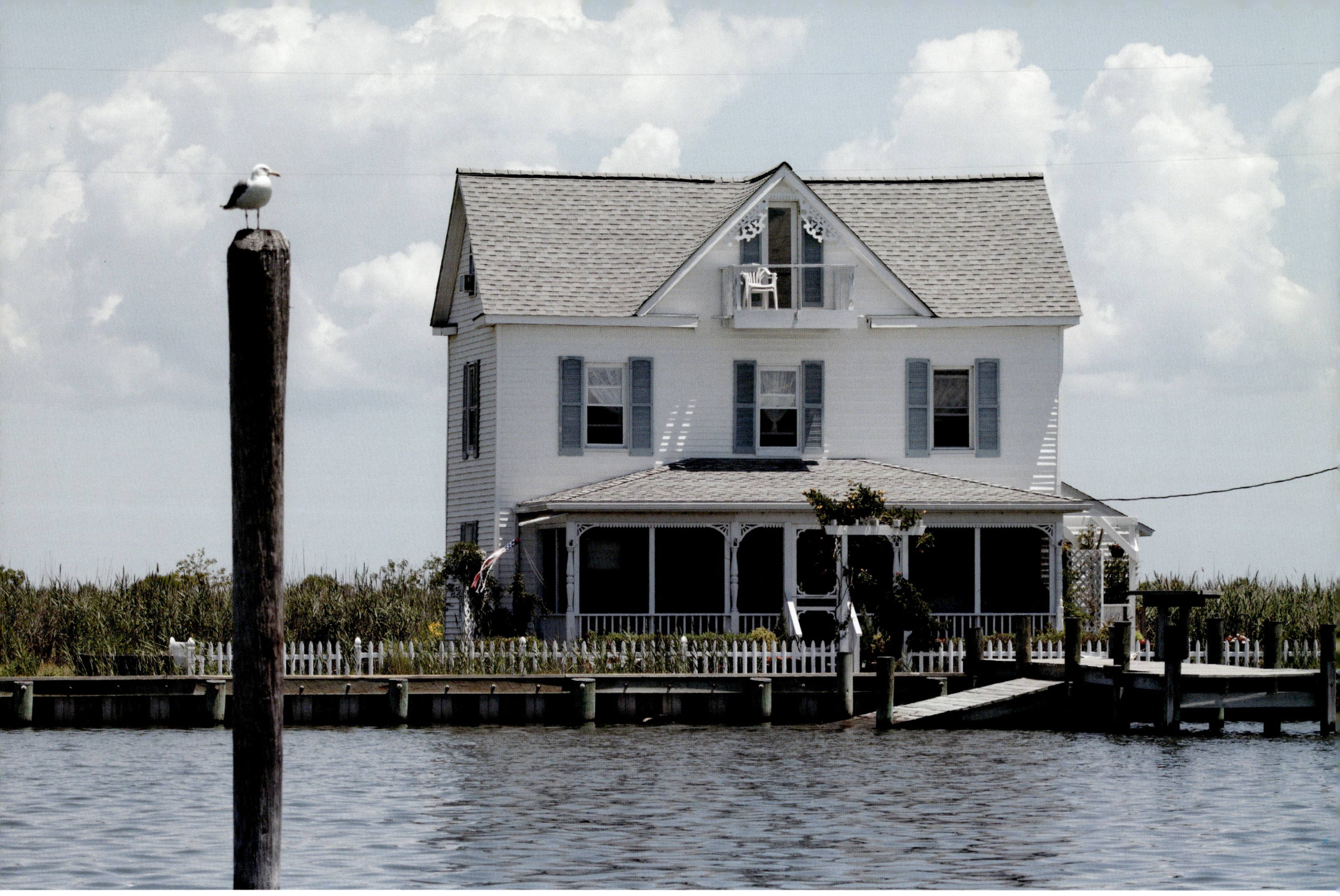

The Inn of Silent Music in Tylerton on Smith Island
is surrounded by water on three sides.

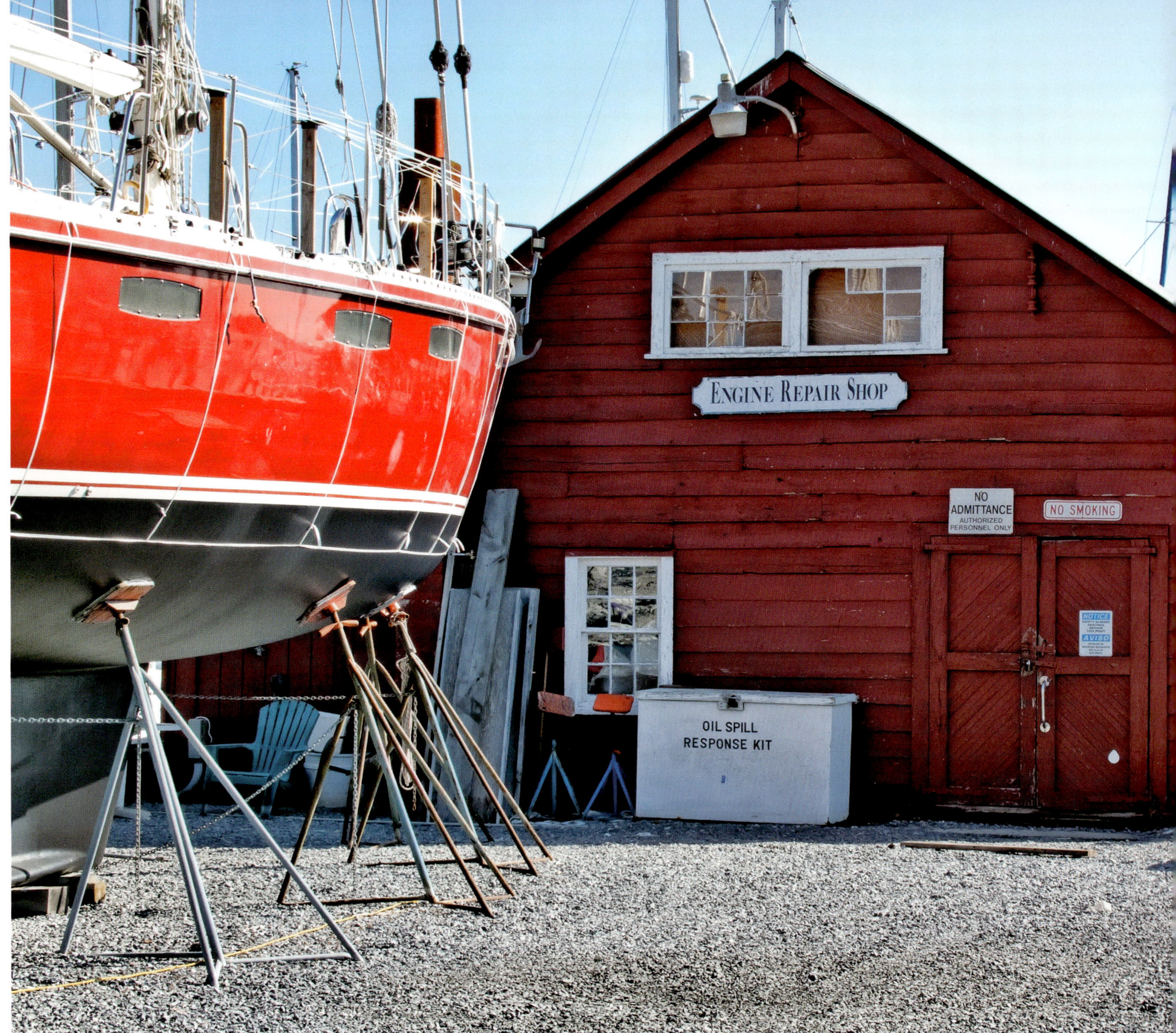


Engine Repair Shop in Oxford, Maryland.

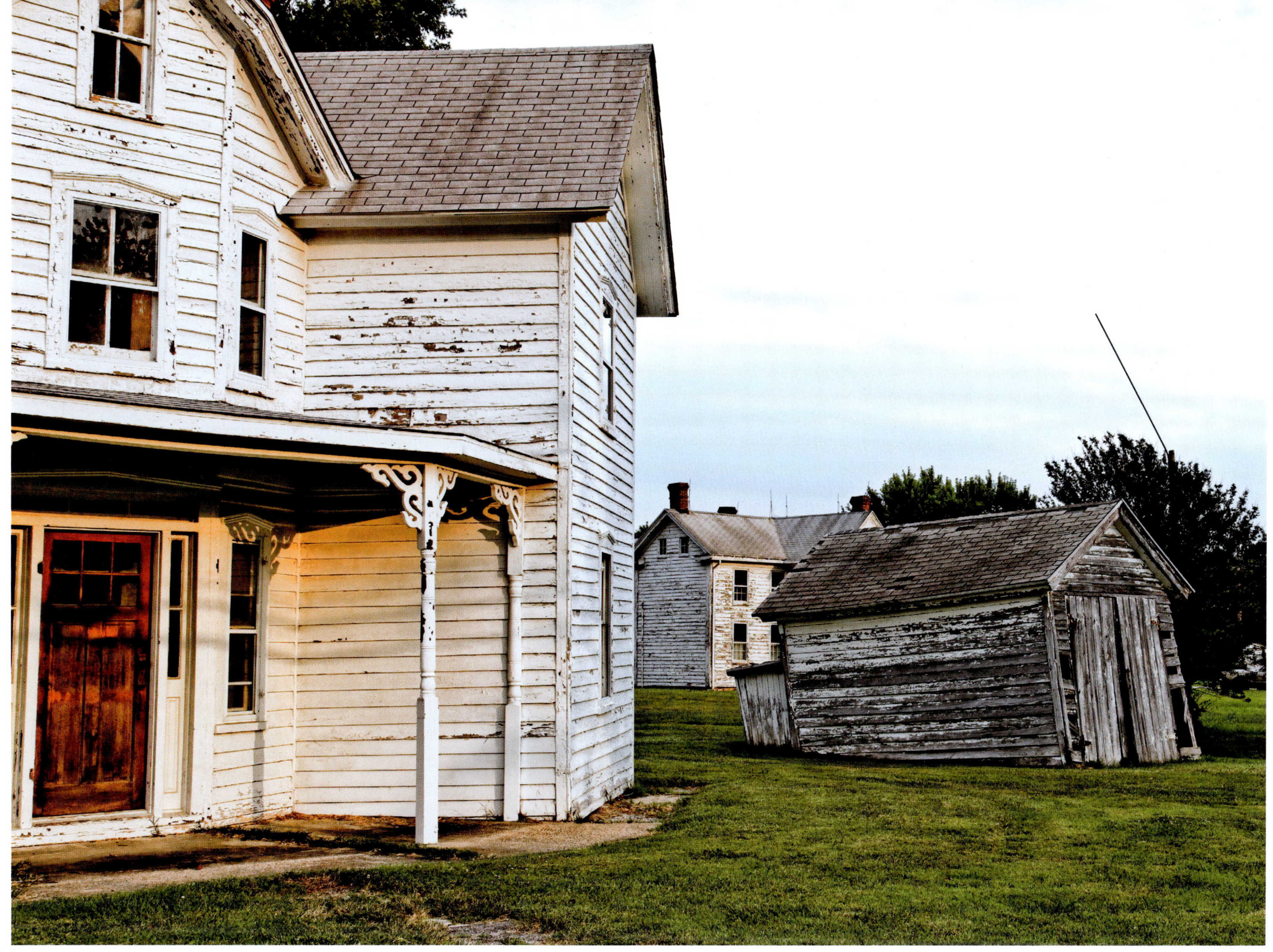

The Lee House on Tilghman Island, built circa 1890.

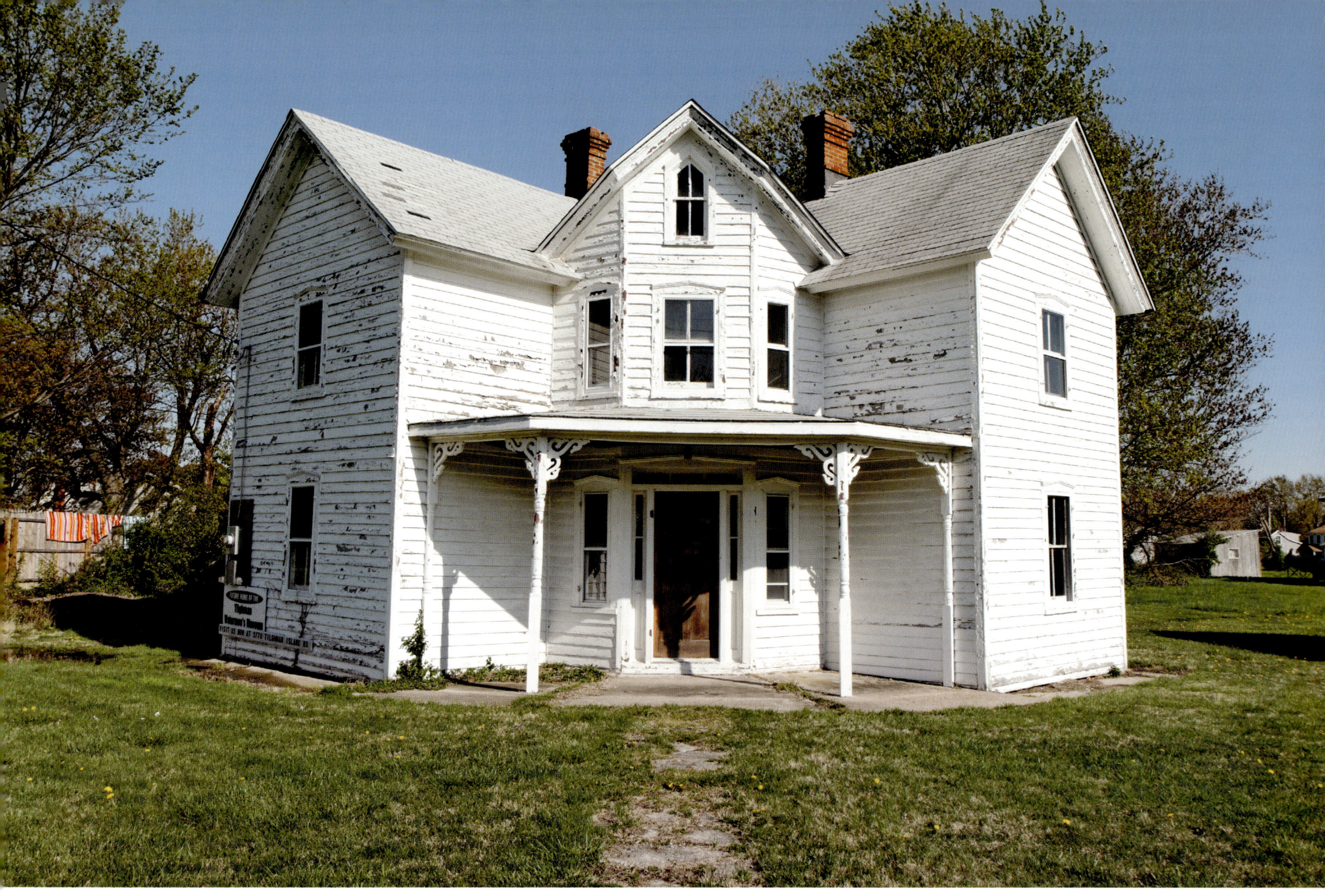

The Lee House, one of seven remaining examples of this unique design, is said to catch the breeze from any direction.

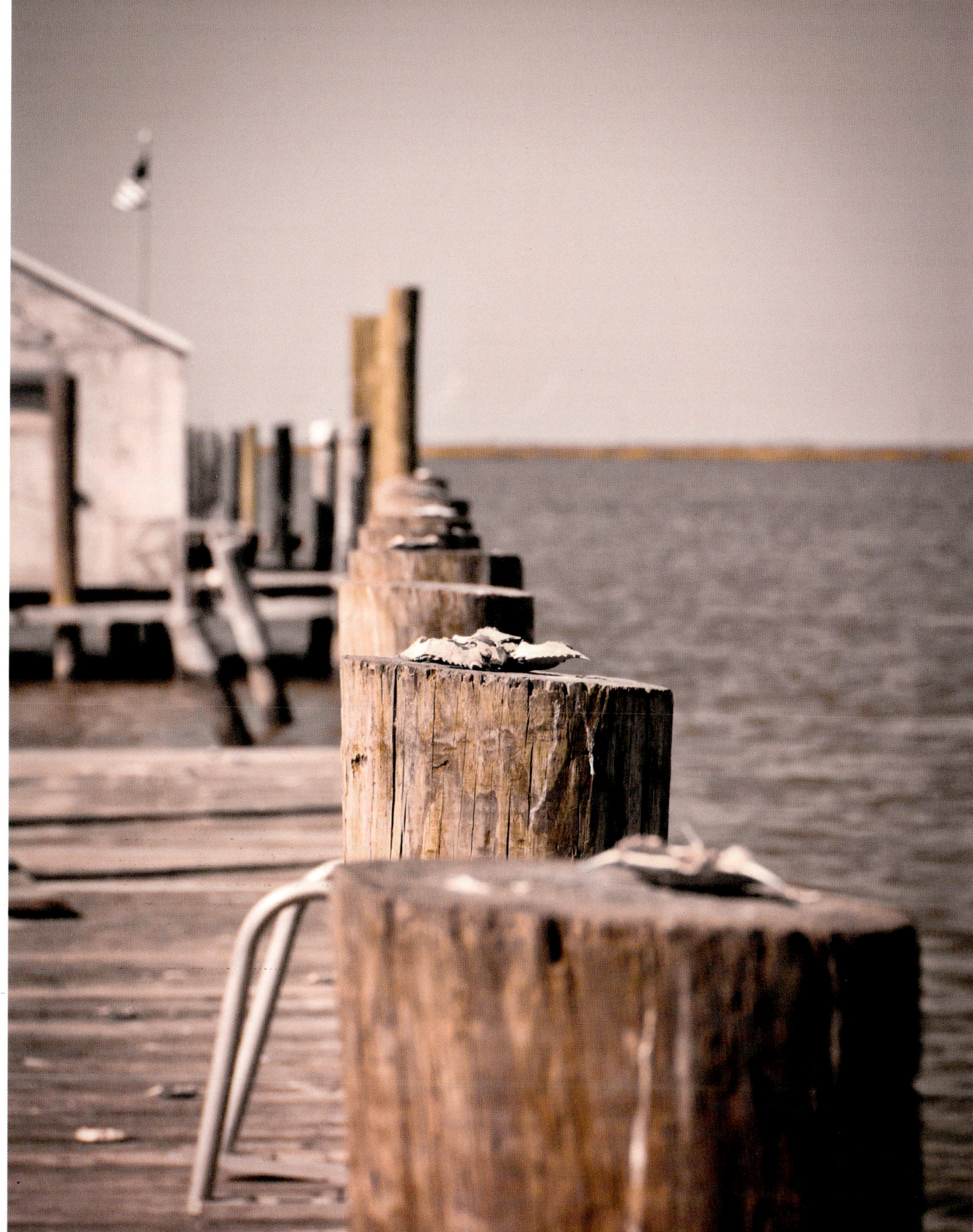

Blue crab shells top the pilings along the pier on Tylerton, Smith Island.

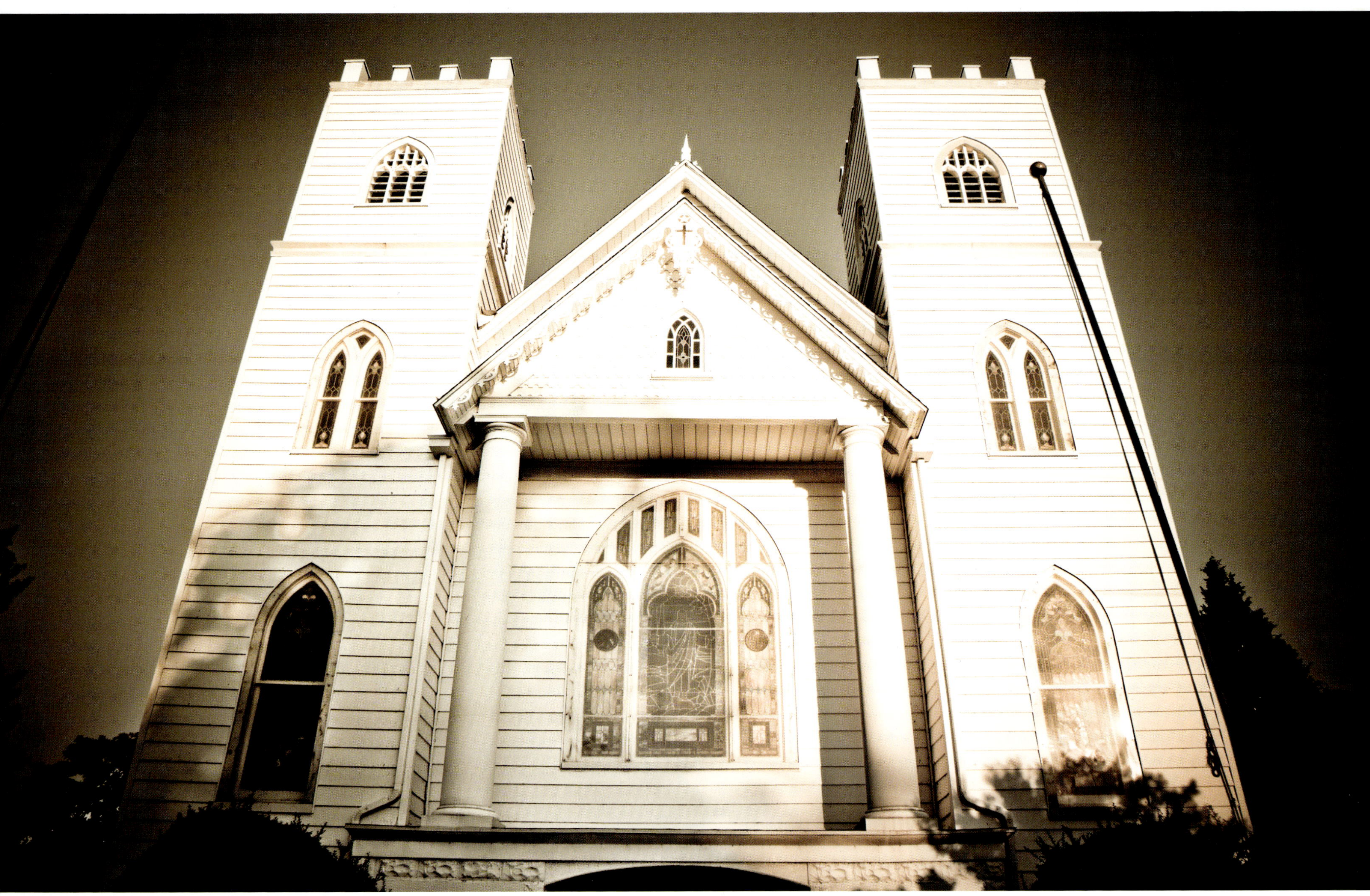

Tylerton's Methodist Church

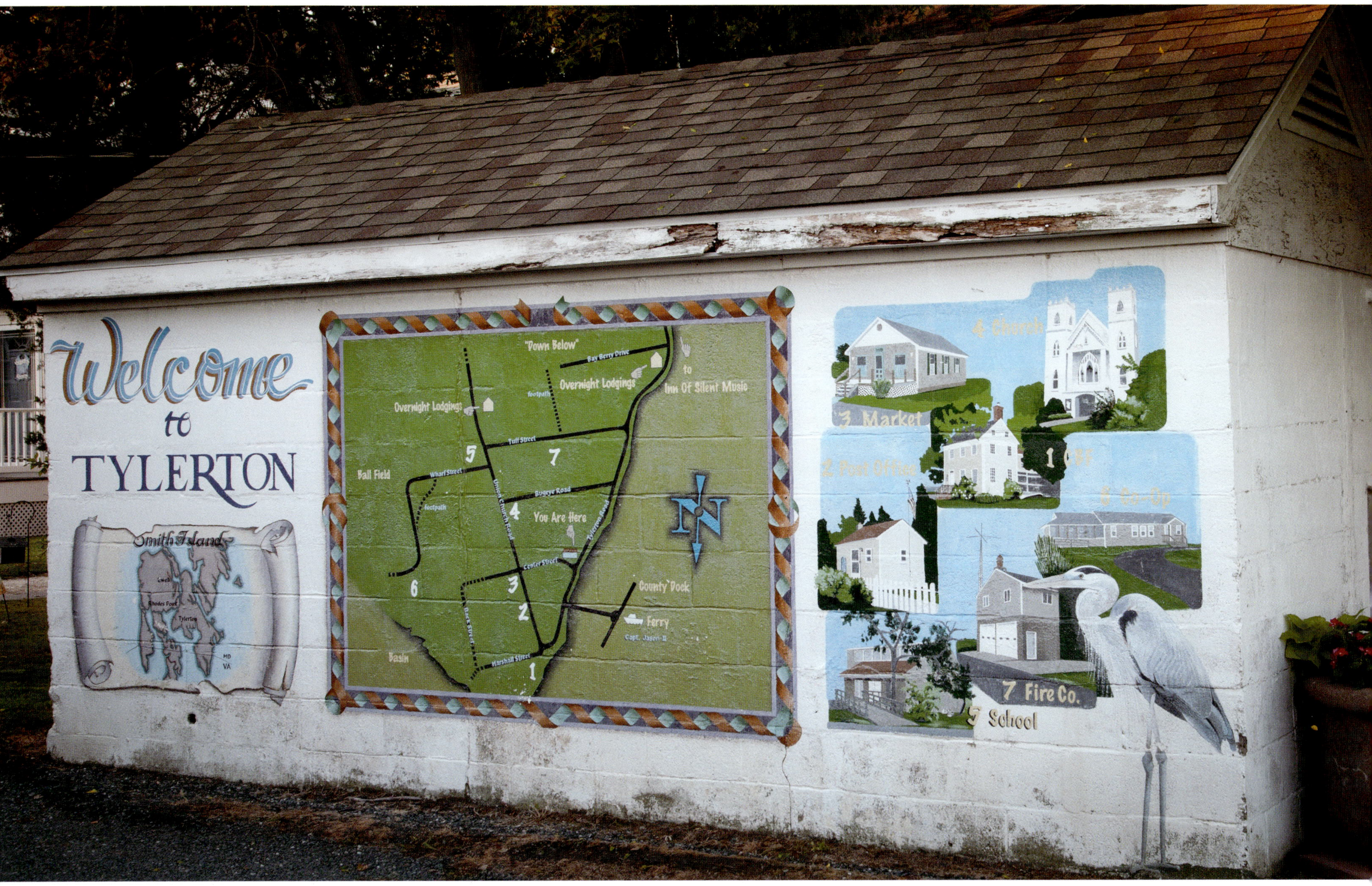


There is no getting lost in Tylerton.

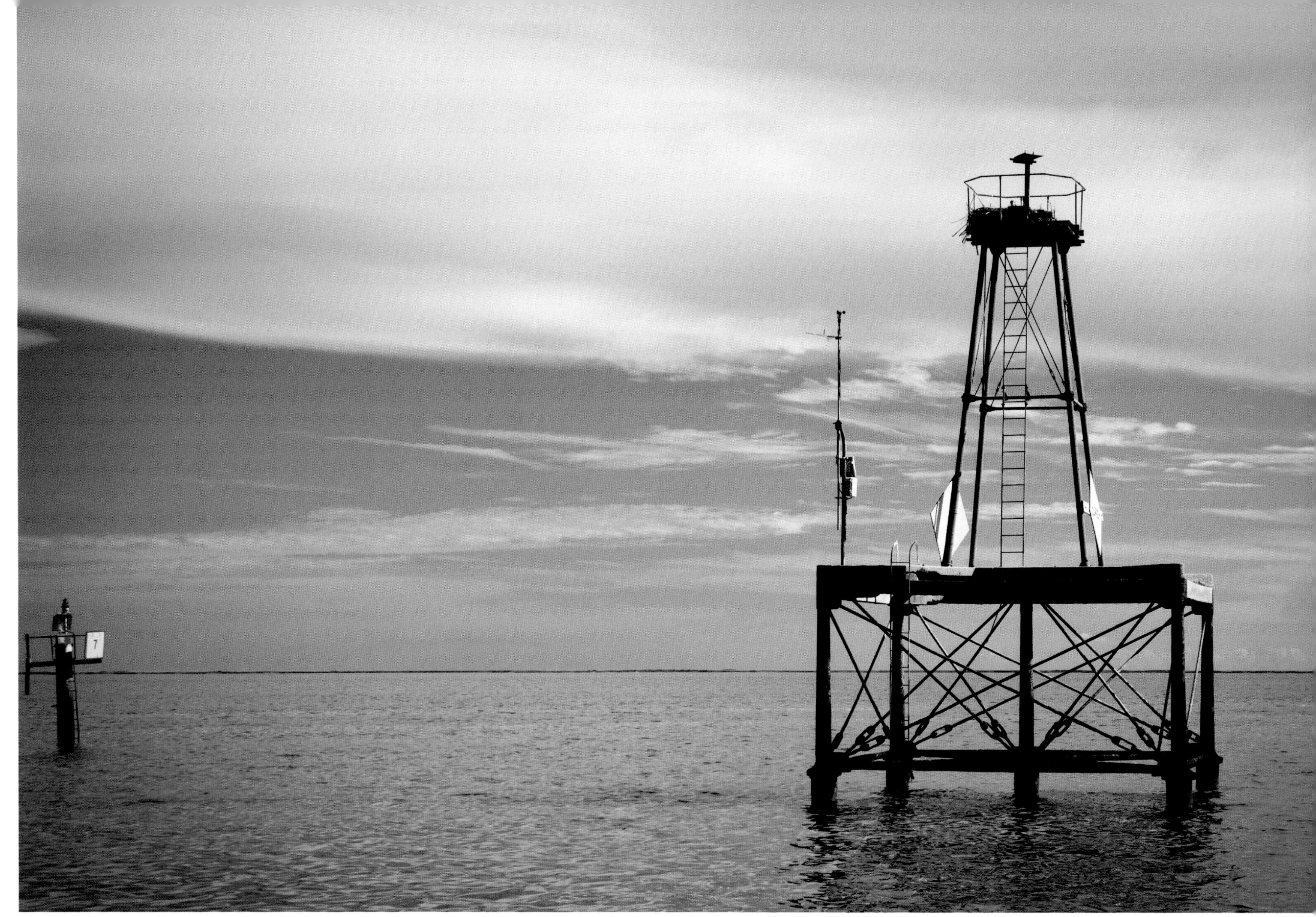

The #7 Spider Buoy off Crisfield, Maryland.

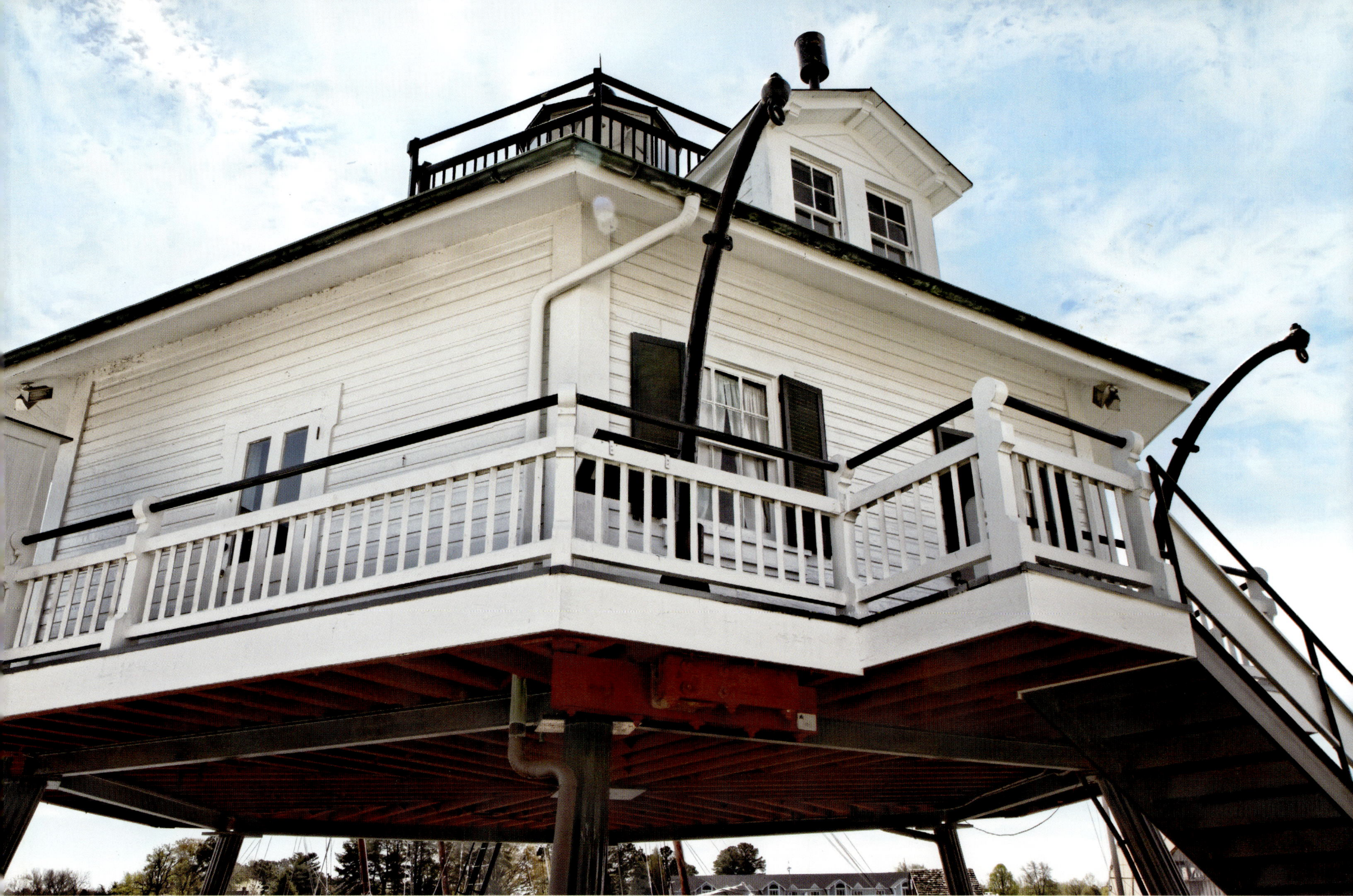

The Hooper Strait Lighthouse, now ashore at the Chesapeake Bay Maritime Museum in St. Michaels, Maryland.

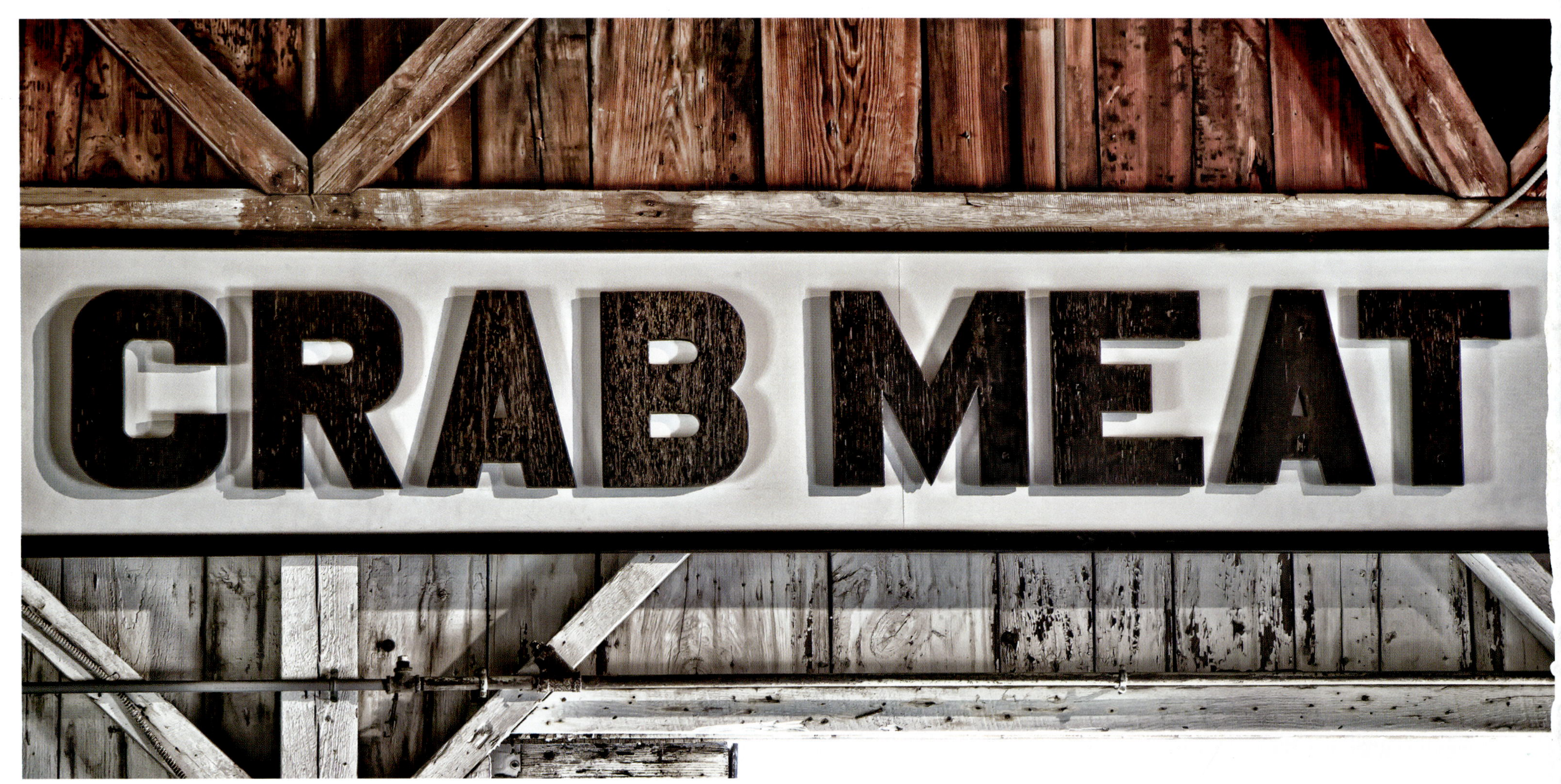


A crab meat sign hangs in the small boat shed at the Chesapeake Bay Maritime Museum.

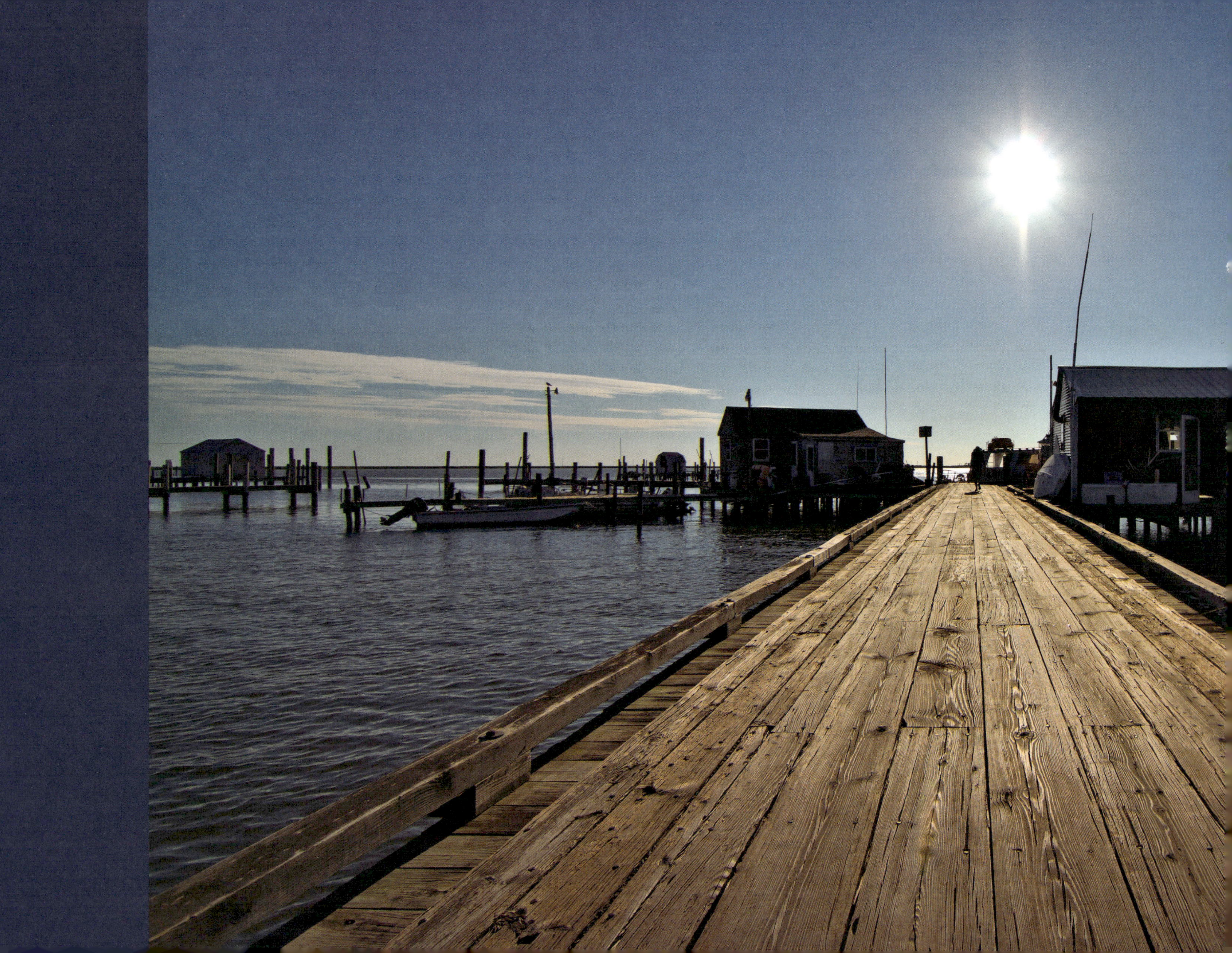